EAST AND WEST

To president
Yuli Guo.

With my compliments
and best wishes
Y-J. Choi
May 16 / 2013

EAST AND WEST
UNDERSTANDING THE RISE OF CHINA

Y. J. CHOI

Guo Yuli
New York
2013. 5. 16

iUniverse, Inc.
Bloomington

East and West
Understanding the Rise of China

iUniverse books may be ordered through booksellers or by contacting:

iUniverse
1663 Liberty Drive
Bloomington, IN 47403
www.iuniverse.com
1-800-Authors (1-800-288-4677)

Because of the dynamic nature of the Internet, any Web addresses or links contained in this book may have changed since publication and may no longer be valid. The views expressed in this work are solely those of the author and do not necessarily reflect the views of the publisher, and the publisher hereby disclaims any responsibility for them.

ISBN: 978-1-4502-6542-3 (sc)
ISBN: 978-1-4502-6541-6 (ebk)

Printed in the United States of America

iUniverse rev. date: 12/28/2010

NOTICE

Persons attempting to find academic rigor in this book will be dismayed; Persons attempting to find moral judgment in it will be disappointed; Persons attempting to find East-West prioritization in it will be disillusioned.[1]

The Author

CONTENTS

Part II: Expressions

Part III: Adaptations

PREFACE

As a young man in the 1970s, I left medical school in Seoul and took a job as a foreign service officer in Paris. Immersed in a Western country for the first time, I was astounded by what I saw. Why were Easterners and Westerners so different in outlook? Why did Asia remain undeveloped and poor when the West was rich and developed? Why, in fact, were our civilizations so vastly different at all? I could not free my mind from such recurring questions.

If we possessed differing abilities according to our race, then no further questions were necessary—everything could be attributed to biological destiny. But my four-year study of medicine convinced me that, as *Homo sapiens*, people of all races shared the same abilities and potential. Our differences must therefore derive from the variety of our interactions with our environment, which constitutes the context of our civilization. In search of an answer, my trips to Venice in the spring of 1975, and to Stockholm in the summer of that year, offered me a valuable clue: the sea, an open and expanding world.

The West's orientation to the sea was a marvel to the Eastern eye. From the Piazza San Marco in Venice, the center of the predominant Mediterranean naval power for many centuries, one can sail directly out to sea; from the stone steps of the City Hall of Stockholm, the origin of astonishing Viking expeditions, one can even dip one's toes in the sea!

Indeed, the Mediterranean and the Baltic are the only bodies of water in the world that bring the sea to one's doorstep. The tranquility of the Mediterranean allowed Western seafarers to hone their navigational skills; whereas the Pacific, the largest of the world's oceans, remained so inhospitable that easy and regular access to it had to await the nineteenth century. The accessibility of the Mediterranean and the Baltic, by contrast to the vast and hostile Pacific, seemed incredible to me.

I began to see, in this environmental condition, the impetus behind Western civilization. With such an intuition, I began to collect materials and insights to develop my theory further. Piece by piece, I assembled a great deal on the environmental contexts, historical development, and cultural manifestations of Eastern and Western civilizations, at the center of which Man, as a living organism, followed the ultimate biological principle: self-preservation.

The essential point is that Western men, having mastered the sea, came to possess an "expansive" perspective on their relation to the world; Eastern men, on the other hand, confined to the continent, developed instead a "circumscribed" perspective. From these perspectives evolved diametrically opposed guiding principles: Unity for the East and Separation for the West. In the East, the concept of Unity put the emphasis on harmony among various elements; in the West, the concept of Dialectics between separated entities gave rise to an emphasis on the freedom of one being from others. Due to its focus on Dialectics and Freedom, the West came to value Law in the sphere of action; the East, by contrast, established Ethics. These respective principles were founded on, and reinforced by, Agriculture and Education in the East, and Commerce and Religion in the West. These foundations were undergirded in turn by a meritocratic examination system in the East, aiming at the management of the empire, and by the ideals of individual initiative and legal compact in the West, aiming at the expansion of the empire. A table of the contrasts between East and West may be drawn up as follows:

	EAST	WEST
Context	**Continental: Closed; Circumscribed**	**Maritime: Open; Expansive**
Means of Self-Preservation	**Ethics**	**Law**
Underlying Tendency	**Unity, Assimilation, Harmony**	**Separation, Dialectics, Freedom**
Societal Mechanism	**Agriculture and Education**	**Commerce and Religion**
Societal Values	**Meritocracy with Examination System**	**Individual Initiative with Legal Compact**

The apparent simplicity of the above distinctions is belied by my tremendous difficulty in explaining Eastern civilization to my Western colleagues. Over the years, I have repeatedly found that Eastern culture—its philosophy, literature, and even history— is difficult to explain to Westerners because it is so different; common ground is hard to find. For example, Eastern literary classics are virtually untranslatable into Western languages, as they lose most of their nuance and flavor in the new tongue.

The easiest means to compare the two civilizations arose naturally during my conversations with Western colleagues: this was to locate Western parallels to the constituent elements of Eastern culture—Taoism and Judaism; Confucianism and Christianity; Sun Tzu and Carl von Clausewitz; Xun Zi and Spinoza; Han Fei and Machiavelli; Admiral Cheng Ho and Vasco da Gama; the games of Go and chess, and so on. The discovery of these pairs and their attendant illuminations counts among the most exhilarating experiences of my life.

Meanwhile, one of the most remarkable historical phenomena of the twentieth century continued to unfold: the rise of East Asia. The economic growth of the Confucian countries—first Japan, then the Four Tigers (Korea, Taiwan, Hong Kong, and Singapore), and China, with Vietnam not far behind—seized the world's attention and curiosity. By the new millennium, the ascent of China in particular, by virtue of its sheer rapidity and global impact, had become a phenomenon of epochal importance.

Naturally, articles and monographs have been produced in great numbers to explain this phenomenon. The greatest attention, however, has been given to law, free market, and democracy, and the narrative has been one of rationalizing forces flowing out from the West into a slumbering East Asia. Differences in culture and civilization have received little consideration, despite their direct impact on economic development, as history continues to show.

For a long time, I searched in this deluge of material for answers to those questions lingering in my mind since the seventies: How different are our civilizations, and why? Although I discovered many excellent arguments and insights into Eastern civilization, I found little that treated it on an equal footing with that of the West. The intellectual scope of the West remains a prisoner, in this respect, to a Eurocentric tradition. One day it dawned on me:

if such a book did not exist, why not write it myself? This book is thus an attempt to explain the cultural implications of China's ascendancy—and that of Confucian East Asia in general—by means of a systematic comparison between Eastern and Western worldviews.

As I broadened the scope of my research, a new phenomenon of historic importance unfolded. Following the demise of communism and the collapse of the Soviet Union, the twenty-first century has ushered in widespread economic and cultural globalization. As soon as we began to grapple with the significance and implications of these changes, we realized that the benefits of globalization were accompanied by emerging transnational problems: climate change, weapons of mass destruction, shortage of fresh water, international terrorism, the advent of failed states, and communicable diseases, such as avian influenza.

Transnational problems demand transnational solutions; mankind must now cooperate to an unprecedented degree to diagnose and address these threats. The stakes are frighteningly high, since these issues have, in essence, an evolutionary dimension: the collateral effects of mankind's success now threaten its very survival. One might conclude that the world is no longer comprehensible by an expansive Western worldview, as its resources appear all too limited and peaceful coexistence all too essential. In short, the entire world—both East and West—appears, for the first time in human history, increasingly closed and circumscribed, with all the consequences such a state might entail. Mankind may be experiencing a paradigm shift, the implications of which the last chapter of this book will elaborate.

As the nations of the world embrace the Western "expansive" perspective based on law, the world as a whole, pinched for space and resources, has paradoxically become more closely circumscribed. For this reason, Eastern values based on ethics are not merely venerable contingencies in a world globalized under the Western aegis of democracy and the free market. Rather, they may constitute the best reflection of human experience, both in its successes and in its failures, within the circumscribed framework that increasingly characterizes the present century.

From this perspective, Eastern civilization may be able to make a crucial contribution to solving our impending challenges. Of course, any such contribution could not occur in isolation, but only by interaction with other civilizations. But to understand Eastern civilization in its own terms will form the necessary first step to assessing the cultural tools available to us; for this purpose, cross-cultural comparison may be the most effective means. What are the merits, limitations, and potential strengths of our respective civilizations?

This book is written in the hope of shedding some light on the Eastern approach to a circumscribed environment. This way of thinking is, in many ways, the polar opposite of the Western way, as explained by Professor Richard Nisbett: "Two utterly different approaches to the world have maintained themselves for thousands of years. These approaches include profoundly different social relations, views about the nature of the world, and characteristic thought processes."[2]

In the first part of this book—chapters 1 to 4—we shall compare the fundamentals of the Eastern and Western civilization. As the basic categories of comparison, this book uses three primary relationships: Man and Nature; Mind and Body; Man and Man. With regard to the relation between Man and Nature, this book compares Eastern Taoism with Western Monotheism, and suggests that the two cultures' definitions of the relationship are diametrically opposed to each other: Taoism contextualizes Man in Nature, whereas Monotheism separates Man from Nature. Next we will examine how Mind (or Spirit) enjoyed an unequivocal supremacy over Body in the West, whereas the two were complementary terms in the East, as conceptualized in the Yin-Yang philosophy. Finally, this book evaluates the relationship between Man and Man: despite the virtually identical teachings of Confucian Humanity and Christian Love, each civilization built its foundation within the dictates of its environmental context—ethics for the circumscribed East and law for the expansive West.

	EAST	WEST
Man-Nature Relationship	**Tao (道): Man as part of Nature**	**God ordains Man to rule over Nature**
Mind (Spirit)- Body Relationship	**Unity: Mind (reason, 理) -Body (force, 氣)**	**Spirit, as essence of God, is separated from Body**
Man-Man Relationship	**Humanity (仁): Man-Man Harmony via Ethics**	**Love your neighbor and obey your God: Freedom via Law**

In the second part of this book—chapters 5 to 7—we shall compare the actual manifestations in their respective culture of the fundamentals of the East and West. We shall continue the examination of the Eastern and Western civilizations, contrasting, from a historical perspective, their ethical systems and religions, cultural characters and attributes, and thought processes and behavioral patterns.

I could find no better terms than Yin and Yang to describe the contrast in character between Eastern and Western civilizations: the Eastern character displays typical Yin attributes—receptive, laissez-faire, equanimous, inclusive, integral, suggestive, introverted, and synthetic; whereas the Western character exudes classic Yang attributes—assertive, activist, dynamic, exclusive, dialectic, instructive, extroverted, and analytical. On the positive side, the Yang Western civilization produced the rule of law guaranteeing individual freedom, whereas the Yin Eastern civilization produced a culture of ethics focusing on social harmony; on the negative side, the West suffered from a tyranny of Spirit—religious and ideological absolutism—whereas the East suffered instead from a tyranny of Man, i.e., despotism.

	EAST	WEST
Role Model	**Junzi** (君子): Noble Man	**Hero**
Modus Operandi	**Wuwei** (無爲): Non-Interventionism	**Activism**
Character of Civilization	**Ethics-Yin** (陰): receptive, laissez-faire, equanimous, inclusive, integral, suggestive, introverted, synthetic	**Law-Yang** (陽): assertive, activist, dynamic, exclusive, dialectic, instructive, extroverted, analytical
Strengths	**Rule of Ethics** with **Social Harmony**	**Rule of Law** with **Individual Freedom**
Weaknesses	**Tyranny of Man** (Despotism)	**Tyranny of Spirit** (Absolutism)

In the third and final part of this book—chapters 8 to 10—we shall move on to an examination of how the two cultures adapted to the Industrial Revolution and its aftermath. I will introduce the concept of the paradigm shift from "military" to "commerce" to facilitate the reader's understanding of the challenges facing mankind in the new millennium. The book concludes with some reflections on the impact of the Industrial Revolution on mankind's future, the magnitude of which has barely been grasped.

At the genesis of this work, my motivation—especially from the 1990s onwards—was sustained and encouraged by the North American forums and colleges where I was invited to present my ideas. My special appreciation goes to Ambassador Stephen Bosworth, dean of the Fletcher School of Tufts University near Boston, who invited me to lecture for a semester on the comparison of civilizations in 2004 and again in September 2007, when I completed the first draft of this manuscript.

Based on this manuscript, the first edition of the current book was published by Yonsei University Press in 2008. Since then, some readers have pointed out the need for more explanation of Eastern culture. This second edition therefore contains more detailed examinations of the philosophies of Junzi (君子, Noble Man) and Wuwei (無為, Non-Interventionism), and of their critical roles in the East's adaptation to the Western paradigms following the Industrial Revolution. The draft for this edition was completed in Abidjan in February 2010.

The rough edges of the manuscript were rounded by my excellent editors—Allen Ellenzweig, Paul Lee, Benjamin Pickard, and Anthony Ossa-Richardson.

Y.J. Choi
Abidjan — February 2010

PART I: FUNDAMENTALS

CHAPTER 1

Context: Maritime West vs. Continental East

"Europe and China ... as the most cultivated and distant peoples stretch out their arms to each other, those in between may gradually be brought to a better way of life."

Leibniz

"The sailor relies upon himself amid the fluctuations of the waves, and eye and heart must be always open.... We see the nations freed from the fear of Nature and its slavish bondage."

Hegel

Mare Nostrum vs. Central Plain

How and why have human beings developed different civilizations? If Easterners and Westerners were in fact peoples with inherently different biological capacities, we would be able to assign the problem to evolution alone. This was the solution adopted by many important Western thinkers of the Enlightenment, from Hume to Kant and Hegel.[1] But if, on the other hand, we are members of the same species—*Homo sapiens*—with the same mental capacities, as Western genetics has now surely proven, then cultural differences must have originated from man's varying interactions with his environment. These interactions between Man and Nature ultimately gave rise to distinct civilizations.

Environmental Distinction between West and East
How do the environments of East and West differ? Western civilization began and developed around the sea, whereas Eastern civilization—denoting, in this book, China, Japan, Korea, Taiwan, Hong Kong, Singapore, and Vietnam—developed in a heartland. There was little connection between the two, due to their separation by the highest mountain chain in the world, the Himalayas. Kept apart by this "roof of the world," the West developed its culture partly as a result of lively interactions with the Middle East and India, which were inaccessible to the East.

In comparing the two cultures, it will be useful to consider their respective geographies. Let us imagine a map of world civilizations from two to three thousand years ago. I suggest this period because this was when the civilizations of East and West first acquired their distinctive characters. Such a map would show only two cultural regions at either end of the Eurasian continent:

the Western part comprised southern Europe, the Middle East, and India, as well as northern Africa; while the Eastern part embraced China, Korea, Japan, and southern Mongolia. East and West were linked by a single trade route, hardly visible on the map—the Silk Road.[2]

Indeed, the separation of these two regions at the two ends of the Eurasian continent gave rise to the long-lasting distinctness of their respective cultures. It was only during the past two to three centuries that the West's respect for the East evaporated, in favor of a Eurocentric world vision, following its conquest of the entire known world in the wake of the Industrial Revolution. In fact, some early modern philosophers admired Eastern civilization and expressed hope for the future of mankind.

Gottfried Wilhelm Leibniz (1646–1716) clearly expressed this optimism: "I consider it a singular plan of the fates that human cultivation and refinement should today be concentrated, as it were, in the two extremes of our continent, in Europe and in China, which adorns the Orient as Europe does the opposite edge of the earth. Perhaps Supreme Providence has ordained such an arrangement, so that, as the most cultivated and distant peoples stretch out their arms to each other, those in between may gradually be brought to a better way of life."[3]

What were the seeds of these two civilizations? How did they begin, and how did they grow to maturity? Our imaginary map as illustrated in Figure 1-1 would show that by the third century BC, Europe, the Middle East, and India interacted via trade, invasions, and war. Despite cultural and linguistic differences, these civilizations knew much of each other. Of East Asia, however, they knew virtually nothing beyond its existence. The reverse was also true: the East knew little of the West except for the vague idea that it existed.

Fig. 1-1. The Known World about 250 BC
(Source: H.G. Wells, *The Outline of History*, vol. I (New York: Doubleday
& Company Inc., 1949), 304. Map by James Francis Horrabin.)

If we focus on Europe, we find that it was formed around the
Mediterranean Sea. On the other hand, the East remained alone,
firmly rooted on the East Asian continent without interaction
with Europe, the Middle East, or even India. We may therefore
conclude that the sea constituted the West's central location, and
that it represented primarily an opportunity; whereas for the
East, it represented an obstacle. One may even go so far as to
say that the Mediterranean gave *birth* to the West, after which
the Renaissance—its *rebirth*—led the West to the Atlantic, and
eventually to the Pacific.

The Eastern world remained isolated by the Himalayas to the
west, the unnavigable Pacific to the east, deserts and tundra to the
north, and jungles to the south. But what distinguishes East Asia
from other agricultural regions is that the space circumscribed

by these obstacles was large enough to produce a complete and sophisticated civilization.[4] The West, on the other hand, with its easy access to the sea, was able to expand beyond its immediate physical borders. In light of these respective environments, we can figuratively refer to the Western world as "expansive" and to the Eastern world as "circumscribed."

To illustrate: for the Romans, the center of the world was the Mediterranean or *Mare Nostrum* ("our sea"), whereas for the Chinese, the center of the world was deep in the heartland, *Chungwon* or Central Plain. Rome fought the three Punic Wars against Carthage (First, 264–241 BC; Second, 218–202 BC; Third, 149–146 BC) to assert its dominance of the Mediterranean— maritime supremacy meant overall control of the Mediterranean world. The Central Plain played the same geopolitical role in the East, from the first emperor of China in the third century BC to Mao Zedong in the twentieth century AD: whoever occupied the Central Plain had command of the Eastern world.

Western Water vs. Eastern Land in Mythology

The environmental differences between these civilizations are apparent even from their respective creation myths. These narratives make clear the cultures' fundamental contrasts in their priority of land or sea. According to a typical Eastern myth, the earth appeared before the sea, while the foundational story in Judeo-Christian theology asserts the reverse. Genesis says: "Let the waters under the heavens be gathered together into one place, and let the dry land appear. God called the dry land Earth, and the gathering together of the waters He called Sea." Surrounded by the Mediterranean, the Red Sea, the Indian Ocean, the Black Sea, the Baltic Sea, and the Atlantic Ocean, the West naturally imagined the world to be a flat disc with water surrounding the land. Thus, in the West, water is the primordial element and earth is secondary—separate from water.

By contrast, in Chinese mythology, earth is the primordial element and water appears later. *Pangu* (the Creator) "cracked the primal egg with an ax, and the light, clear part of the egg floated up to form Heaven while the cold, heavy part stayed down and formed Earth [land]."[5] One recurring difference between East and West should be emphasized: the East shows conformity whereas the West demonstrates diversity. It is therefore crucial to distinguish mainstream from marginalized elements in Western culture. In this case, the East's focus on the earth has been consistent, while the West has produced many opinions and views, including an emphasis on water.[6] The key point is that water has achieved dominance in the West through a dialectical process among various elements, including fire, earth, air, and so on. As we shall see, this dialectic constitutes the pattern of Western civilization as opposed to the assimilative and consistent nature of Eastern civilization.

Earth was considered the crucial element of the universe by early Eastern thinkers, while many of their Western counterparts considered water to be the crucial element. Thales of Miletus (ca. 620–546 BC), the first known Greek philosopher, attributed the origin of all things to water. Although there were many differing views in the West about the fundamental element of the universe, the proponents of water had the most influence.[7] On the other hand, the East was uniform in pointing out land as the crucial element of the universe. This Western view may have had its source in the creation of the Mediterranean Sea, which was formed by a vast influx of seawater from the Atlantic Ocean through the Straits of Gibraltar over the course of thousands of years, making an indelible impression on the people living on the sea's rim.

Although Eastern history was also punctuated by many stories of deluges and inundations, its mythology places little emphasis on water or the sea, or on stories of a deluge. On the other hand, such myths and stories abound in the West. For example, the story of Noah's Ark is not unique to Genesis; similar stories of a deluge appear in the mythologies of all the Mediterranean peoples, including the Greeks. The similarities between the Judaic story of Noah's flood and the Greek story of Deucalion's flood are unmistakable.[8] By contrast, the importance of Earth is paramount in Eastern culture. Of the five fundamental elements in Eastern teaching, Earth occupied the central position. The color reserved for the use of the emperor was the yellow associated with Earth as opposed to the purple of the West, a color derived from the marine murex.[9] It is also worth noting that the body of Pangu, according to Chinese mythology, is dispersed to form the various parts of the Earth.

Birth of the West in the Mediterranean
Greek civilization originated and developed in and around the Aegean Sea, the northeastern area of the Mediterranean. The Roman Empire, meanwhile, expanded throughout the Mediterranean, *Mare Nostrum*: although it also expanded northwards, to cover what is today France, and part of Britain—as well as east to the Balkans—it remained centered around the Mediterranean. At its zenith, the empire covered every shore of the Mediterranean—North Africa, the Middle East, and Southern and Western Europe. The Mediterranean was truly a Roman Sea and served as the hub of the empire for trade, transport, and communication. Even after the fall of the empire in the fifth century, the Western world still revolved around the Mediterranean: the peoples of Northern Europe continued to accept and follow the traditions of Rome, although civilization to the north became more rural and fragmented after

the sixth century, with stronger local traditions and less connection to Rome, until the revival of papal power in the eleventh century. The waning of the Eastern Roman Empire based in Constantinople resulted in the weakening of its ties with Italy; this in turn forced the Papacy to strengthen its ties with Northern Europe.

It was only after the eighth-century Muslim conquest of the Middle East, North Africa, and Spain, breaking the trade route of the Mediterranean, that the West's political center of gravity moved away from the sea to the north. The emergence of the Carolingian dynasty (ca. AD 751–987) coincided with the rise of Islam. As Henri Pirenne observed in his book *Mohammed and Charlemagne*,[10] the Papacy had no alternative but to make an alliance with Charlemagne, since it no longer had the military assistance of Byzantium, then fighting desperately for its own survival against the advancing power of Islam. In the Dark Ages, the Mediterranean constituted a barrier rather than an opportunity for the Christian West. The western parts of the sea almost constituted a Muslim lake. The Islamic naval expansion in the Mediterranean would continue to its height in the sixteenth century under the Ottoman hero, Hayreddin Barbarossa. Between the Battle of Preveza in 1538 and that of Lepanto in 1571, the entire Mediterranean lay under Ottoman control.

During this period, the Vikings became active. Originating on the shores of the Baltic Sea, the Vikings emerged as the dominant maritime power in the West, expanding their influence to the whole of Northern Europe as well as parts of Southern Europe and North Africa. The extraordinary vitality of the Vikings carried them even to North America, via Greenland, some five centuries before Columbus. But climate change caused longer and harsher Greenland winters, rendering that passage too inhospitable for transatlantic use; migration therefore ceased before the Vikings could establish sufficient numbers on the new continent.

The advance of the Vikings into the Mediterranean must have helped to revive maritime trade and transport by weakening Islam's grip on the sea. In the thirteenth century, moreover, Muslim power was also in decline in the East, due to the rise of the Mongol Empire, which extended to Persia, Baghdad, and Damascus. The subsequent *Pax Mongolica* greatly facilitated the expansion of international trade as far as Europe. During this period, the West received and further developed such important technologies as gunpowder, paper, printing, and the compass. Thanks to this renewal of Mediterranean life and increased international trade, the West was ultimately able to emerge from the Middle Ages and usher in the Renaissance and the Age of Discovery.

It is no coincidence that it was not Venice—an Eastern Mediterranean maritime power trading with the Ottoman Empire—but the Western powers of Genoa, Spain, and Portugal that first began to explore the opportunities presented by the Atlantic. The fall of Constantinople in 1453 to the Ottomans deprived the West of the Black Sea trade. But by this time, seafaring had made an important advance: maritime powers could now use sails, as well as the magnetic compass and gunpowder imported from the East, instead of depending on galleys propelled by oars. This availability of new technology coincided with the emergence of nation-states in the West, which provided extraordinary vitality through mutual competition. The early rivalry between Portugal and Spain was a case in point. Thus, the West, which was born and grew in and around the Mediterranean, could now venture into a much larger ocean, the Atlantic, and eventually into the largest and the most inhospitable ocean on earth, the Pacific. The sea presented opportunities to the West, as it offered an open trade route with easy access to transport and communication. As a result, Western civilization naturally developed with all the characteristics favored by an expansive worldview.

Birth of the East in the Central Plain or "All within the Four Seas"

Eastern civilization, by contrast, was overwhelmingly landlocked. As we have already seen, four barriers determined the environment of the Eastern world: the Pacific Ocean to the east, the Himalayas to the west, the Gobi Desert to the north, and jungles to the south. The importance of the Central Plain in Chinese culture is clear even in the language used to describe it. In the Chinese language, "all within the four seas"—that is, the East Asian landmass—denoted everything in the world. Westerners, on the other hand, with their expansive and centrifugal perspective, spoke of the "four corners of the world." The sea was perceived as a barrier throughout the Chinese world. Figures 1-2 and 1-3 demonstrate clearly how the West was formed around the sea, the Mediterranean, whereas the East centered on a landmass, the Central Plain.

Fig. 1-2. Roman Empire: *Mare Nostrum*	**Fig. 1-3. Han Empire:** *Central Plain*
The Roman Empire at its greatest extent under Trajan in 117 AD. (http://en.wikipedia.org/wiki/File:Roman_empire.png)	Boundary of the Han empire and its Western Protectorates, ca. 220 AD. (http://www.metmuseum.org/toah/hd/hand/hd_hand.htm)

The vastness of the Central Plain, with its large population supported by intensive rice cultivation, provided the East a circumscribed continental environment opposed in character to the West's maritime, expansive environment. The size of the population determined the magnitude of the civilization that developed: both East and West had sufficient numbers of inhabitants to evolve a full-fledged civilization. The geography of the East also facilitated the syncretic and eclectic tendency among Eastern philosophical schools to intermix, borrow from, share with, and assimilate each other's core concepts. This constitutes a clear contrast with the Western schools of philosophy, which had a tendency to evolve in an exclusive, competitive, and dialectic way more than an eclectic and syncretic fashion.

It is true that eclecticism was common in early Western philosophy, especially among the Roman intellectual elite. Judaism and Christianity, likewise, absorbed many influences from other religions and pagan philosophy, especially Platonism. In the Renaissance, again, conscious eclecticism became very popular, but theological and metaphysical dialectics constituted the mainstream of the history of philosophy. From a broad perspective, therefore, the West evolved around exclusionary dialectics more than eclectic syncretism. A comparison of the relationship between Judaism and Christianity on the one hand and Taoism and Confucianism on the other attests to this. We shall examine this aspect more in detail later.

Thus separated, the two civilizations—the one maritime and the other continental—were conceived and developed without significant interaction until modern times, when sea routes became available. The only connection between East and West was the Silk Road, which passed through the narrow gap between the western Himalayas and the northern Gobi Desert. On this road passed such important cultural contributions as domesticated plants and animals: plant grafting techniques traveled from East to West, and the tamed horse traveled from West to East. But there was little else: the pass was so narrow, and communications so infrequent, that formative interaction was necessarily limited. Even the transmission of so central an invention as gunpowder had to await the trade routes created by the vast Mongolian continental empire.

One may wonder why the Eastern world did not venture into and beyond the Pacific Ocean. But despite its name, the Pacific, with its high tides and deadly typhoons, was simply unnavigable in ancient times. Even the Atlantic, which was smaller and less formidable than the Pacific, was not explored by the West until the Renaissance. Despite their maritime experience, neither Greeks nor Romans dared venture into the Atlantic, although there are records of sporadic and isolated Atlantic sallies by the Phoenicians and Carthaginians. It remained largely unexplored until Europeans had acquired the requisite technology, along with the skill they had honed over thousands of years on the Mediterranean and Baltic seas.

The vital impetus that its expansive maritime environment gave the West thus marks the fundamental difference between East and West. Even now, to Eastern peoples, nothing is more astounding than places like Venice and Stockholm, where one can sail out to sea from one's own front door. Easterners had vast maritime experience of their own—for instance, during the Korean Silla, Chinese Tang and Song, and Japanese pre-Tokugawa periods—covering East Asia, Southeast Asia, the Indian Ocean, and even the East African coast. But, besides such rare exceptions as Admiral Cheng Ho's, these activities remained at local and individual levels without the active involvement of the central government. We shall examine this important aspect more in detail in chapter 7.

Eastern culture is replete with myths and stories about agriculture and related concerns and phenomena, such as irrigation, flood control, famine, and hunger. Although much of Western mythology is also agricultural in origin—relating to the pattern of crop cycles—the West in the end graduated from this agricultural fixation through navigation. On the other hand, the East adhered to this agricultural fixation. The administration of these problems, domestic management as opposed to external expansion, constituted the major preoccupation for the ruling class of any East Asian country throughout its history. The outcome was a remarkable emphasis on social stability or even immobility. China, Japan, Korea, and Vietnam have been settled on their land without significant change for over a millennium.

The almost exclusively land-based character of Eastern civilization is also evidenced by its near-total lack of any "exploitative" naval expeditions or battles fought on the open sea. There have been several exceptions: the Japanese pirates who raided Korean and Chinese coastal areas from the thirteenth century for about three-hundred years; Admiral Cheng Ho's extraordinary naval expeditions in the early fifteenth century; and the battle between Korean and Japanese fleets during the Japanese invasion of Korea toward the end of the sixteenth century. There were important "naval" battles in Chinese history, but most of these occurred on rivers, like the famous Battle of Red Cliffs in 208, or on lakes, such as the Battle of Lake Poyang in 1363. The mainstream historical events of the Chinese world were almost exclusively decided on land battles.

By contrast, the history of the West reveals many epoch-making naval expeditions and battles. These include the Battle of Salamis in 480 BC, which put an end to Persia's attempt to conquer the Greek mainland; the Battle of Actium in 31 BC, which finally sealed the fate of the Roman Republic and ushered in the empire; the rise of Muslim corsairs in the Mediterranean after the demise of the Roman Empire in the West; the Age of the Vikings from the late eighth to the eleventh centuries, during which the Vikings raided and conquered the Atlantic coast of Europe, the eastern Mediterranean, and the Black and Caspian seas; the Age of Discovery inaugurated by Columbus in 1492 to the Americas, and by Vasco da Gama in 1497 to Asia; the Battle of Preveza in 1538 and the Battle of Lepanto in 1571 between Ottoman and European forces for the control of the Mediterranean; the Battle of Gravelines in 1588, which marked a lasting shift in the naval balance in favor of the English fleet, at the expense of Spain's formerly invincible armada; and the Battle of Trafalgar in 1805, which confirmed Britain's naval supremacy.

Not until the twentieth century did we see epochal naval battles involving Eastern powers, such as the Battle of Tsushima in 1905, in which the Japanese defeated the Russian fleet, and the Second World War's Battle of Midway in 1942, with the American fleet defeating the Japanese. Otherwise, the East remained mainly circumscribed within its continental borders, almost exclusively relying on land and agriculture, with the cultivation of rice predominating.

Expansive West vs. Circumscribed East

How did sea and land make their distinctive contributions to Western and Eastern civilizations, respectively? In the East's circumscribed continental environment, man's skills were almost exclusively agrarian. By contrast, in the West's expansive maritime environment, seafaring and commerce were as important as agriculture. Until the beginning of the twentieth century, the Eastern world remained fundamentally agricultural, while the Western world evolved largely through navigation. Although agriculture was crucial in the West up to the Industrial Revolution, seafaring and expansion truly distinguished West from East and, for that matter, from all other civilizations in the world.

With a view to putting East and West in perspective, it is important at this point to broaden our scope in time and space. How did mankind, in its long journey on our planet, almost simultaneously—two to three thousand years ago—begin to formulate distinct civilizations and religions in so many regions of the earth? What led to the formation of these continental agrarian and maritime civilizations?

From Hunter-Gatherer to Animal Husbandry and Agriculture

Billions of years of evolution finally produced a creature that was bipedal and walked erect: a development directly linked to both the use of hands and increased brain capacity. This crucial breakthrough is thought to have occurred around 50,000 years ago. A species with approximately the same brain size as that of modern humans, and with a comparable linguistic faculty, *Homo sapiens* (intelligent man) began to roam the earth. Language was at the root of human societies and civilizations as we know them today. *Homo sapiens* had to wait 40,000 years, until the end of the Fourth Ice Age, when they could move from their nomadic hunter-gatherer lifestyle to a sedentary pattern of agriculture and animal husbandry.

This transition from a hunter-gatherer society to an agricultural one brought about a revolutionary change in human affairs. Meanwhile, invented around 3000 BC, writing marked the beginning of human *history*, as opposed to prehistory. With the advent of writing and the dawn of the first urban communities, humans were faced with new political, social, ethical, and philosophical problems. Knowledge began to increase, setting in motion a cultural evolution as opposed to a merely biological one. Finally, around two to three thousand years ago, this accumulation reached "critical mass" in societies all across the globe. It was at this stage that most of the major religions and schools of philosophy appeared: Judaism, Zoroastrianism, Hinduism, Taoism, Confucianism, Buddhism, Christianity, and Islam.[11]

Domestication of Plants and Animals

This crucial cultural evolution began with the domestication of plants and animals. The first agricultural revolution began around 8000 BC. The five major grains—rice, wheat, barley, corn, and sorghum—were domesticated around this time. The next stage in the agricultural revolution occurred about 4000 BC with the introduction of fruits and nuts. The most important fruit-bearing plants were the olive, grape, pomegranate, date, and fig, all of which require cultivation for at least three years before they become productive. Fruit cultivation was possible only after humans had lived a settled lifestyle long enough to discover the secrets of fruit trees. Evident in the history of Mediterranean trade and the wars of the Greco-Roman era, the importance of the olive and the grape in early Mediterranean civilization can hardly be exaggerated.

Along with agriculture, humans learned how to domesticate animals. Crucial animal husbandry started around 8000 BC. The first wave of domestication included the five most important animals—horse, cow, pig, sheep, and goat; by the fourth millennium, all current domestic animals (around fourteen types in total, including the aforementioned five) had been accommodated to man. Since then, no further successful domestication of animals has occurred.[12]

Following this, the third and last revolution in agriculture occurred around 3000 BC, with fruits that required grafting techniques: the apple, pear, plum, and cherry; while these fruits are labor-intensive, they assure a large production. It is believed that these grafting techniques were first developed in the East before spreading to other regions. At this stage, mankind seems to have exhausted the possibility of any further domestication of agricultural products. For more than ten thousand years, millions of people all over the world had experimented with all kinds of plants for possible domestication. But around three to four thousand years ago, all the plants that could be domesticated had been, and no significant new plant domestications have occurred since.[13]

Nomads: Attila the Hun, Genghis Khan, Timur

The domestication of the horse possessed a particular significance, for it was the most effective means of overland transport until the invention of the motor car in the early twentieth century. Horse-mounted nomads enjoyed mobility overwhelmingly superior to that of settled city dwellers and were virtually invincible when unified under effective leadership. In many ways, nomadic raiders resembled pirates, their maritime counterparts. Based on their mobility, their tactics were "hit and run," and their aims were the same: plundering as many riches and taking as many slaves as they could. When they could muster sufficient numbers, they occupied sedentary agricultural tribes or nations and ruled as overlords.

They were invariably victorious in wars against "civilized" nations until the use of the cannon was mastered by the latter in the sixteenth century. Attila the Hun (406–453), Genghis Khan (1162–1227), and Timur (1336–1405) built great empires. Genghis Khan, with two million Mongols, built the greatest empire in human history. Its imperial administration and military discipline amazed Marco Polo. Contrary to prevalent negative Western perceptions of Genghis Khan, the ruler left an enduring positive legacy by his empire's contribution to the birth of the modern world. Professor Jack Weatherford explains, "In nearly every country touched by the Mongols, the initial destruction and shock of conquest by an unknown and barbaric tribe yielded quickly to an unprecedented rise in cultural communication, expanded trade, and improved civilization.... Seemingly every aspect of European life—technology, warfare, clothing, commerce, food, art, literature, and music—changed during the Renaissance as a result of the Mongol influence. In addition to new forms of fighting, new machines, and new foods, even the most mundane aspects of daily life changed as the Europeans switched to Mongol fabrics, wearing pants and jackets instead of tunics and robes, played their musical instruments with the steppe bow rather than plucking them with the fingers, and painted their pictures in a new style."[14]

Nomadic empires, however, were short-lived; their exciting lifestyles and epic sagas died away, as their cultures did not favor the creation of a civilization as enduring as those of geographically rooted nations. In the modern era, nomadic horsemen lost their comparative advantage against the long-range cannons of city-dwellers.

East and West: Centrality of the Eurasian Continent

Despite repeated nomadic incursions, invasions, and occupations from the center of the Eurasian "continent," the East and West continued growing and enriching their respective civilizations at the two extremities of the Eurasian continent. For their development, the Eurasian continent, as a cause of cultural stimulation, played a crucial role. Without its geographic centrality, the two civilizations would have had less global importance. What is the nature and significance of this centrality?

In his book *Guns, Germs, and Steel*, Jared Diamond offers a convincing and insightful theory.[15] The large expanse and east-west axis of the Eurasian continent provided mankind with the most favorable environment for producing complex civilizations. Such a setting was characterized by a long crop season, a different sort of animal husbandry, species diversity, and the opportunity to interact with new inventions from other regions. The advantage of the Eurasian continent in terms of plant and animal domestication with respect to other continents had far-reaching implications for its cultures. The abundance of agricultural and animal products enabled Eurasia to create a far more advanced social life and achieve fruitful exchanges with other civilizations.

When Europeans reached America, the Inca and Aztec civilizations were, in many respects, still Stone Age, having not yet developed metalworking. Africa and Oceania were at a comparable level of development. As Diamond forcefully demonstrates, animal husbandry spawned the spread of germs and, with them, new communicable diseases, such as smallpox, plague, cholera, measles, tuberculosis, and malaria. These diseases are all of animal origin and clearly came to mankind through the domestication of animals. All of these illnesses caused high rates of fatality in the Eurasian continent during the past millennia. Similarly, when

Europeans arrived in America and Oceania, new germs to which the indigenous peoples had not been exposed—due to the absence of domestication—killed around 90 percent of the existing human populations. These are key factors in explaining the centrality of the Eurasian continent in producing civilizations.

Environmental Determinism vs. Man's Supremacy over Nature
Here an important question arises. Are we to accept the claim of some that environment shapes destiny in a deterministic manner? Fundamentally, the answer must be yes, if we accept that man is part of nature, and that nature is Tao or God. But within a limited time and space, the answer must surely be no: unlike other animals, man is endowed with the mental capacity to overcome to a certain degree his environment's immediate restraints. It is this aptitude that allows hope and courage to flourish, leads to marvelous adventures, provides an outlet for human curiosity, and achieves the most dramatic results. The West's discoveries and conquests attest to this.

But at the same time, this limited victory over nature encourages the illusion that we can conquer nature and master the world. Only now do we understand that mindless exploitation of nature is endangering our survival. If, on the other hand, we accept environmental determinism at the tactical level, too, then humans remain totally passive within their environment—an attitude manifest in Eastern civilization. Also found in Western Stoicism, this attitude downplays or discourages mankind's natural curiosity and fosters stagnation, servility, and fatalism. The issue, therefore, is learning to strike a balance between tactical elation and strategic equanimity.

Environmental determinism may be particularly repellent to many Westerners who have been taught by religion and philosophy that man reigns supreme over nature. It is undeniable, however, that civilization is created by man's interaction with his environment. From a broader perspective, the preponderance of nature and climate over human affairs must not be underestimated. Also, one's attitude to and perception of the environment's importance crucially affects one's view of the natural world. The belief in man's superiority will produce an arrogant and reckless approach to nature, which may prove catastrophic for our continued existence in a post-industrialized world.

Among all the civilizations that have appeared in Eurasia, no two civilizations are as diametrically opposed as the East and West. Perhaps this is due to their different origins and mutual isolation: the West has been in constant contact with the Middle East and India, while its interaction with East Asia was virtually nonexistent until the seventeenth century, when Western Jesuits established numerous missions to China. We know very well of the West's ventures into the Middle East and even into India during the Greco-Roman period: the wars between Greece and Persia, the expedition of Alexander into India. But the West through all this period had virtually no record of any interaction with the East, with perhaps the sole exception of the silk trade. The role of geography was crucial in the East and West's long isolation from each other and in the unfolding of their respective histories; it is this which makes our comparison between Eastern and Western civilizations a vital one.

Expansive World vs. Circumscribed World

In isolation from one another, each region developed its own culture. Western civilization rests on the twin pillars of Judeo-Christian religion and the Greco-Roman intellectual tradition, while Eastern civilization is founded on Taoism and Confucianism, as well as the relative latecomer Buddhism, incorporated into Eastern culture after the first century AD. It is fascinating to ask how and why two regions populated by the same human race have produced such vastly different cultures. If we are content to believe that God gave us our various religions and cultures, we can accept theological dogma and abandon further questions. But if we have enough curiosity to explore further, we can go in search of deeper explanations.

Following the irresistible temptation for adventure and the centrifugal tendency provided by maritime opportunities, the West ventured into the unknown and continued until it had conquered or at least explored the entire globe. From the West's perspective, the history of the world can be rendered in broad strokes as a shift from the Mediterranean Era—with the rise and dominance of Greece and then the Roman Empire—to the Atlantic Era, characterized by the emergence of Europe, and finally to the preeminence of North America, which linked the Atlantic to the Pacific. Together with North America, the emergence of East Asia may now herald the beginning of a "Pacific Era."

While the West has been generating this unstoppable advance, the East has been waiting, suffering from chronic hunger, enriching its culture, and expanding its territory inwards rather than outwards: while all other empires prospered by extension (and ultimately perished by overextension), Eastern countries prospered, at times stagnated, and survived for thousands of years by focusing on self-preservation. The Chinese Empire is a case in point. Its acquisition of new territories was mostly due to its centripetal attraction rather than centrifugal expansion.[16] For example, the Mongols and Manchus were drawn into the Central Plain with its vast population and territories, and became its inhabitants, sharing its culture and losing the individuality of their own cultures.

A similar pattern of assimilation occurred in the West when the Normans invaded England in 1066 and their culture became fused to the native Saxon one, which itself incorporated Roman and Celtic elements. The same happened with the numerous encounters of Goths and Lombards with Romans and Celts throughout the continent. Yet mainstream history shows that the West has grown according to the centrifugal force encouraged by its expansive worldview, whereas the East has grown with the centripetal force specific to a circumscribed worldview. But by reaching the East, the West's journey has ended: there is no more to explore! By this final discovery, and by conquests across the rest of the globe, the West transformed its expansive world into a circumscribed one.

Shaping of Cultural Fundamentals: Law vs. Ethics

As we have observed, all the great teachers of mankind appeared around two to three millennia ago. This phenomenon we attributed to the emergence of a "critical mass." At that period, people began to think about the society of men they had themselves formed. What was to be done? The freshness of their wonder, dismay, and enlightenment would never be repeated. That period presented a unique opportunity for the development of religious and ethical schools, just as Classical Greece would provide an opportunity for the evolution of plastic arts and poetry, or the Renaissance, much later, for these and other forms of artistic expression.

The great teachers, at that critical period, must have considered the critical mass—villages blossoming into tribes and countries with kings, priests, armies, farmers, herders, sailors, markets, raids, and wars. All of them sought a way to lead the critical mass toward order, peace, and self-preservation amid constant fears of piracy and warfare. Laws, both divine and human, and ethics were the two fundamental concepts that they found to be best for this end of self-preservation. As indicated by the earliest law code of Hammurabi, ca. 1700 BC, law appeared earlier than ethics, at least in a codified form. No religion or school of thought of laws and ethics recommended disorder, war, hatred, and conflict (i.e., self-destruction). There was a clear difference, however, in their solutions between law and ethics as the primary means to achieve their goals: expansive worldviews gave priority to laws and circumscribed worldviews gave priority to ethics.

In the West, one becomes adventurous, courageous, and extroverted by virtue of one's urge to explore and exploit the world. Westerners thus acquired, step by step, all those character traits that encourage and justify such exploration and expansion. The upshot is that Western civilization has become an extroverted and expansive civilization based on law and force. In such a civilization, individual initiative guaranteed by law is cherished, and individual liberty becomes the ultimate value. It goes without saying that there were periodic fluctuations in the West. For example, medieval society, before the rise of the merchant class, was not chiefly capitalistic in character, but feudal and hierarchical—"circumscribed" in political and religious terms, much like the East. Yet, from a broad perspective, the mainstream West remains characterized by expansion. Ethics and harmony between individuals will be of secondary importance as the prospect of immediate and endless profit urges and favors initiative and freedom. Law and force were the major tools to be employed.

In this world, a tendency to exploitation and absolutism, as embodied by Western conquerors and prophets, including medieval theologians and modern metaphysicians, accompanied the positive values of individuality and personal liberty. Conquerors and prophets must be absolute, extreme, clear-cut, and unambiguous in their leadership and in their divinely ordained missions and enterprises, whether conquest or prophecy, dogma or philosophy. Such an absolute approach motivates and produces victory and conquest—whether material or ideological—much more effectively. The positive aspects of Western civilization like individual initiative and freedom are the flipside of its negative characteristics: exploitation and absolutism.

By contrast, in the circumscribed Eastern worldview, the need for a peaceful and harmonious society became much more important than the impulse to expand; the maintenance of order constituted the primary concern for Oriental thinkers and leaders as well. And their situation dictated a reliance on ethics, better suited than law to peace and stability. An urge to expand in this context would necessarily have instigated conflict and war to the detriment of all involved. For the purpose of "enlightened" self-preservation, Easterners acquired those cultural traits that promoted social harmony: "Chinese social life was interdependent and it was not liberty but harmony that was the watchword—the harmony of humans and nature for the Taoists and the harmony of humans with other humans for the Confucians."[17] It was thus only natural that the East has given rise to an introverted civilization reliant on ethics.

Such characteristics were further reinforced by the East's predominant mode of production, agriculture. The cultivation of rice remained the single most important industry in the East until the nineteenth century, when the West arrived, bringing with it industrialization and new technology. Prior to that, the wealth of the nation, as well as that of the individual, was measured by the amount of rice production it (or he) controlled. Rice production, though labor-intensive, can support a population four times larger than that supported by other types of grain.[18] This explains the population density of the East and its subsequent impact on cultural and social development, including the absence of slavery as an exploitative institution.[19]

But again, this positive aspect of Eastern ethics (i.e., the absence of exploitation) constitutes only one side of the coin. We must also examine what happened when this rule of ethics broke down, as it did periodically throughout the East's history. Despite its solid system of ethics, Eastern culture was unable to produce any mechanism of checks and balances, which would have enabled it to deal with the recurrent problem of despotism until the nineteenth century. On the other hand, Western civilization was based on the rule of law from within, and the rule of force from without. The rule of law could not be established as long as it required rule by force outside its perimeter, and it appeared only when rule by force had been eliminated during the twentieth century.

Western Dialectics vs. Eastern Unity

The role played by contrasting physical environments in the evolution of Eastern and Western civilizations can hardly be overemphasized. Land and sea played key parts in generating antithetical cultural frameworks. It appears that the concepts of Dialectics for the West and Unity for the East were the elemental seeds, from which blossomed the defining features of these respective civilizations.

Western Sailing: Man-Nature Dialectics

Civilization, as we have said, emerges from man's interaction with his environment. First, however, he must define his position with respect to Nature. This basic relation influences the two other fundamental relations: between Spirit and Body as well as between Man and Man. The maritime West and the continental East defined these relationships in opposing ways. Western civilization emphasized the individual based on a separation between Spirit and Body, a tendency initiated by the exaltation of the power of the Spirit.

How did this pattern of separation and ensuing dialectics occur in the West? The process of self-assertion and individuation is succinctly described by Hegel in his book *The Philosophy of History*: "The Phoenicians discovered and first navigated the Atlantic Ocean.... This opens to us an entirely new principle.... Babylonia had its determinate share of territory, and human subsistence was there dependent on the course of the sun and the process of Nature generally. But the sailor relies upon himself amid the fluctuations of the waves, and eye and heart must be always open.... At this point we see the nations freed from the fear of Nature and its slavish bondage."[20]

In the Preface, I shared my astonishment at the settings of Piazza San Marco and Stockholm City Hall. My surprise was initially due to their miraculous accessibility to the sea: the Mediterranean and the Baltic are the two seas that are virtually immune to tides thanks to the protection from the Atlantic Ocean provided by the Straits of Gibraltar and the Danish Strait. By contrast, Seoul's nearest seaport, Inchon, which has been well-known since Douglas MacArthur's landing during the Korean War, suffers extreme tidal shifts: "Tidal shifts at Inchon were sudden and dramatic; the range of spring tides was from an average of twenty-three feet to a maximum of thirty-three. At ebb tide the harbor turned into mud flats, extending as far as three miles from the shoreline."[21] In such an environment, it was not easy to venture out to the sea to experience the Hegelian freedom "from the fear of Nature and its slavish bondage."

The amazement that Piazza San Marco and Stockholm City Hall, as shown in Figures 1-4 and 1-5, impart to Easterners allowed me to imagine all the maritime adventures of the West: Athens, Rome, Venice, the Vikings, Christopher Columbus, Vasco da Gama, the Invincible Armada, the British Royal Navy, and the American Pacific fleet. As someone who was almost exclusively formed and conditioned by continental Eastern civilization, what stunned me in those places was the essence of the West: liberty. In hindsight, what I actually marveled at in Venice and Stockholm were the ideals and material expressions of this Western concept: liberty guaranteed by the rule of law; individual freedom and initiative, democracy, science, prosperity, arts and architecture, and so on. All these wonders were conveyed to me so powerfully that it was only much later that I began to pay attention to the other side of liberty: Rule by Law or Rule by Force. From this realization, I began to comprehend the material extensions of the concepts of exploitation and conflict: endless warfare from antiquity to the Middle Ages and through to the modern era, the slave trade, religious dispute, imperialism and colonialism, theological dogma, metaphysical and ideological absolutism, and so forth. All of these Western wonders and shortcomings arose from man's separation from Nature, symbolized by his "simple" act of setting out to sea.

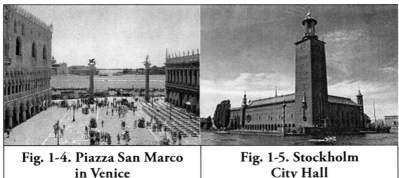

Fig. 1-4. Piazza San Marco in Venice (http://en.wikipedia.org/wiki/ File:Venezia_piazza_s.Marco_2.jpg)	Fig. 1-5. Stockholm City Hall (http://en.wikipedia.org/wiki/ File:Townhallstockholm.jpg)

Western Religion: Spirit-Body Separation

Already in Hegel's description, the separation between Man and Nature is made by the sailor's mind or Spirit. This presupposes a separation between Mind (Spirit) and Body. If we consider the nature of seafaring and navigation, it is clear that every captain of a ship becomes a kind of king and discovers the freedom and temptation to create his own kingdom. Plato, in Book Five of his *Republic*, uses the parable of the pilot on a ship to describe the relationship of a philosopher-king to his subjects. The West still uses a similar metaphor in contemporary politics, since *governor* comes from the Latin *gubernator* (from Greek *kubernetes*), meaning a ship's pilot. Those in positions of authority commonly claim to have been invested with their power by a deity or other supernatural being. While every tribe or nation tends to create its own god or gods, the temptation and rewards are incomparably higher for those in a maritime civilization than for those living inland.

As previously noted, all of the tribes and nations around the Mediterranean devoutly worshipped their own gods. There was no shortage of deities, since each nation grew by annexation or conquest, and in the process absorbed the gods of the other tribes or nations. Because each group thought its own gods supreme, conflict between the gods, and so between their worshippers, was inevitable. These gods were all naturally conceived of as spiritual, rather than corporeal beings.

Hegel claimed that "the spirit of the seafaring people teaches how to dominate Nature."[22] The hidden mechanism for the spirit was the invention of gods, who were supposed to have handed Nature over to Man. In the West, Spirit is separated from Body, and Man from Nature—God is the indispensable element in both separations. And the secret of the genesis and essence of the Western religions, Greco-Roman polytheism and monotheism alike, may be in their anthropomorphic development. The Western gods and God acted as moral and spiritual allies to the Western heroes, sea captains and conquerors.[23] The gods therefore had to be anthropomorphized. The Homeric heroes of *The Iliad* and *The Odyssey* were so inextricably linked with gods that at times it is difficult to distinguish who's who.

The West: Dialectics between Spirit and Body

In Western civilization, the interplay between religious zeal and secular interests is evident, embodying Spirit and Body, respectively. In a way, its intellectual history, from myth, to theologies, to

EAST AND WEST ♦ 43

metaphysics, and finally to ideologies, can be interpreted as the record of an evolutionary dialectic between these two forces: that is, as the journey of the Spirit, and as the reaction of the Body to the domination of Spirit. We shall examine this aspect in detail in chapter 3.

The West's conquering heroes and seafaring captains share the same intrepid spirit as well as unwavering admiration throughout Western history. This constitutes one of the most important contrasts with the East, as the latter valued scholar-officials rather than military heroes. We shall see that there is a fundamental link between conquering captains and the maritime culture, which separates Spirit from Body. Montesquieu observed that the first Mediterranean sailors must have been pirates.[24] H.G. Wells similarly thought that, given the facts of human nature, man would plunder whenever possible and would trade only when necessary.[25] War and conquest bring enormous profits and are therefore to be encouraged. Conquest and exploitation became a European enterprise in which all countries joined, leading the West to eventually occupy much of the world. The sea captains, conquerors, and prophets had become the leading figures of Western civilization, as the guardians of rule by law inside and rule by force outside—this was its most pronounced difference from the civilization of the East, which had been founded instead on a rule of ethics.

In the West's journey from antiquity to the modern era, the role of Spirit was crucial: it provided religious and ideological motives and justifications for expansion. Law or God's decree (that is, *fas*, as the Romans had it, or *natural law—lex naturalis*—as later formulated), created by Spirit, was the dominant tool, eclipsing ethics in providing stability as well as the legitimation of outward expansion. At the same time, the concept of Law contributed to the development of individual freedom in Western civilization by asserting an authority greater than the king's, resulting eventually in a separation between religious and secular powers.[26] Eventually, as the Western world was transformed from an expansive one to a circumscribed one, the concept of freedom, and the separation between religious and secular powers—or Church and State—provided a balance of authorities, leading to mankind's greatest institution, democracy. This signified the advent of a universal rule of law, replacing the former system of rule by law inside and rule by force outside.

The West: Separation-Dialectics-Freedom Based on Law
To confirm these separations between Man and Nature and between Spirit and Body, one need only look at the two aforementioned pillars of Western civilization—Judeo-Christian religion and the secular Greco-Roman tradition. According to the former, God created Nature and gave it to Man to rule—the two are arranged in a hierarchy. In Genesis, God says, "Let us make man in our image, after our likeness: and let them have dominion over the fish of the sea ... and God said unto them, 'Be fruitful, and multiply, and replenish the earth, and subdue it."[27] Genesis also reveals the relationship between Spirit and Body: "The Spirit of God moved upon the face of the waters"[28]—thus graphically representing the separation of Body (matter) from Spirit. The teachings of the Bible are strongly based on this separation: "And fear not them which kill the body, but are not able to kill the soul: but rather fear him which is able to destroy both soul and body in hell."[29]

Greco-Roman philosophy is also predicated on separation. Socrates, Plato, and Aristotle all taught the separation and subsequent alienation of Spirit from Body as well as that of Man from Nature. Aristotle had a different view from Plato regarding Spirit and Body: Plato emphasized the importance of Spirit over Body, but Aristotle focused rather on the dialectics between the two. Yet from a broad perspective, Aristotle also founded his entire study on the premise of Spirit-Body separation. This Greek attitude becomes evident when compared to Spinoza's philosophy, which we shall examine in greater detail in chapter 3. Their major areas of concern were God, the Soul, the *Idea*, and Eternity, and their considerations of these subjects provided fertile ground both for medieval theology and for modern Western metaphysics.

Seen from this angle, the history of Western philosophy is an aspect of the history of religion and theology, at least until the seventeenth century, when it became more specifically metaphysical and epistemological in character. The result of these distinctions was the creation of individuated concepts: God, Nature, Man, Spirit, Body. The fragmentation of these ideas was compensated for by the extraordinary vitality and dynamism of Western dialectics. Every critical Western achievement—science and industry, commerce and the market economy, personal liberty and liberal democracy—is born from this separation and dialectic development. But at the same time, these achievements are inseparable from the dogmas that were the source of religious wars, and from the political ideologies of the nineteenth and twentieth centuries, which almost ruined the West's progress. Separation and individuality are the fundamental and pervasive attitudes of a maritime civilization.

The East: Unity-Assimilation-Harmony Based on Ethics
In Eastern agrarian civilizations, Nature remained supremely important. In the absence of navigation, there is no exaltation of the Mind, Spirit, or Soul. Spirit is not dissociated from Body, nor

is Man separated from Nature. In premodern Western thought, by virtue of a god in whose image man was created, mankind occupies the central position in the cosmos. The Universe must revolve around the Earth, and the Earth must work for Man. When Copernicus, Galileo, and Kepler argued otherwise, they were vehemently attacked and persecuted by theologians and religious authorities. The Western scientific world has since acknowledged their discoveries, although Western culture as a whole remains reluctant to accept the demise of anthropocentrism.

In the East, however, Man is an integral part of nature, rather than standing above it, in the center of the universe. As we see in traditional forms of Eastern painting and poetry, mankind blends into an omnipotent and all-embracing Nature. Certain strains of Western thought suggest a similar picture: pantheism, Spinoza, Romanticism, but these do not constitute the mainstream.

Eastern civilization accepted Nature as an unchanging principle, instead of positing an anthropomorphic theism. Man's place in the cosmos was to follow the Way of Nature, identified as Tao in the East. This approach is almost identical with Spinoza's language, *"Deus sive Natura,"* God or Nature. Because Man cannot understand the essence of Nature itself, he must learn through such natural phenomena as the cyclical change of seasons or the waxing and waning of the moon. Thus, the Way of Nature connects man to the eternal and unchanging—but not *supernatural*—principle. Although Western philosophy constantly invoked the study of natural phenomena as a path to understanding God, its religious doctrines of Nature, premised on a supernatural God, were simply too overwhelming for the West to accept nature as it was.

In Eastern culture, the Yin-Yang philosophy is accepted by virtually all schools of thought, although it is associated in particular with Taoism. This ancient and fundamental concept of

Eastern thought implies unity, harmony, and interconnectedness between opposites: sun/moon, summer/winter, male/female, paternal/maternal, active/passive, creative/receptive. Although one can find a similar philosophy in the West, including Heraclitus' unity of opposites, this was not the norm. Assisted by the primary Eastern concept of Unity, the relationship between Mind and Body was elaborated via the concept of harmony and interconnection. As opposed to the separation/division that constitutes the primary concept of Western civilization, this union/connection represents the foundation of Eastern thought.

In the East's civilization of Harmony, the qualities of modesty, moderation, humility, and balance become recommended human virtues instead of the vitality, absolutism, and extremism of the West. Greek philosophy highly valued moderation, as expressed in its emphasis on Sophrosyne and in the constantly quoted maxim of Delphi, *meden agan*, or "nothing in excess." Accordingly, Aristotle proposed the Golden Mean: moderation and balance as against extremes and absolutes. Plato also extolled the virtue of temperance in *Republic,* Book IV, and elsewhere. At the same time, it must be pointed out that both Plato and Aristotle premised their philosophy on a separation between Spirit and Body: Plato proposed the philospher-king and Aristotle propounded the theory of tabula rasa, which later inspired, by their emphasis on the role and immense possibility of spirit, much of the Western theologies, metaphysics, and ideologies. Thus, through Western dialectics, ultimately inspired by these philosophers, the ancient ideals of Sophrosyne, the Golden Mean, and temperance lost much of their vigor in favor of absolutism and extremism from the Middle Ages through to the modern era. It is only now, after the demise of the Age of Ideologies, that the West is refocusing on the values of modesty, moderation, humility, and balance.

Inertia and Despotism in the East

When the concept of unity prevails in the relations between Mind and Body and between Man and Nature, the result is not dialectics but assimilation. The peaceful pattern of societal development, as well as the self-preservation and longevity of the East, is a natural outcome of assimilation. And through this mechanism, Eastern civilization produced ethics in contrast to the laws of the West.

However, such a society is also susceptible to inertia, the negative aspect of harmony. Inertia and complacency made Eastern peoples powerless against despotism until the arrival of new concepts and institutions from the West: personal liberty, the rule of law, checks-and-balances, free market, and democracy. The history of the East is, admittedly, less bloody than that of the West, and it did not suffer, as the West did, from tyrannies of Spirit—the almost incessant conflicts and wars grounded in theology, metaphysics, and ideology. But while the East was spared these atrocities, it was subject instead to the insipid and tasteless tyranny of Man. Its relatively uneventful history is frequently punctuated by the arbitrary rules of its emperors and kings, as they could easily turn a blind eye to, or even openly violate, the unwritten covenant of the rule of ethics. This was most frequently manifested as a de facto abdication of responsibility; while indulging various personal and petty appetites, they left the actual running of the empire entirely to a handful of personal advisors, including eunuchs. The increased role of the eunuchs in times of disorder attests to this periodic breakdown of ethics in the East.

The pairing of Harmony and Inertia also explains the relative lack of dynamism in the history of the East, compared to Liberty and Conflict in the West. While the latter kept expanding until it could go no further, capturing wealth and slaves and establishing trade, the East remained fixated on agricultural cultivation, which resulted in an inescapable poverty for the majority of the population. It was only with the arrival of Western industrialization and capitalism that the East began to enjoy for the first time in its long history a material prosperity that freed its large population from hunger and poverty.

Western Law vs. Eastern Ethics: Freedom vs. Harmony

The third and last relationship—between Man and Man—involves sensitive ethical considerations and cannot be as clearly defined as the first two. But here, again, Eastern culture has shown a tendency to interpret the relationship in terms of unity, producing ethics, whereas Western culture has posited division and produced laws.

This contrast exists even today, exemplified in the relationship between labor and management. In the West, labor and management were for a long time cast as opposing forces, while from the beginning the East saw them as symbiotic. Although Eastern labor-management relations have generated contention, they have been largely grounded on the concept of harmony. This contrast comes into sharper relief when we examine the Western history of the same relationship. Here it has largely been perceived as a relation of conflict, since the interests of each party have been deemed fundamentally incompatible. Maritime culture led Western man to see the world as divided and separated, and to emphasize the individual, while agrarian, continental culture encouraged Eastern man to focus on the relationships between individuals, emphasizing unity and connection.

In an agricultural setting, men depend on nature while actively pursuing an ethic of social harmony through assimilation. Agricultural production depends on climate and other natural conditions. The movements of the sun and moon as well as seasonal changes have an overwhelming influence on the thinking of agrarian people, who see in nature the obvious reality of cyclical change and value the relationship between man and nature rather than separating the two into individual entities. This attitude also provides Eastern man with the opportunity to observe and learn about nature as it is, without distortion. This attitude proved particularly instrumental in producing a practical system of ethics in the East, by enabling it to preserve the concept of the whole Man as related to the harmony of Mind and Body. The Roman poet Juvenal left us a very useful maxim: *Mens sana in corpore sano*, a healthy mind in a healthy body. Although this important statement indicates the same ideal as that of the East, it remained as a maxim rather than being developed into a full philosophy. We shall examine this aspect in chapters 3 and 4.

Just as the observation of Man as a holistic entity, guarded against distortion and dissection, led the East to ethics, so its observation of Nature as a holistic entity, eliminating superstition and miracles, provided it with a solid and rational basis for the rule of ethics. The brightest moment of the day, midday, contains the beginning of darkness; the darkest moment of the day, midnight, contains the beginning of light. The winter solstice has the longest night but from that moment on, the days becomes longer until the summer solstice. The summer solstice has the longest day of the year but thenceforth the nights become longer. Thus, the zenith is the beginning of decline, and the nadir is the beginning of ascent. In a circumscribed environment, one realizes that the best way to ensure order and stability is by harmony based on a rule of ethics, rather than on rule by law or by force. In such a setting, one is quick to realize the futility of excessive competition and conflict as leading to mutual loss. One will also realize that success contains the germ of one's own downfall, and that failure contains the seed of one's ascent. One can find a similar concept in the West as expressed by Boethius and the Wheel of Fortune, *Rota Fortunae*.[30] In the long run, decline and ascent, zenith and nadir, form a whole. This understanding of connectedness and relatedness is far deeper and more pervasive in a circumscribed environment than in an expansive one, where individual assertion is more pronounced, providing crucial impetus for action and expansion.

The Eastern focus on coexistence encourages the deep philosophical understanding expressed in the idea: "contraries are complementary," reinforcing the primacy of harmony over individual liberty. This is the polar opposite of mainstream Western thinking, which follows the maxim: "contraries are opposites." Such Western premises naturally place individuality over relationships. The Yin-Yang philosophy, denoting harmony and complementarity, is pervasive in both Taoism and Confucianism as well as in all other philosophical schools of the East. Because the extremes are the beginning of return, the East teaches one to be wary of extremism, which it defines as unnatural, and suggests that we take the golden mean, instead of leaning toward extremes.

As we shall see, both civilizations have their respective strengths and achievements as well as their shortcomings. As mankind enters the third millennium AD, we have begun to see a rapprochement between West and East on the basis of their strengths and achievements, having dealt with their respective weaknesses, often with great suffering and conflict. We can see the potential synergy, rather than the incompatibility, between the Eastern rule of ethics and the Western rule of law, consolidating the free market and democracy.

Chapter 2

Man and Nature:
Western God vs. Eastern Tao

"The Ethiopians say that their Gods are black-skinned; the Thracians say that theirs are red-haired ... Horses would draw the figures of their Gods like horses, and oxen like oxen, and would depict their bodies on the model of their own."[1]

Xenophanes

"The Creator ... His hair became the grass and herbs ... his eyes, Sun and Moon ... As for the fleas on his body, these became the diverse races of humankind."[2]

Eastern Creation Myth

Western Theism vs. Yin-Yang Deism

In the previous chapter, I attempted to demonstrate that the differences between Eastern and Western civilizations originated from their different environmental contexts: the land in the East and the sea in the West. We have further explored how these contrasting environments helped man to produce the fundamental concepts of these respective civilizations: unity in the East and separation in the West. These core concepts manifested themselves in all three cardinal relationships relating to mankind: between Man and Nature, between Spirit and Body, and between Man and Man.

The result was a greater individuation and liberty of entities in the West—Nature, God, Man, Spirit, Body. This Western dynamic, with the basic aim of self-preservation, was regulated by the concept of "rule by law inside and rule by force outside" until these elements were combined as the universal rule of law during the twentieth century. By contrast, emphasis in the East was placed on the relationship between such entities, thus relying on harmony as the basis for civilization. This dynamic, with the same aim of self-preservation, was regulated for over two millennia by the rule of ethics, periodically disrupted by a spell of authoritarian despotism; the East was able to break this cycle only with the influence of the Western rule of law in the twentieth century.

In the West, the idea of God has been essential in legitimating man's separation from nature and his domination both of his environment and of other men. In this chapter, we shall examine the implications of this monotheistic and anthropomorphic religion by contrasting it to the Eastern concept of "Tao," which is at once natural and rational, without recourse to the category of the supernatural.

We shall then examine how the Western concept of God sustained man's subjugation of nature and its relationship to his expansive worldview. Creation theology was later augmented by the Darwinian theory of evolution, positing an evolved man within a created nature. We will contrast this Western creationism-evolutionism with Eastern cosmology-transformism, as expressed in the *I Ching* and in the concept of Yin-Yang, which was incorporated into Taoism as one of its core tenets.

Greco-Roman Era vs. Warring-States Era

The post-Renaissance West owes its civilization to the Atlantic. But this period is only a renaissance, that is, a rebirth. The first birth of the West was Mediterranean, and its two central elements— Judeo-Christian religion and Greco-Roman philosophy—were both created around the Mediterranean. The blossoming of various Greek philosophies was rendered possible by a long period of intense competition among Greek city-states. And the rise of Roman law came about with the strife that accompanied its extraordinary expansion.

The birth of Western civilization roughly coincided with that of the East, which covered five centuries of intense competition and incessant warfare among various nations. This era began with the waning of the Zhou dynasty and ended with the reunification of China under the Qin dynasty; in China it can be divided into the Spring and Autumn Period (eighth to fifth centuries BC) and the Warring States Period (fifth to third centuries BC). During the Spring and Autumn Period, Zhou kings maintained their nominal title with actual powers belonging to powerful feudal hegemons; during the Warring States Period, the remaining Zhou authorities had all but disappeared as the hegemons began to consolidate their own kingdom, calling themselves kings, equal to Zhou. Nations vying with each other provided a fertile ground for the blossoming of philosophy—this phenomenon is referred to in the East as the "Hundred Flowers Competing for Fame."[3] As we know, all important Eastern schools of philosophy—including Confucianism, Taoism, Legalism, Mohism, and Yin-Yang, as well as Sun Tzu's *Art of War*—were developed during this period. Just as the various pre-Socratic philosophers travelled from city to city in search of an audience, so Confucius, Mencius, Sun Tzu, and others travelled from kingdom to kingdom. The same would happen again in modern Europe, with Machiavelli, Hobbes, Voltaire, and so on, who travelled between different nations.

The two great eras of intense competition among numerous entities, the city-states of Greece and the kingdoms of China, and the blossoming of various philosophies in the East and West, are to be matched one and a half millennia later only by the modern age of the West when numerous nation-states competed against each other, providing fertile ground for new ideas to germinate.[4]

Thus, in both East and West, such great teachers and religious leaders as Lao Tzu (the founder of Taoism), Confucius, Socrates, the Buddha, Jesus, and Mohammed appeared successively, and Mosaic Judaism was codified following the rebuilding of Solomon's Temple in 516 BC. The key difference was that the West, in its expansive maritime environment, emphasized religion and law, whereas the East, in its circumscribed and agricultural environment, relied on education and ethics for self-preservation.

As observed in the previous chapter, it was around this period that mankind accomplished major innovations in cultivation and animal husbandry; increased productivity allowed population densities to reach a critical mass, creating a plethora of new moral and socio-political problems. These problems were ultimately answered by ethics in the East and law in the West, but both solutions shared a single guiding principle—that of self-preservation. The central distinction stemmed from the presence or absence of a supernatural being or God.

Yin-Yang and *I Ching*

The Yin-Yang (陰陽) philosophy is the key to understanding the Eastern relationship between Man and Nature. The Chinese words originally denoted the sunny (Yang) and shady (Yin) sides of a mountain. A description of this principle first appeared in fourteenth century BC in China, as an explanation of cosmological premises without recourse to the supernatural entity. Transformation and complementarity are two essential aspects: The transformation principle implies both change and stability; the complementarity principle undergirds all the phases of creation.

Greco-Roman polytheism must have developed in about the same period, with its first literary attestation in Homer, around the ninth or eighth century BC. Egypt and Babylon already had polytheistic religion by 2000 BC, while the Minoans (based on Crete before 1450 BC) seem to have worshipped a number of goddesses. Moses is also thought to have imparted his laws to the Israelites around the same time. The first five books of the Jewish Bible, also called the Torah in Hebrew, or the Pentateuch in Greek, seem to have been completed and codified—a process traditionally ascribed to Ezra—around the fifth century BC. Although there is little definite evidence for the dates, one can safely assume that a monotheistic religion was first systematized in this time frame. In China, as we have noted, the principles of Yin and Yang were developed into a systematic philosophy during the Spring and Autumn and Warring States Periods, and thence penetrated virtually all schools of thoughts.

Although the terminology of Yin-Yang was created and disseminated from the end of the second millennium BC, its genesis can be traced back even further, to the legendary origins of the *I Ching*, said to have been delivered by a sage of the third millennium BC. For two millennia, as its basic elements, the *I Ching* used not Yin and Yang but unbroken (–) and broken (--) lines, which it called Firm (or steadfast, 剛) and Soft (or yielding, 柔). Yin and Yang were incorporated only around 1000 BC as the terms began to gain wider currency; they harmonized perfectly with Firm and Soft, the former identified with Yang, and the latter with Yin. In the process, there occurred a subtle but intriguing reversal of priority: *I Ching* placed Firm before Soft, whereas Taoism placed Yin before Yang. This switch reflects the paradigm shift in the East during the first millennium BC from "law and force" to "ethics."

Taoism initially made use of the 'Firm-Soft' dichotomy of the *I Ching*, rather than Yin and Yang; it was only during the first millennium, after the arrival of Buddhism with its metaphysical character, that Taoism began to incorporate the current labels and their attendant cosmology. This conjoint Eastern cosmology postulated an Ultimate Being (*Taiji*, 太極, "ridgepole"), prior to which was an Ultimate Non-Being (*Wuji*, 無極, "ridgepole-less"). The Ultimate Non-Being can be construed as the broken line of the *I Ching*, and the Ultimate Being as the unbroken. From the Ultimate Non-Being arose Yin and Yang, just as the Firm line creates two entities in any spatio-temporal dimension by defining above/down, right/left, front/back, and past/future.[5] And from this primary Yin-Yang arose many forms and manifestations, both natural and human. The Taoist diagram ☯ is meant to evoke this cosmogony: from Ultimate Non-Being proceeds Ultimate Being, which in turn gives rise to Yin and Yang; the primal Yin contains the seed of Yang and the primal Yang contains the seed of Yin, which explains the dynamic and reciprocal relation of all things under Heaven.[6]

Above is a very brief synthesis of the Eastern cosmology, which can be gleaned from the combined *I Ching*, Yin-Yang philosophy, and Taoism. Let us not attach too much importance to its metaphysical or epistemological implications; let us rather, since our aim is to understand the relationship of Man to Nature, direct our attention to the entirely natural character of Eastern cosmology. To this end, we shall contrast the natural foundation of Eastern culture to the supernatural basis of Western cosmology and religion.

Cosmology: Supernatural Theism vs. Natural Deism

The philosophy of Yin-Yang and *I Ching* is quite similar to the Deism developed in the West during the Age of Enlightenment. Tao, like the God of the Deists, is an eternal principle that does not intervene in human affairs, nor does it produce miracles or supernatural phenomena. The Deists considered these latter aspects of Christianity to be irrational, but since they were arguing in reaction to theism, they did not develop their ideas into a fully fledged system of thought. On the other hand, the very similar Eastern deism continued to evolve. For this reason, the supernatural-natural pairing captures better the West-East contrast than the theism-deism one. What sort of new thoughts, and new ethics, might have evolved from deism? Eastern philosophy provides an answer to this intriguing question.

During the period when the concept of Yin-Yang was being established, the West remained dominated by polytheism. The anthropomorphic character of its deities provides a profound contrast to the thoroughly natural character of Eastern culture and was even more pronounced in Greco-Roman polytheism than it was in Judeo-Christian monotheism. With regard to the relationship between Man and Nature, there is little difference between polytheism and monotheism: both are predicated on the separation of Man from Nature and of Spirit from Body, and the superiority of each first term to each second. We need not elaborate on this point, as it is so well known from the global domination of Western paradigms.

On the other hand, the non-supernatural character of Eastern cosmology, with its harmonious Man-Nature relationship, has hardly been stressed enough. There is no implication of the supernatural or religion in Yin-Yang philosophy and in all the other Eastern schools of thought. This aspect puzzled Enlightenment thinkers, who asked how a country without God's blessing could be so affluent, and how a non-religious system of ethics was possible at all.[7] In the entire Yin-Yang philosophy, there are no theistic attributes or elements whatsoever—no mention of a supernatural entity, spirit, god, demon, or life after death. Rather, it begins and ends with the observation of nature, of which both Yin and Yang are parts. This focus on nature and natural manifestations freed the East from reflections on supernatural entities, miracles, theology, metaphysics, and ideology. Assuredly, there were many deities, like Pangu, and many who worshiped them, but, as we shall see with Xun Zi in chapter 3, these were treated as useful cultural ornaments rather than having any serious theological or metaphysical implications.

The same is true of the *I Ching*. Even though this and most other Chinese classics occasionally mention *Shen* (神, spirit, god, demon, deity, spiritual), the word has a different meaning from that of the Western *Spirit* and, like the word for *Heaven* (天), lacks any connotation of theism. As the *I Ching* evolved from a cosmology and divinatory practice into a full philosophical system during the first millennium BC, *Heaven* was increasingly used to represent a higher principle in opposition to *Earth*. Nonetheless, it had no theological or metaphysical connotations, indicating instead the sublime and noble; for example, the Mandate of Heaven was to become an Emperor, while Rejection by Heaven follows a violation of Tao or Humanity. Heaven (noble principle), Earth (mundane affairs), and Man (as the sole actor) constitute three primordial entities: when the *I Ching* developed its trigrams, each of its three components represented Heaven, Earth, or Man.

As nature itself is the Supreme Being and man's ultimate point of reference, man must closely observe natural phenomena and human affairs, rather than trying to control it by associating himself with a supernatural being. This emphasis was particularly developed in Taoism, as a philosophy contextualizing man within nature. Yin and Yang provided the basis for all of Eastern philosophy, including Taoism and Confucianism, with their characteristic focus on humility before, and harmonious coexistence with, Nature. By contrast to this, monotheism provided the West with its focus on the active assertion of self and religious absolutism.

Opposites: Yin-Yang "Cherish" vs. Monotheistic "Crush"
There are many valid and useful explanations of the fundamentals of Yin-Yang philosophy. But in contrast to Western monotheism, its most essential features can be reduced to two. The first is its notion of complementary opposites. The second one is its syncretistic perspective. To repeat, there were similar concepts in Greece, for instance, the concept of Unity of Opposites, or the *coincidentia oppositorum* of Heraclitus (ca. 535–475 BC), but Heraclitus' ideas made few inroads in the mainstream of Western thought. Among Greek thinkers, it was rather Plato and Aristotle, whose main

focus was the importance of Spirit over Body, who influenced medieval theology and modern metaphysics. Consequently, we shall compare the Western monotheistic exclusionary dialectics with the Eastern Yin-Yang inclusionary complementarity.

The Eastern mind perceives all natural phenomena within the framework of Yin-Yang: summer and winter, day and night, man and woman, waxing and waning of the moon, life and death, and so on. As these pairs illustrate, everything in the universe has its opposite, without which it cannot exist: Yin creates Yang and Yang activates Yin, neither meaningful without the other. This concept, symbolized by the *taijitu*, the circular diagram of Yin and Yang, underlies all Eastern philosophy. In the West, dualism has likewise been acknowledged by philosophers since antiquity, but mainstream Western culture invariably takes the two elements as contrary or oppositional terms. Eastern culture is founded on the premise that "opposites are complementary"; Western culture is based on the premise that "opposites are contrary."

Yin-Yang is the conceptual opposite of almost everything represented by Western monotheism. As we shall see, Western monotheism exhibits Yang characteristics and attributes, such as assertiveness and dynamism, whereas Eastern philosophy exhibits Yin attributes like receptiveness and equanimity. Each set of traits manifests the underlying character of their respective civilizations. But the most conspicuous contrast is evident in their treatments of the notion of "opposite." Western monotheism, with its principle of exclusion, resolved to crush pagans, idolaters, atheists, and heretics, all of whom it understood as the enemies of God; hence, many Greek and Roman temples were destroyed after the adoption of Christianity as the official religion of the Roman Empire in the fourth century. The philosophy of Yin-Yang, on the other hand, cherishes opposites, as one cannot exist without the other. Yin and

Yang are not only abstract principles, but part of nature. And since man is part of nature, human affairs also must follow the Yin-Yang pattern. Taoism thus connects man with nature and focuses on establishing a social and political ethos based on reciprocal opposites. This we shall examine in greater detail below.

Syncretistic Yin-Yang vs. Exclusionary Theism

The second feature that puts Yin-Yang in direct contrast to Western monotheism is its syncretistic character. During the first millennium BC, the school of Yin-Yang, which then concentrated on astrological divination, coexisted with Confucian, Taoist, Mohist, Legalist, and Fatalist Schools. But it failed to develop into a philosophical system, perhaps because the East, with its hostility to the supernatural, did not favor divinatory practices. Rather, it was other philosophical schools, such as Taoism, which propagated the doctrine of complementarity at the heart of Yin-Yang.

This phenomenon of assimilation with resultant syncretism is not unique to Yin-Yang. Humanity (仁) and Tao ('way', 道) had been in general use throughout the East before their elaboration as Confucianism and Taoism, respectively. Taoism, with its emphasis on ethics, reinforced the Eastern tendency of putting Yin before Yang. This stands in stark contrast to Western culture, which, with its emphasis on divine and human law, always prioritized Yang over Yin.

The shape of the Yin-Yang diagram first appeared not in the East but in the West.[8] It was in the fifth century AD that a Roman legion began to use it as an emblem decorating its shields, as illustrated in Figures 2-1 and 2-2.[9] But given the nature of Roman culture, this usage of the symbol involved no assimilation of the meaning of Yin-Yang. Western theism, be it polytheistic or monotheistic, is fundamentally in contrast with Yin-Yang, which denies any supernatural intervention in physical and human affairs. We find a similar attitude among the Western Epicureans, who denied supernatural intervention in human affairs. But as we know, this school had little impact on the mainstream of Western thought, which was dominated by theology and metaphysics.

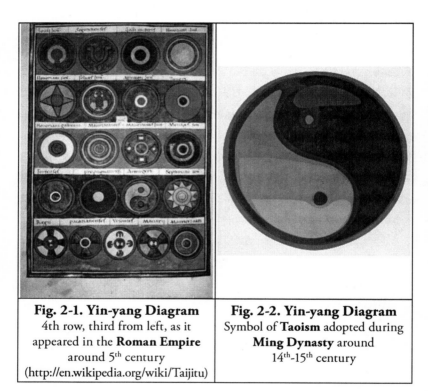

Fig. 2-1. Yin-yang Diagram	Fig. 2-2. Yin-yang Diagram
4th row, third from left, as it appeared in the **Roman Empire** around 5th century (http://en.wikipedia.org/wiki/Taijitu)	Symbol of **Taoism** adopted during **Ming Dynasty** around 14th-15th century

The role of Yin-Yang in Eastern culture is approximately comparable to that of Judeo-Christian cosmology in the West: Christian monotheism constituted the theological backbone of the Middle Ages, the metaphysics of the modern era, and the ideologies of post-modernity. As we shall see, monotheism contributed to the growth of the West's twin concepts of Liberty and Conflict, whereas in the East, Yin-Yang reinforced attitudes of unity and harmony in Taoism with respect to the Man-Nature relationship, in Confucianism with respect to the Man-Man relationship, and in Li-Ki (理氣) with respect to the Mind-Body relationship. Naturally, there is a clear contrast in the role of the two principles in their respective cultures. In the East, Yin-Yang was assimilated and accepted by all schools; in the West, anthropomorphic monotheism was accepted by religious and philosophical schools, before being rejected by many aspects of the Enlightenment.

It is tempting to imagine that the two ideas had a common origin: both expressed the existence of an ultimate order or being in the natural world. This is not altogether fanciful, given Yahweh's initial strong resistance to Moses' appeal for anthropomorphic transformation: "Moses hid his face, because he was afraid to look at God" (Exodus 3:6); the theophany at Sinai has God hidden in a great smoke: "But," the Lord said, "you cannot see my face, for no one may see me and live." Then he said, "There is a place near me where you may stand on a rock. When my glory passes by, I will put you in a cleft in the rock and cover you with my hand until I have passed by. Then I will remove my hand and you will see my back; but my face must not be seen." (Exodus 33:20–23) This demonstrates the existence of a pre-anthropomorphic representation of Yahweh, who responded, "I am what I am" when asked his name. Yet due to their environmental differences, East and West evolved in opposition. At the heart of the difference was the anthropomorphic development of Western monotheism. We shall examine this in detail in the following chapters.

Infallible God vs. Ineffable Tao

In defining the relationship between Man and Nature, Tao and God provided the East and the West with their respective frameworks. But while Tao remained natural and ineffable, God, as a supernatural being, became anthropomorphic and infallible.

Tao, Taoism, and Taoteking

The Taoteking (道德經, Tao and its Power), the canon of Taoism, is comparable to the Old Testament in terms of its role in, and importance to, Eastern civilization. The West missed an early opportunity to learn of Taoism, when the Jesuit missionaries brought back only Confucianism during the seventeenth and eighteenth centuries; in the nineteenth century, the West's confidence in its own spirituality was so powerful that everything deemed "unspiritual," including Taoism, was discarded immediately. Thus, Taoteking appeared to most Western minds as archaic and mystifying.

There were at least three reasons for this reaction. The first was a matter of style. Taoteking in its entirety is composed of poems or aphorisms, reserved in the Western intellectual tradition for anecdotal and nonsystematic inspirations. Although there are many aphoristic and fragmentary works in the Western tradition, from the Wisdom books of the Old Testament (Proverbs, Ecclesiastes, Wisdom) to the *Adages* of Erasmus, the *Maximes* of La Rochefoucauld, the *Fragments* of Schlegel and Novalis, and the apothegms of Nietzsche, none comes close to the high level of initial inscrutability of Taoteking. Inscrutability, at least initially, arises from the work's ambiguity and ambivalence: "The passages of Taoteking are ambiguous, and topics range from political advice for rulers to practical wisdom for people. Readers do well to avoid making claims of objectivity or superiority because the variety of interpretation is virtually limitless not only for different people but for the same person over time. Also, since the book is eighty-one short poems, there is little need for an abridgement."[10] But we must also observe the merits of the Chinese ideogram as a means of writing. Being synthetic and integral as opposed to analytic and dialectic, the ideogram can conserve and convey meanings in a way unavailable to alphabetic languages.

The second reason for Western incomprehension was the work's age—it was written about two and a half thousand years ago, the same period as Homer and the Old Testament. Yet Taoteking claims its relevance to such contemporary paradigms as the free market and democracy. Without proper introduction, translation, and explanation, it would be very difficult for many Western minds to see such relevance. We shall see this aspect in the following chapters. The third reason was the incompatibility between Eastern philosophy and the traditional Western mind, trained within the framework of theology, metaphysics, and ideologies. Thus, the Taoteking could be easily assumed as an object of study by academic intellectuals, but had little appeal to the general public.

Prima facie, the book appears a simple collection of loosely connected aphorisms, with the occasional insight but little more. But, as Taoteking repeatedly observes, appearances can be deceiving. Tao is often impenetrable at first glance. With this in mind, let us examine the true substance of Taoteking. First, let us consider its "aphoristic" nature. The book concerns Tao and its Forces. It is so short that the word "chapter" for each of its eighty-one segments is misleading. For instance, the shortest chapter, number 40, is composed of two sentences: "Returning is the mode of operation of Tao; yielding is the usefulness of Tao. All things under the heaven are born of being; being is born of non-being." These are more like poems or epigrams. The entire work more closely resembles a single chapter composed of eighty-one paragraphs. Each chapter, however, may be annotated indefinitely. The meaning of even a single word eludes easy comprehension— let alone the work as a whole.

Taoteking is attributed to a single individual, Lao Tzu (老子, literally meaning "old sage"), but, as specialists have argued, it is more likely to be a collection of insights and thoughts from many thinkers and observers of a similar tendency over centuries. Every sentence and every paragraph offers a conclusion, with no logic or explanation. For this reason, Taoism is best understood not as an "ism" or ideology, but as a school. Whereas an ideology presents itself as the truth, higher than man, the purpose of a school is heuristic, to serve man; Taoteking emphatically denies that objective truth is within human reach. Legend has it that Lao Tzu, having been enlightened, was about to leave this world. When a peasant saw Lao Tzu departing, he asked him for a souvenir for this world. Lao Tzu left Taoteking.

The innumerable Eastern literati who have studied Confucius' books would be greatly puzzled if asked, "Do you believe in Confucianism?" It would be like asking a man reading a book on the French language if he was a Frenchist. Just as one can speak French, English, and many other languages, so one can study the teachings of Confucius, Tao, and Buddha at the same time; the teachings are at the service of man, not the other way round.

Accordingly, since Confucius, Lao Tzu, and Buddha have left us great insights and wisdom, it is preferable for us to absorb as much of their teachings as possible, rather than focusing on one to the exclusion of others. From an Eastern perspective, its syncretism is rational, and it is rather Western religion that is full of mysticism, superstitions, and irrational dogmas; to a Westerner, its own religion and ideology are rational, and Taoism, with its strange symbols and words, is superstitious, irreligious, and irrational. The difference is paradigmatic: one cannot accept both as long as one maintains an exclusionary frame of mind, which prevents us from overcoming the barrier. The Western focus on "isms" is a remnant of the exclusionary character of medieval theology, modern metaphysics, and ideologies—one is encouraged to have faith in a single body of thought, with any deviation deemed heretical. The Eastern notion of a "school," on the other hand, encourages a syncretistic or eclectic attitude, as it is only natural that one tries to benefit from all schools. It is greatly hoped that with the demise of the Age of Ideologies, we can also overcome our exclusionary mind-set. It is a tall order, but, as illustrated by the domination of the inefficient "qwerty" keyboard arrangement, nothing is predetermined. There are always possibilities and uncertainties.

Wuwei and Taoism

If Taoteking is comparable to the Old Testament, its core principle of Wuwei (無為) can be compared to God's Law in the role each played in their respective civilizations. But their aims are almost diametrically opposed. If the Word of God is the Ultimate Being, Wuwei of Tao is the Ultimate Non-Being: "The sage manages his affairs with Wuwei" (Taoteking 2); "Act with Wuwei, and everything falls into place" (Taoteking 3); "Relying on Wuwei, Tao achieves everything" (Taoteking 35); "Teaching without instructing, acting with Wuwei: this is the highest art of the sage" (Taoteking 43). Wuwei literally means "no action" and can be translated in various terms, including nonaction, inaction, without action, action without action, effortless action, soft action, invisible action, laissez-faire, and action by default. Each represents part of Wuwei but none fully grasps its meaning. I will therefore use the term Wuwei itself, rather than a translation, with "non-interventionism" as an alternative when discussing the free market and political economy.

Here are some examples of Wuwei in operation: "The sage has no plan of his own; he uses the plan of the people" (Taoteking 49); "As the sage acts with Wuwei, he does not fail; as the sage possesses nothing, he loses nothing" (Taoteking 64); "The sage relies on Wuwei, people will act. The sage relies on equanimity, people will be peaceful. The sage relies on no decrees, people will enjoy abundance. The sage relies on no ambition, people will be innocent" (Taoteking 57); "The sage knows without moving; understands without looking; achieves without acting" (Taoteking 47).

The philosophy of Wuwei was firmly established more than two millennia ago in an environment of constant warfare between nations. Its proponents identified a lust for power and wealth as the main cause of conflict, both between individuals and between nations. The teaching of Taoism is about returning to the pre-greed state. Thus, Wuwei was founded on the fundamental premise of the Ultimate Non-Being, which precedes the Ultimate Being. Wuwei thus advocated the ideal of emptiness rather than plenitude, arguing that in the beginning there was nothing: "All things are born of being; being is born of non-being" (Taoteking 40).[11] In the West, one may find a similar concept in the theory of "Chaos" of Hesiod and Genesis. Christianity claims that the Creation was *ex nihilo*, from nothing: "In the beginning, the Earth was without form and void."[12]

Yet there is a critical contrast between the two: in the West, Chaos or Void is described with a negative connotation as opposed to the subsequent Order or Creation. Thus, the real importance for the West is not non-being but being: "In the beginning there was the Word, and the Word was with God, and the Word was God."[13] On the other hand, in the East, Ultimate Non-Being or Wuji is more fundamental than Ultimate Being or Taiji. Order and Word are no better than no-Order and no-Word. Wuwei argues that words, as expressions of greed more than altruism, are the source of disorder more than order. In that sense, one understands why Tao must remain nameless (Taoteking 1). For the sake of peace and harmony, then, man should always remember the merit of his preverbal state—a state of nothingness. The ultimate reference point for humanity must therefore be non-action, rather than action. The Confucian golden rule, "Do not do unto others what you do not want them to do unto you," shares the fundamental non-interventionism of Taoism. The golden rule of Christianity, by contrast, is active: "Do unto others as you would have them do unto you."

But Taoism does not stop there. It acknowledges the necessity of living in this world and using actions and words, provided that they are not considered more highly than no action, no words; that is, Wuwei. Among Greek thinkers, Carneades (ca. 214–129 BC) espoused a very similar philosophy. He did not believe in metaphysics, as he thought that the search for truth by abstract and speculative reasoning would lead man neither to wisdom nor to enhanced knowledge. Yet he did believe that relative truth can be discerned by man, and that it would enable him to live and act correctly. Unlike the West, where ideas like this became marginalized, in the East they constituted the mainstream. Confucianism, to be precise, played the role of being, order, word, and action as opposed to the Taoist principle of non-being. The important aspect in this relationship is that the two schools of thought, Confucianism and Taoism, acknowledged their respective roles. Confucianism accepts Wuwei as its mode of action: "Managing a state by virtue is illustrated in the Pole Star; as it keeps its place in stillness, all the other stars find their place."[14] "The Book of Poetry contains three hundred poems for us. They can be condensed in one concept— having no depraved thoughts."[15] Both Confucianism and Taoism value non-codified ethics over codified laws, as the latter, despite good intentions, risks being overshadowed by greed and thus giving rise to depraved thoughts.

We shall discover in the following chapters, especially in chapter 9, Wuwei's role in the East's assimilation of the free market and political economy, as it had long been the modus operandi of Eastern civilization. Wuwei includes an understanding of the nature around us, of human nature, of the desirable form of government, and of the relationship among nations.

Context of Taoism: Circumscribed East

Taoism and Confucianism constitute two pillars, or Yin and Yang, of Eastern civilization. One cannot understand the East without knowing Taoism, since it is this which defines the East's conception of the Man-Nature relationship. But while Confucianism was introduced to the West and admired by Enlightenment thinkers, Taoism has been largely ignored. The Jesuits at that time were received exclusively by those scholar officials who had passed the imperial examination, the curriculum of which was then limited to the Confucian canons. And when the West finally made full contact with the East, its spiritual, economic, and military superiority led it to dismiss as outmoded the cultural and ethical values of the East. But neither the present economic rise of the East, nor its ethical contributions, can be grasped without reference to Taoism, especially its core principle, non-interventionism.

In order to grasp the essence of Taoism as a collection of fundamental insights on nature, man, and government, we must examine the context in which it developed. This was a period of constant warfare between nations lasting about five centuries, comparable to the modern West with its centuries of international conflict since the Renaissance. Although two thousand years apart, there are two crucial differences between the warring periods of East and West.

The first is that Western nations, as we have already seen, have lived and fought in an expansive world, whereas Eastern nations were engaged in a circumscribed world. The West has always viewed glory in victory and promoted statecraft for the sake of self-preservation and short-term profit; the East, for the sake of self-preservation and long-term benefit, understood the futility of victory and kept statecraft to a minimum. Unlike the West, where warfare and piracy brought wealth and slaves, and where a Hobbesian attitude of "war of all against all" prevailed, wars in the East brought no slaves or plunder, and even its victories were deemed Pyrrhic. Taoism identified greed as the core motivation behind warfare; we shall see how this insight provided the essential basis of Taoteking.

The second point concerns the relevance of this attitude to the twenty-first century, which has become a circumscribed world. It should be remembered that the Western situation is only the culmination of a paradigm of conflict lasting over two millennia. By contrast, the East, even in its "warring states" period, has lived within a circumscribed perspective for the same amount of time. The relevance of Eastern philosophy arises from this similarity in terms of cultural context between the East of the first millennium BC and our world today. With this in mind, let us examine the true nature of Tao, by exploring its differences from the Western notion of God.

Ineffable Tao vs. Infallible God

It is undeniable that the Book of Tao, written more than two millennia ago, contains a certain amount of mysticism, but it is also true that Tao and Yin-Yang have a rational foundation—perhaps even a scientific one.[16] Their means of expression are deliberately vague, ambiguous, and mystical because they aim to convey not knowledge but wisdom, which is seldom clear-cut. Therefore, Taoteking and many other Eastern classics can be given multiple interpretations, not only by different readers, but even by the same reader at different times.

To repeat, Tao represents Nature and, in essence, *is* Nature. Further, it demonstrates that Man is part of Nature, which in turn is one and the same as God. The first chapter of Taoteking starts: "The Tao that can be told is not the eternal Tao. The name that can be named is not the eternal name.... Ever desireless, one can see the essence; ever desiring, one sees the manifestations." And it ends: "The sage never tries to store things up. The more he does for others, the more he has. The more he gives to others, the greater his abundance. The Tao of heaven is pointed but does no harm. The Tao of the sage is work without effort."[17] We can find a similar approach in the Greek thinkers like Plotinus and the Pseudo-Dionysius, in the Jewish concept of "*Ein Sof*" (Infinite or Nameless Being) or "*Ein*" (Nothingness), and most importantly in the Western tradition of Apophatic or negative theology, the *Via negativa*. Ein Sof is quite comparable to Taoist Ultimate Being and Ein to Ultimate Non-Being. Yet again, these Yin Western attempts remained at the margin of the Yang assertive mainstream and Cataphatic (positive) theology, since Western religion was increasingly based on revelation, incarnate Logos, and anthropomorphic evolution.

By contrast to the East, Western civilization demands a separation between Man and Nature, both of which were created by God, the essence of Spirit—an idea utterly foreign to Taoism. Thus, the Bible begins with the Creation and closes with the Book of Revelation, which describes the end of the world and the Last Judgment. As the Supreme Judge, the Western God interferes in human affairs as a god of justice; Tao, as Nature itself, does not interfere in human affairs—man is to accept and follow Tao, which is beyond human morality.

The first monotheistic religion emerged in Egypt in the fourteenth century BC, when, during the reign of Pharaoh Akhenaten, the sun was worshiped as the sole divinity, Aten. The next is the religion of the Israelites, which was formed toward the end of the second millennium BC. Then, we have Zoroastrianism in Persia (ca. sixth century BC to seventh century AD), which worshipped fire as the sign of Ahura Mazda, the Wise Lord. But the monotheistic religion most influential in the West was that of Moses.[18] According to experts, several centuries separate Moses from Ezra. Perhaps this period witnessed the crucial anthropomorphic transformation of the Western God. During these eight centuries, the story of Moses absorbed many elements from other tribes and regions—for example, the creation of the universe, the Deluge, the Exodus.

In the beginning, God resisted Moses' plea for definition. When Moses asks the name of God, God denies any definition beyond his existence, saying merely "I am what I am."[19] God has no name, no form, being beyond definition. It follows then that men are forbidden to make images of God. In this sense, Moses' original concept of God was similar to that of Tao in its ineffability: "Tao cannot be heard; what is heard is not Tao. Tao cannot be seen; what is seen is not Tao. Tao cannot be spoken; what is spoken is not Tao."[20] A creature cannot know its creator. The creator can be perceived as Nature or God but must otherwise remain essentially unknown. Nor can man name or define his creator. Otherwise, the relationship between creator and creature is broken. God's first account of Himself, "I am what I am," as well as his repeated warnings against images, has a profound meaning. It can be interpreted as an injunction to resist the temptation of defining God by anthropomorphism. Figures 2-3 and 2-4 illustrate respectively Lao Tzu and Moses.

Fig. 2-3. Lao Tzu (6ᵗʰ century BC)	**Fig. 2-4. Moses (14ᵗʰ century BC)**
According to legends, Lao Tzu leaves China on his water buffalo (http://en.wikipedia.org/wiki/Laozi)	*Moses with the Tablets*, by Rembrandt. (http://en.wikipedia.org/wiki/File:Rembrandt_Harmensz._van_Rijn_079)

In fact, the ineffability of God is a fairly common point in many aspects of mystical Jewish and Christian thought as well as Greek philosophy, as we have noted above. But as we shall see, the expansive environment made it impossible for the West to preserve the ineffable character of its God. In this environment, personal conviction served as a means to enhance one's confidence as one ventured into the unknown, but a belief in an eternal and absolute God encouraged people to adapt facts into particular patterns, as Bertrand Russell appeared to imply when travelling China and appreciating Eastern culture: "I know of no other civilization where there was such open-mindedness, such realism, and such a willingness to face the facts as they are, instead of trying to distort them into a particular pattern."[21]

God or Tao, as the absolute being or principle of the cosmos, must be ineffable and infallible—two qualities that are necessarily bound together. Tao had no need to insist on infallibility, since it emphasized ineffability. But ineffability is compromised as soon as the absolute principle becomes anthropomorphic. Thus, when God became manifest and anthropomorphic in Christ, the West had to insist on the infallibility of its God, and of his earthly representative, the pope. Pseudo-Dionysius (ca. AD 500) is known to have warned against presenting god or angels in human form, since this encourages us to confuse the two.

Equanimous Tao vs. Anthropomorphic God

Despite this similar point of origin, however, the Western and Eastern concepts of nature diverged radically. While Tao remained ineffable and indefinable, the Western God was given multiple definitions with anthropomorphic characteristics. Eventually answering Moses' requests, God gives his name, Yahweh, to Moses and speaks with Moses on Mount Sinai. He allows himself to be defined: God of Justice, God of Wrath, and God of Jealousy. His burning finger engraves the Ten Commandments upon two stone tablets. Later, at Joshua's request, God halts the passage of the Sun to allow Israel to triumph.[22] As such, the deity continued to undergo anthropomorphic transformations; he performs numerous miracles and invites human prayers and worship. Western religion stipulates that man was created in the image of God.

An Eastern mind would argue the reverse, agreeing instead with such pre-Socratic philosophers as Pseudo-Dionysius and Xenophanes of Colophon (ca. 500 BC), who composed verses on divine anthropomorphism. He writes in one of his works, "The Ethiopians say that their Gods are snub-nosed and black-skinned, and the Thracians that theirs are blue-eyed and red-haired. If oxen and horses had hands and wanted to draw with their hands or to make the works of art that men make, then horses would draw the figures of their Gods like horses, and oxen like oxen, and would depict their bodies on the model of their own."

The anthropomorphism of Western deities stands in complete contrast to the profound ineffability of the Eastern analogue, Tao. Taoism maintains its ineffability. Taoteking literally means "the Way and its Virtue": "All things arise from Tao; they are nourished by Virtue."[23] By presenting the Way as an eternal principle, of which only external manifestations are within our reach, Taoism discourages absolutism, such as religious dogma, metaphysics, ideologies, miracles, and superstitions. And while Taoism acknowledges the existence of an eternal principle, it repeatedly warns against confusing manifestation with essence, which is precisely what the Western anthropomorphic God does.

For some, the Taoist split between principle and manifestations may seem equivalent to the Platonic distinction between Truth (Knowledge) and Opinion, or the world of Forms and the material world around us. But in truth these are exactly opposite, in that the Platonic distinction was made to emphasize the importance of Truth, which constitutes man's ultimate objective, whereas the Taoist distinction was made to warn man against any futile efforts or arrogant and monstrous claim of custody of Truth. Plato says, "You can and must find the Truth, never be satisfied with opinions and manifestations"; Taoism, by contrast, says, "Try to discern precious manifestations even though they are not the eternal truth." Tao is unknowable in its essence but observable in its manifestation.[24] The West's search for knowledge, essence, and truth, relying on the philosophy of the ancient Greeks, did produce a positive accumulation of knowledge and the development of science. But at the same time, the idea of the human possibility of attaining Truth (i.e., the denial of ineffability) also contributed to the creation of monstrous ideologies in the West.

The following quotations from the Taoteking illustrate the indefinable quality of Tao: "The Tao that can be told is not the eternal Tao.... Desireless, one sees the essence; desiring, one sees the manifestations" (as we have already seen, this is the very first sentence of Taoteking and sets the tone for what follows)[25]: "Stand before it and there is no beginning; follow it and there is no end. Stay with the eternal Tao; move with the present"[26]; "Tao is subtle, mysterious, profound, and responsive; the depth of its knowledge is unfathomable. Because it is unfathomable, all we can do is to describe its manifestations"[27]; "Once the whole is divided, the parts need names. There are already enough names. One must know when to stop. Knowing when to stop averts trouble."[28]

In the East, the Tao remains integral and all-inclusive. For example, opposites, such as just and unjust, as well as good and bad, are all included in the Tao. Taoism regards these divisions as merely human constructs. Consequently, Tao embraces both good and evil, both just and unjust, both mercy and mercilessness: "If Tao is just, to what does the unjust belong? If Tao is good, to what does the bad belong? Tao is the source of both good and bad. Tao is the blessing of the just and the protection of the unjust."[29] Consequently, Tao promotes equanimity and control of self. Tao advises that control of self must precede control of others, since ethics, not law, must stand as the guiding principle of human relations.

Since the Judeo-Christian God is proclaimed as a God of Justice, the West has spent much time and energy attempting to solve the intractable problem of injustice and evil. But this Western division between just and unjust, good and evil also gave rise to its unique dialectic development and evolution: the dynamic interaction between the two entities, combined with the historic power struggle between the nobility and the monarchy, was finally instrumental in the production of valuable concepts and institutions, such as checks and balances, the rule of law, individual liberty, and democracy.

By rejecting division, Tao remains integral and inclusive. This trait has given Eastern civilization harmony and stability as well as inertia and complacency. Unknowable, Tao remains beyond human definition, but it encourages humility and agnosticism, the acceptance of chance and uncertainty in both natural and human affairs. Eastern man, while remaining agnostic, must attempt to discover relative truth, which, according to the fundamental tenet of the *I Ching,* is specific to given circumstances. As we have briefly seen, one can find a very similar epistemology in Greek philosophy, including that of Carneades, who denied absolute truth but allowed probable truth. But this attitude, being antithetical to that of Plato and Aristotle, was completely marginalized in Western mainstream philosophy and labeled as radical skepticism. We shall examine Carneades in more detail in chapter 6.

In the East, the denial that absolute truth could be attained was taken on by Taoism, while the task of seeking relative truth was left to Confucianism. According to the legend, Confucius did meet with Lao Tzu and recognized the profundity of his thinking.

Whereas Eastern thinkers warned against mistaking relative truths for absolute ones, the expansive Western mentality encouraged men to treat their truths as absolute, and manifestations as essence.[30] In the West, revelations, convictions, beliefs, or faiths are needed to justify one's actions.[31]

Spinozist God and Eastern Tao: Man-Nature Unity

If one has difficulty understanding Tao by reading Eastern texts, one has only to consult *Ethics* of Baruch Spinoza (1632–1677), whose characterizations of God are remarkably similar to those of the Tao by Lao Tzu. Indeed, Spinoza's understanding of human nature also is almost identical to that of the East. We shall examine the human nature aspect in chapter 3. Spinoza defines God in the first book of his *Ethics* as follows: "a being absolutely infinite"; "indivisible"; "not susceptible to passions"; "having no particular goal in view"; "having no volitions or desires"; "Nature itself." Spinoza further explains in the fifth book: "The mind's highest good is the knowledge of God, and the mind's highest virtue is to know God"; "God does not love or hate anyone"; "No one can hate God"; "Love towards God cannot be turned into hate"; "He, who loves God, cannot endeavor that God should love him in return." In all these definitions, God closely corresponds to the concept of Tao. Spinoza was identified by some Western thinkers, such as Nicolas Malebranche (1638–1715), with the Eastern philosophers. The *Ethics* could not be published in his lifetime, and for a century after his death his work was a byword for radicalism and even atheism, though much of this opprobrium stemmed from his critical-historical arguments in the *Tractatus Theologico-Politicus* (1670).

The following paragraphs demonstrate the similarity between Spinozism and Taoism: "By Tao, one means a being absolutely infinite; Tao, or substance, consisting of infinite attributes, necessarily exists; Tao, substance absolutely infinite, is indivisible. Besides Tao no substance can be granted or conceived. Whatsoever is, is in Tao, and without Tao nothing can be, or be conceived; Tao is efficient cause not only of the existence of things, but also of their essence; all things are in Tao, and so depend on it, that without it they could neither exist nor be conceived. It is impossible, that man should not be a part of Nature; the mind's highest good is the knowledge of Tao, and the mind's highest virtue is to know Tao; Tao does not love or hate anyone. For Tao is not affected by any emotion of pleasure or pain, consequently it does not love or hate anyone; the power, whereby each particular thing, and consequently man, preserves his being, is the power of Tao or of Nature. Thus the power of man, insofar as it is explained through his own actual essence, is a part of the infinite power of Tao or Nature, in other words, of the essence thereof. No one can hate Tao; he who loves Tao cannot endeavor that Tao should love him in return. Some assert that Tao, like man, consists of body and mind, and is susceptible to passions. How far such persons have strayed from the truth is sufficiently evident from what has been said." This passage has been stitched together entirely from propositions in Spinoza's *Ethics*, only replacing "God" with "Tao."

A rational explanation for this similarity across time and space is that both Tao and Spinoza identify God with Nature. Spinoza remains arguably the most important modern philosopher who made this identification in a systematic way. There were modern Western philosophers before Spinoza who had understood God as an immanent principle in the world: for instance, Giordano Bruno (1548–1600). Lucilio Vanini (1585–1619) meanwhile argued that God was identical to Nature and that both denoted simply the principle of motion in matter. Both Bruno and Vanini were burned at the stake for heresy and atheism. Before Spinoza, Thomas Hobbes (1588–1679) was already questioning the validity of revelation and the theory of Hell and Paradise, at the risk of being excommunicated. Spinoza was also certainly familiar with the Apophatic theology of Moses Maimonides (1135–1204). Spinoza was the culmination of this strand of dialectic Western philosophy.

In an expansive Western environment, action brings wealth and fame, and is based on conviction and faith. A centrifugal force prevails: man moves outward, and exploration and conquest become his principal goals. In this world, Man needed God to justify and reinforce his inner drives. God is superior to Nature, his creation, and so, by identifying himself with God, man himself becomes superior to Nature and to other men (i.e., non-believers). This conviction or faith was facilitated by anthropomorphism and remained useful as long as the West ventured into an expansive world. The religious zeal of missionaries and conquistadors in the Age of Discovery is well known. These men firmly believed in their mission to fulfill God's divine commands; the price they paid was alienation and separation from Nature.

An Eastern mind would readily agree with Spinoza when he says that these Western assertions are not God's will but human desires. Spinozism holds that "Nature does nothing on account of an end. That eternal and infinite being we call God, *or* Nature, acts from the same necessity from which he exists. For we have shown that the necessity of nature from which he acts is the same as that from which he exists. The reason, therefore, *or* cause, why God, *or* Nature, acts, and the reason why he exists, are one and the same. As he exists for the sake of no end, he also acts for the sake of no end. Rather, as he has no principle or end of existing, so he also has none of acting. What is called a final cause is nothing but a human appetite insofar as it is considered as a principle, or primary cause, *of* some thing."[32]

Spinoza lamented, as most Eastern minds would have done, that religion had acted more as a divider than as a unifier of mankind. Given the Yin character of his analysis, Spinoza would have been praised by the thinkers of the East. In the Yang West, however, he was persecuted as an atheist, pantheist, and heretic. His masterpiece, *Ethics*, could only be published posthumously, and this and other works were banned in the West for centuries. Many great Western philosophers admired Spinoza secretly and borrowed freely from him, but were forced to denounce him publicly—Goethe being a rare exception. This was due to the influence of monotheistic Christianity and fear of ecclesiastical and secular retribution. As long as the Western environment remained expansive, Yang tenets prevailed.

Evolution vs. Transformation

Under the influence of religion, the West retained its religious creationism until the nineteenth century. Creation stories are treated more like myths in the East, rather than being taken seriously. In the nineteenth century, the Darwinian theory of evolution shocked the West, which in some ways is still struggling with the aftermath of the conflict. As scientific theory and research is conspicuously lacking in the history of the East, there is no clear counterpart to the theory of evolution. But with respect to its ethical and practical implications, we can compare the concept of "transformation" in the *I Ching*.

Evolution of Man: Recapitulation

Humanity's evolutionary history is almost as old as the history of the earth itself: three to four billion years. Although the "theory of recapitulation" does not correspond to the actual evolution of the human embryo, at least early embryonic stages follow the same pattern common to other species: a fetus, as we know, begins with a single cell, the *ovum*, and then becomes a multicellular organism, successively transforming into forms that are jellylike, fishlike, reptile-like, and mammal-like before finally assuming its humanoid form.

Five-hundred million years ago, the earth was populated by fish and proto-amphibians, and so we can call this period the Age of Fish. All fish have fins with five bones in each, and their body fluid's saline density (0.8 percent) is the same as that of sea water. From this period, mankind inherited five fingers and 0.8 percent saline blood density, which, along with body temperature, is regulated by the remarkable mechanism of homeostasis. Had the fish of 500 million years ago possessed six bones instead of five in their fins, mankind may have had six fingers and, consequently, used a base-12 numerical system instead of the decimal one.

The Age of Fish was succeeded by the Age of Dinosaurs. The first land animals are thought to have emerged around 350 million years ago; dinosaurs dominated the earth between 200 and 70 million years ago. From these reptiles and birds, humans acquired the "R-complex": the reptilian brain. This is the oldest part of the human brain, responsible for the regulation of basic needs, drives, and instincts. Then, around 60 to 70 million years ago, the dinosaur suddenly died out, whether from a meteoric collision or a sudden climate change.

The Age of Dinosaurs was succeeded by the Age of Mammals. For the first period of approximately 100 million years, small mouse-like mammals led a hide-and-seek existence, eating seeds and insects on the forest floor, and being eaten in turn by carnivorous dinosaurs. The extinction of dinosaurs allowed them to climb the evolutionary ladder; some abandoned the ground life and adopted the safety of the trees—thus were born the first anthropoid apes.

Humans inherited from these mammals the "limbic system," which is responsible for the regulation of desire, passion, and emotion. The limbic system is called the old brain as opposed to the neocortex, or new brain. The latter deals with rational thinking, problem solving, planning, and organization; however, these functions require stimulation from the limbic system, a relationship we shall examine in detail in chapter 3, along with its critical implications. Although the neocortex is unique to mankind, the limbic system is common to all mammals; the functions it regulates are those we often describe as the animal aspects of mankind.

Contemporary Mankind: *Homo sapiens sapiens*

The apelike anthropoids faced another important evolutionary challenge about 20 million years ago when climate change brought about the development of savannahs. Our remote ancestors must have hesitated at the edge of the forests, unable to decide whether or not to venture out. In the end, they could not resist the temptation of the savannah, just as their ancestors had succumbed to that of the trees. The plains encouraged them to stand erect, which they achieved after millions of years—at which point they also began to use their hands and evolved a larger brain. Anthropologists call these intermediary ancestors *Ramapithecus*.

From *Ramapithecus* evolved *Homo habilis* (the first to use tools), then *Homo erectus* (walkers). This chain of evolution seems to have taken place in Africa. One to two million years ago, *Homo erectus* crossed the narrow land bridge from Africa and marched toward Europe and Asia. Peking Man (600,000 years ago), Java Man (600,000 years ago), and Heidelberg Man (500,000 years ago) all belong to the *Homo erectus* species. Next, *Homo sapiens* (intelligent man) emerged, and this species eventually replaced *Homo erectus*.

The transition from *Homo sapiens* to *Homo sapiens sapiens* (contemporary mankind) is presumed to have taken place some 50,000 years ago. *Homo sapiens sapiens* is a subspecies of *Homo sapiens* and had cousins like the Neanderthals (*Homo sapiens neanderthalensis*), Solo Man, and Rhodesia Man. Unlike *Homo sapiens sapiens*, these cousins failed to prosper and eventually disappeared. Their failure was perhaps due to overspecialization in their environment. The most tantalizing question remains whether or not *Homo sapiens sapiens* itself has now specialized too much— that is to say, whether it will destroy itself by its own success.

Eastern Creation Myth vs. Western Creationism

The 1860 debate between Thomas Huxley (1825–1895) and Bishop Samuel Wilberforce (1805–1873) was a historic clash between evolutionary theory and the theology of creation.

Huxley defended Darwin's theory of evolution while Wilberforce advocated the Bible's creation theology. Despite the incredible advance of science and accumulation of knowledge since this confrontation, creationism is still very much alive among the religious members of the West.

Creationism had flourished in the West for a millennium and a half, with little challenge, partly for fear of religious persecution. God created the world, sea, land, and then man—first male, then female. The Bible also recounts in great detail the genealogy of important persons, prophets, and kings, up to the birth of Jesus Christ. It was therefore considered possible to calculate the age of the earth and the date of Creation. Such attempts produced a range of dates, from approximately 5000 to 3000 BC. This calculation was made in the Middle Ages and remained widely accepted until the nineteenth century. Even Isaac Newton was no exception: not only did he firmly accept creationism, but he himself undertook to verify the prevailing date calculation. Newton arrived at a date of about 4000 BC.

The East has quite a different creation story, and one that was long accepted as myth. Nonetheless, it reflects the East's basic perception of the relationship between Man and Nature, and remains clearly compatible with the cosmology developed by assimilation with Taoism, Yin-Yang, and *I Ching*. The common theses are that Man is part of Nature, and that there is no supernatural creator.

According to one Eastern creation myth, there was nothing in the beginning but a formless chaos. Then this chaos coalesced into a cosmic egg for about 18,000 years. From the egg, Pangu (盤古) emerged to create the world. He separated Earth and Sky with a swing of his giant axe on the egg. To keep them further separated, Pangu continued to push the sky up further every day for 18,000 years. After the 18,000 years had elapsed, Pangu was laid to rest. His breath became the wind; his eyes, the sun and moon; his body became the mountains, his blood the rivers, his fur the trees, and the fleas on his fur became the animals, including the human races of the earth.

Fig. 2-5. A Caricature of Charles Darwin	**Fig. 2-6. A Portrait of Pangu** (盤古)
with an ape body symbolizing evolution, when "Darwinism" became widely accepted in the 1870s (http://en.wikipedia.org/wiki/Darwinism)	Mythological Creator of the Universe from the Chinese Encyclopedia of 1609 (http://en.wikipedia.org/wiki/File:Pangu.jpg)

Religious Creationism vs. Scientific Evolutionism

Western creationism is now widely relegated to the domain of faith. But even if one accepts Darwin's theory of evolution, one cannot specify the precise moment of the origin of life on earth. Did the millions of species alive today evolve from a single original organism? How did this organism come about? Did it emerge "naturally" on earth? Or did it come into existence by an act of creation? Faith serves a special purpose, dealing with questions unanswerable by reason and science. But one must realize that it is only by faith that we can accept the old theory of creation, and that this fails to answer the evidence of certain undeniable facts.

Charles Darwin (1809–1882) convincingly argued that man emerged by evolution rather than simple creation. But at the same time, he accepted God's initial creation of nature and life. The final sentence of *The Origin of Species* reads: "There is grandeur in this view of life, with its several powers, having been originally breathed by the Creator into a few forms or into one; and that, whilst this planet has gone cycling on according to the fixed law of gravity, from so simple a beginning endless forms most beautiful and most wonderful have been, and are being, evolved."[33]

Darwin firmly established that all species on earth emerged through evolution: "Although much remains obscure, and will long remain obscure, I can entertain no doubt, after the most deliberate study and dispassionate judgment of which I am capable, that the view which most naturalists entertain, and which I formerly entertained—namely, that each species has been independently created—is erroneous."[34] His theory holds that: 1) Species appear on earth not by creation but by evolution; 2) evolution occurs by means of natural selection; 3) natural selection is gradual. The first and second points are undeniably great discoveries, but the third point caused considerable controversy in the nineteenth and twentieth centuries.

Darwinian Gradualism and Western Progressivism
In formulating his theory, Darwin accepted the fundamental tenets of Western civilization—namely, the concept of separation, which necessarily entails a struggle for life as well as gradualism.

In fact, gradualism and the struggle for life require one another within a system of thought. And progressivism provides the philosophical justification for both conflict and gradualism. Without progressivism, which promises paradise or utopia, conflict cannot be justified. And progressivism cannot stand without support from gradualism, i.e. the belief in causality.

Conflict also has no basis without separation. That *Natura non facit saltum* ("Nature does not make leaps") was universally accepted in the nineteenth century, as was only natural since the Age of Ideologies was founded on progressivism and gradualism.[35] It was also natural that most who believed in the dictum of "Nature does not make leaps" accepted creationism: because Nature is created by God, and because God operates without uncertainty, probability, ambiguity, or chance, it should not make leaps. God is omnipotent, while a jump presupposes uncertainty and chance beyond the scope of divine omnipotence. Gottfried Wilhelm Leibniz (1646–1716) explains how disorder and imperfection should not exist in nature created by God: "All the different classes of beings which taken together make up the universe are, in the ideas of God who knows distinctly their essential graduations, only so many ordinates of a single curve so closely united that it would be impossible to place others between any two of them, since that would imply disorder and imperfection."[36]

In both Darwinian evolutionism and Christian creationism, a "leap" means a gap in evolution or creation between species. If one accepts leaps in evolution or creation, that means one accepts uncertainty and chance because one does not know when and how the next leap will occur. The concept of "the great chain of being" or *scala naturae* ("ladder of nature"), which was developed during the Middle Ages, is intimately related to gradualism: all creatures in the world are classified according to their degree of perfection toward God. And the spirit-body separation is the basis of "the great chain of being" classification. This vision of gradual hierarchy toward spiritual perfection was deeply ingrained in the minds of the Western people of the nineteenth century; they could hardly accept the concepts of leap, chance, or uncertainty. These Yin concepts are tantamount to agnosticism, which is anathema to Christian religion. Thus, gradualism was the conceptual framework within which Darwin proposed his theory. As the succeeding debates demonstrated, however, the gradualism of natural selection has now lost most of its support.

But in the intervening century and a half, great damage was inflicted upon the world as his gradualism, with its implied struggle for life, was extensively repeated and misused by extreme ideologies, including fascism and communism, as Social Darwinism. Without Darwinian gradualism, all such ideologies of progress lack a valid basis. Karl Marx was ecstatic when he learned of Darwin's theory. His enthusiasm was expressed in a letter to Friedrich Engels: "It is remarkable how Darwin recognizes among beasts and plants his English society with its division of labour, competition, opening-up of new markets, 'invention,' and the Malthusian 'struggle for existence.'"[37] Later, in a letter to Ferdinand Lassalle, Marx wrote that the theory of natural selection provided a foundation for his philosophy, by making class struggle an inevitable historical step.[38] Similarly, Hitler in *Mein Kampf* states that evolutionary theory gives the Nation the responsibility to foster the best and the strongest, while restraining the bad and the weak, according to the eternal laws governing the universe.[39]

The concept, *Bellum Omnium contra Omnes* ("War of all against all"), is also inherent in Darwin's theory of evolution, as he explains in *The Origin of Species*: "In the next chapter, the Struggle for Existence, amongst all organic beings throughout the world, which inevitably follows from the high geometrical ratio of their increase, will be treated of. This is the doctrine of Malthus, applied to the whole animal and vegetable kingdoms."[40] Darwin's reference was to Thomas Malthus's *Essay on the Principle of Population*, and his own *Origin of Species* indeed followed Malthus's framework. Malthus (1766–1834) had argued that population growth will always outrun resources of nutrition and space, necessitating competition.

Along with the gradualism embodied in the dictum, "Nature does not make leaps," the conflict-oriented nature represented by "War of all against all" constitutes one of the two pillars of modern Western philosophy. Darwin describes how "natural selection is daily and hourly scrutinizing, throughout the world, every variation, even the slightest; rejecting that which is bad, preserving and adding up all that is good; silently and insensibly working, whenever and wherever opportunity offers."[41] It appears that the cultural importance of gradualism in Darwin's theory was specifically tied to the Western conception of the Man-Nature relationship. Its significance and ultimate demise demonstrates the importance of civilizational bias; the gradual turn toward a more Eastern understanding of that relationship reinforces the broader phenomenon of a turn toward Yin in the West.

Gradual Evolutionism vs. Punctuated Equilibrium

Darwin firmly believed in the existence of "missing links" and assumed that fossil evidence should show the gradual progress of evolution. Darwin held that natural selection accumulates minute, continuous, and useful changes and that it cannot bring about sudden shifts. Furthermore, he thought that the validity of the principle that Nature does not make leaps had been proven by contemporary science, and thus, that it applied equally to the theory of natural selection.

Gradualism is one of the basic principles underpinning Western science and philosophy since the Enlightenment. This gradualism underpins causality and determinism, excluding a priori any room for probability and chance. Darwin accepted it matter-of-factly. Thomas Huxley, who defended Darwin's evolutionism in his famous debate with Wilberforce, strongly warned Darwin against this belief in a letter he sent to Darwin the day before the publication of *The Origin of Species*. Huxley said that he was ready to be burned at the stake to defend Darwin's evolutionism, but was also compelled to observe that Darwin was inviting unnecessary problems by accepting the principle that "nature does not make leaps."[42] Such Yin concepts as agnosticism, probability, chance, and uncertainty remained unacceptable to Darwin, for whom the process of natural selection must be gradual, since Nature was created by God. In this sense, Darwin was a true Christian despite all the accusations that he was an atheist. It goes without saying that Darwin might have postulated a non-anthropomorphic God; even so, that God is a supernatural entity, and not identical to Nature.

Thus, gradualism ensured God's place in Nature. The West had to wait almost a century and a half to embrace Yin concepts and purge gradualism from Darwin's theory. Darwin believed that creatures more primitive than *Homo sapiens* must have existed as missing links. These links, he assumed, simply awaited discovery. However, the fossil evidence has proved otherwise; no such missing links have been found.[43]

The late paleoanthropologist Stephen Jay Gould has proposed a revised theory of evolution, which he calls "punctuated equilibrium." Discarding gradualism, he suggests that we accept the fossil evidence without any distortion: species appear and disappear suddenly, but during their existence they remain virtually unchanged for millions of years.[44]

This repudiation of gradualism also de-emphasizes the vision of a conflictual nature so important to Darwin. Gould claims that members of the same species compete within the framework that was fixed at the origin of that species; consequently, their struggle produces little evolutionary change and so possesses far less significance than it had done for Darwin. This new theory is analogous to the "quantum leap" theory of subatomic physics. Evolution occurs in jumps, rather than gradual changes, just as electrons move abruptly between energy states: electrons make leap swiftly from "excited state" to "ground state and remain most of the time in the ground state until the next leap.

If the missing links do not exist, then we can accept such concepts as probability and chance. And so if nature does make leaps, then gradualism must be abandoned as one has to accept uncertainty and probability. The fact that the evolutionary mechanisms advanced by Darwin have now been discredited does not at all render his discovery worthless. Goethe (1749–1832) once wrote that the strength of a great idea belongs to its author, while its weakness belongs to the time in which he lived. Darwin's idea was powerful enough to withstand the challenges and scorn of those who derided him: "Your evolutionism says that men are descendants of apes. Then, on which side of your family was the ape?" But although he opened the door to a new understanding of man's history, he also accepted some of the mistaken concepts of his time. The West finally shed this legacy when it became a circumscribed world, having completed its conquests in the twentieth century.

We are left with a complex explanation: mankind emerged through evolution, but it has since been transforming only as a means to adapt to its diverse environments—a transformation which, in most cases, involves no significant evolutionary shifts.

When and how the next step of evolution will occur is beyond our grasp. It is only with this revised theory of evolution of punctuated equilibrium that the West has begun to accept agnosticism.

Human Races: Non-Evolutionary Transformation

Grave errors have been made in history by mistaking human races for separate species. Social Darwinism or racism has confused transformation among subspecies with the evolution between species. Members of *Homo sapiens sapiens*—in different regions with distinct climates—simply developed different characteristics within the boundaries of a single subspecies. Such characteristics include skin and eye color as well as the shape of the nose, eyelids, and lips. Such apparent differences notwithstanding, we all belong to the same subspecies, namely *Homo sapiens sapiens*.

Anthropologists describe black people as "the sons of the African sun": the dark skin, coiled hair, and thick lips are all protective characteristics that they acquired while living under strong sunlight. The same is true for white people: when mankind began to inhabit the North, the amount of melanin in the skin decreased, so that in the reduced sunlight, vitamin D could be synthesized more easily. Simultaneously, the eyes of Nordic peoples lost their melanin density and became pale, taking on a greenish or grey color.

The peoples of East Asia needed protection from cold, dry weather, especially during the winter season. Small noses and mouths were useful for warming and moisturizing air before it reached the lungs. The epicanthic fold in the eyelid was also useful for protecting the eyes from desert dust and cold air. Thus, different races are the outcome of adaptation to different climates. Naturally, they also developed distinctive civilizations and cultures that reflected these environments.

Here lies the problem: the gap between the non-evolutionary transformation of human races and the Lamarckian evolution of culture is rapidly widening. Now, due to globalization, people can easily acquire aspects of other civilizations, provoking interactions between their distinct features. This unusual dynamism is the defining characteristic of the present century, the era of globalization. Humankind seems to be engaged in changing the environment too fast for its biological evolution to keep pace. We shall examine this crucial aspect in chapter 10.

Eastern Transformism: *I Ching*

Eastern civilization possesses nothing like the West's elaborate creation theology, nor Darwin's theory of evolution. But it has developed a rational cosmology containing solid ideas and concepts about how the universe, nature, and man came into being and how they work. The *I Ching* concept of transformation is similar to the "theory of flux" propounded by Heraclitus of Ephesus (fifth century BC): while the universe and everything in it is in constant flux, it is not necessarily progressing toward perfection. Heraclitus, unsurprisingly, also claimed "the unity of opposites," which is the fundamental tenet of Taoism and *I Ching*. We have already examined the cosmology of the *I Ching*, Yin-Yang, and Tao. The basis of this was the *I Ching*, as it explains the fundamental tenets of transformism, with its ethical and political implications.

The *I Ching* is the oldest of the Chinese classics. This canon constituted, along with the Book of Poetry, Book of Rites, Book of History, and Spring and Autumn Annals, five works codified by Confucius himself. Because of its universal value and its non-political nature, the *I Ching* was the only text among the Five Confucian Classics that was spared from destruction by the First Emperor. It took a thousand years before it finally acquired a definite shape, around the twelfth century BC. The Zhou dynasty (1122–256 BC) relied heavily on it for its philosophy, administration, literature, and poetry. It appears that the *I Ching* itself went through a qualitative transformation during the first millennium BC, before which it was essentially a book of oracles and divination. With sixty-four hexagrams, it served the nobility to reflect and decide on the possible course and changes of future events. Later, the work became a philosophical textbook, imparting wisdom in natural and human affairs. This shift was due principally to the commentaries (the Great Treaties) attached to the original text.

Both Lao Tzu and Confucius knew the *I Ching* and appear to have studied it seriously. The aphorisms of Taoism have a deep resonance with its philosophy; Confucius reportedly wrote a detailed commentary on it. The tenets of these schools thus constituted the foundation upon which all of Eastern culture was built. The primary teaching of the *I Ching* is the idea of perpetual change or transformation. This change is founded on the order of nature— an unknowable ultimate principle that is made manifest through eternal metamorphosis. Both Taoism and Confucianism accepted this teaching. Confucius repeated to his disciples: "Everything flows on and on like this river, without pause, day and night."[45] From this insight arises the practice of "putting things into perspective," more common in the East than in the West. "When one loses perspective, one will find worries near at hand."[46]

With this realization of eternal change, without recourse to new evolutionary values, one is inclined to equanimity and calm consideration. In the game of Go, strategic and long-term thinking is essential. Strategy is important in chess as well, but the scope for strategic thinking is certainly more limited in comparison with the game of Go. In the *I Ching*, one is motivated to identify the hidden order in random events. A thousand years of reflection and wisdom went into the development of the *I Ching*. In its new form, the sixty-four hexagrams came to explain the diverse manifestations of the cosmos by permutations of Yin and Yang. This permutation occurs at random, everywhere and every day. Unlike the Western model of mechanical world order based on causality, *I Ching* presumes that there is no strict causality in nature, which underlies all these transformations. Man, along with the forces of Heaven and Earth, participates actively in the process of transformation. Nonetheless, the immanent principle of change remains beyond his grasp: he can deal only with its manifestations.

Western Evolutionism vs. Eastern Transformism

This principle of transformation can be summarized in three parts: transformation occurs by dynamic interaction between opposites; opposites are fundamentally complementary; transformations are random and undirected. The *I Ching* shares the first two propositions with Yin-Yang; we have already analyzed their significance. In this section, as we compare this Eastern concept with Western creationism and evolution, its third aspect—that of undirected change—stands in polar opposition to its Western counterparts.

The *I Ching* does not recognize the existence of a Creator, nor does it use any term analogous to "creation." It does not even mention a supernatural being. The origin of the universe itself is part of the transformation. The expressions Ultimate Non-Being and Ultimate Being indicate situation or status, not action. The *I Ching* makes no reference to the end of the universe. As the universe is limitless, transformation would go on forever. Since there is no Creator, there is no supernatural intervention in human affairs, no Heaven or Hell, and no divine punishment or reward. Nature, in the East, is indifferent to human beings.

As Taoism defines it: Nature (Tao) provides a blessing to the just and protection to the unjust. In the East, there is, instead of reward and punishment from above, only conformity to Tao, which brings inner satisfaction, and violation of Tao, which brings inner dissatisfaction and hinders self-fulfillment. Self-fulfillment is to the Eastern mind what heavenly reward is to the Western mind.

In the *I Ching*, ethics is about correctly assessing one's situation, with a view to making the appropriate decision and taking responsibility for its consequences. One chooses not between good and evil, but between fortune and misfortune. The concepts of "good" and "evil" are included within a larger conception of fortune and misfortune. As there is no pure Yin or pure Yang, and each is easily transformed into the other, there is no room for rigid, Manichean dichotomies of good and evil. As such, Eastern transformation is about practical ethics and politics—contextual solutions—rather than theology or metaphysics. Yin and Yang are not static, but contain the seeds of each other: hence, there is no destiny, but only free possibility and uncertainty. For the Western mind, inclined to regard Yin-Yang philosophy, Taoism, and *I Ching* as mere mysticism, it may be helpful to observe that the computer uses a binary numeral system equivalent to Yin and Yang, in that all activity derives from the permutation of 1 and 0.

The transformation described in the *I Ching* is, as we have said, both random and undirected, and cyclical rather than linear. As with the Moon, it eternally alternates between waxing and waning: there is no progress or perfection—nothing irreversible or teleological. The Eastern understanding of change can thus be compared to the variations in *Homo sapiens sapiens*, which are temporary and context-responsive, rather than directed and evolutionary.

Eastern Divination vs. Western Oracle

The *I Ching* began around five millennia ago as a book of oracles. Because of its nontheistic culture, the East, instead of visiting shrines for oracular pronouncements, consulted this book. The West also possessed many non-oracular forms of divination, from augury and geomancy to astrology and sortilege, but these practices appear to have remained in the domain of myth and divination, whereas *I Ching* evolved into a fully fledged philosophy.[47] Its philosophical character was enriched by several commentaries.

One finds traces of fortune-telling here and there in the book, such as "If you head towards the northwest it will bring fortune and towards the southeast will bring misfortune." Because of this, the *I Ching*, when introduced to the West, was sometimes called a Book of Divination. But we must be cautious in using this term, for the *I Ching's* approach to divination is quite different from the Western notion of an oracle: the latter refers to a divine prediction of events whereas the former guides man's involvement in the transformation of events, by teaching him to clearly assess the situation and make good decisions.

The *I Ching*, as a tool of divination, was thus meant to give direct advice to a man in a particular situation. As such, it can be read for guidance when one encounters a difficult problem. The *I Ching* aims to restore the reader's perspective and help him to understand the necessity of change. It is therefore erroneous to see the *I Ching* as a mere fortune-telling book. Eastern culture considers divination to be in vain: everything depends on human wisdom, judgment, decision, and action, in search of, and in conformity with, the eternal principle of transformation.

But as Spinoza observed, the multitude is apt to cling to superstition; they desired a book of divination and so the *I Ching* was frequently used for simple fortune-telling in Eastern markets.

This demonstrates the same vulgarization found in all cultures: the Humanity of Confucianism, the Love of Christianity, and the Nirvana or Compassion of Buddhism. Because the *I Ching* offers wisdom rather than prophecy, it warns the reader not to consult it if he already knows the answer to his problem. One should not use it to check one's own solution, for this would only lead to confusion. Rather, it should be humbly consulted when one cannot find any other clue or inspiration.[48]

But despite its heuristic nature, the *I Ching* is not easy to use, since its structure and tenets remain archaic, even though its primary insight is supported by contemporary science. Since the *I Ching* concerns change, if one does not find what one needs, one may consult a supplementary hexagram by substituting the "variable" line for its opposite, whether Yin or Yang. One will thus arrive at a new hexagram, with a new set of suggestions and perspectives. In short, the *I Ching* deals with "what is to be done." The chosen hexagram describes one's situation and offers possible courses of action. By contrast, the Western oracular tradition is about "what is going to occur." This contrast seems to have arisen from the distinction between theistic and secular viewpoints.

Transformism: Chance and Probability

Should we regret our lost paradise, in which gradual progress was believed to guarantee optimal results? No: such regret can be grounded only in nostalgia. As Gould has argued, "Humans are pattern-seeking animals. We must find cause and meaning in all events—quite apart from the probable reality that the universe both does not care much about us and often operates in a random manner. I call this bias 'adaptationism'—the notion that everything must fit, must have a purpose, and in the strongest version, must be for the best." Contrary to the old Western belief in God's providence, sustained in a new way by secular optimism about evolutionary progress, the hidden mechanism of the universe may be random, and so hardly optimal.

This revised perspective concedes that evolution may not have produced the best possible results, and that chance and uncertainty are as much part of the universe as progress. This need not be cause for regret, however; we may enjoy the uncertainty and imperfection of life. As Taoism teaches, imperfection entails change and hope, while perfection can lead only to decline: "Great accomplishment seems imperfect, yet it does not outlive its usefulness. Great fullness seems empty, yet cannot be exhausted. Great straightness seems twisted. Great intelligence seems stupid. Great eloquence seems awkward."[49] An Eastern mind would have enjoyed Gould's ironic equanimity: "But why fret over lost optimality? History always works this way.... If a portion of the African jungles had not dried to savannahs, I might still be an ape up a tree. If some comets had not struck the earth (if they did) some 60 million years ago, dinosaurs might still rule the land, and all mammals would be rat-sized creatures scurrying about in the dark corners of their world.... If history were not so maddeningly quirky, we would not be here to enjoy it. Streamlined optimality contains no seeds for change."

Classical progressivism was sustained by a mechanical model of the universe, as embodied in Newtonian physics. The Newtonian view provided the conceptual framework for modern Western metaphysics, but this framework has since been expanded to include newly discovered phenomena, such as relativity theory and quantum physics. Must we now abandon our previous confidence? On the contrary: the new concepts of chance and probability have created fresh opportunities and have been instrumental in the emergence of today's information revolution.

Progressivism vs. Ecology

Western progressivism has been encouraged in no small measure by its theology and metaphysics, and by man's physical superiority over nature. But many of the problems we face today have been created by man's mindless exploitation of nature. Environmental degradation and unsustainable economic development, along with weapons of mass destruction, constitute the century's most serious challenges. But these are only epiphenomena of the blind and fanatical competition among nations, as well as individuals, for economic gain. A humble acceptance of man's unity with nature should be the first step toward a satisfactory solution to these challenges.

Western science, with its self-critical nature, soon embraced Copernican heliocentrism, with the attendant diminution of man's symbolic status in the universe. But the philosophical propositions of Spinoza, whose role in human science is comparable to Copernicus's heliocentrism on natural science, are yet to be fully accepted in the West. Unlike Eastern culture, which was founded on the Taoist unity of Man and Nature, Western culture seems still to struggle with the notion that God created Man to govern Nature. There appear to be two schools of thought in the West. One expects a new religion to rethink the old with a view to protecting the environment: "Our science and technology have grown out of Christian attitudes toward man's relation to nature, which are almost universally held not only by Christians and neo-Christians but also by those who fondly regard themselves as post-Christians. Despite Copernicus, all the cosmos rotates around our little globe. Despite Darwin, we are not, in our hearts, part of the natural process. We are superior to nature, contemptuous of it, willing to use it for our slightest whim.... What we do about ecology depends on our ideas of the man-nature relationship.

More science and more technology are not going to get us out of the present ecologic crisis until we find a new religion, or rethink our old one."[50]

The other school of thought surmises that the Christian religion indeed contains provisions to protect the environment: "True Christianity is supposed to free a man from his natural self-centeredness and turn his mind toward the welfare of others. The Christian should not be interested in the exploitation of the here and now. Having dominion over or control of something, should mean its protection rather than the improper use of it."[51]

I am inclined to trust the second school of thought; the overarching spirit of the Bible is about protection rather than exploitation of the things over which one has dominion. The fundamental modus operandi of Western culture is separation-dialectics-freedom, as we have already seen; it therefore presupposes two individuated elements—in this instance, one for the exploitation of the environment and the other for its protection. While the West was expansive, it privileged exploitation; now in a circumscribed world, it will slowly but surely move toward protection. The strong contemporary Western focus on ecology attests to this.

Likewise, regarding the Man-Nature relationship, the West is rapidly closing the gap with the East, as it has almost reached the conclusion enshrined in Taoism—that man is part of nature, and that their relationship should be seen not as one of conflict, but as one of harmony. After all, Western science hardly supports an anthropomorphic deity.

CHAPTER 3

Mind and Body:
Western Spirit vs. Eastern Man

"The mind and the body are one and the same thing, which is conceived now under the attribute of thought, now under the attribute of extension."[1]

Baruch Spinoza

"Heaven works by an eternal principle: it does not exist because of Sage, nor does it disappear because of Despot: Complying with it is the way to prosperity; defying it is the way to misfortune."[2]

Xun Zi (荀子, 310–237 BC)

Western Dichotomy vs. Eastern Holism

Mankind's future depends on our management of two crucial relationships: between Man and Nature, and between Man and Man. But this in turn depends on our self-management—that is to say, a balance between Mind and Body. The relationship of these two, as understood in the East and West, is the subject in the present chapter.

Building Block of Civilization: Man vs. Mind

"Man is the measure of all things: of things which are, that they are, and of things which are not, that they are not." This famous saying of Protagoras indicates that man is at the center of civilization, be it Eastern or Western. In examining the Western man-nature relationship, we found that Western man sees himself in control of his own destiny and that of the world: God, in whose image he was created, placed nature under his dominion. This proposition is predicated on a separation of spirit from body; since God is spiritual, so man must be spirit in essence, rather than body. This notion was the driving force behind Western expansion: it would hardly be an overstatement to say that, in the West, Mind stood for Man, and that the building block of Western civilization was Mind rather than Man himself. I shall elaborate on this critical point later.

In the East, the relationship between Mind and Body is viewed holistically: man is seen as a harmony of the two elements, rather than simply mind or spirit alone. From this perspective, we can say that man, not mind, is the building block of Eastern civilization. Eastern Mind-Body holism and Western Mind-Body dichotomy constitutes perhaps the most fundamental contrast between the two civilizations. This fundamental contrast also explains why such branches of thinking as theology, metaphysics, epistemology, and ontology have been either absent or futile and why ethics and politics free from theological and metaphysical influence have flourished in the Eastern civilization. How did man arrive at such diametrically opposite ways of conceptualizing himself? It is only natural that the separations of man and nature, and of mind and body, have the same cause: both require a supernatural entity. I can think of no better reason for the differing views of East and West than their environmental contexts. The expansive West was in need of supernatural empowerment as well as justification for its expansion; the circumscribed East needed to make the most of Man, since he is without supernatural aid.

Man has always been fascinated by the functions of his own uniquely large brain—functions variously called spirit, mind, soul, reason, and psyche. As each of these is more pronounced in the West, due to the identification of spirit with God, the Westerner will be inclined to distinguish these terms more sharply than an Easterner. However, unless we believe that spirit is an entity specifically created by God for Man, and that it exists in a specific location in the brain, we must accept that all these functions are based in the neocortex (new brain), which is much larger in humans than in other animals. These functions give rise to the problem—how are we to define human nature or the human mind?

Why has the soul been praised as noble in Western theology and metaphysics? Must we strive to promote the spirit and reject bodily desires? If so, has this been ordained by God, or by evolution? Is man a "spiritual" being, guided by a supernatural divinity, as mainstream Western thought tends to assert? Are Spirit and Body destined to remain in conflict? Or is it rather, as Easterners believe, that the conflict is between man's own desires and passions? Do mind and body pull us in different directions according to contrasting desires and passions? Can we control this process—for instance, can we cause reason to dominate?

The Genesis of the Western Spirit

In chapter 1, we examined Hegel's insight into the separation of Man (and *Geist*) from Nature. He was the inheritor of a rich tradition: based on Judeo-Christian religion and Platonic philosophy, the West founded its civilization on the perceived primacy of Spirit over Body. This fundamental premise is found in Genesis, in which "the Spirit of God moved upon the face of the waters."[3] Here, God is a spiritual being; and since Man was created in His image, Man, too, must essentially be a spiritual being. The Platonic *logos*, meanwhile, connotes reason, possessed by the mind, but not the body. Plato believed in innate ideas; Aristotle, by contrast, proposed that the mind was empty at birth. Although Aristotle did not accept the actual existence of a soul without a body and acknowledged a much greater role for the body than Plato had done, he still built his philosophical system on the premise that the soul and body are two distinct entities. And his focus on the soul is evident, for instance, in his classification of man into four categories—*virtuous, vicious, continent,* and *incontinent*—according to the perfection of the rational soul. Looking from inside, the contrast between Plato and Aristotle appears great—for instance, Aristotelian teleology vs. Platonic idealism, but from outside, their difference is contained within the same framework. Both Plato and Aristotle built their philosophical systems on the premise of Soul-Body separation (we shall discuss this more in chapter 4). This Western notion is in polar contrast to the East, which did not see such a separation.

Western Christianity reinforced this separation of Mind from Body, putting the former above the latter. Bodily and corporal needs, passions, and instincts were considered base, if not downright evil: "God is the opposite of the darkness of Sin, the *Spirit* that contrasts with the *Flesh*. For Paul, the *Spirit* is the power of God's love for humanity, the driving force of the Christian life. The term *Flesh* is used to sum up the state of humanity when in opposition to God. *Flesh* is backed by other dark forces."[4]

This dichotomy between Spirit and Body was emphasized time and again in Western history, always maintaining the primacy of the former. The last words of the Roman Emperor Julian is one such example: "Friends and fellow-soldiers, the seasonable period of my departure is now arrived, and I discharge, with the cheerfulness of a ready debtor, the demands of nature. I have learned from philosophy how much the soul is more excellent than the body; and that the separation of the nobler substance, should be the subject of joy, rather than of affliction.... I now offer my tribute of gratitude to the Eternal Being, who has not suffered me to perish by the cruelty of a tyrant, by the secret dagger of conspiracy, or by the slow tortures of lingering disease."[5] We have already suggested that the rationale behind this preference was a need to legitimate one's actions with supernatural—that is, divine—authority. This required an environment favoring individual initiative and liberty: such an environment was provided by the Mediterranean. In an expansive, seafaring world, action engendered profit and success, and the individual became supreme. H.G. Wells shrewdly pointed out: "Very soon the seafaring men must have realized the peculiar freedom and opportunities the ship gave them. They could get away to islands; no chief or king could pursue a boat or ship with any certainty; every captain was a king."[6]

Journey of the Western Spirit: from Descartes to Hegel

This Spirit-Body dichotomy was inherited by Renaissance Europe. The West, at liberty in its expansive world, and intent on conquest, had to invoke the supernatural power of the Spirit. Since the modern West took it for granted that human nature was essentially spiritual, early modern European philosophy gave rise to a metaphysics that gave Spirit the role of guiding human history. Mainstream philosophers thus focused on the ontology, epistemology, and phenomenology of Spirit as opposed to matter.

The first important philosopher to voice this tendency was René Descartes (1596–1650), who advocated a fundamental separation of spirit and body, locating the nexus of the two in the brain's pineal gland. He declared, *"Cogito ergo sum"* ("I think, therefore I am"), proclaiming the domination of thought over extension, spirit over body, in Western metaphysics.[7] This assertion troubled Spinoza, who sought to unify mind and body, and dedicated a lengthy paragraph of his *Ethics* to the problem: "Descartes maintained that the soul, or mind, was especially united to a certain part of the brain, called the pineal gland, by whose aid the mind is aware of all the motions aroused in the body and of external objects, and which the mind can move in various ways simply by willing."[8] But, as we know, it was Descartes and not Spinoza whose basic metaphysics was openly embraced by European philosophy.

Western minds, especially those familiar with the history of its metaphysics, will find this too sweeping and cursory an overview. I plead guilty as charged. After all, I am an Easterner, and attempt only to present an Eastern reading of the intricate yet obvious journey of Spirit in the modern West.[9] Let us observe the principal points in its development:

> In the mid-seventeenth century, Descartes introduced Spirit separated from the Body to Western metaphysics, arguing that the former, an immaterial entity, interacts with the body via the pineal gland. This spirit is unique to mankind and does not obey the laws of physics.

In the later seventeenth century, Gottfried Wilhelm Leibniz (1646–1716) exulted in the "Spirituality" of mankind; he considered it natural that man could understand the universe, since man is himself a little universe—a microcosm made in the image of God, an idea accepted in the West since antiquity. For Leibniz, man is preeminently a spiritual being, and Spirit was created by God.

A century later, Immanuel Kant (1724–1804) advanced "Reason," pure or practical, as the ultimate entity, founding his transcendental idealism on Reason, which was another metaphysical expression of Western Spirit.[10]

In the nineteenth century, G.W.F. Hegel (1770–1831) presented "Absolute Spirit" as the guiding principle of human history. He inherited the long-held Western belief that the Spirit was created by God with the special purpose of managing natural phenomena. For Hegel, history is understood as humanity's progression toward full self-consciousness and self-actualization of God, the "Absolute Spirit."[11]

With Hegel, the Spirit became absolute truth in the West, as *logos* had been in Greek antiquity with Plato. As long as this spirit remained metaphysical and abstract, it could do no harm to ordinary people. When it was invoked in worldly affairs, the story was quite different. What happens when someone claims to be the custodian of his age's "Absolute Spirit," its *Zeitgeist*? Hegel claimed that Napoleon embodied his era's *Zeitgeist*; many ideologies flourished in the same period, all claiming absolute truth, eventually leading to conflicts of unprecedented scale in the twentieth century.

One might argue that these ideologies are regrettable distortions of Western philosophy. This may be true, and the West did produce the best institutions of social organization: democracy based on individual freedom, and the free market based on individual initiative. But its original values barely survived the onslaught of extreme ideologies like Marxism and fascism, which would not have evolved without the conflicts arising from the absolutism of Spirit in Western philosophy.

Machiavelli: Reaction to Medieval Theology

Given the overwhelming dominance of Spirit over Body in Western values, it should not be surprising that some thinkers revolted, placing Body over Spirit. The Renaissance produced the first Western books since the Middle Ages to deal with politics and society without reference to God or religion. These were the works of Niccolò Machiavelli (1469–1527), which offered an unusually realistic secular perspective on human nature. Machiavelli initiated "realpolitik" and left an indelible mark on Western politics, both domestic and international. Before Machiavelli, Western politics had revolved around Platonic idealism and scholastic Christian theology. Machiavelli reacted against these systems, which he deemed too abstract.

The Catholic Church had represented the reign of Spirit in the West during the Middle Ages and naturally condemned Machiavelli's masterpiece, *The Prince*. In the same vein, his work was openly condemned by many Western thinkers of the early modern period, although it was widely read and disseminated in secret. Machiavelli came to stand for deception, cunning, and manipulation. It was only in the nineteenth and twentieth centuries that the West openly recognized Machiavellian realpolitik. We can see parallels here to the reception of Spinoza and David

Hume, both of whom rejected the Western prioritization of the Spirit. Both of them, charged with heresy, had to conceal their work from the Church. Both men's ideas would have to wait until the nineteenth century to enjoy open support.

This struggle between political realism and political idealism can best be understood within the framework of Western mind-body dialectics. Machiavelli's ideas, as a reaction against the preeminence of Spirit, naturally emphasized the Body. Discussion of the moral aspect of human behavior is conspicuously absent in his arguments; instead, he advises action that is daring, preemptive, and decisive, with little regard for ethical scruples. It was this advice that generated the most serious criticism of Machiavelli, but as Goethe pointed out, the shortcomings of a genius are due to his era and should not eclipse his merits. The culture of Renaissance Italy, in which Machiavelli developed his philosophy, arose partly in reaction against the suffocating medieval tyranny of Spirit. In this period, popes—including Cesar Borgia's father—married and had children, and every means was accepted in their election; principalities and republics rose and fell overnight; foreign powers intervened with no moral scruples or principles whatsoever. In short, it was a world in which the maxim "all's fair in love and war" was accepted and practiced.

Notwithstanding, Machiavelli's observations on human nature were highly astute, and many considered his new approach to the subject to be scientific. His secular and materialistic views provided a balance to the prevailing religious views of human nature, which were founded exclusively on Spirit.

But man cannot exist as an amoral being: "Man does not live by bread alone."[12] Men naturally seek a balance between spiritual and temporal forces, rather than taking an extreme position on either side. Machiavelli's realpolitik is based on ruthless realism and fails to provide a balanced or wholesome approach to human nature. His ideas were not incorrect but incomplete: his realistic understanding of humanity from a legal perspective must be complemented by ethics if one wants a balanced view. In accepting and even recommending the ruthless and amoral will of princes, Machiavelli anticipates Nietzsche's more generalized and philosophical *will to power*.

Nietzsche: Reaction against Metaphysics as the Spirit of the Modern Era

In early modern Europe, medieval theology began to be replaced by metaphysics; this, too, was founded on a separation between Body and Spirit or Mind. The latter dominated mainstream early modern thought, as represented by Descartes, Leibniz, Kant, and Hegel, and so another revolt against Spirit was inevitable. This we can find in the work of Thomas Hobbes (1588–1679), whose political theory was grounded on a secular and materialistic analysis of human nature. In the next two centuries, several new thinkers, recognizing the power of the passions in shaping behavior, reacted against metaphysics and instead championed the body as opposed to the blind domination of the spirit.

Friedrich Nietzsche (1844–1900), Arthur Schopenhauer (1788–1860), and Ludwig von Feuerbach (1804–1872) are among these philosophers of "reaction." From their perspective, modern metaphysics was simply a transformation of earlier theology; Leibniz and Kant were accused of having distorted the truth, while Hegel's grand philosophical systems were ultimately no more than scholastic dogma. In hindsight, we can see that these philosophers contributed involuntarily to the development of extremist movements like fascism, just as the metaphysicians influenced the emergence of ideologies like communism.

Among the radical thinkers, the preeminent figure was Nietzsche, whose critique of Western metaphysics provided a healthy antidote to the emphasis on Spirit. Bertrand Russell called this movement of the Western Spirit toward absolutism a march toward madness. But Nietzsche repeated Machiavelli's mistake, by marching to the opposite extreme, that of the Body. As a reaction to German idealism, he founded his philosophy of the "will to power" on the notion of "exploitation." This responded to extremism with extremism, proposing a disconnected Body instead of a disconnected Spirit. For this reason, Nietzsche's works, so scintillating in their critique of metaphysical absolutism, could offer no solution to the problem of tyranny of spirit, except by proposing an equally extreme reaction from the body.

Nietzsche attempted to prevent the imminent weakening and disintegration of the Western "rule by law and force," or Master ethics, by clinging to any last vestige of such ethics. He did not want to give up the simple and powerful Master ethics of the West as embodied in the Roman Empire. Indeed, the laws and ethos of the empire allowed the Caesars absolute freedom to exploit others, especially those outside of Rome: the more they pillaged and enslaved, the greater their glory and wealth. Nietzsche explains this very clearly: "Life itself in its essence means appropriating, injuring, and overpowering those who are foreign and weaker."[13] Absolute "rule by force" with no regard for ethics, nor contaminated by the arguments of the weak, represented for him an ideal and natural condition for the West.

Eastern Metaphysics: Li-Ki

As the East never saw Man in terms of a Mind-Body dichotomy, there is no Eastern theology or metaphysics based on this. However, there has been an Eastern attempt to analyze human nature. This analysis was called Li-Ki (理氣) and became popular among scholars from the Song dynasty (AD 969–1279). Li-Ki, however, is the only exception to the rule, since studying the relationship between Spirit and Body necessarily involves a certain amount of metaphysics. Buddhism developed in an Indian intellectual atmosphere, which had an unusually strong metaphysical tendency. This was introduced to the Sinic world in the first century and brought with it a taste for metaphysics; it finally flourished in China during the Tang dynasty (AD 618–907), becoming the official state philosophy. But the succeeding Song dynasty reverted back to Confucianism, giving birth to neo-Confucianism, which, from the tenth to the thirteenth century AD, absorbed the metaphysics of Buddhism and produced the philosophical school of Li-Ki. Li represents principle, reason, or mind, whereas Ki represents force, drive, or passion. Li-Ki philosophy, which was particularly prominent in Korea, aims to understand the fundamental aspects of the universe.

Zhu Xi (朱熹, 1130–1200), the most important neo-Confucian scholar, argues that Tao is expressed as Li in Nature, and this Li is shrouded by Ki. On the other hand, Wang Yangming (1472–1529), who lived during the Ming dynasty and is considered the second most important figure in neo-Confucianism, claimed that Li is within man: Mind has an innate moral knowledge, which we access through meditation. Enlightenment therefore comes intuitively, not by reasoning. These two schools of Li-Ki concepts and discussion spread to Korea and Japan, where they also thrived, and attained great refinement, especially in Korea.[14]

As such, it may be an oversimplification to categorically equate Li with Mind (or Spirit) and Ki with Body, although these remain the closest parallels to the Western concepts. As a result, the two terms are often translated as Spirit and Body. Neo-

Confucianism describes the relationship as follows: "Li and Ki must be considered as a dualistic but single entity. They must be seen as separated and at the same time united."[15] The resemblance to Spinozism is plain: "The mind and the body are one and the same thing, conceived at one time under the attribute of thought, and at another under that of extension." Zhu Xi remarked that "Ki is the origin of energy and movement. Li has no motivation of its own. Li only provides order and principle to Ki." Here again, we can parallel Hume's concepts of reason and passion: "Reason is, and ought only to be, the slave of the passions, and can never pretend to any other office than to serve and obey them." The following Eastern description of Li and Ki demonstrates their symbiotic relationship: "Li is the coordinator of Ki and Ki is the provider for Li. Without Li, Ki has no outlet and without Ki, Li has no support."[16] Here, man is a holistic being of body and soul, rather than simply of soul, as in the West.

Western Scholasticism vs. Eastern Neo-Confucianism

The intellectual world of the medieval West evolved from an attempted synthesis between Christian theology and ancient Greek philosophy. As the West had lost most of its Greek heritage, it had to borrow from the Muslim world, and especially from Moorish Spain, which had preserved many of the Greek classics. This attempt at synthesis gave rise to the scholasticism that flourished from the eleventh to the fifteenth century, up to the Renaissance.

It is curious that, unbeknownst to both parties, a similar phenomenon occurred in the East around the same time. During the Song dynasty (960–1279), the East developed, as we have seen, an attempted synthesis between Buddhism and ancient classical philosophies, especially Confucianism and Taoism. The strong metaphysical flavor of Buddhism brought fresh stimulus to Eastern culture. The resulting synthesis gave rise to neo-Confucianism.

The two legacies, Eastern and Western, are also comparable. In the West, scholastic philosophers, in their efforts to reconcile Christian theology with Greek rationalism, borrowed principally from Plato and Aristotle among the latter: the Franciscan order (founded in 1209) focused on the Platonic, innatist ideas of Saint Augustine (354–430), while the Dominican order (founded in 1215) propounded an Aristotelian, "tabula rasa" view of the soul, producing the theology of Thomas Aquinas. The universities founded across Europe at this time formed the basis for the intellectual evolution of Europe through the Renaissance and modernity.

Similarly, in the East, neo-Confucianism revived the thought of ancient philosophers, especially Confucius and Mencius; it also established academies across the country and codified the Four Canons of Confucianism: *The Analects of Confucius, Mencius, The Doctrine of the Mean*, and *The Great Learning*. Neo-Confucianism became the official philosophy of Eastern countries—China, Korea, Japan, and Vietnam—and remained the official creed of those nations until the early twentieth century. For more than half a millennium, the four classics constituted the core educational curriculum in those countries and the basis for civil service examinations.

Original Sin vs. Three Years of Mourning

In terms of intellectual influence, Zhu Xi can be compared with Thomas Aquinas. Just as the latter's *Summa Theologica* dominated the philosophy of the Middle Ages, so the former's Four Canons dominated that of the Song dynasty. Interestingly enough, there developed a tendency in neo-Confucianism to consider Li as good and Ki as evil—similar to Scholasticism's characterization of noble Spirit and evil Flesh, associating the latter with original sin.

| **Fig. 3-1. Zhu Xi** (朱熹, 1130–1200) The leading Neo-Confucian scholar during the Song Dynasty (960–1279) (http://en.wikipedia.org/wiki/Zhu_Xi) | **Fig. 3-2. Thomas Aquinas** (1225–1274) The leading philosopher and theologian of scholasticism (http://en.wikipedia.org/wiki/Thomas_Aquinas) |

Thomas Aquinas is known for having extolled the body as well as the soul, following the influence of Aristotle: the human being is both body and soul, intrinsically joined. In the same vein, Thomas Aquinas differed from Saint Augustine in his replacement of concupiscence by privation of grace as the central element of original sin: "the sin of Adam was one thing but the sin of children at their birth is quite another, the former was the cause, the latter is the effect." The significance of Thomas Aquinas in liberating concupiscence (e.g., human bodily desire) from original sin is not to be underestimated, especially in light of the fact that such Protestant reformers as Martin Luther and John Calvin persisted in equating original sin with concupiscence. Yet the point to be made here is not to illustrate the difference between Saint Augustine and Thomas Aquinas or Franciscans and Dominicans or Catholicism and Protestantism, however significant they may look from the inside. The purpose of this book is contrasting East and West. Seen from outside, Aquinas, like all other Western theologians, supported a distinction between spirit and body, and thus all of them varied within the same framework of spirit-body separation and original sin.

In the East, a long and fierce battle had arisen over the practice of mourning for three years upon the death of one's parents. There is the strong possibility that Confucius' original injunction on filial duty was about parents caring for children: "When asked what filial piety was, Confucius responded, parents are anxious lest their children should get sick."[17] Then Confucius explains about children's duty toward their parents. But in other places, the three-year mourning period was explicitly mentioned. Since Confucianism made it mandatory, all sorts of variations, interpretations, and practices plagued the Eastern world with social condemnation and the threat of impeachment. Even as early as the time of Confucius, Mohists were firmly opposed to this practice on the grounds that it was impractical and inflicted pain on the people; as Confucianism became the state philosophy, gender difference was instituted between father and mother—the death of the mother while the father was still alive did not deserve the full three-year mourning.

Empress Wu of the Tang dynasty eliminated this gender discrimination by decreeing the same mourning period for both parents; neo-Confucianism naturally reinforced the three-year mandatory mourning practices. Even as late as the Qing dynasty, a central political figure almost lost his power when he shortened the mourning period of three years upon his parents' death; during the Korean Yi dynasty, there was a similar controversy over the duration of the mourning period of a Queen Mother.

Both Western Scholasticism and Eastern neo-Confucianism met with criticism for their common shortcomings—rigid formalism and narrow-mindedness. Scholasticism demonstrated its emphasis on theology and original sin, resulting in the accentuated separation of spirit from body and severe condemnation of the latter. Such an intellectual environment did not favor intellectual freedom: this had to wait for the Renaissance. Similarly, neo-Confucianism was criticized for its limitations and tendentiousness; its critics often compared it unfavorably to Han learning or syncretism, which had allowed competing interpretations of Confucius to coexist. For example, Han learning had valued Xun Zi (荀子, 310–237 BC), whereas neo-Confucianism condemned him in favor of Mencius. Both Scholasticism and neo-Confucianism were attacked for placing too much emphasis on abstract speculation detached from everyday reality.

The Western mind could fortunately overcome and transcend Thomism after the Renaissance, whereas the East remained faithful to Zhu Xi until the nineteenth century, when the West arrived with new ideas. In a sense, one may discern a long-term pattern of opening and closing the mind, both in the West and East: the Western mind broadened during the Greco-Roman era, closed for about a millennium during the Middle Ages, and reopened in the Renaissance. The Eastern mind first opened during the Western Zhou dynasty (770–221 BC), remaining open for a millennium until the Tang dynasty (618–907); it closed during the Song dynasty (960–1279) and finally reopened in the nineteenth century with the arrival of the Western influence in the East.

Western Renaissance vs. Eastern Closing of the Mind

When we expand our perspective, we find a stark contrast between the medieval West and the Song dynasty in the East. The West would have its Renaissance with incredible energy and curiosity, resulting in astounding achievements and discoveries in science, literature, and the arts. This energy was directed toward the New World, ushering in the Age of Discovery that stimulated and contributed to such subsequent Western developments as the Reformation, the Enlightenment, and eventually, the Industrial Revolution.

But the fifteenth and sixteenth centuries saw similar levels of exploration and incursive pressure from both East and West. In the early fifteenth century, Ming-dynasty China (1368–1644) launched an Eastern maritime enterprise similar to the Western Age of Discovery—Admiral Cheng Ho's seven epic expeditions to the Indian Ocean and Africa. This parallels the Western maritime adventures of the period: Vasco da Gama to Asia, Christopher Columbus to America, and Magellan around the world. Perhaps both East and West needed a new horizon: the West lost its Mediterranean trade routes with the fall of Constantinople in 1453, while in the East, the Ming Empire barely defeated the Mongol Yuan Empire (1271–1368), but the Mongols continued to threaten from the North.

Similar maritime enterprises did not achieve similar results; these were partly determined by the cultural differences between East and West. The West evidently enjoyed the impetus of the Renaissance, as well as the benefit of the *Pax Mongolica*, which, however, little helped the East, except in the area of military discipline. As we have seen, thanks to the *Pax Mongolica* connecting East and West over land for the first time in history, such key Eastern inventions as paper, printing, the magnetic compass, and gunpowder were introduced to the West; these inventions made crucial contributions to the Renaissance and, in particular, to its oceanic navigation.

Without such a boost, the East fell into decay and inertia. Although the Ming dynasty is considered successful in having organized a peaceful society with flourishing arts and literature, it failed to channel its energy into exploration and expansion. Content with looking inward, the dynasty showed signs of complacency and stasis. Petty domestic power struggles among scholar-politicians began to predominate, especially in China and Korea. In this process, the various metaphysical Li-Ki schools of neo-Confucianism played a key role. Along with the teachings of Buddhism, these schools acquired a taste for the argumentation inherent in metaphysics, thus diluting the traditional attitude of syncretism and eclecticism; this resulted in accusations of heresy. Naturally, two schools competed with each other: the Li school resembled the Idealists of early modern Europe, while the Ki school resembled the European natural philosophers or Deists. Each school built and sponsored its own academy; as civil servants were selected through a national examination, students or teachers of those academies, when successful, eventually became officials and brought their metaphysical bickering to the court.

In the seventeenth century, while the West was ravaged by sectarian conflict, such as the Thirty Years' War and the English Civil War, the East also saw its political power struggles spring into life. Scholarly disputes were often colored by political motives, as scholar-politicians mobilized different schools and sects to impeach each other. This began in the Song dynasty and continued into the Ming dynasty and beyond. When Korea imported neo-Confucianism from the Song dynasty, it also imported this custom of impeachment; the politics of its Yi dynasty were especially dominated by this internecine practice of impeachment, which thankfully disappeared as the dynasty died out. The East thus slipped deeper and deeper into metaphysical and intellectual inertia as the West was emerging from its own.

Neocortex vs. Limbic System

Having examined in the previous chapter what contemporary science reveals about human evolution, let us now discuss what it tells us about human nature and the Mind-Body relationship. We have seen that evolution can be traced as far back as the evolution of the earth, suggested by our observation of the human embryo and the theory of recapitulation. From the Age of Dinosaurs, humankind inherited the ancient brain, and from the Age of Mammals, the old brain. Then, evolving into *Homo sapiens*, the human brain reached its current size of about 1,600 to 2,000 cc, which is extremely large in proportion to its body. Most of this increase in volume can be attributed to the development of the neocortex, or "new brain." What can we learn about human nature and the mind from this "new brain"?

Neocortex and the Human Mind

The human brain has three parts: an ancient brain (the R-complex), an old brain (the limbic system), and a new brain (the neocortex). Humans share the ancient brain with all reptiles and birds, the old brain with all mammals, and the new brain with later mammals. But the size and function of the new brain is unique to humans. Although the chimpanzee has the second largest new brain, it remains only a tenth the size of man's. According to contemporary medicine, the new brain is responsible for reasoning—the "higher function of the nervous system."

Figures 3-3 and 3-4 illustrate respectively the Neocortex (New Brain) in four lobes and the Limbic System (Old Brain) inside the Neocortex.

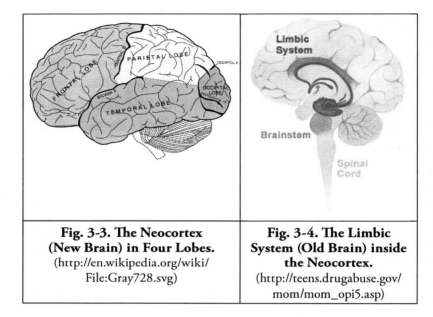

| Fig. 3-3. The Neocortex (New Brain) in Four Lobes. (http://en.wikipedia.org/wiki/File:Gray728.svg) | Fig. 3-4. The Limbic System (Old Brain) inside the Neocortex. (http://teens.drugabuse.gov/mom/mom_opi5.asp) |

It is the size and function of the new brain, and especially of its frontal lobes, which differentiates *Homo sapiens* from all other mammals. The "higher function of the nervous system" includes such mental functions as language, association, judgment, recognition of consequences, imagination, memories (both short- and long-term), and interaction with the limbic system. In short, the frontal lobes of the neocortex are the origin of what we call the mind—spirit, soul, and reason. It might therefore be suggested that the best approach to understanding the Mind-Body relationship would be to investigate the human brain, especially the newly formed neocortex.

The terminology, however, can be quite confusing: mind, spirit, soul, psyche, or reason, each has a different usage and role in literature, philosophy, and religion. Spirit, in particular, has a special significance as an eternal entity associated with

God. But in a broader sense, these terms are interchangeable. The same is true of the group of functions variously called emotion, passion, instinct, drive, and desire—these are all at once finely distinguished and interchangeable.

Let us not be caught up in ontological or epistemological niceties. Spirit and soul are not possessed by any animal other than Man, and so we must accept that this principle arises from the new brain. Given the presence of a rudimentary new brain in other animals, and since many of those animals demonstrate certain functions of consciousness, we may not entirely agree that spirit, or soul, or mind is unique to mankind. But the "mind" that we are dealing with here is whatever enables us to create a civilization. Figuratively, we can equate this with the new brain.

The new brain's frontal lobe has particular importance as the center of the higher functions of the nervous system. Even in more sophisticated mammals, the frontal lobe failed to form a "critical mass" to enable them to possess a mind remotely like that of man.

Limbic System (Old Brain): Emotion or Human "Body"

What, then, is the function of the old brain (i.e., the limbic system)? Contemporary medical science gives the following succinct description: "The deep limbic system lies near the center of the brain. Considering its size—about that of a walnut—it is power-packed with functions, all of which are critical for human behavior and survival. From an evolutionary standpoint, this is an older part of the mammalian brain that enabled animals to experience and express emotions. It freed them from the stereotypical behavior and actions dictated by the brain stem, found in the older reptilian brain."[18] We might note here that the pineal gland, considered by Descartes to be where the mind meets the body, belongs to the old brain. Modern medical science has shown that the pineal gland, through its production of melatonin, regulates the function of sleep.

The limbic system is responsible for emotion, passion, instinct, drive, and desire. The ancient brain, meanwhile, governs basic regulatory functions, such as breathing, sleeping, and appetite. For the sake of simplicity, let us categorize the ancient brain together with the old brain. From this perspective, the functions operated by both the ancient and old brain are those of the body, while the functions of the new brain relate to the mind or spirit.

Human Mind: Innate Ideas vs. Tabula Rasa

Man is neither purely spiritual nor purely physical; what then are human nature and the nature of the human mind? Does the human mind possess innate ideas (Plato) or is it a blank slate at birth (Aristotle)? Our mind has always been a subject of intense debate and theorization in the West, given its acceptance of a mind-body duality. The West has tended to identify the mind as the essence of human nature and to attribute to it an unlimited ability. Modern Western philosophy has shown two distinct views on the nature of the mind: the rationalists, whose theories were predicated on innate ideas, and the empiricists, whose ideas derived instead from a "tabula rasa" conception of the mind, denying innate ideas, contrary to Christian theology, which saw original sin as innate. But both rationalists and empiricists agreed that mind and body were distinct.

As empiricism evolved, the relationship between mind and body also evolved. John Locke (1632–1704), while taking a step toward denying innate ideas, still believed in the superiority of the spirit to the body. For Locke, the mind represented the "self" as the "the conscious thinking thing."[19] Although he accepted that "the body too goes to making the man,"[20] nonetheless he put a conspicuous emphasis on the mind. This hierarchy between mind and body was rejected by David Hume (1711–1776) and later empiricists, who stressed the body over the mind, or passions over reason. Reason, they argued, must be the slave of the passions: morality excites passion, and increases or diminishes actions; reason provides justification for action; consequently, for them, reason cannot be behind morality. But throughout this period of empiricism, the Mind-Body separation remained intact.

Western Mind: Neocortex without Limbic System

The belief in Man as an essentially spiritual being encouraged him to accept challenges and overcome obstacles—paradise could be realized in this world. Through his own efforts and with God's help, Man can be purely altruistic, transcendental, and free from bodily desires. Such a belief gave rise to many innocent and well-intentioned proposals, ideas, and ideologies. But none of these lasted, since they were grounded in an incorrect notion of human nature; such noble endeavors turned out to be only the beginning of a long journey toward disillusionment, and eventually to unprecedented destruction and tragedy. In the real world, a blind faith in human ability led not to paradise but to hell, as the twentieth century demonstrated.

Mainstream Western thought tended to interpret the body not as an indispensable aspect of man, but as a source of vices to be overcome. Man was made in the image of God and must strive to become like Him. Spinoza lamented that "philosophers look upon the passions by which we are assailed as vices, into which men fall through their own fault. So it is their custom to deride, bewail, berate them.... The fact is that they conceive men not as they are, but as they would like them to be. As a result, for the most part, it is not ethics they have written, but satire."[21]

Nietzsche, likewise, observed the error of Western metaphysics: "People everywhere are rhapsodizing, even under the guise of science, about future social conditions that will have lost their *exploitative character*—to my ear that sounds as if they were promising to invent a life form that would refrain from all organic functions."[22] As Nietzsche understood, human nature is neither a blank slate nor a mere neocortex, nor is it a malleable vessel of innate ideas. For the neocortex cannot function without a limbic system, nor reason without passions, the soul without the body.

Will to Power: Limbic System without Neocortex

But Nietzsche's position is also extreme, albeit in the opposite direction. Whereas the metaphysicians had dreamed of a human nature consisting only of reason, Nietzsche instead postulated a nature comprised of "noble" instinct and passion. Nietzsche claims: "Life itself in its essence means appropriating, injuring, overpowering those who are foreign and weaker; oppression, harshness, forcing one's own forms on others, incorporation, and at the very least, at the very mildest, exploitation.... *Exploitation* is not part of a decadent or imperfect, primitive society: it is part of the fundamental nature of living things, as its fundamental organic function; it is a consequence of the true will to power, which is simply the will to life."[23]

The problem is that Nietzsche's view of human nature does not extend beyond this point: exploitation, the will to power, nobility as opposed to herd morality, and no more. He thus commits the same error as Machiavelli—both emphasized the limbic system at the expense of the neocortex. The "amoral self-interest" of Machiavelli or the "will to power" of Nietzsche would be better served if the first became an *"enlightened* self-interest" or the second an *"enlightened* will to power." This is simply because Man cannot escape being a "social," altruistic, and spiritual animal. Machiavelli's Prince and Nietzsche's Zarathustra each lack a fundamental element of human existence.

Ideology: Innate Ideas or Acquired Ideas Written on Tabula Rasa

All philosophies, ideologies, and political and economic systems are built on a particular conception of human nature. Of course, these cannot stand the test of time if that conception is erroneous. Communism and fascism provide two good examples: both have lost credibility because they were founded on mistaken notions of human nature. Communism accepted a tabula rasa theory of human nature and dreamed of an altruistic society, promising to "invent a life form that would refrain from all organic functions."[24] Worse, it justified extreme measures as a means to achieve this utopia. Because this utopia never arrived, the extreme measures became a permanent fixture; having built its entire system on an untenable view of human nature, its demise was inevitable.

The nineteenth century was the Age of Revolution, full of utopian theories and ideologies, each claiming that mankind's problems could be resolved through reason. This innocent and commendable attitude soon degenerated into extreme ideologies that all shared a dichotomy of Spirit and Body. The three great wars of the twentieth century—the two world wars and the cold war—were fought under ideological banners, namely, imperialism, fascism, and communism. The degree of atrocity and destruction of each war was proportionate to the magnitude and intensity of the ideology that justified and amplified it.

As a reaction against communism's absolute faith in reason, fascism resorted to an equally extreme faith in instinct, intuition, and passion, pursuing racial self-interest based on the theory of "war of all against all." Moral scruples were ignored as the domain of the weak, much in line with Nietzsche's thinking. But the human sense of morality and justice—the conscience—is a biological imperative and cannot simply be discarded. Since fascism was based on a false perception of human nature, it could not survive long. It must be admitted that these two extreme ideologies, communism and fascism, were only aberrations in Western civilization, which also produced the liberal democracies that defeated them both. But insofar as the extremes were the products of Western civilization, they reveal the extreme perceptions of human nature underlying that civilization. Having experienced a bloody and tragic twentieth century as the culmination of a dialectic interaction between Spirit and Body, the West, at the outset of the new millennium, is finally changing its views on human nature, although very slowly. The West can no longer ignore the cumulative evidence of its own science.

Such dialectics, however, have also contributed to the growth of science and liberal democracy. The point here is not to contest the extraordinary achievements of the West, but to note that these achievements have been inseparable from the West's shortcomings.

Encephalization: Mind-Body Holism

From a scientific point of view, then, what is the relationship between new and old brains, or Spirit and Body? Contemporary medicine claims: "The subsequent evolution of the surrounding cerebral cortex in higher animals, especially humans, gave the capacity for problem solving, planning, organization, and rational thought. Yet, in order for these functions to occur one must have passion, emotion, and desire to make it happen. The deep limbic system adds the emotional spice, if you will, in both positive and negative ways."[25]

Current thought, meanwhile, holds that "the dichotomy which is implied by mind and body does not exist in the organism," and continues, "The mind and body are equivalent and inseparable expressions of life itself—the two aspects of psychosomatic existence."[26]

We have seen how contemporary versions of evolutionary theory reject the traditional separation of Man and Nature. The same is true of contemporary medical findings, which challenge the separation between Spirit and Body. By these discoveries, Western knowledge is undermining the guiding concept of its civilization. The relationship between the old brain and the new is surprisingly similar to the symbiotic relationship between Body and Spirit. As medical science describes it, "The neocortex is sitting over the limbic system in the same way as a jockey riding a horse with hardly any reins. Actually the bridle is very weak, as the frontal lobe of neocortex and the limbic system are linked through neurons."[27] This metaphor of the jockey and horse is noteworthy; the limbic system provides the necessary drive, while the neocortex provides coordination. Faced with this discovery, the West has had to distance itself from its view of separateness and dialectics between Spirit and Body, and adapt instead to a unity of the two. In the words of Bertrand Russell, echoing Hume, "Desires, emotions, or passions (you can choose whichever word you will) are the only possible cause of action. Reason is not a cause of action but only a regulator."

Western anatomists have found clues to understanding the relationship between mind and body: old brain and new brain are physically linked by neurons and are interdependent. These neurons are proof of "encephalization": that some of the functions of the old brain have been integrated with the new brain. For example, the frontal lobe of the neocortex is responsible for data collection, analysis, and judgment, integrating some functions of the limbic system. But the fact that reason can affect instinct implies that instinct can also affect reason, making encephalization a mixed blessing.

Medical science has discovered that the sexual function is particularly encephalized in humankind and is thus widely influenced by social and psychological conditions. But because encephalization works both ways, human activities are also strongly influenced by sexual desire. Darwin dedicated a new chapter in *The Descent of Man* to sexual selection, comparing it to natural selection.[28] Freud, likewise, with his theory of libido, dealt with the sexual function in humans. All in all, the encephalization between the neocortex and the limbic system serves as physical evidence for the interconnectedness of spirit and body: "The physiological and psychological aspects are integrated and inseparable."[29] A dichotomy between these two entities cannot hold in contemporary medical science.

The Third Way: Psychosomatic Being

The scientific definition of a "psychosomatic being" occurred only in the twentieth century. This definition is, in a way, an expression of the phenomenon of encephalization. Some Western philosophers, however, had an inkling of this definition long before it was formulated by scientists. These rare "third roaders" accepted a unity of Spirit and Body, acknowledging that passions were among the most basic components of human nature, and that the role of reason is to act as manager for the passions, rather than suppressing them.

Plato appears to show a similar attitude when he argued in *The Republic* that Reason is the charioteer who guides the passions (e.g., appetite and spiritedness), much like the jockey mentioned above. But his emphasis is precisely the opposite. In Plato, reason is the undisputed master, having full power over the passions as its slave, whereas among the moderns, passion is the master and reason is only its manager, having no source of action of its own. Hume's argument that reason must be the slave of passions explains this. From this perspective, reason is more a manager *for* the passions rather than the manager *of* the passions.

Hobbes appeared to have taken the very first step, indirect but unequivocal, by challenging the absolute supremacy of Spirit over Body. Voltaire, Lessing, and Adam Smith followed. Other British empiricists, such as John Locke and David Hume made critical contributions in this respect. It was their ideas, in the end, which contributed to the emergence of the free market and democracy; these saved Western civilization from the onslaught of extremism.

But in terms of clarity, Spinoza and Lessing stand out. Spinoza famously established that "the mind and the body are one and the same thing, which is conceived now under the attribute of thought, now under the attribute of extension." Spinoza stands as the most important Western philosopher to propound the unities of Mind and Body, and of Man and Nature, and to preach an ethics of harmony among men. Spinoza's position in Western philosophy is equivalent to that of Copernicus in Western science. Western science eventually accepted the Copernican revolution. But mainstream Western philosophy, with its conflict between spirit and body, long shunned—and still has yet to fully embrace—Spinoza's revolution. Hegel mentioned that all philosophers must start with Spinoza, but his entire metaphysics remained indebted to Descartes, that is, to a separation of Spirit and Body. Gotthold Ephraim Lessing (1729–1781), and later Bertrand Russell (1872–1970), tried to present a syncretism of the two Western extremes of Spirit or Body. As we have already seen, Russell believed passion to be the source of action, with reason as its guide. Lessing, who was closer to Spinoza, postulated that the soul is nothing but the body thinking itself, and the body is nothing but the extension of the soul. Lessing also famously quipped that man is "nothing but a carnivorous animal with a megalomaniacal perception of his own mental capacity."

These thinkers conceived of man—to put it in modern terms—as a "psychosomatic" being, with an encephalization between neocortex and limbic system. But in an expansive Yang environment, they could never hope to penetrate the philosophical mainstream, which was occupied by theologians and metaphysicians. In such a world, which naturally favors extremes, the Golden Mean has no place. However, now that the world has become circumscribed, a shift from extremes to mean is inevitable. After heavy sacrifices, the West has finally purged itself of both fascism, which promoted blind faith in instinct, and communism, which encouraged blind faith in reason. It appears that, with the end of history (to borrow the words of Francis Fukuyama) of the Western Spirit, that is, with the end of the West's dialectical struggle between Spirit and Body, it has finally repudiated its long-standing tendency to spiritual absolutism.

Western metaphysics—pure reason, independent of present material concerns—is the father of later ideologies. But what is a pure Spirit completely dissociated from the Body? Voltaire (François-Marie Arouet, 1694–1778) doubted its existence: "Metaphysics—*Trans naturam*—beyond nature. But what is that which is beyond nature? By nature it is to be presumed that one means matter. But metaphysics relate to that which is not matter.... Spirit, which the world has always talked of, and which mankind appropriated, for a long period, a body so attenuated and shadowy, that it could scarcely be called body, but from which, at length, they have removed every shadow of body, without knowing what it was that was left."[30]

Precursors

Besides these thinkers, there are, of course, many examples of Western figures who intuitively grasped Man as a whole without falling into the metaphysical trap of the Mind-Body dichotomy. These appear to have intuitively denied either innate ideas or a tabula rasa theory, hinting instead at the principle of self-preservation. Here are few such examples:

Pericles, in his eulogy, as described by Thucydides, for those who fell during the Peloponnesian War: "Mankind is tolerant of the praises of others so long as each hearer thinks that he can do as well or nearly as well himself, but when the speaker rises above him, jealousy is aroused and he begins to be incredulous."[31]

Spinoza in *Ethics*: "We see, therefore, that for the most part human nature is so constituted that men pity the unfortunate and envy the fortunate, and [envy them] with greater hate the more they love the thing they imagine the other to possess. We see, then, that from the same property of human nature from which it follows that men are compassionate, it also follows that the same men are envious and ambitious."[32]

H.G. Wells in *The Outline of History*: "From what we know of mankind, we are bound to conclude that the first sailors plundered when they could, and traded when they had to."[33] (For that matter, Montesquieu also thought that the first sailors must have been pirates.)[34]

These three thinkers observed the evolutionary character of human nature. Self-preservation, as they understood, remains Man's fundamental *raison d'être*. In order for man to attain his own self-fulfillment and social harmony with other beings, his drives must be guided by reason. This is a crucial departure from the other mainstream Western philosophers and theologians and metaphysicians who trusted reason to the detriment of the passions. From this perspective, it was only natural that the Westerners who were mostly influenced by Plato and Aristotle emphasized the importance of Knowledge based on spirit-mind separation, rather than falling under the influence of other Greek philosophers like Heraclitus (ca. 535–475 BC) and Carneades (214–129 BC), who appear to have had a more natural and balanced view on human nature.

As our examination of the functions of the old brain and new brain have shown, and as these latter Western thinkers first pointed out, the passions are only the causes of human action, while reason exists to regulate them. Reason is not concerned with ends, but with choosing the right means to an end established by desire. Spinoza defines the ultimate end as self-preservation: "the endeavor after self-preservation is the primary and only foundation of virtue." Reason exists to make the "right choices" in the constant human endeavor of self-preservation.

Aristotle and Thomas Aquinas: Spirit-Body Balance within Spiritualist Framework

When we examine the journey of Western thought over the last two millennia in terms of the domination of Spirit (most Western theologians and metaphysicians, or proponents of the neocortex), the reaction of Body to this domination (Machiavelli and Nietzsche, or proponents of the limbic system), and the "third way" psychosomatic thinkers (Spinoza and Lessing, or proponents of encephalization), some question may arise about Aristotle and Thomas Aquinas: where do they belong?

Aristotle excelled in his knowledge and understanding. The comprehensiveness of his intellectual system is indeed extraordinary, comprising ethics, politics, logic, biology, science, and so on. He was really "a man who knew all there was to know in his time." He influenced many thinkers, including Thomas Aquinas. Indeed, the two philosophers have enjoyed a unique position in the history of Western ideas. They belong with the mainstream Western proponents of the Spirit, represented by theology and metaphysics, but at the same time, within this framework, they expounded the importance of the Body. As we have briefly seen, Aristotle has the merit of counterbalancing Plato's overemphasis on Spirit, Ideas, and Forms with his stress on the role of the Body. In the same vein, his tabula rasa theory also provided a counterbalance to Plato's *innate idea* theory. Aquinas sought to free man from guilty feelings about his bodily desires (i.e., *concupiscence*) by replacing them with something mental (i.e., *privation of grace*) as the central element of the original sin.

From this perspective, Aquinas and Aristotle have offered new perspectives to many contemporary Western thinkers, since they belong neither to the tradition of modern metaphysics, nor to that of those against metaphysics, such as Nietzsche. Recent thinkers from Ayn Rand and Etienne Gilson to Robert Greene and Alasdair MacIntyre have rediscovered several aspects of their thought, being naturally critical of both Kant and Nietzsche. Rand's emphasis on rational self-interest and MacIntyre's interest in teleological virtue-ethics fit nicely between the two strands of thought, each represented by Kant and Nietzsche.

Given the overwhelming and still-powerful legacy of the Western Spirit, and given that Christianity remains the religion of most Westerners, the moderate doctrines of Aristotle and Aquinas may still retain more mass appeal than the "radical" ideas of Spinoza or Hume. One finds a similar logic in Lynn White's search for the origin of, and solution to, contemporary ecological problems. White identified Western religion's doctrine of domination of Man over Nature as ordained by God as the root cause. But his remedial model remains within the framework of Western religion—Saint Francis of Assisi, the patron saint of animals and the environment.[35]

But again, seen from within, the philosophy of Aristotle and Aquinas may have a unique place: Aristotle recognized the role of the Body much more than Plato did. It may be the same with Aquinas. He recognized the role of the Body much more than Saint Augustine. Thomas Aquinas went through great difficulty during his late life because of his emphasis on the role of the Body, relying on Aristotle, but he was eventually canonized. This episode proves both the uniqueness of Aristotle-Aquinas as well as their eventual grouping with the proponents of the Spirit. Thus, seen from the outside, both of them clearly belong to the broad spectrum of proponents of the Spirit in the Western history of ideas. Aristotle-Aquinas sought a Spirit-Body balance within the Spiritualist context.

In regard to the putative irrelevance of Spinoza, a true "third way" thinker to most Westerners, one recalls Kuhn's intriguing description of a paradigm shift. In his book, *The Structure of Scientific Revolutions*, he describes how the truth of heliocentrism discovered by Aristarchus (ca. 310–230 BC) had to wait for about 1,800 years to be successfully revived by Copernicus and Kepler. Until the Age of Discovery, mankind felt more comfortable with the geocentric theory of Aristotle and Ptolemy, regardless of its truthfulness, as long as the sphere of action remained confined to the Mediterranean: "Cleanthes (a contemporary of Aristarchus and head of the Stoics) thought it was the duty of the Greeks to indict Aristarchus on the charge of impiety for putting in motion the hearth of the universe ... supposing the heaven to remain at rest and the earth to revolve in an oblique circle, while it rotates, at the same time, about its own axis."[36] In a way, to most people, the truth of heliocentrism remained "less relevant" than the comfort of egocentrism—until they needed it.

The End of History of the Western Spirit

With the demise of the Age of Ideologies, the West has now completed its spiritual history. The dynamic and bloody dialectics between Spirit and Body has finally drawn to a close. We might even speak of an "end of history," that is, of the history of the Western Spirit, thanks to Western science and the continued efforts of the "third roaders." With the closing of the world, Mind and Reason must reunite with Body and Passion for our self-preservation.

The vast majority of Western history, literature, philosophy, and religion remains to remind us of their traditional separation of Mind and Body—over two thousand years cannot be forgotten so easily. But it is clear that we have passed a threshold. All ideologies—the penultimate illegitimate products of a Spirit-Body dichotomy—have disappeared with the wars of the twentieth century. Democracy and the free market—the final legitimate product of Western dialectics—have prevailed. The Industrial Revolution, and its concomitant transformation of the world from an expansive to a circumscribed one, has ushered in a paradigm shift of historic proportions, which will be treated in the final chapter of this book. Nobody can deny the new paradigm: even Western religion, which has long asserted its own exclusive truth, has come to accept its coexistence with other religions and schools of thought.

Now as the West has completed its journey of the Spirit, what will happen to its various theories of human nature? And what is the

Eastern understanding of human nature, and how does it contrast with those of the West? For the most part, the West interpreted human nature on the premise of mind-body separation, accepting no boundary to the capability of human nature: it had boundless potentiality according either to the nature of innate ideas or to the ideas based on tabula rasa. Paradise, in other words, is within human reach. On this, the East is in staunch opposition to the West, for it sees that human nature works within the framework of self-preservation, just like Nature and Tao. No ideas to the contrary can be either innate or acquired. As self-preservation in man tends to mean a greedy self-interest, and as each man and generation must learn the value of altruism from scratch, man must aim for the best possible management of human nature and society, instead of pursuing paradise, which remains illusory. Let us examine this Eastern understanding of human nature using Xun Zi and Spinoza as examples.

Human Nature: Spinoza vs. Xun Zi

It appears almost impossible to introduce an Eastern way of thinking to Westerners. This is because Western man is currently in the same place Eastern man found himself in two thousand years ago. Some Westerners may think that the East is yet to begin its Mind-Body dialectics, but it is fairer to say that the West has finally arrived at the truth of Mind-Body unity. Xun Zi in the East, and Spinoza in the West, are evidence of this.

Junzi: Eastern Man vs. Western Mind

It is very difficult to compare Eastern and Western views of the mind-body relationship, since the two views overlap very little. The West began with Spirit, separated from Body, and after two millennia, it arrived at Man as a unity of Spirit and Body, but it was precisely with Man that the East started its journey at the same time. Nothing similar to the West's rich theology and metaphysics exists in the East, since Spirit was never separated from the Body. The brief period of Li-Ki metaphysics is all that the East can show in this respect—and this was an aberration, signaling the closure of the Eastern mind and squabbling between factions.

But since the East began with Mind-Body unity, it possessed a rich literature and philosophy of Man based on a distinct understanding of human nature, in its ethical and political aspects, devoid of religious, supernatural, metaphysical, or ideological interference. The enormous difficulty in introducing Eastern Man to the Western mind derives from the fact that the latter has no counterpart to serve as a reference.

This obliges me to introduce two Eastern terms used to describe Man; although they lack exact translations, it is impossible to understand Eastern culture without them. The two terms are "Junzi" (君子, ruler's son) and "Xiaoren" (小人, small person). Junzi-Xiaoren forms an inseparable pair in Eastern culture, like Yin and Yang. Junzi has been translated in various terms, including "gentleman," "superior man," "prince," "nobleman," and "noble man"; Xiaoren has been translated as "small person," "common man," "inferior person," "ordinary person," and "petty man." As they have no precise counterparts in the West, it is natural there are no satisfactory Western words to translate them. Although Noble Man for Junzi and Petty Man for Xiaoren come close, they fail to capture the *nature, human nature, ethics,* and *politics* embodied in the Junzi-Xiaoren pairing. Consequently, we shall use the terms Junzi and Xiaoren, with Noble Man and Petty Man as occasional alternatives. Although Junzi and Xiaoren are referred to mostly in Confucianism, they are shared among all other schools of Eastern thought. Taoism, for example, prefers to use the pairing Sage and Multitude, but these are almost identical to Junzi-Xiaoren, the only difference being that if Junzi is practical, the sage is philosophical.

In this section we shall examine the Eastern understanding of human nature, as encapsulated in the duality of Junzi and Xiaoren, which permeated its entire culture. As Xun Zi extensively developed Confucianism in this direction, we shall refer mostly to his ideas in our examination of Junzi. In doing so, we shall juxtapose Xun Zi and Spinoza since their thought systems are in essence very similar. On the other hand, the comparison between East and West in this respect shall be undertaken in chapter 6. We shall compare Junzi as the Eastern role model with Hero as the Western role model. In doing so, we shall also examine the part played by Junzi in the East's assimilation of democracy and individual freedom.

What Man Should Be vs. What Man Is

The Eastern thinkers attempted to explain human nature by observing Man as he is. On the other hand, the West approached Man as he *should be*: God ordained Man to emulate Him, a spiritual being, without bodily constraints. By contrast, the result of the Eastern holistic approach is a number of synthetic expressions for Man, according to his dominant desire: Sage, benevolent man, man of Tao, of courage, of propriety, of knowledge, as well as Junzi and Xiaoren. Various schools of thought vied to interpret and compare them, and so these types dominate the canons and classics of Eastern literature. Junzi and Xiaoren found their way into almost all kinds of literature and daily conversation in the East, comparable to the figures of the Christian and Pagan in Western culture. Junzi denotes the accomplished and pragmatic man, who acts and chooses between his desires according to reason, preferring altruism; Xiaoren denotes the common man who spends much of his time lost in his passions, preferring greed and profit.

One must also bear in mind the critical difference in human nature as perceived by Eastern men and by the "third roaders" of the West. Although the latter also postulated Mind-Body unity, they arrived at this conclusion by combining elements already divided conceptually; unity was their conclusion, not their starting point, and they offered almost no further elaboration on man's behavior and place in society. By contrast, since Eastern thought began with mind-body unity, it could develop and accumulate a vast number of observations about Man as expressed and manifested in his social behavior.

This approach enabled the East to produce a conception of man that was ethical yet practical, as proven later by Western science. Perhaps the Eastern focus on man as a manager of his desires was due to its orientation on the past, as opposed to the West's orientation

on the future. Belief in paradise and the promised land that should
or could be realized in the future would drive us to concentrate on
what man should be rather than on what man is. We concluded in
chapter 2 that unless this orientation was ordained by God, the best
explanation for this contrast was in the environmental differences
between the two civilizations: an expansive environment is more
apt to produce belief in the future.

Understanding of Human Nature vs. Malleability of Human Mind

The contrast outlined above has radical consequences. The Western
prescriptivist approach assumes that man can be altered, whether by
penitence, grace, law, or evolution, and that he *should* be altered for
the better. The Eastern descriptivist approach, on the other hand,
aims simply to clarify man's actual nature, rather than to alter it—
this is achieved by education, training, and enlightenment. There
were virtually no significant Eastern philosophers who considered
human nature to be a blank slate. Because the Spirit was not separate
from the Body, there was no way to imagine human nature as
malleable. Instead, Eastern philosophers accepted the premise that
mankind was born with a fixed nature (i.e., self-preservation). Some
thought this nature generally good, others generally bad.

The principle of self-preservation was not recognized by
mainstream Western thinkers, since for them, human nature
remains malleable one way or the other (i.e., the innate idea theory
or tabula rasa). But if we conceive mind and body as unified, neither
has any meaning independent of the other. Eastern Man is not
a duality of mind and body, but a single psychosomatic being
struggling with various emotions and desires. Eastern Man perceives
himself constantly pulled by conflicting desires or passions, which
are neither mind nor body alone. His everyday task is to negotiate

these desires, and his life's work is to attain self-understanding and, thus, dominion over desire. In proportion to his progress, he acquires a greater degree of choice between these various desires, which include altruism. Most people, as Xiaoren, have no idea which path to take, remaining dominated by certain passions and blind to others. Only a few people, Junzi, by nature and by dint of education, training, and practice, can dispassionately survey their options and choose the right path for their self-interest, altruism.

Xun Zi's Thoughts

Xun Zi and Spinoza lived about two thousand years apart. However, they presented almost identical views on human nature as well as man's place within Nature. Spinoza's life is so well known that we need not repeat it at length here: his Jewish family was persecuted and expelled by Lisbon Christians; he was excommunicated from his own Jewish community in Amsterdam because of his belief; he was disowned by his family for his "betrayal" of the Jewish community; yet he miraculously succeeded in composing an ethical treatise that transcended all religious constraints and prejudices, and excelled over all others in clarity and focus. Xun Zi of the East comes close to Spinoza, a feat achieved by few other thinkers. In chronological terms, it was Spinoza whose views resembled those of Xun Zi. Had Xun Zi been known in the West in Spinoza's time, the latter could have claimed hardly any originality.

Xun Zi's life (310–237 BC) coincided with the height of internecine conflict in the East, which had already lasted almost five centuries. He thus had a unique opportunity to contribute to Eastern culture, and this he seized. Like Lao Tzu and Confucius, he also saw human greed and national disorder as the chief problems of his time. He proposed ethics as a remedy against greed, and law against disorder. His view of the Man-Nature relationship resembled Taoism, and his view of the Man-Man relationship resembled Confucianism.

The two portraits in Figures 3-5 and 3-6 reveal the difference in personality between Xun Zi and Spinoza. The former was blunt and argumentative, rare qualities among the Eastern philosophers, and his explicit critiques, bordering on attacks, of his fellow thinkers were highly unusual in his *milieu*. The constant warfare of the period may explain his bluntness and political realism. He also served as a high-ranking political official in one of the warring states. Spinoza's portrait, by contrast, conveys his amiable and compassionate personality, accommodating in everyday affairs, if not in religious beliefs.

Fig. 3-5. Xun Zi (荀子, 310–237 BC) (http://www.iep.utm.edu/x/xunzi.htm)	Fig. 3-6. Baruch Spinoza (1632–1677) (http://en.wikipedia.org/wiki/File:Spinoza.jpg)

During the Han dynasty, Xun Zi was considered the most important Confucian scholar, second only to Confucius himself. His chief merit lay in expanding and clarifying Taoist and Confucian views with his realist perspective. He also argued that Nature or God does not care about man's fate, but rather constitutes an eternal principle, with which man must comply for his own self-preservation. There is no divine punishment or reward involved. Xun Zi defined human nature as intrinsically problematic but acknowledged that everybody who wanted to could improve himself; this was a leap forward from Confucius: "Men are the same by birth; men are set apart by learning." Xun Zi's realism acknowledged the dominant role of the prince and the attendant utility of law, in addition to the traditional Confucian benevolent prince and system of ethics. He offered the East a new point of departure in the development of law, but his thought was rejected by Zhu Xi and other scholars of the Song dynasty, and so the door to intellectual innovation was closed when it most needed to be open.

Xun Zi and Spinoza I: Nature

Xun Zi's book is also called *Xunzi* and is composed of thirty-three chapters. Most notable for our comparison to Spinoza are chapter 17 on Heaven and chapter 23 on Human Nature. Let us first compare his conception of Heaven to the God of Spinoza's *Ethics*. I shall explain Xun Zi's thought more than that of Spinoza, since it is less well known to the West, and even perhaps in the East.

Eastern thinkers, like Spinoza, saw human nature as a holistic composite of Mind and Body, both a reflection and a part of Nature. Because of this, man aims at self-preservation, just as Nature does, but according to mainstream Western thought, man was given a choice between Spirit and Body, and so had difficulty accepting the idea of self-preservation. This is so because self-interest as an expression of self-preservation was either condemned or praised.

In his treatise on Heaven, Xun Zi writes: "Heaven works by an eternal principle: it does not exist because of Sage; nor does it disappear because of Despot: Complying with it is the way to prosperity; defying it is the way to misfortune (17-1); Achieving without acting, realizing without seeking, this is the way of Heaven (17-2); One cannot know Heaven except through its expressions and manifestations (17-4); Order and disorder, do they depend on Heaven? Sun, Moon, and Stars followed the same principle under Sage and Despot alike; but order was with Sage and disorder was with Despot; Order and disorder, they do not depend on Heaven (17-5); Heaven does not dispose of winter because people complain about the rigors of winter; Earth does not diminish its size because people complain about long distances; Junzi does not change his virtue because Xiaoren complains about it (17-6); Junzi focuses on that which depends on him; he does not waste his efforts on that which depends on Heaven. Xiaoren does not focus on that which depends on him; he wastes his efforts on that which depends on Heaven (17-7); Perceiving strange natural phenomena as strange is correct; perceiving them with awe and respect is incorrect (17-8); It will rain with rain ceremony; it will rain without rain ceremony: Junzi accepts it as ceremony; people do it as superstition: As ceremony, it is useful; as superstition, it is ominous (17-9)."[37]

Now, let us see how Spinoza defined the man-nature relationship in his *Ethics*: "It is impossible, that man should not be a part of Nature... The power, whereby each particular thing, and consequently man, preserves his being, is the power of God or of Nature (IV, Prop. IV); He, who loves God, cannot endeavour that God should love him in return. (V, Prop. XIX); Some assert that God, like a man, consists of body and mind, and is susceptible to passions. How far such persons have strayed from the truth … it is the height of absurdity to predicate such a thing of God, a being absolutely infinite (I, Prop. XV); Everyone thought out for himself, according to his abilities, a different way of worshipping God, so that God might love him more than his fellows, and direct the whole course of nature for the satisfaction of his blind cupidity and insatiable avarice. Thus the prejudice developed into superstition, and took deep root in the human mind; and for this reason everyone strove most zealously to understand and explain the final causes of things; but in their endeavor to show that nature does nothing in vain, i.e. nothing which is useless to man, they only seem to have demonstrated that nature, the gods, and men are all mad together … nature has no particular goal in view, and that final causes are mere human figments.… Hence anyone who seeks for the true causes of miracles, and strives to understand natural phenomena as an intelligent being, and not to gaze at them like a fool, is set down and denounced as an impious heretic by those whom the masses adore as the interpreters of nature and the gods (I, Appendix)."

The similarity between Xun Zi and Spinoza needs no further elaboration. Their essential position can be summarized thus: God (Tao) is indifferent to man, but it is in man's interest to observe the Way of God (Tao). Consequently, both agree that the chief victims of miracles and superstitions are those who greedily covet temporal advantages.[38] The Way of God (Tao) is reflected in human nature. These shared ideas could be compared to the deism later developed by Western thinkers of the Enlightenment. There is one fundamental difference: for Xun Zi, deism was the starting point. He advanced further to human nature, ethics, and politics; Western deism is the end point. It began as a reaction to mainstream theism and consequently failed to evolve beyond a critique.

Xun Zi and Spinoza II: Human Nature

Let us now compare human nature as interpreted by Xun Zi and Spinoza. Xun Zi: "Human nature is bad; man is born with it; it pursues profit and pleasure which give rise to conflicts, to the detriment of mutual accommodation: it falls prey to jealousy and hatred, which beget injuries to the detriment of sincerity and mutual trust (23-1); Emotions are troublesome … most people are under the whim of emotions, only the wise are not (23-13); Confounding human nature and learning was the reason behind the assumption that "human nature is good" (23-3); As an experiment, let us eliminate all possibility of restraints by authorities, improvement by ethics, discipline by laws, and dissuasion by punishment: now let us see how the multitudes get along together: In that case, the strong will injure and cheat the weak; the majority will harm and destroy the minority; ethics and order will be lost; society will immediately march into perdition (23-7); One has no choice concerning human nature; it can only be differently manifested: The way of its manifestation is not innate; this is at one's disposal: With strenuous learning, practice, and habit, human nature can be differently manifested (8-16)."

Spinoza defines human nature as follows: "Man is necessarily always a prey to his passions (IV, Prop. IV); Desire is the essence of a man, that is, the endeavour whereby a man endeavors to persist in his own being…. Men do not abide by the precepts of reason (IV, Prop. XVIII); Human infirmity in moderating and checking the emotions I name bondage: for, when a man is a prey to his emotions, he is not his own master, but lies at the mercy of fortune: so much so, that he is often compelled, while seeing that which is better for him, to follow that which is worse (IV, Preface); Most writers on the emotions and on human conduct seem to be treating rather of matters outside nature than of natural phenomena following nature's general laws.... They believe that he disturbs rather than follows nature's order, that he has absolute control over his actions.... They attribute human infirmities and fickleness, not to the power of nature in general, but to some mysterious flaw in the nature of man, which accordingly they bemoan, deride, despise, or, as usually happens, abuse (III, Preface)."

Both philosophers believed that in man there is always a dynamic interaction of passion and reason (body or spirit). The best description of this state is the Yin-Yang concept described in chapter 2. Reason contains a part of passion and passion a part of reason. Depending on one's temperament, reason or emotion can dominate, but each always contains the germ of the other. For Xun Zi and other Eastern thinkers, one of the most important challenges was to express a man's state: who was dominated by reason and who by passion? The Junzi-Xiaoren pair was an answer to precisely this problem, on which most Eastern thinkers agreed.

Confucius himself had not elaborated on human nature; he probably (and correctly) believed that defining it as good or bad would only lead to unnecessary and harmful metaphysical disputes: human nature must be beyond good and evil, as is Nature herself. He did, however, emphasize the importance of education and training; "By nature men are similar; by learning men are wide apart." This is comparable to Locke's idea on education: "of all the men we meet with, nine parts of ten are what they are, good or evil, useful or not, by their education."

Xun Zi and Spinoza III: Ethics

The most critical aspect of the ethics of these two philosophers is their emphasis on learning, understanding, and acting. As seeking self-preservation is innate to human nature by definition, we cannot condemn it, nor repent for it; instead, we must learn to manage it. Spinoza perceives understanding as providing liberty, while Xun Zi gave education the role of guiding Li, which is unique to mankind: "Fire and water have Ki but do not have life. Grasses and trees have life but do not have perceptivity. Fowl and beasts have perceptivity but do not have Li (sense of right and wrong, duty, justice). Men have Ki, life, perceptivity, and Li."[39] This description of the Eastern *scala naturae* is very similar to Aristotle's three souls: *vegetative, perceptive,* and *rational.* The difference was that Aristotle was speaking from a metaphysical perspective, whereas Xun Zi wanted to emphasize the importance of education. Let us now examine how Xun Zi and Spinoza stressed this point.

Xun Zi: "Ethics arises from learning and the action of the sage; it is not born with human nature.... The sage accumulates reflections, habituates actions, and then gives rise to ethics and laws: Ethics and laws arise with the Sage; they are not born with human nature.... The sage is the same as the multitude with respect to his nature; The sage differs from the many with respect to his actions (23-5); Unattended and given free license, human nature and emotions are bound to create conflicts, disorder, and violence: they can be tamed and controlled only through ethics, following the instruction of teachers and principles (23-1); The man in the street can become a sage, by means of benign ethics and transparent law (23-11); A man becomes sage by learning and actions; why, then, cannot everybody achieve this? Because although one *can* achieve it, one is not *forced* to achieve it: Xiaoren can become Junzi, but does not wish to: Junzi can become Xiaoren; he does not wish to: Junzi and Xiaoren do not become each other, not because they cannot, but because they are not forced to (23-12); Junzi has three concerns: To neglect education when young would lead to ineptness when old; to neglect education when old would lead to incomprehension when dead; not to share in times of abundance would lead to no relief in times of poverty (30-8)."

Spinoza suggests that human freedom comes with understanding: "Men who are governed by reason—that is, who seek what is useful to them in accordance with reason—desire for themselves nothing, which they do not also desire for the rest of mankind, and, consequently, are just, faithful, and honorable in their conduct (IV, Prop. XVIII); He who lives under the guidance of reason, endeavours, as far as possible, to render back love, or kindness, for other men's hatred, anger, contempt, etc., towards him (IV, Prop. XLVI); The free man, who lives among the ignorant, strives, as far as he can, to avoid receiving favors from them (IV, Prop. LXX); Only free men are thoroughly grateful one to another (IV, Prop. LXXI); The free man never acts fraudulently, but always in good faith (IV, Prop. LXXII); Yet minds are not conquered by force, but by love and high-mindedness (IV, Appendix XI); It is before all things useful to men to associate their ways of life, to bind themselves together with such bonds as they think most fitted to gather them all into unity, and generally to do whatsoever serves to strengthen friendship (IV, Appendix XII); But for this there is need of skill and watchfulness. For men are diverse (seeing that those who live under the guidance of reason are few), yet are they generally envious and more prone to revenge than to sympathy. No small force of character is therefore required to take everyone as he is, and to restrain one's self from imitating the emotions of others (IV, Appendix XIII); Blessedness is not the reward of virtue, but virtue itself; neither do we rejoice therein, because we control our lusts, but, contrariwise, because we rejoice therein, we are able to control our lusts (IV, Prop. XLII); If men had not this hope and this fear, but believed that the mind perishes with the body, and that no hope of prolonged life remains for the wretches who are broken down with the burden of piety, they would return to their own inclinations, controlling everything in accordance with their lusts, and desiring to obey fortune rather than themselves. Such a course appears to me not less absurd than if a man, because he does not believe that he can by wholesome food sustain his body for ever, should wish to cram himself with poisons and deadly fare; or if, because he sees that the mind is not eternal or immortal, he should prefer to be out of his mind altogether, and to live without the use of reason; these ideas are so absurd as to be scarcely worth refuting. If the way which I have pointed out as leading to this result seems exceedingly hard, it may nevertheless be discovered. Needs must it be hard, since it is so seldom found. How would it be possible, if salvation were ready to our hand, and could without great labor be found, that it should be by almost all men neglected? But all things excellent are as difficult as they are rare."[40]

Both Xun Zi and Spinoza accept that most people would naturally remain and behave as Xiaoren. In understanding and reiterating the virtues of Junzi, both stressed the importance of friendship, since the environment created by one's associates is crucial in the process of educating oneself.[41] For this reason, Xun Zi remarks: "If you do not know a man, look at his friends; if you do not know a ruler, look at his attendants." We have the same old Western proverb: "You may know a man by his friends." Spinoza: "Only free men are thoroughly useful one to another, and associate among themselves by the closest necessity of friendship. Only such men endeavour, with mutual zeal of love, to confer benefits on each other, and, therefore, only they are thoroughly grateful one to another (IV, Prop. LXXI, Proof)." Both accept, moreover, that even Junzi always has the germ of Xiaoren inside him: such is human nature. Social status and nobility of birth, however, have nothing to do with the matter. Altruism for Junzi is the equivalent to greed for Xiaoren. Junzi will pity, not despise, Xiaoren, since he knows how difficult it is to manage desires by reason.

Xun Zi and Spinoza IV: Politics

Although the two philosophers show close resemblances in their views of Nature-God, human nature, and ethics, they differed in their emphasis on the value of role models. Spinoza cites the "free man" as a role model, but does not elaborate, since his chief concern was theological and metaphysical, rather than practical. His concept of the "free man" served more as a reaction against the Christian model of virtue than as an ideal in its own right. Xun Zi, by contrast, offers extensive definitions and explanations of the role model, Junzi, comparing it to the anti-role model, Xiaoren, and examines the position and behavior of each in society. This Junzi-Xiaoren pairing carries heavy political implications. And Xun Zi, following the Confucian tradition, understood politics as an extension of ethics. Aristotle had a similar attitude, but the unity of ethics and politics is much more pronounced in the East.

In any society there must be an ideal to which people can aspire: this is the foundation of education, social ethics, and eventually politics. When a civilization intensely focuses on one ideal, it naturally develops an anti-type in opposition to this ideal. Spinoza thus presented the "free man" as the ideal and the "multitude" as his antitype. But these two terms simply embody the more abstract concepts of bondage and freedom. Xun Zi, on the other hand, operated within the Eastern framework of pragmatic and concrete analysis of ethical norms: the Junzi-Xiaoren pair.

Easterners strove for almost two millennia to approach the ideal of Junzi, just as Westerners strove to be good Christians.

Here are a few examples of Junzi and Xiaoren, as articulated by Xun Zi: "Junzi advances every day; Xiaoren regresses every day: Efforts from them are the same; results from them are the opposite (17-7)[42]; Junzi's actions are always beneficial, whether he is capable or not; those of Xiaoren are always detrimental, whether he is capable or not: Junzi, when capable, leads people with clemency and rectitude; when incapable he serves people with humility and esteem: Xiaoren, when capable, uses people with arrogance and insolence; when incapable, he harms people with jealousy and resentment (3-3): Junzi avails himself of ideas and things; Xiaoren makes himself available for ideas and things (2-5): Junzi when spirited practices Tao and the Way of Heaven; when unspirited he practices awe and restraint: when intelligent he becomes resourceful and competent; when unintelligent he remains correct and orderly: when employed he shows integrity and rectitude; when unemployed he shows respect and probity: when delighted he becomes harmonious and rational; when worried he becomes equanimous and reasonable: when fortunate he expresses his delight; when unfortunate he practices prudence and caution: Xiaoren, when spirited, displays arrogance and violence; when unspirited he practices perversity and malice: Consequently, Junzi always advances, while Xiaoren always regresses (3-6); When faced with good, one must examine whether he possesses it; when faced with bad, one must be concerned as to whether he possesses it (2-1); Junzi is easy to know but difficult to understand; he acquires respect but is never threatened (3-2); He takes pleasure in virtue; he compliments others but does not flatter them: He takes pleasure in what is right; he addresses others' wrongs, but does not denounce them (3-5)."

Does Junzi have worries? According to Xun Zi, no. Junzi always takes pleasure: "Junzi takes pleasure in his efforts when achievement is not possible; he takes pleasure in his achievement when it is possible; he always takes pleasure in his life, and does not let himself worry even for a single day; Xiaoren worries about failure when achievement is not possible; he is afraid of losing what he has when achievement is possible; he always worries in his life, and he does not let himself take pleasure even for a single day."

As he lived amid constant warfare among nations that continued for several centuries in a circumscribed environment, Xun Zi also touched upon "international politics." He developed an idea of how relations among nations could improve under a king who reigned as the provider of peace and stability based not only on a superior military force but also on the consent of other nations. This aspect shall be examined in chapter 5 as we compare the concept of the Eastern Hegemon-king with the concept of the Western Hero-conqueror.

Human Nature: Epistemology and Ethics

Some Eastern philosophers, such as Mencius (372–289 BC), believed human nature to be intrinsically good, given Man's benevolence, altruism, sense of honor, and justice. But this good nature could be corrupted by a bad environment; education was necessary to protect men from this negative influence. Mencius was well known for his claim that people had the right to overthrow a tyrant, which was also a popular subject of Western discussion in the seventeenth century and which can be found among some medieval theologians. This doctrine was revolutionary at a time when rulers treated subjects simply as a means to attain their goals. As such, Mencius' idea resembles Immanuel Kant's claim that human beings must treat others as ends, not means. Both philosophers shared a view of moral will, or moral law.

Xun Zi, a fierce opponent of Mencius within Confucianism, saw human nature as bad, full of negative emotions, such as jealousy, hatred, and greed; only by ethical education could man overcome this nature and achieve self-fulfillment and social harmony. Unlike Mencius, Xun Zi did not believe in the moral law of Heaven, instead understanding Heaven as Nature, indifferent to human affairs; this conception he shared with Confucius, who had famously said that man should focus on affairs of Man rather than concentrating on matters of Heaven or God. Although Mencius and Xun Zi had different views of human nature, they both put emphasis on the necessity of education and learning.

It must also be pointed out that the terms "bad" and "good" used by Eastern thinkers more than two millennia ago were more often used to express what they "liked" or "disliked." Some Western thinkers, including Spinoza and Russell, also thought that, in the final analysis, the pairing of just and unjust, as well as that of good and bad, boiled down to like and dislike. Thus, the Eastern usage of the same terms for bad and dislike, and for good and like, requires explanation from both epistemological and ethical perspectives. In the Eastern view of human nature, there was no concept of just or unjust, and consequently, there were no suggestions of sin or punishment. There was no absolute categorization or definitive judgment on the matter. The term that was used by Xun Zi and Mencius to indicate human nature (性) also had the broader sense of a "tendency." In this context, it is more correct to say that, for Xun Zi, human nature "tends" to be bad rather than good, whereas for Mencius, human nature "tends" to be good rather than bad. This "tendency" of human nature carries a critical importance in terms of the role of ethics in a capitalist free market, as we shall see in chapter 9.

According to the Eastern thinkers, including Xun Zi and Mencius, Man's negative qualities, like his positive qualities, simply tend to follow the way of Nature, that is, toward self-preservation. Spinoza made a similar claim: "The striving to preserve itself is the very essence of a thing.... Striving to preserve oneself is the first and only foundation of virtue. For no other principle can be conceived prior to this one and no virtue can be conceived without it."[43] In the final analysis, desires are man's only source of action and, as such, must be value-neutral. As sources of action, they are only to be guided and coordinated by reason, and if this is achieved, they result not in bondage but in liberty. For instance, both greed and altruism are passions; Xiaoren, who fails to regulate them, remains in thrall to his greed, whereas Junzi, who regulates them correctly, becomes free through altruism.

Xun Zi's justification of the Hegemon-king, along with his belief that human nature tended to be bad, prompted some of his disciples to join the Legalist School, with its extreme vision of a just society grounded on a draconian legal system. Such a legacy complicated Xun Zi's reputation in the history of Chinese philosophy. The Han dynasty (ca. 206 BC to AD 220), with its famous syncretism, regarded him as one of the great teachers of Confucianism, while the Song dynasty (AD 960–1279), with its rigidity and narrow-mindedness, labeled him a heretic. His Legalist disciples, such as Han Fei and Li Ssu, probably contributed to this latter unfavorable opinion.

Regardless of this narrow interpretation, however, Xun Zi's teaching was fundamentally Confucian. Instead of confining it, Xun Zi had expanded it by providing a flexible and innovative interpretation of its values. His emphasis on education follows the essence of Confucianism, as opposed to the Legalist School, which advocated severe punishment and a strict rule of law. Compare Xun Zi's oft-quoted maxim on education: "If wood is pressed against a straightening board, it can be made straight; if metal is put to the grindstone, it can be sharpened; and if the refined person studies widely and examines himself every day, his wisdom will become lucid and his conduct faultless."[44]

CHAPTER 4

Man and Man:
Western Law vs. Eastern Ethics

> "Do unto others as you would have others do unto you."
>
> Jesus Christ

> "Do not do unto others what you do not want others to do unto you."
>
> Confucius

Christianity and Confucianism

Christianity and Confucianism, more than any other cultural elements, defined their respective civilizations. Due to its straightforward acceptance of monotheism, the West based its understanding of interpersonal relationships on the ideal of liberty, rather than of harmony. This principle of liberty (and attendant separation) is the third and final aspect of the Western conceptual triad that we analyze in this book. An equivalent triad is found in the East, based not on liberty and separation but on unity and harmony.

Confucianism focused almost exclusively on the Man-Man relationship without any supernatural mediation and, consequently, proposed ethics as the principal means of governance. By contrast, Christianity had the double task of providing a Universal ethics and of founding this ethics on the Judeo-Christian lawgiving God; it thus relied on both ethics and law, with far-reaching consequences for Western civilization.

Although unlike Christ, Confucius did write his teaching; it was decades, even centuries later that the Confucian teachings were compiled in their present form as the Confucian canons. In the process, the original teachings must have gone through substantial additions and modifications. These additions and modifications are all ultimately attributed to Confucius as statements clarifying his original views. Thus, instead of citing the individual names of Confucius, Mencius, Xun Zi, and other great Confucian teachers, we will simply use "Confucianism" to mean the shared teachings of the Confucian tradition.

Taoism and Confucianism: Complementarity

As we have seen, Taoism defined the relationship between Man and Nature, while Confucianism defined that between

Man and Man. The common basis of both is ethics, grounded in Tao—the eternal principle of Nature—and elaborated by Confucianism in a social context. Neither school recognized the existence of any supernatural entity, which puzzled Western Enlightenment thinkers: how was a system of ethics possible without God? As both emerged almost contemporaneously from the same background of ongoing warfare, both were concerned primarily to identify and remedy the principal cause of human conflict. Taoism identified princely greed as the cause, whereas Confucianism, which identified disorder as the cause, understood the problem rather as a general breakdown in a system of ethics. Confucianism counsels learning the ethics of self-management for the individual, the family, the state, and even the world, while Taoism counsels the philosophy of Wuwei based on Tao, for both man and state. In this respect, Confucianism and Taoism remained complementary and constituted the Yang and Yin of Eastern civilization.

The Confucian canons can be compared to the Western Bible, in terms of their significance within their civilization: "In China, the canon's formation coincided with the expansion of the Chinese empire and the consolidation of bureaucracy. Confucianism and the Confucian canon came to Korea and Japan at a time when both countries were in the process of consolidating monarchical power in the early history of their unified states. Administrative and penal codes, cosmology and rituals, the recruitment and education of officials, inculcation of social virtues, historiography in Korea and Japan—all were influenced by the Confucian canon and its ideology."[1] Taoism is also essential to Eastern thought, since it defines man's relationship to nature; it serves as a complement to Confucianism, and the two together may be compared to the Old and New Testaments.

Here one crucial point must be stressed. Monotheistic religions or ideologies are built on the premise of a supernatural being or transcendental ideals, to which man is supposed to submit and sacrifice for the sake of a promised paradise. Eastern ethics recognizes no such entity or ideals, instead being humanist in character. It is impossible to be both Jewish and Christian, Protestant and Catholic, or Communist and Fascist, but Easterners have no problem embracing both Taoism and Confucianism, as well as other schools—they are encouraged to choose the best aspects of each school, with the overall goal of self-cultivation and self-realization. Philosophy is at the service of man, not vice versa. This important point is succinctly made by Confucius: "Truth does not make Man great; Man can make Truth great."[2] A similar view is shared by Taoism and most other Eastern schools.

Judaism vs. Christianity: Dialectics

In the West, it was primarily Judaism that defined the relationship between Man and God, and Christianity which defined that between Man and Man. Both religions cannot coexist in the Western mind: one must choose between them, or others. The same was true even within Christianity, for example, with the Great Schism of 1054 or the Protestant Reformation of the sixteenth century, and so on. A brotherly or eirenical attitude toward other religions left many open to marginalization or, worse, charges of heresy: excommunication, or even execution.

This separatism, however, engendered a dialectics between individuals and encouraged freedom of thought and indeed freedom itself. Within an expansive environment, freedom was more important than harmony, as it encouraged action and entrepreneurial results. Western man, who successfully ventured out to sea, into the unknown world, became sovereign and readily claimed supernatural authority for his sovereignty. Ideological and religious differences soon became unbridgeable, and human society had to be regulated by law, divinely legitimated, instead of ethics.

Universal Ethics: Confucian Humanity, Christian Love, Buddhist Compassion, and Islamic Brotherly Love

The fundamental teaching of Confucianism is Humanity (*Jen*, 仁—a reduplication of the character denoting man, 人). *Jen* denotes the ideal relationship between Man and Man; we shall translate it as "Humanity," or sometimes "Benevolence," to avoid confusion with other senses of "humanity." When asked to define the word, Confucius responded: "*Jen* is to love mankind."[3] Humanity is central to Confucianism, in the same way that "Love thy neighbor as thyself" constitutes Christ's central teaching. In fact, all major religions established a similar doctrine: Compassion in Buddhism and Brotherly Love in Islam. All agree on the importance of harmony among men. Perhaps such a unity reveals a biological need for ethics and moral law in human society based on self-preservation.

Let us briefly return to 2000 BC, when the domestication of plants and animals was practically complete—an achievement that enabled and initiated urban life. Mankind confronted, for the first time in its history, the problem of social relations. Innumerable ideas must have been proposed and put to the test, but all must have reached the same conclusions: that man cannot live alone; that self-preservation requires altruism; and that enlightened self-interest is in the best interest of society as a whole. Confucius asks, "I cannot live among birds and beasts; if I do not live among mankind, who am I?"[4] One finds a similar question in the West, when the Talmud asks, "If I do not live for myself, who will do it for me? If I live only for myself, who am I?" All solutions, then, converge on the principle of love, and this is not so much simple exhortation as a promotion of enlightened self-interest. As we have since learned, mankind has had the same basic nature since its evolutionary emergence about 50,000 years ago and will probably continue to do so for millions of years. Likewise, the key moral rule established by the great teachers of four millennia past will remain with us.

Ethics vs. Religion

Confucianism was rigorously humanistic. When asked about death, Confucius replied, "We do not even know about life. How can we pretend to know about death?"[5] About the spirits, he said, "We do not even know how to serve man, so how can we pretend to serve the spirits?"[6] On wonders and miracles, he remarked, "To live in obscurity, and yet practice wonders, in order to be mentioned with honor in future ages: this is what I do not do."[7] This attitude marked a rejection of metaphysics, religious dogma, and miracles.

Confucius was very clear on this point: after defining humanity as loving mankind, he defined knowledge as, "to know mankind." But having humanity is not a goal, rather it is an inviolable and universal rule—a guide to man's goal or *raison d'être*, that is, self-fulfillment and improvement, a state of striving to further one's understanding and situation. According to Confucianism, nothing is more important than self-fulfillment: one is born with a certain potential, which it is one's lifelong duty to discover and realize. Pledging oneself to a specific faith or dogma creates two problems for the Confucian: that faith may serve a goal other than self-fulfillment, and may require one to violate the principle of humanity against those of other faiths. Consequently, such a pledge is tantamount to abandoning the Confucian ideal. Perhaps this explains the low rate of adherence to religion or ideology in East Asia, even today. Some may claim Communist China as a counterexample, but this is mistaken: Chinese communism is being thoroughly "sinicized," not vice versa. We shall shortly examine this issue in detail.

It is therefore fairer to regard Confucianism as a source of ethics than of religion. In the same vein, it is quite mistaken to describe Confucius as a lawgiver, as Western philosophers have done, for Confucius repeatedly stressed the primacy of ethics over law. To Western minds, this may sound unusual, since even the great Voltaire and other Enlightenment philosophers wondered at the possibility of a secular ethics in the East. But Confucianism has no church, no ecclesiastics, no dogma, and no supernatural being. Without dogma, Confucius succeeded in making Humanity the one cardinal rule. Legend holds that Confucius met the founder of Taoism, Lao Tzu, and expressed respect for him. The significance of this story is that Confucianism accepts the fundamental precepts of Taoism—Tao is not within human reach, but its manifestations are. This element of Taoism influenced Confucianism in its rejection of dogma, miracles, and superstition. The profound rationality of this Eastern humanism made such an impression on Western Enlightenment philosophers that some of them, such as Voltaire, praised Confucius as the only teacher of mankind who did not try to deceive people.[8]

The mainstream Eastern role model is Junzi. Junzi shuns physical force and acts with modesty in times of success, and with fortitude in times of distress. Both Taoism and Confucianism recommended moral over physical force as the best means of self-preservation, and the virtues of fortitude and equanimity: "When resting in safety, Junzi does not forget that danger may come; when in a state of security he does not forget the possibility of ruin; when all is orderly, he does not forget that disorder may come." These Confucian teachings recall Pericles, who calmed the Athenians when they grew arrogant in times of success, and who encouraged them in times of adversity. The Eastern role model, Junzi, serves his country with exemplary leadership, a pattern equally applicable in private and family life: "Confucian education from the start was focused on the self-cultivation of those who would become leaders in society, and much of what is said in *The Analects, Mencius, Xun Zi*, and in other classic texts would still be applicable to leadership in the modern world."[9]

| **Fig. 4-1. Confucius (551–479 BC)** (Source: *Confucius the Scholar*, http://commons.wikimedia.org/wiki/Image:Confucius_the_scholar.jpg) | **Fig. 4-2. Jesus Christ** (Source: *Christ Pantocrator*, http://web.ceu.hu/medstud/basiliscus/Daphni0001.htm) |

Thus, the Eastern role model is the man who can "control himself, raise his family, serve the nation, and pacify the world."[10] Voltaire was fascinated by Confucius for this very reason: "By what fatality, perhaps shameful for western nations, is it necessary to go to the extreme east to find a simple sage, without ostentation, without imposture, who taught men to live happily 600 years before our common era, at a time when the entire north knew nothing of the alphabet, and the Greeks had hardly begun to distinguish themselves by wisdom? This sage was Confucius, who, alone among the ancient legislators, never sought to deceive mankind. What finer rules of conduct have ever been given on earth? He teaches: Regulate a nation as you regulate a family, a man can govern his family well only by setting an example; Make it your business to forestall crime in order to diminish the need to punish it; Love man in general, but cherish those who are good; Forget wrongs, never kindness; I have seen men incapable of learning, I have never seen any incapable of virtue. We must admit that no legislator has enunciated truths more useful to mankind."[11]

Unlike Western thinkers, Confucius did not believe in suppressing desire to achieve a higher spiritual status. Instead, his aim was to reconcile the individual's desires with those of others. Life was to be pleasurable for all men: not hedonistic pleasure, but the kind of pleasure man finds in nature, in true friendship, or in the search for wisdom. In this context, it is very revealing to compare the sacred books of the two civilizations, particularly the beginnings of each book. The classic of Confucianism starts with the pleasures of this world: "Isn't it delightful to learn and put it into practice?" and "Isn't it a pleasure to have a friend come from afar?"[12] This is a stark contrast with the New Testament, which begins with the genealogy of Christ: "forty-two generations from Abraham: fourteen from Abraham to David; fourteen from David to the Babylonian captivity; fourteen from the Babylonian captivity to Jesus Christ."

Although Humanity remains the fundamental principle of Confucianism, a Confucian mind is taught to place more value on finding pleasures in life than on practicing Humanity or acquiring knowledge: "One who practices Humanity is better than one who knows, and one who finds pleasure in life is better than one who practices Humanity."[13] The West, on the other hand, emphasized obedience to the decree of God; this duty which revolved around conflicting edicts is also fundamentally different from Socratic faith in Knowledge, which states, "Man errs only through ignorance."

Christianity: Law vs. Ethics

Jesus offered the same doctrine as Confucius—"Love thy neighbor as thyself." But unlike Confucianism, Christianity exhibits a dialectical tension. Perhaps this is due to the fact that later Christians had to codify Jesus' teaching as religious dogma to ensure its continued relevance in an expansive world. One would like to believe that the fundamental teaching of Christ is *agape*, and that Christianity abides by it. However, since Judaism preceded Christianity, Jesus' doctrine had to be built upon Moses' legalistic monotheism: "Think not that I am come to destroy the law, or the prophets: I am not come to destroy, but to fulfill."[14] Religion as an institution divides believers from non-believers. How, then, can we reconcile Jesus' universal love with Moses' law, which is reserved for the believers? As Enlightenment philosophers observed, the two fundamental precepts of Christianity, charity and faith, are perhaps in fundamental contradiction. The only solution is to suggest that love is the only faith, but then religion would lack any solid institutional basis. Saint Paul, for one, is equivocal on this point, since he sometimes emphasizes love ("And now abideth faith, hope, charity, these three; but the greatest of these is charity"[15]) and other times stresses faith ("Therefore we conclude that a man is justified by faith without the deeds of the law"[16]). This shows a clear difference from the Confucian attitude that Faith is part of Love: "When Humanity is concerned, do not defer to the teacher[17]; Man can expand the Way: the Way cannot expand the man."[18] Although Jesus taught something very similar—"The Sabbath was made for man, and not man for the Sabbath" (Mark 2:27)—it cannot be denied that the central theme of the New Testament is "love the Lord thy God." Here also, tension and dialectics are evident. Perhaps this Western dialectics between law and ethics may have been necessary in an expansive world, but it had no place in a circumscribed world.

In much of the West's history, those who did not profess Christianity were anathema: if a man was justified by his faith and not by his deeds, he remained a heretic as long as he failed to recognize the Christian God, no matter how many good deeds he performed. The reverse is true in Eastern civilization, since the Eastern equivalent of atheism is "violation of Humanity" or "violation of Tao." Thus, a man was to be judged by his deeds, not his faith. If love has greater value than faith, then Confucians, Buddhists, and Muslims who practice benevolence should be regarded as sharing the same key value as Christians. From the Eastern point of view, this constitutes the central dilemma for the monotheistic religions.

One might think that if the entire world professed a single religion then love would become that religion's only dogma, but this is simply an illusion. The absolutism of a monotheistic faith naturally divides not only different religions, but also different sects within the same religion as soon as any individual or group claims absolute truth. Western history reveals many instances of bloody sectarian struggles within religions. Here we can clearly see the contribution of Confucianism, which unequivocally recommends unity and harmony among men, as the one and only ethical principle above any creed or law.

Despite Christ's Golden Rule, institutional religion had to emphasize faith as much as charity, if not more. Actually, such law as is contained in the Ten Commandments remained all powerful: "You shall not bow down to them or worship them for I the Lord your God am a jealous God, punishing children for the iniquity of parents, to the third and the fourth generation of those who reject me, but showing steadfast love to the thousandth generation of those who love me and keep my commandments" (Exodus 20:5–6). It is far from obvious whether Christianity has acted in history as a unifier or a divider among mankind. Clearly, despite its violent divisions, it has played a unifying role within the Western world and beyond. Innumerable people have drawn enormous comfort from Christ's teaching: "Blessed are the poor in spirit ... Blessed are they that mourn ... Blessed are the meek ... Blessed are ye, when men shall revile you, and persecute you ... Come unto me, all ye that labour and are heavy laden, and I will give you rest. Take my yoke upon you, and learn of me; for I am meek and lowly in heart: and ye shall find rest unto your souls. For my yoke is easy, and my burden is light ... And lead us not into temptation, but deliver us from evil."[19]

Furthermore, we know of many heart-warming instances of Christian benevolence and compassion toward others, regardless of race or religion. At the same time, history abounds with instances of Christianity being used as a tool of Western imperialism or sectarian dispute. This Law-Ethics dualism of the Western attitude toward social relations has caused considerable human conflict, between religions and individual sects: the Crusades, the sale of indulgences, the Inquisition, the Thirty Years' War, the Saint Bartholomew's Day massacre, and the persecution of Puritans, which resulted in their emigration to the New World. Their new nation quickly enacted a rule: "Congress shall make no law respecting an establishment of religion."[20]

Law and Ethics

"Love your neighbor and obey your God" proved very difficult to follow. Indeed, Christianity raised the complex issue of the relationship between law and ethics. As expounded in the Bible, law and ethics are supposed to work together, which appears a tall order since the two are far from interchangeable: "Though law often embodies ethical principals, law and ethics are far from co-extensive. Many acts that would be widely condemned as unethical are not prohibited by law—lying or betraying the confidence of a friend, for example. And the contrary is true as well. In much that the law does it is not simply codifying ethical norms."[21]

Law is indeed a powerful mechanism. But what is to be done in those areas not covered by law? This question becomes all the more relevant as law is fundamentally about prohibition. Although such cardinal legal concepts as the presumption of innocence may already exist in early codes like that of Hammurabi, nonetheless, these codes, like the Decalogue, essentially concern prohibition and punishment. "If a man kills another man's son, his son shall be cut off; If a son slaps his father, his hand shall be cut off; If anyone steals the minor son of another, he shall be put to death; If a man strikes a pregnant woman, thereby causing her to miscarry and die, the assailant's daughter shall be put to death; If a man put out the eye of another man, his eye shall be put out" (from the Code of Hammurabi); "Do not have any other gods before me; You shall not make wrongful use of the name of the Lord your God, for the Lord will not acquit anyone who misuses his name; You shall not murder; You shall not commit adultery; You shall not steal; You shall not bear false witness against your neighbor" (from the Ten Commandments).

Consequently, what is unlawful may be otherwise permitted.

The second problem concerns the management and implementation of the law. As we shall see in the following chapters, if one accepts that human nature seeks greed more often than altruism, then we realize that law may easily be used as an instrument for private interest rather than public interest, for which it was originally intended. This aspect of law was perceived as its essential weakness by the Eastern thinkers who privileged ethics. In contrast, ethics is safe from being the tool of greedy individuals and can be freely promoted without danger. Its weakness, rather, lies in the difficulty of enforcing it, especially under despotism. Thus, neither law nor ethics alone can provide sufficient answers to the problems inherent in human relations. Rather, both must work together in a complementary manner—law by prohibition; ethics by recommendation.

The relationship between law and ethics remains puzzling: "It becomes tempting to think that we might give up trying to clarify the philosophical relationship between law and ethics, and look to a legal stipulation of what a person's duties are (or aren't). Only how should law take the lead this way, with no compelling ethical defense for such an action? ... The problem, we can now see, is not an inability to know what law and ethics are. The problem is that we cannot state where one ends and the other begins."[22] As we have seen, in Christianity law and ethics coexist, although the former was prioritized over the latter. But this happened because the West was living in an expansive environment; now that we live in a circumscribed environment, law and ethics can work together. Ethics alone failed to prevent despotism, while law failed to alleviate greed; both are therefore required for an ideal society, the one serving as recommendation, the other as prohibition.

Christian Ethics and Confucian Ethics

Western ethics is thus founded on two contrasting principles: Moses' dictum "Eye for eye, tooth for tooth,"[23] and Jesus' command to "Love your enemies ... and pray for them which spitefully use you, and persecute you."[24] Here we can note another saying of Jesus: "Ye have heard that it hath been said, an eye for an eye, and a tooth for a tooth: but I say unto you, that ye resist not evil: but whosoever shall smite thee on thy right cheek, turn to him the other also."[25]

But neither is easily practicable to the ordinary man. Moses' dictum had suited the powerful, but the audience of Jesus lived under Roman occupation, and his message was better adapted to the political weakness of his audience. Nietzsche made a similar point in *The Genealogy of Morals*—Christianity is an ethics suited to the ruled, not to those who rule. Whatever our interpretation, both messages were too extreme and had to be moderated in practice.

Eastern ethics offers a third way between the extremes of Moses and Jesus. Confucianism advises: "Good for good; rectitude for bad,"[26] an ethical principle applicable both in personal life and in politics. But even this apparently practical principle is not easy to follow. Men tend to forget received good and remember received evil. Consequently, most men, being Xiaoren, tend merely to despise evil, without trying to rectify it, for that involves an effort of humanity—and most, likewise, fail to reciprocate good. It is in this sense that we understand Confucius' claim that "Only Junzi can truly love as well as hate others."[27]

Yet beyond the descriptive and circumstantial additions, the Christian ethics remains fundamentally "love thy neighbor as thyself," which is a Universal ethics for mankind. "Love your enemy" is subsumed in "love thy neighbor as thyself," as attested by the parable of the Good Samaritan. From this perspective, Confucian and Christian ethics constitute one and the same Universal ethics: Love, Humanity, Compassion, or Enlightened Self-Interest. Nietzsche's interpretation of Christian ethics, cited above, misses precisely this point, which is not surprising, as his entire ethics system was based on Master ethics as opposed to Universal ethics.

Universal Ethics vs. Master Ethics

Besides Christian ethics, the West has the Greek ethics of Plato and Aristotle. Socrates, Plato's teacher, is known to have been the first Greek thinker who focused on ethics. Although the ethical ideas of the ancient Greeks appear similar to those of the East, in fact they are polar opposites.

Greek Philosophers and the One Hundred Schools of Thought

In chapter 2, we briefly compared classical Greece to the Eastern Warring States Period, both of which gave man a uniquely fertile environment for various philosophies to flourish. These periods may be called the golden age of philosophy for both East and West. As we examined, the Eastern one was named the One Hundred Schools of Thought, and all sorts of philosophy, including Confucianism and Taoism, vied for influence. Quite similarly, Greece enjoyed the same flowering and contending of various philosophies: Thales, Anaximander, Pythagoras, Protagoras, Heraclitus, Empedocles, Anaxagoras, Democritus, Xenophanes, Parmenides, Socrates, Plato, Aristotle, the Cynics, the Epicureans, the Stoics, the Skeptics ...

Interestingly, both eras demonstrate a clear division: the Greek era can be divided into the pre-Socratic and Hellenistic periods. The division seems to have largely been provoked by Alexander's conquest of most of the known world; the Chinese Golden Age is divided by the Qin-Han unification of China under a single empire. During the pre-Han period, such schools as Legalism and Mohism were as influential as Confucianism and Taoism; after this, the former lost much of their influence.

There is great similarity, again, between pre-Socratic Greek philosophy and Confucian-Taoist philosophy. Both valued

Sophrosyne, self-control, moderation, and balance as the chief virtues: "Nothing in excess" and "Know thyself" were inscribed at the temple of Apollo in Delphi, as the ancient Greek philosophers believed that no man could completely understand soul or thought. More importantly, Spirit and Body existed in equilibrium in the pre-Socratic period.

Yet a critical difference already existed between East and West: in the Greek West, the Spirit-Body separation was already evident. Logos, Nous, Soul, and polytheism were firmly established in the expansive West. On the other hand, in the East, thinkers were focusing almost exclusively on ethics and politics: there were no marked interests in natural science or metaphysics. Most probably, such limitation and concentration was due to more than five centuries of constant warfare. This East-West contrast may be epitomized by the pronounced activities of the school of warfare in the East, including Sun Tzu, and by the pervasive influence of religion in the Greek West: Anaxagoras' description of the sun as a fiery mass larger than the Peloponnese earned him opprobrium for contravening the established religious doctrine. He had to flee.

Most significantly for our comparison, a subtle but crucial change occurred with Plato, who began to place a greater emphasis on the importance of the Soul with respect to the Body. Plato had learned from Parmenides that the void cannot exist, as nothing comes from nothing: the One is unchanging and eternal. This was in polar contrast with the Taoist prioritization of Non-Being over Being. More importantly, perhaps, Parmenides distinguished between the Way of Truth, eternal and unchanging, and the Way of Opinion, false and deceitful. He thought that only through Logos, pure reason, would one understand the Way of Truth.

This thinking was developed by Plato and transmitted to the mainstream of Western philosophy: "When the mind's eye rests on objects illuminated by truth and reality, it understands and comprehends them, and functions intelligently; but when it turns to the twilight world of change and decay, it can only form opinions, its vision is confused and its beliefs shifting, and it seems to lack intelligence." "The philosopher is in love with truth, that is, not with the changing world of sensation, which is the object of opinion, but with the unchanging reality which is the object of knowledge" (Plato, *The Republic*). The relentless search for objective truth has since characterized the West. Although other Hellenistic philosophies like Stoicism and Epicureanism had some influence in the history of the Western philosophy, Plato and Aristotle, with their rigid separation between Spirit and Body, came to dominate the mainstream. The Hellenistic world in the wake of Alexander's conquest of the world needed the Western Spirit the same way as the Age of Discovery and subsequent world domination needed the Western Spirit. Thus, the balance between Spirit and Body preserved among pre-Socratic thinkers gradually yielded within the mainstream to an outright supremacy of Spirit over Body.

Universal Ethics vs. Master Ethics

In the West, Man's relation to man—ethics and politics—were first articulated by Socrates, Plato, and Aristotle, and in a detailed and systematic way. These can be found in Plato's *Republic*, *Laws*, and many other works, and Aristotle's *Ethics* and *Politics*. Aristotle proposed courage, temperance, generosity, magnanimity, and sincerity as virtues of the Golden Mean. Confucianism also stresses such virtues as sincerity, loyalty, modesty, fortitude, and courage, and recommends the Doctrine of the Mean: "To exceed is as bad as to fall short"; "Pleasure not carried to the point of debauchery, grief not carried to the point of self-injury." The

Aristotelian emphasis on self-realization also appears quite similar to Confucian stress on self-fulfillment. Consequently, one may find a similarity between Confucian and Aristotelian ethics.

Yet, this similarity is deceptive and conceals a more fundamental contrast between East and West: Universal vs. Master ethics. The purpose of self-realization in Aristotle is personal happiness, preserved for the elite citizen-masters, excluding slaves, women, and barbarians; the purpose of Confucian self-fulfillment is the better service of one's family, community, state, and world—self-fulfillment was established as a warning against seeking recognition from outside. This goes as well for the virtues of sincerity, temperance, magnanimity, fortitude, and so on; for Aristotle, these virtues are the virtues of master-citizens. Slaves, women, and barbarians are not included in his ethical thinking. They were simply left out. Aristotle's Master ethics is not so much moral ethics as the observation of his society from the master-citizen's angle.[28] From that perspective, his philosophy was meant to be a scientific analysis of the ethical structure of Greece as it was, rather than a reflection of universal moral ethics. And the key to understanding Aristotelian ethics is the supremacy of Soul over Body.

Let us examine several examples of Aristotle's Master ethics:

On Slavery: "Where then there is such a difference as that between soul and body, or between men and animals (as in the case of those whose business is to use their body, and who can do nothing better), the lower sort are by nature slaves, and it is better for them as for all inferiors that they should be under the rule of a master.... And indeed the use made of slaves and of tame animals is not very different; for both with their bodies minister to the needs of life"; "That some should rule and others be ruled is a thing not only necessary, but expedient; from the hour of their birth, some are marked out for subjection, others for rule."[29]

On Barbarians: "Among barbarians no distinction is made between women and slaves, because there is no natural ruler among them: they are a community of slaves, male and female. That is why the poets say: 'It is correct that Greeks rule Barbarians'; for by nature what is barbarian and what is slave are the same."[30]

On Woman: "It is the best for all tame animals to be ruled by human beings. For this is how they are kept alive. In the same way, the relationship between the male and the female is by nature such that the male is higher, the female lower, that the male rules and the female is ruled."[31]

Master Ethics: Expansive Environment

Bertrand Russell wrote that: "Aristotle left out the whole sphere of human experience with which religion is concerned."[32] He also regarded Aristotelian ethics as repulsive. Seen from the perspective of Universal ethics, whether Christian or Confucian, one can only agree with his assessment. But Aristotle might have been amoral in his writing on ethics—he simply wrote down what he observed. Aristotle is known to be the last man to know everything there was to be known in his own time. Indeed, he studied and wrote on almost everything: anatomy, astronomy, economics, embryology, geography, geology, meteorology, physics, zoology, aesthetics, government, metaphysics, politics, psychology, rhetoric, theology, literature, poetry, and ethics. In his writings on all of these, he seems to have rationalized the situations of his elite master-citizens, slaves, barbarians, and women, and labeled them as ethics. Either humankind was not his concern or his fellow master-citizens represented the entirety of humankind, while slaves, barbarians, and women were like low animals without soul, or very little of it.[33]

Without moral judgment, Aristotle's descriptions of his elite citizens' mores naturally produced a "Master ethics." In the

West, this coexisted with Christian Universal ethics, producing a dialectics between the two. Consequently, the West projected two ethical ideals, Christian and Hero. As a Master ethics requires law and force to deal with its enemies—slaves and barbarians— heroes represented law and force rather than ethics in Western history. Indeed, this history is full of stories of the subjugation of barbarians and the repression of slave by heroes.

As part of this dialectics, Aristotelian Master ethics has long played an important role in the West, from the Romans and the medieval Church to Nietzsche and the Fascists of the last century.

In contrast to this, the Cynics and the Stoics supported an ethics encompassing all of mankind—with the exception of slaves—based on the belief that all men share an innate dignity, independent of social status. Consequently, they described men as citizens of the world. But their ideas served the expansive West less well than the Master ethics of Aristotle; it was only when the world became circumscribed that the West began again to prioritize a Universal ethics, which produced democracy, human rights, and economic assistance to foreign countries. Yet, nostalgia lingers on. Still today, thinkers return to Aristotle when they yearn for a Master ethics.

It would be anachronistic to judge Aristotle's views by a modern standard. To repeat Hume: "Morals excite passions, and produce or prevent actions. Reason itself is utterly impotent in this particular. The rules of morality, therefore, are not conclusions of our reason." Human nature is a constant; our greedy inclination is to prefer Master ethics to Universal ethics whenever possible. It is only in a circumscribed world that Master ethics becomes less relevant than Universal ethics. Thus, it may be quite possible that, one day, with the reversion of the current circumscribed environment to an expansive one, man will rediscover the relevance of Master ethics.

Master Ethics, Theology, and Metaphysics

The Aristotelian Master ethics was sustained in the West by mainstream theology and metaphysics, which followed its separation between spirit and body. This subtle but decisive mechanism allowed Middle Ages theology and modern era metaphysics to enthusiastically embrace Aristotle and Plato: the common base was Spirit-Body separation. Just as Aristotle denied barbarians a soul, and so excluded them from his system of values, so theologians denied pagans a place in their system, and ideologues later rejected dissidents. The consequences of such exclusionary practices are only too well known.

Eastern philosophy, by contrast, does not suffer from the same problem, since it denies that any human being may claim absolute truth; claiming truth by any individual would come as a result of a theological or metaphysical process that would be initiated by Spirit dissociated from Body. There is therefore little room for prophets or extreme ideologies in the East. Confucius refused to cloak himself in mysticism: "To live in obscurity, and yet practice wonders, in order to be mentioned with honor in future ages—this is what I do not do."[34] His doctrine of the Golden Mean translates literally as "the doctrine of being in the middle and commonplace." From this perspective, Eastern ethics has a similar ideal to that of British "common sense"—a wariness of absolutist metaphysics and ideologies. As we shall see in chapter 5, Benjamin Franklin arrived at the same conclusion and pointed out the uselessness of metaphysics, instead recommending such values as *truth*, *sincerity*, and *integrity* grounded in common sense.

The influence of religion, metaphysics, and ideology on Western culture is so overwhelming that it is difficult to imagine it without them. A comparison between Spinoza and Kant will make this clear, since Eastern ethics shares its foundation with the former but not with the latter. Kant explained in metaphysical terms: mankind is born with an innate sense of moral duty; this sense leads reason to generate ethics and religion; freedom and God precede moral law and ethics. Spinoza, on the other hand, had argued for the unity of Mind (reason) and Body (passion), and for that of Nature and Man. Consequently, his ethics emanated from the biological need for self-preservation, rather than being preordained by God.

Junzi remains a realistic ideal that everyone can strive to achieve, including kings and emperors. Here we have a clear contrast between East and West, since a potentially catastrophic twist is inherent in Plato's philosopher-king concept. As we know, Plato's Academy was closed by the Roman Emperor Theodosius, who regarded Platonism as a danger to Christianity. Subsequently, Plato was lost for more than a millennium to the Western intellectual world until the end of the Middle Ages. It was Aristotle who influenced medieval theology almost exclusively, as witnessed by the work of Thomas Aquinas. After the Middle Ages, Plato's authority was revived and began to dominate Western metaphysics, which largely insisted on a separation between spirit and body. Plato's philosopher-king, the ideal of an enlightened reason unencumbered by corporal passions, now offered the modern West the role model which it had sought. We have described the journey of the Western spirit from Descartes, Leibniz, Kant, and Hegel, to arrive at the level of Absolute Spirit. Subsequently, the idea of a philosopher-king flourished and gave way to the "enlightened despot," embodied in Frederick the Great, and finally the totalitarian leaders espoused by Nietzsche and his twentieth-century descendents.

Metaphysicians, Junzi, and Xiaoren

I am emphatically not arguing that Plato intentionally advocated the advent of mad ideology. On the contrary, like Kant and Hegel, he offers us many profound insights into man and nature. But seen from the outside, there is an undeniable journey of the Western Spirit, alienated from the body, from Plato's *Idea* to modern metaphysics, and finally to the mad man, the fanatical ideologue. Enlightenment philosophers like Voltaire, who fought bravely against religious bigotry and fanaticism, were overwhelmed by the post-Enlightenment metaphysicians who, with much ingenuity, converted theology into metaphysics and religion into ideology. The Enlightenment freed the West from theological absolutism and religious bigotry but could not free it from metaphysical absolutism and ideological fanaticism.

Seen from the East, Western totalitarian ideologies share many essential characteristics with Western religion, especially, in their separation of the spirit from the body, their promise of utopia and their absolutism. The major difference was of course that, unlike religion, which advocated love, totalitarian ideologies advocated violence, to the point of making it a duty. That is how and why Western ideologies ended up producing the Mad Man. The Mad Man characterization was shared by some Western thinkers and writers. Bertrand Russell thought that the post-Kantian evolution of Western metaphysics was a march toward madness; Karl Popper, meanwhile, argued that Plato was indirectly responsible for the rise of grotesque totalitarian ideologies like communism and fascism.

Unlike the West, the East did not experience this metaphysical transformation of man. Since Junzi realizes the difficulty of controlling one's own desires and that, as long as he lives with his body, he must eat and sleep, he accepts Xiaoren's plight with compassion, rather than dismissing it out of moral outrage. Junzi does not aim at eliminating Xiaoren from this world, as he knows that it is impossible. As life repeats itself, most men would always act as Xiaoren. As he knows that he cannot, and does not need to embody a pure spirit, he does not bother aiming for a utopia in which all men would be noble. He knows that such a world would be as "hellish" as a world where all men would be Xiaoren. Like Yin and Yang, Junzi exists because of Xiaoren and vice versa: the one requires the other. This is a marked difference between East and West.

Western Exclusionism: From Ancient Rome to the Modern Era
The narrow-mindedness of the Middle Ages was due partly to the exclusivity of Christianity, which superseded Greco-Roman polytheism during the fourth century AD, following the conversion of Constantine the Great in 312. Constantine's Edict of Milan put an end to the persecution of the Christians, but it was only in 380, when Theodosius decreed Christianity the sole official religion of the empire, that pagan temples were closed, sacked, and destroyed, and many were converted into Christian churches.

The religious intolerance of monotheism was thereafter demonstrated. For 1,500 years after Theodosius, the Catholic Church remained staunchly exclusionist. In the seventeenth century, the West began to free itself from religious bigotry and fanaticism. The Church's attitude, of course, had little in common with Jesus' injunction to "love thy neighbor." All ideas and writings in opposition to the Church were proscribed, and violators were excommunicated or burned at the stake.

The East's focus on harmony was again reinforced by the introduction of Buddhism. It was then in disarray, just as the Roman Empire declined as Christianity began to flourish.

But while the syncretistic East incorporated Buddhism, the exclusionary West simply replaced the old pagan deities with the new religion of Christianity. The common ground was a desire for self-preservation. There also was a great deal of Western syncretism, as Christianity adopted various pagan legends, iconography, and rituals, and the Church Fathers adapted pagan philosophy for their own needs. But it was ultimately exclusion, not syncretism, which characterized Christianity in its institutional aspect. Thus the process of Western syncretism could better be expressed as an exclusionary dialectics. In practical terms, the Christian ideal reigned in the West while Junzi led the East. Christian and Junzi constituted the building blocks of their respective civilization and so defined their culture for two thousand years.

As religious power and state power were not clearly separated in the West until after the Enlightenment, the practice of exclusion effectively combined religious and secular means. The power struggle between Church and State continued throughout the Middle Ages between the Papacy and the Holy Roman Empire—for instance, Emperor Henry IV vs. Pope Gregory VII (the Investiture Controversy); Frederick II Hohenstaufen vs. Pope Gregory IX; the Guelphs vs. Ghibellines; and Louis IV vs. Pope John XXII. Even the Church itself was divided, as with the Great Schism and the Avignon Papacy. Thomas Hobbes, Spinoza, and Voltaire are only a few thinkers who had to flee religious or political persecution and wrote their works at great personal risk. Even scientists were forced to conform to religious dogma, as the case of Galileo illustrates.

Exclusionism is everywhere, and common to a degree to all races and nations. What characterizes the West was its absolutism. As Voltaire observed, the Church pushed intolerance to an extreme: "The Romans permitted all cults, even that of the Jews, even that of the Egyptians.... Why did Rome tolerate these cults? Because neither the Egyptians nor even the Jews tried to exterminate the ancient religion of the empire.... It is undeniable, however, that the Christians wanted their religion to be the dominant one. The Jews didn't want the statue of Jupiter in Jerusalem; but the Christians didn't want it in the Capitol.... It was their view that the whole world should be Christian. They were therefore necessarily the enemies of the whole world, until it was converted."[35]

Monotheism and Exclusionism

How did this Western attitude arise, and why did it endure for so long? If the Church was correct, then we may simply accept that it was God's way: the entire non-Christian world was to be defeated or converted. But we may also offer a historical explanation: the necessity of fierce conviction in an expansive environment, whose dominant mode was anthropomorphic religion. This explains why the zenith of Western exclusionism coincided with the Age of Discovery, a period of restless expansion and conquest. With this suggestion in mind, we are intrigued to note that, with the recent development of a circumscribed world, the West has finally begun to reject its ancient attitude. The construction of mosques and Eastern temples in Western countries, and even the open toleration of other religions, is a recent phenomenon.

The foregoing is well known to most Westerners. Less well known is how this attitude spoiled a golden opportunity to spread the Word to the East. By the end of the seventeenth century, the East was already open to Christianity. The Chinese emperor was particularly enlightened and respected the West's scientific and artistic achievements. Here is the story of how the West's attitude backfired: "In 1692, when Fr. Tomas Pereira requested tolerance for Christianity, the Kangxi Emperor was willing to oblige, and issued the Edict of Toleration, which recognized Catholicism, barred attacks on their churches, and legalized their missions and the practice of Christianity by Chinese people. But the good will did not last. Controversy arose over whether Chinese Christians could still take part in traditional Confucian ceremonies and ancestor worship, with the Jesuits arguing for tolerance and the Dominicans taking a hard-line against foreign 'idolatry.' The Dominican position won out with Pope Clement XI, who, in 1705, sent Charles-Thomas Maillard De Tournon as his representative to the emperor, to communicate the ban on Chinese rites. On 19 March 1715, Clement issued the Papal bull *Ex illa die*, which officially condemned Chinese rites. In response, the Kangxi Emperor officially forbade Christian missions in China, as they were causing *trouble*."[36]

This Western intolerance worked in the case of the Roman Empire but failed with the Eastern empires. What made it fail here? Perhaps one can find an answer in its inability to understand the importance of syncretism, and specifically of Junzi, in the East.

Eastern Syncretism: Confucian-Taoist-Buddhist

As we have already seen, the syncretism intrinsic to Eastern culture has made it immune to religious struggles between Taoism, Confucianism, and Buddhism, or among their individual sects. These "Three Ways" coexisted harmoniously. By contrast, such cohabitation is unthinkable among monotheistic religions, such as Christianity, Judaism, and Islam. There were exceptions; for example, there was much of this "cohabitation" in Andalusia during the thirteenth to fifteenth centuries. But this occurred under very specific political circumstances in which tolerance was of greater advantage to the rulers and existed only between men, rather than within a single person. The reason is very simple: each claims absolute truth, preventing any explicit syncretism with other faiths. No monotheistic religion, including Christianity, has resolved this dilemma between charity and faith. Religion acts to unify men when it emphasizes love, but divides men when it emphasizes faith.

Today, however, Christianity is encountering difficulties. While the Western world remained expansive, and committed to conquest and exploitation, the Church naturally provided much of its missionary impetus. But now that the world has become circumscribed, Christianity puts more stress on charity than on faith. It is therefore not surprising that Christianity has become tolerant as it has never been before, repudiating much of its former exclusionism and absolutism.

Before we end our comparison between Confucianism and Christianity, we should observe that religion satisfies a deep psychological need, regardless of the challenge posed by science to its doctrines and absolutism. No matter how educated, men will never be able to act very reasonably: many will continue to find comfort in faith, if not in institutionalized religion. This explains why the largest religious institutions (Catholicism and Islam) are growing, not shrinking. It is also important to emphasize that Christianity made a crucial contribution to the emergence of Western individualism, rule of law, and democracy; these are essentially alien to the East. It cannot be said, for instance, that Confucianism was inclined toward personal liberty or the rule of law. Freedom and democracy were the hard-won fruits of the West's absolutist dialectics between Spirit and Body: these achievements we shall study in subsequent chapters. Let us focus in this section on Eastern ideas about human relations. The syncretistic attitude, which constitutes one of Junzi's essential virtues, is difficult to explain to a Western mind fully indoctrinated in monotheism. Just as Eastern eyes are astonished at the sight of the Piazza San Marco or Stockholm City Hall, so a Westerner will be amazed at Eastern pictures depicting the harmonious coexistence of different religions.

The painting of the three vinegar tasters in Figure 4-3 explains Eastern syncretism as a variation in perspective. What the picture tries to demonstrate is the following: Lao Tzu accepts the taste of vinegar as natural and so enjoys it; Confucius finds it sour and so seeks to rectify the taste; Buddha finds it bitter and recommends overcoming it, just as one tries to transcend the sufferings of life. But the central message of this syncretistic approach is that all three teachings (i.e., Tao, Humanity, and Compassion) point to one fundamental truth for mankind. The same is true of the painting of three masters laughing by a river in Figure 4-4. Three figures, representing a Taoist, a Confucian scholar-official, and a Buddhist monk, instead of posturing as competing adversaries, are united in a casual and friendly manner, apparently enjoying the beautiful scenery after having crossed the dangerous Tiger Stream, and are engrossed in a philosophical discussion. As Richard Nisbett explains: "The Chinese orientation toward life was shaped by the blending of three different philosophies: Taoism, Confucianism, and, much later, Buddhism. Each philosophy emphasized harmony and largely discouraged abstract speculation."[37]

Indeed, syncretism is difficult to understand for Westerners, whose culture is founded on monotheism. To a mind accustomed to refer all beliefs to Christianity, the eclecticism of Eastern culture may be interpreted as a superstitious mysticism. Consequently, the two images mentioned above will be viewed by Westerners with incredulity. Would a Western artist paint a picture of Moses, Jesus, and Mohammed as three great teachers preaching the same fundamental truth?

Fig. 4-3. Lao Tzu-Buddha-Confucius: The Vinegar Tasters (http://en.wikipedia.org/wiki/File:Vinegar tasters.jpg)	Fig. 4-4. Confucianism-Taoism-Buddhism: Three men laughing by a river stream (http://en.wikipedia.org/wiki/File:Huxisanxiaotu.jpg)

Orientation toward Past vs. Future

One of the most significant differences between Confucianism and Christianity lies in their respective emphases on this life and the next. Confucius remarks again and again that the purpose of life is better management of worldly affairs. He sets out man's goal unequivocally: "control oneself; raise one's family; serve the state; bring peace to the world." Management of one's self, family, state, and world constitute man's ultimate and supreme value— nothing else. Reflection on the afterlife is discouraged, as it leads nowhere. The drawback of this attitude is a lack of progress, which is sacrificed for the sake of harmony and stability. Confucianism suggests that the perfect management attained by men of the past declined with the diminishment of ethical standards.

This attitude gave the East a clear orientation toward the past for the sake of order, stability, and harmony, to the detriment of progress and future-oriented innovation. By contrast, the orientation of Christian culture is clearly toward a future paradise, in which all the sufferings of this world will finally be over. These sufferings, it claims, were caused by original sin, which to overcome requires penitence and faith. Those who accept the faith receive heaven as a reward; those who do not are punished in hell. This attitude ensured that Christians spared no efforts in pursuing progress and improvement, just as Easterners strove for management both of oneself and the empire.

Life: Man in Nature vs. Supernatural God

Confucianism focuses on Junzi and the attainment of happiness in this life, without recourse to supernatural beings; its wisdom is grounded in practical management of everyday affairs: "Isn't it a pleasure to learn and practice? Isn't it delightful to have a friend from afar? ... Junzi does not murmur against Heaven, nor grumble against men.... Junzi cultivates himself with a view to serving others and the people of the nation.... Without understanding the sense of mission, one cannot become Junzi; without understanding ethics, one cannot establish true characters; without understanding words, one cannot know men."[38] This life is the only one we can be certain about. In this respect, Eastern culture is thoroughly humanistic and secular.[39]

Christianity, with its single, anthropomorphic God, is threatened when that God is called into question. Consequently, one of two attitudes is usually adopted: if God does not exist, he must be created, or, if God does not exist, everything is permitted, including licentious abandonment and utter depravity. This Western dilemma follows from the premise that God created Man to govern Nature, and that Man is therefore in conflict with Nature. Such a dilemma does not exist in the East because Tao, which connects Man to

Nature, remains intact even when faced with the most advanced Western science. Man is part of Nature, and Tao shows him the virtues to follow lest he be alienated from it.

The dilemma facing the West was expressed by Albert Einstein: "A man's ethical behavior should be based effectually on sympathy, education, and social ties and needs; no religious basis is necessary. Man would indeed be in a poor way if he had to be restrained by fear of punishment and hope of reward after death."[40] But Western history and ethics are imbued with anthropomorphic theism—when Robinson Crusoe is shipwrecked on an uninhabited island, his first action is to seek Divine intervention and find God's response in the Bible: "Call on me on the day of trouble, and I will deliver, and thou shall glorify me." Einstein does not agree with the Western view of divine intervention: "I cannot imagine a God who rewards and punishes the objects of his creation, whose purposes are modeled after our own—a God, in short, who is but a reflection of human frailty. Neither can I believe that the individual survives the death of his body, although feeble souls harbor such thoughts through fear or ridiculous egotisms."[41] He aligns himself with a Spinozist God, along similar lines to the Taoist conception explored in chapter 2: "I believe in Spinoza's God who reveals himself in the orderly harmony of what exists, not in a God who concerns himself with the fates and actions of human beings."[42] What can be done in the face of atheism? For Einstein, a profound humility toward the cosmos can and should provide us with a genuinely religious feeling; here we can detect a kinship between contemporary Western science and Eastern ethics.

Tyranny of Man (Despotism) vs. Tyranny of Spirit (Absolutism)

We have discussed the apparent paradox of Western culture: its encouragement of freedom and rationality as well as Man's separation from Nature and his submission to God. Over the course of Western history, we see evolving dialectics resulting from the need for freedom and for religion.[43] Indeed, the concept of God has played a critical role in developing personal liberty away from secular tyranny in the West. This concept fostered a system of law that emphasized justice independent of temporal authority. One can already see the germ of this concept in ancient Greece. Antigone speaks to Creon in Sophocles' tragedy *Antigone*: "It was not Zeus that had published me that edict; not such are the laws set among men by the justice who dwells with the gods below; nor deemed I that thy decrees were of such force, that a mortal could override the unwritten and unfailing statutes of heaven. For their life is not of today or yesterday, but from all time, and no man knows when they were first put forth." This concept of "natural law," above the human sovereign, was absent from Eastern civilization, which as a result was in thrall to the whims of emperors and dynasties. Such a deficiency gave rise to harmony in the East, but also stagnation. When the latter prevailed, ethics broke down and harmony entailed inertia, fatalism, and submission to despotism.

Since emperors lacked an aristocracy or priesthood, and since they were advised and surrounded by scholar-officials, who always reminded them of their responsibility as father figures toward their subjects, inept emperors invariably left the daily management of the empire to the inner circle of their advisers, which included eunuchs. Eunuchs posed a particular problem in the history of China for over two millennia. Any emperor who wanted to alienate the scholar-officials because they advised the sovereign to govern the country as a father manages his family, and who wanted to have his own way against this cardinal ethics, empowered eunuchs against scholar-officials. When eunuchs took power, good governance was naturally lost and disaster struck the empire. One typical example was what happened to General Yuan Chonghuan (袁崇煥 1584–1630) toward the end of Ming dynasty. He was a victorious general during the last years of Ming China. He repeatedly defeated the invading barbarians (e.g., the Manchu power that challenged Ming China). Succumbing to jealousy to the point of violating the rule of self-preservation, the eunuchs in power lured General Yuan to an audience with the emperor and killed him. Having this last obstacle thus eliminated by Ming China herself, the Manchu easily conquered the Ming and established its own dynasty in China—the Qing Empire.

Fig. 4-5. Flavius Stilicho (ca. 359–408), Roman General http://en.wikipedia.org/wiki/Stilicho	Fig. 4-6. Yuan Chonghuan (袁崇煥 1584–1630), Ming General http://en.wikipedia.org/wiki/Yuan_Chonghuan

An almost perfectly similar case occurred during the last years of the Roman Empire. General Stilicho successfully checked the invading barbarians (e.g., the Goths with Alaric at the head). Jealous of his success and power, the emperor, in collusion with his palace sycophants, lured General Stilicho to a trap and killed him. Seeing his only valid enemy thus eliminated by the Romans themselves, Alaric finally conquered the Roman Empire and sacked Rome in 410—the eternal Rome that did not allow foreign occupation for over a millennium. General Yuan and General Stilicho, two patriots long remembered, stand tall in their respective histories. Their military genius, integrity, courage, and patriotism were exceptional but both perished by the tyranny of man. They are over a millennium apart. While the West resolved the problem of man's tyranny through religion and law, the East remained vulnerable to this recurring curse until it relatively recently absorbed new paradigms from the West.

Western freedom, meanwhile, has been constantly threatened by religious dogma and ideological fantasies. In the twentieth century, which saw the rise of extreme ideologies, Western freedom was placed in grave peril—religious and secular authorities and ideologues usurped the rule of law to reinforce absolutism, with disastrous consequences. Fortunately, the Age of Ideology is over. We can draw from the past century a lesson already recognized by Voltaire: "Those who can make you believe absurdities, can make you commit atrocities." Voltaire learned this principle from the internecine religious strife of sixteenth-century France, and the strife across Europe that followed; the Thirty Years' War can legitimately be called the first pan-European war, as almost all nations participated. The result was widespread slaughter, all in the name of religion.

Twentieth-century history demonstrates that Voltaire's warning against fanaticism was largely ignored. World War I—the result of blind imperialism—resulted in massive carnage among "civilized" Europeans, leaving more than seven million dead after four long years of battle. Several decades after its conclusion, World War II broke out, mobilizing the dual ideologies of communism and fascism. Tens of millions of people were butchered, including a large number of civilians—this time in the name of "total war." Such is the negative side of metaphysics and ideology, which can be encapsulated in one word—absolutism (i.e., spiritual tyranny).

A drawback of the reign of Spirit is its division between Us (believers) and Them (non-believers). This division was amply demonstrated by the ideologies of the twentieth century. The case of religion is more complicated. Marx characterized religion as the opiate of the masses, but this view was cynical and simplistic. Unlike ideology, religion is founded on the premise of neighborly love, proclaiming unity among men. This is what keeps religion, unlike ideology, alive today, despite its dogmas. More specifically, it imparts a sense of meaning, social belonging, and even personal salvation. But as an institution, it means freedom for "us," not for "them": the distinction between Christian-insiders and heathen-outsiders is inevitable. Due to its inability to separate the teaching of charity from its dogmatic and ecclesiastical structures, it always fails to be universal. To repeat, even if everybody were convinced of the superiority of one particular religion, it would inevitably be divided into numerous sects and denominations, as history has demonstrated.

Politics: Universal Ethics vs. Master Ethics

Just as Confucianism considers ethics and politics simultaneously, Taoism embraces the two as one. The common ground is the concept of Junzi, who leads by example. Confucianism focuses on exemplary behavior. To cite once again: "When occupying a high situation Junzi is not proud, and in a low situation he is not insubordinate. When the kingdom is well governed, he is sure by his words to rise; and when it is ill governed, he is sure by his silence to attract forbearance."[44] Taoism focuses on both man and nation: "Possessing body and soul but only embracing the one, can you avoid separation? Loving all men and ruling the country, can you lack intelligence? Understanding and being open to all things, can you afford negligence?"[45] This is quite different from Western dualism, which postulates: "Render therefore unto Caesar the things which are Caesar's; and unto God the things that are God's."[46]

It is true that Western conceptions of ethics have always been closely linked to politics, from Aristotle and Plato onwards: for Plato, for instance, the self was a microcosm of the *polis*. Christian writers all through the Middle Ages focused on wise governance, which began with ethics. Many Western philosophers, for instance, have, like Confucius, been actively involved in politics, from Plato at the court of Dion of Syracuse, to Leibniz in the entourage of George I. But as we have seen in the previous section, their ethics was that of the Master as opposed to a Universal ethics, which remained separate from politics. What Plato and Aristotle tried to apply in politics is not Universal ethics but the Master ethics excluding the majority of humankind, which included all slaves, barbarians, and women. In that sense, in the West, Universal ethics remained separated from politics until recently. From this perspective, what Jesus said could also be understood as indicating the separation between Roman Master ethics and Christian Universal ethics.

Confucius himself practiced active participation in government, since for him self-realization could only be achieved through experience and social interaction. Men constitute society, and society requires government, which, in turn, entails politics. Consequently, the books of Confucianism place an equal emphasis on politics and ethics. Both share the same basis, namely exemplary behavior and action. Confucianism emphasizes the resolution of conflict in human relationships, which necessarily involves both ethical and political considerations. Confucianism regards Wisdom as more valuable than knowledge, as illustrated by the saying: "Junzi, the Noble Man, possesses three ways: Benevolent, he is free from anxiety; Knowledgeable, he is free from perplexity; Courageous, he is free from fear."[47] Overcoming anxiety, perplexity, and fear is the result of wisdom. Knowledge may lead to debate, but this process only reinforces one's prejudices, while wisdom leads to equanimity and harmony, both within the individual and in society as a whole.

Thus, in a circumscribed world, wisdom rather than knowledge serves the purpose of self-preservation. Although Western philosophers have never tired of praising "wisdom," sometimes even over knowledge, they relied on Socratic knowledge, divine revelation, and Aristotelian Master ethics, which ultimately valued power over wisdom. The natural outcome of prioritizing wisdom is a development of sound ethics and politics. Confucius therefore aimed at cultivating the personal ethics and political guidance of Junzi, who, as a leader by example, valued humanity, integrity, rectitude, and sincerity. In his view, harmony and peace reign when each acts according to his place.

As already noted, Confucius writes that "The ruler should act like a ruler; the minister, a minister; the father, a father; the son, a son."[48] He repeatedly warns of the danger of Xiaoren, who can gain an audience by clever talk and disingenuous conduct: "Junzi recognizes and praises the admirable qualities of others; he does not point out the weaknesses of others. Xiaoren does just the opposite."[49] Again, he says that "Junzi is concerned with his own lack of ability, not with what others think of him."[50] Because ethics and politics are treated equally, Confucianism and Taoism never depart from a pragmatic approach to the treatment of both. Thus, in the East, Universal ethics and politics remained firmly united.

In the West, the relationship between ethics and politics went through a complex evolution: for two millennia, politics remained separated from Universal ethics, and joined instead to a Master ethics. Plato proposed the harmony between ethics and politics in his definition of justice in his *Republic*. Aristotle also stressed the interconnectedness between ethics and politics.[51] Thomas Aquinas grounded his politics in ethics, heavily influenced by Aristotle. Thus, as we have seen, the ethics propounded by Plato and Aristotle are only relevant to a small group of elite citizens, rather than all of mankind; ancient Greek politics are structured accordingly.

Church vs. State

This combination of politics with Master ethics in the West manifested itself as a struggle between Church and State: during the Middle Ages, the Papacy constantly claimed secular as well as spiritual power, provoking endless disputes with kings and emperors who also demanded exclusive secular powers. In recent centuries, a separation between state and religion has increasingly become the norm. Consequently, ecclesiastics are supposed to remain aloof from the worldly affairs of politicians. And with this separation, politics, at last free from religious dogma, began to be united with Universal ethics. But the legacy of spiritual power combined with Master ethics remained strong in the West. Stendhal (Marie-Henri Beyle, 1783–1842) entitled one of his novels *Le Rouge et Le Noir* (*The Red and the Black*). Red, the color of a cardinal's robe, stands for spiritual power; and black, the color of a general's uniform, stands for secular power.

As examined earlier, the separation of Church and State did make a crucial contribution to the advent of democratic institutions in the West. But its separation of ethics from politics was also the origin of many intractable problems, including the distinction of "us versus them." Indeed, the three most violent periods of European history—the Hundred Years' War of the fourteenth and fifteenth centuries, the Thirty Years' War of the seventeenth century, and the ideological wars of the twentieth century—demonstrate the results of a division between politics and Universal ethics and the union between politics and Master ethics. A politics divorced from Universal ethics but united with Master ethics could easily claim that different ethical standards are to be applied in different circumstances, or to different adversaries. Western politics often enjoyed reinforcement and legitimation from religion in the application of these varying standards. In the East, as ethics and politics were one, no political violence could claim ethical justification, especially not in the name of religion or ideology.

It is only now after the West has suffered innumerable religious and ideological wars that it has settled upon union between politics and Universal ethics. It appears that the Church-State separation was a precondition for the transition from Master ethics to Universal ethics in the West. Again, it is intriguing that this transition is occurring as the world transforms from an expansive to a circumscribed one.

Sinicization of Buddhism and Communism

In the Period of Disunity (third to sixth centuries AD), Buddhism became a very strong presence in many Eastern countries; during the Tang dynasty (seventh to tenth centuries AD), it became the state philosophy of China. The Eastern world was thus rejuvenated with the impetus of the new religion. After the sixth century, the East was culturally active, while the West entered what we call the "Dark Ages." The upshot of this Eastern renaissance was the "sinicization" of Buddhism, which the East reshaped without changing its own essential characteristics.

Almost fifteen-hundred years later, China was once again swept up by a foreign system of belief: communism. It may be too early to predict the outcome of this adoption of Western ideology on Chinese soil, but it is not far-fetched to suggest that communism will be "sinicized" just as Buddhism was.

Brahmanism vs. Buddhism

Buddhism grew out of Hinduism in India, just as Christianity grew out of Judaism in the Ancient Near East. Hinduism aims to escape material life and extinguish desire through the practice of self-denial and self-mortification. Its doctrine of reincarnation—the transmigration of an eternal soul from one body to another after death—supports the separation and privileged status of Soul (called "Atman" by Hindus) over Body. Although the Hindu *Atman* is different from mainstream Western conceptions of the soul, in that it has *direct* participation in Brahman, both Atman and soul arise from the neocortex, not from the Body. In Hinduism, Brahma represents the universe and is essentially a spiritual being. Because Atman is Spirit trying to attain the status of Brahman, the Body represents an obstacle.

India's environment, where water and food are so scarce, must have given rise to the practice of self-mortification in much the same way that different physical environments have fundamentally shaped Western and Eastern civilizations. Nirad Chaudhuri, in his book *The Continent of Circe*, summarizes the effect of the Indian environment on Hinduism: "What, however, nobody seems to suspect is the possibility that this impressive mortification of the flesh … might have been due to the climate and weather of India. Now, if the dust of the country showed itself to be inescapable, the easiest way to resist it was to demonstrate that it did not matter.… These men seemed to be determined to conquer their environment by inflicting more discomfort on themselves."[52]

But the body is not extinguishable except in death. As the body weakens from self-mortification, the spirit also weakens. Such a struggle cannot produce the intended outcome: a pure spirit devoid of all bodily desires and needs.

Buddha's Enlightenment: *Mens Sana in Corpore Sano*

In ancient India, hunger remained the preoccupation of most people. Many lacked plentiful harvests and fasted by necessity rather than religious duty. Fasting thus became a sine qua non of spiritual leaders of the period, as a demonstration of religious devotion to those in their care. Such a practice, elevated to the level of religious piety, must have contributed to social stability and peace. The Buddha (Siddhartha Gautama, fifth century BC) initially followed this course; during this period, he became one of the most renowned among those practicing fasting and self-mortification.

One day, however, Siddhartha shocked his followers by renouncing these disciplines. His enlightenment was a realization that the true relationship between Spirit and Body was unity, not separation: *mens sana in corpore sano.* H.G. Wells explained it convincingly: "He amazed and horrified his five companions by demanding ordinary food and refusing to continue his self-mortifications. He had realized that whatever truth a man may reach is reached best by a nourished brain in a healthy body. Such a conception was absolutely foreign to the ideas of the land and age."[53]

We encounter a remarkable similarity between this Buddhist enlightenment and Confucius' realization: "I tried thinking all day not eating, and all night not sleeping; it was without gain, and not equal to learning."[54] Siddhartha's enlightenment on the harmony of spirit and body led to his insights into the harmony among men, and then, by a natural progression, to the essence of Buddhist teaching: compassion. Confucius's preoccupation was the disorder generated by constant warfare, which he perceived as the primary cause of people's suffering. The Buddha's chief concern, however, was the suffering caused by hunger and desire. Confucius proposed a revival of the lost order by means of ethics, whereas Siddhartha advocated a renunciation of desires in favor of compassion. Taoism shares the same point of departure— namely, desire, although it advocates not renunciation but self-management by ethics, since desire is intrinsic to human nature. Naturally, when Buddhism was introduced to the East, it was espoused in Taoist language.

Buddhist Compassion: Man-Man Unity

The Buddha, like Confucius, focused on everyday life; when asked about metaphysical problems—for example, whether the world is eternal or not, whether spirit and body are one or two, whether saints live after death or not—he replied that his teaching did not attempt to resolve such questions. These doctrinal issues are far removed from the real problems faced by men: birth, aging, death, sorrow, and despair. Unlike Hinduism or Judaism, Buddhism does not postulate a distinction between spirit and body, nor did the Buddha preach about the Atman so crucial to Hinduism. Siddhartha did not claim divine status, just as Confucius refused to assume the mantle of a supernatural power.

Indeed, Buddhism repeatedly warns its adherents away from taking relative truth for dogma. Each person must find his own faith and convictions—but must not insist that these are the absolute truth, for this is beyond our knowledge. "Asked by the young Brahmin to explain the idea of maintaining or protecting truth, the Buddha said: 'A man has a faith. If he says *This is my faith*, so far he maintains truth. But by that he cannot proceed to the absolute conclusion: *This alone is Truth, and everything else is false.*'"[55]

Both the Buddha and Confucius concentrated on ways to improve life by alleviating suffering in this world. Seen from this perspective, Buddhism might be understood better as an ethical system, like Confucianism, than as a religion. After all, creating and identifying oneself with an absolute being, as well as borrowing authority from such a being, is essentially egoistic, and thus constitutes the very first step toward separating Man from Man. Waphola Rahula describes this aspect in *What the Buddha Taught*: "Two ideas are psychologically deep-rooted in man: self-protection and self-preservation. For self-protection man has created God, on whom he depends for his own protection, safety, and security, just as a child depends on its parent. For self-preservation man has conceived the idea of an immortal Soul or *Atman*, which will live eternally. In his ignorance, weakness, fear, and desire, man needs these two things to console himself. Hence he clings to them deeply and fanatically. The Buddha's teaching does not support this ignorance, weakness, fear, and desire, but aims at making man enlightened by removing and destroying them, striking at their very root. According to Buddhism, our ideas of God and Soul are false and empty. Though highly developed as theories, they are all the same extremely subtle mental projections, garbed in an intricate metaphysical and philosophical phraseology. These ideas are so deep-rooted in man, and so near and dear to him, that he does not wish to hear, nor does he want to understand, any teaching against them."[56]

By refusing the practice of self-mortification, and by rejecting the existence of Atman, Buddha acknowledged the harmony between body and spirit; and furthermore, by denying Brahmanism, he acknowledged the harmony between men. Buddhist compassion is thus based on a profound sense of human interconnection, similar to the charity or Samaritanism of Christianity, the brotherly love of Islam, and the Humanity of Confucius. In turn, because it is devoid of religious dogma, the Mahayana (Great Vehicle) school of Buddhism, which placed a greater emphasis on Compassion than on Nirvana, was more easily assimilated into Eastern civilization.

Nirvana: Man-Universe Unity

Here we should consider the true significance of Nirvana, to which popular Buddhism attaches such great importance. Indeed, there is a tendency to consider Nirvana the central teaching of Buddhism. The concept of Nirvana originated from Hinduism—in which it is called *Moksha*—and literally means "extinguishment." It is popularly believed that the Buddha attained Nirvana, yet he scarcely ever mentioned it. This discrepancy can partly be explained by the fact that, like Jesus, Siddhartha did not leave a written doctrine; his teachings were compiled centuries later, during which the essence of Buddhism must have undergone many significant transformations, much as Christianity did when it was codified after the death of Jesus. It seems unlikely that Siddhartha viewed individual salvation as the ultimate goal of life, like Hinduism, which seeks salvation through Moksha. Buddha sought the redemption of mankind—not the individual: hence the concept of the "Bodhisattva," the enlightened being who seeks the enlightenment of others. If Buddhist Nirvana adhered to such concepts as "extinction of all desire," "salvation of self," "emancipation from hatred and jealousy," "status of perfect wisdom and bliss," then it would be the same as Brahmin Moksha. Buddha disagreed with the Brahmin emphasis on self-salvation versus compassion for others.

At this time in India, suffering must have seemed omnipresent, but behind all suffering is desire, and so those who sought Nirvana had to first extinguish desire. Buddha's great understanding was that, although the desires behind suffering may be eliminated, the mind cannot remain void. It must be filled with something instead—as Westerners put it, Nature abhors a vacuum. According to the Buddha, selfish desires must be replaced with positive passion linking one with others—and in particular, compassion. Thus, Buddhist Nirvana must be treated in conjunction with compassion. A mind filled with compassion does not distinguish itself from others, and thus experiences oneness with the universe. According to Buddhist tradition, Siddhartha attained Nirvana at the age of thirty-five and then set out to achieve the salvation of mankind.

Buddhism: "Metaphysicization" of the East

Buddhism evolved out of Hinduism, which had a very strong metaphysics. It was only natural that Buddhism, when introduced to the East, carried with it a metaphysical flavor. We may call this process of assimilation "metaphysicization."[57] The process took two paths, transforming the Taoist conception of the Man-Nature relationship, and the Confucian idea of interpersonal relations. As we have seen, Taoist cosmology and the neo-Confucian school of Li-Ki were the chief products of this metaphysicization; Eastern culture was enriched, but also was plagued with futile metaphysical and political squabbles. However, the process remained marginal and did not affect the fundamental tenets of Eastern thought. Just as the East before Buddhism always rejected supernatural interference from its ethics, so afterwards, it rejected the interference of metaphysics.

We have previously described the metaphysical character of Li-Ki, inherited from Buddhism. Yet it is important to note—in clear adherence to the East's fundamental rejection of a supernatural entity—that neo-Confucianism continued to deny the separation of the external world from nature and so failed to absorb such concepts as reincarnation and karma, which Buddhism had inherited from Hinduism. The same was true of Buddhist relics. During the Tang dynasty, which embraced Buddhism as the court religion, a renowned Confucian scholar named Han Yu (韓愈, AD 768–824) risked his life by sending the emperor a letter denouncing the worship of Buddhist relics: "the elaborate preparations being made by the state to receive the Buddha's finger-bone, which he called 'a filthy object' and which, he said, should be 'handed over to the proper officials for destruction by water and fire to eradicate its origin forever.'"[58] In this way, the East absorbed Buddhism according to its own cultural tenets, rather than being overwhelmed by the new philosophy. Hence we refer to the "sinicization" of Buddhism.

Sinicization of Buddhism

The history of the introduction of Mahayana Buddhism into the East clearly demonstrates its sinicization. Indian Brahmins did not welcome the Buddha, just as the Jewish priests did not welcome Christ. After a temporary retreat, Hinduism reestablished itself with renewed strength. To flourish fully, Buddhism had to either undergo a significant transformation, or compromise with traditional Hinduism. The early, compromised form of Buddhism is known to have focused, under the possible influence of Hinduism, on Nirvana and individual salvation. The Buddha's true teaching— Compassion—lost much of its importance here. But a splinter group also formed, focusing on the salvation of mankind as a whole, and thus on Compassion, and this branch became known as the Mahayana or Greater Vehicle. These were reformists and revolutionaries compared to the early Buddhists. An approximate analogy can be detected in the relationship of Protestantism to Catholicism, although the Western schism occurred much later.

The East, accustomed to Confucius' teachings, was ready to embrace Mahayana Buddhism, with its emphasis on compassion, advocating harmony among men. As the East welcomed this new school, it experienced a conflict between Buddhist compassion and Brahmin Nirvana, just as India had done before. But in the East, due to its core tenet of social harmony, compassion prevailed over Nirvana. Buddhist metaphysics did not radically alter, but only enriched, Eastern culture.

In due course, Confucianism regained its previous dominance in the East, as neo-Confucianism. It must be observed that this predominance refers only to its official endorsement; Buddhism had already been assimilated and syncretized with the other local schools of thought. This syncretism occurred not only in society as a whole, with different individuals adopting different ideas, but even within a single person—an Easterner can accept Confucianism, Taoism, and Buddhism all at the same time, since he sees the elements common to all three.

Eastern Culture vs. Communism

The sinicization of Buddhism may be seen as a precedent for the more recent attitude toward communism in the East. The latter is a Western ideology grounded in the separation between classes as a dialectical engine of social change. Such separation is, by nature, incompatible with the Eastern emphasis on harmony. Junzi, the conceptual product of many millennia, cannot simply be converted into a Communist. Although, as we have seen, Taoism and the other ancient schools denied the possibility of absolute truth, communism declared precisely the opposite, claiming such a truth for itself. This "truth" consisted largely of an attack on capitalism and of the idea of class struggle between the proletariat and the bourgeoisie, with the promise of utopia for the former.

The Communist theory of class struggle has now largely been discarded in the Eastern "Communist" countries, which are now actively engaged in creating free market economies. Only in political terms can communism maintain the appearance of control, and it does so perhaps because it continues to provide the necessary framework for the political stability of these countries. Communist countries in the West, such as the Soviet Union and East Germany, perished because they identified the regime with the ideology; with the demise of that ideology, the countries could no longer exist. But in the East, Communist countries possess a much older ideological character—that of Confucius and Tao, unity and harmony. Stalin reportedly compared China to a radish—red (Communist) only on the outside but white (Chinese) inside. A similarly limited engagement with Communist ideology can be found in North Korea or Vietnam. It is increasingly clear that these regimes borrow only the name of communism, along with a few useful elements of state management, all the while reintroducing the fundamentals of traditional Eastern ethics, albeit in a distorted fashion.

Eastern Noninterventionism vs. Communist Interventionism

The incompatibility between the East and communism can be better grasped if one understands the fundamental Eastern tenet of "nonintervention" (i.e., laissez-faire): Taoism preaches non-action, while Confucius advised his followers not to do unto others what they would not have done unto them. Communism, by contrast, advocates extreme interventionism—even political revolution. This Communist political revolution was predicated on the promise of utopia, which would be realized by a transition that justified extreme interventionist measures by the state. These measures, the "Communist Ten Commandments," include the abolition of property, the abolition of inheritance, the confiscation of any property belonging to emigrants and rebels, the centralization of credit in the state, and the centralization of communication and transport.

For an Eastern mind that does not believe in utopia, whether religious or Communist, such a society of "from each according to his capacity and to each according to his needs" would be not only a fantasy but, realistically, a nightmare. Under the circumstances, what are left from communism were the transitional measures (i.e., its Ten Commandments), which would thus become nightmarish permanent conditions. For Eastern culture and people who have long been accustomed to a lack of state intervention, those extreme interventionist measures could not possibly be accommodated.

The East's rejection of this Communist interventionism was manifested by the immediate and enthusiastic popular support for the three paradigmatic declarations of Deng Xiaoping: "Black cat, white cat, the cat that catches the mice is a good cat" (1961); "Truth can better be found in everyday life than in a book written one hundred years ago" (1984); "Socialist market economy and socialism with Chinese character" (1992). In dealing with the innate contradictions of communism, which necessarily entailed radical reform, the Chinese approach stood in stark contrast to that taken in the Soviet Union. Deng Xiaoping relied on the non-interventionist character of the East in his efforts to save China during its tumultuous transition from a Communist to a market economy. Deng's reform was from the ground upwards: he let the people adopt a market economy with timely guidance and leadership. On the other hand, Mikhail Gorbachev's Glasnost and Perestroika policies were reform from the top down: he had no tradition or cultural foundation on which to rely for his well-meaning reforms.

It is off the mark to interpret the success or failure of reform in China and the USSR as owing simply to technical issues; this would be tantamount to ignoring the fundamental cultural differences between the two countries. We cannot say, therefore, that China succeeded only because it opened economically while closing politically (i.e., achieved Perestroika without Glasnost). The free market and democracy go hand in hand. Both rest on the fundamental principle of noninterventionism and individual freedom. What Deng initiated, with the overwhelming support of his people, was a regional "opening and reform" with national implications. Deng's problem was not the choice between opening and reform, but rather the politicians. He had both to fight and to accommodate the Communist ideologues still powerful in Beijing. He knew instinctively that opening and reform (i.e., the free market and democracy) were inseparable. In dealing with this situation, he made the most of China's strategic position by placing the "free market and democratic" region as far as possible from the country's political and cultural center, Beijing. The Special Economic Zone was thus chosen in the South East Coastal region. Furthermore, he allowed individual entrepreneurship and self-interest to run their course by applying the traditional Eastern approach of nonintervention to economic and political life.

Sinicization of Communism

Given the profoundly syncretic tradition of Eastern culture, it is unlikely that its Communist countries will officially repudiate Communist ideology; rather, they will seek to integrate the system with their own traditional fundamentals. What we continue to witness in these countries is the sinicization of communism. It is too early to tell what China will ultimately glean from communism; we can only speculate. If its absorption of Buddhism is a reliable guide, we may expect China to glean four elements from communism: the rejection of greed and profit-seeking; the alternation of power; its mode of governance; and its global view.

First, the rejection of greed and profit-seeking has long constituted one of the fundamental virtues of Junzi. The Communist rejection of these therefore perfectly fits the Eastern tradition. But in the Eastern tradition, rejection of profit-making applies only to leadership as a sign of altruism. Profit-making is the natural tendency of most people, and as such it is condoned as the basic driving force of a society. This is a fundamental difference between Junzi and communism. The sinicization of communism could therefore allow China to absorb free market economics with an ethical countervailing force against greed; the latter may provide an invaluable supplement to the classical capitalist *invisible hand*, enabling China to take measures against the greed of individuals, or a society of individuals, without hampering the basics of the free market. Although the West has similar measures, including welfare systems, import duties, and other regulatory mechanisms, such as antitrust laws, these measures are legal instruments, not ethical tools. Greed cannot be regulated by laws but only condemned by ethics. As we shall argue in chapter 9, the capitalistic West tends to condone greed as a natural part of self-interest, with grave consequences. The robber barons could be protected by laws but not justified by ethics. How, then, would such men—the precursors of modern multinationals—be dealt with in a post-Deng China? This would be an interesting question not only for China but also for the philosophy of the free market.

The second aspect of the sinicization of communism concerns the alternation of power. The traditional East had a fundamental political weakness, which it could never remedy: dynastic power. Communist ideology clearly repudiates hereditary monarchical succession. Clearly, China would have found a solution for the alternation of power anyway. Yet China could make the most of communism for this purpose and seems so far to have succeeded in alternating power efficiently and cost-effectively for several decades.

The third aspect of the sinicization of communism—its mode of governance—is a very sensitive area and still in an experimental stage: can a one-party system be compatible with democracy? Both Taoism and Confucianism explicitly warn Junzi against party formation. We shall examine this aspect in detail in chapter 7. The rationale for this is clear: in the end, political parties always tend to compromise the people's interests for their own. Discerning the people's interest would be all the more challenging, especially given the ambiguous nature of most political decisions and the ready availability of self-justification. Political parties will cling to power according to the principle of self-preservation; the larger the party, the greater its will to power. Although his intention appears to be more to warn American political parties than appreciate Chinese one-party governance, Thomas Friedman hinted at an intriguing alternative: "One-Party autocracy certainly has its drawbacks. But when it is led by a reasonably enlightened group of people, as China is today, it can also have great advantages. That one party can just impose the politically difficult but critically important policies needed to move a society forward in the twenty-first century. It is not an accident that China is committed to overtaking America in electric cars, solar power, energy efficiency, batteries, nuclear power, and wind power."[59] We are all too aware of the dangers inherent in a one-party system: absolute power corrupts absolutely. Might the Chinese experiment of a "one-party democracy," as a sinicization of communism, produce an alternative to the Western multiparty democracy? Or will it become a complete failure?

The fourth aspect of the sinicization of communism is particularly relevant, since China's foreign exchange reserves are increasing exponentially. Will China be able to enlarge its outlook to the world from its traditional orientation around the family? After all, despite its fundamental shortcomings and faults, communism does have a global view, both in terms of time and space.

PART II: EXPRESSIONS

CHAPTER 5

Role Model:
Western Hero vs. Eastern Junzi

"You are the light of the world ... you give light to all that are in the house.... You are the salt of the earth: but if the salt loses its taste, how can you make your food seasoned?"[1]

Jesus Christ

"Mud is used to make celadon, but it is the emptiness of the celadon that becomes useful.... Doors and windows are used to make rooms, but it is the emptiness of the room that becomes useful."[2]

Lao Tzu

Western Sword vs. Eastern Pen

We have now compared the fundamental elements of Eastern and Western culture. Once we established the bases of this comparison—the conceptual environment and three cardinal relations—the profound differences soon became evident.

Of the three relations, the most essential is that between mind and body: the other two depend in turn on this. If Man perceives his own mind or spirit as separate from his body, he is likely to identify Nature with the body and God (or gods) with the mind. Here he enters into the realm of faith, which naturally divides believers from nonbelievers. With faith comes the law of God; in a social context this is reflected as the law of men, which gives rise to a community based around the enforcement of political power.

On the other hand, if Man perceives a unity between his mind and his body, he needs no God or supernatural entity with which to identify the former. Harmony takes precedence over Domination; such a community becomes grounded in ethics. In a circumscribed environment, as in the East, enforcement leads to struggle and disorder, while ethics better serves Man's purpose of self-preservation. The genesis of Western law and Eastern ethics serves as a conclusion to the first part of this book; we can now proceed to the second, which deals with the outward expressions of each fundamental principle.

In the second part of this book, chapters 5–7, we shall contrast those concepts and phenomena that manifest the essences of Eastern and Western culture; here, the only basis for comparison is the degree of importance possessed by each manifestation within its civilization. To make such a contrast worthwhile, it is essential that we overcome our own limitations and prejudices as far as possible; thus, we may not use law or Christianity to understand the East, nor ethics or Confucianism to understand the West. The pejorative concepts of *heathen* and *Xiaoren* lose their value in such a context. Instead, we will compare the human ideals of each culture.

As we have seen, the West produced two role models: Christian, in relation to its Universal ethics, and Hero, in relation to Master ethics. The East, on the other hand, had only one model—Junzi, based on Universal ethics. In this chapter we shall contrast Junzi and Hero; in the next, Junzi and Christian.

The concept of a hero is well-known in the West; Junzi, of course, is not. One can better grasp this key concept by comparing the roles played by the sword and the pen in the respective histories of East and West.

Sword vs. Pen

The Hero, more than the Christian, embodied Western ideals from classical antiquity to modernity—excluding the present. Because Junzi stands for Universal ethics, and Hero for Master ethics, we can draw the East-West division in terms of these two systems. It would be a mistake to suggest that Junzi is "right" and Hero "wrong." Each ideal simply suited its context. Junzi would have seemed irrelevant to most Westerners before the present.

To illustrate this distinction, let us compare some of the most prominent figures of each culture: Alexander, Julius Caesar, Charlemagne, and Louis XIV in the West, and Qin Shi Huang, Tang Taizong, and Kangxi in the East. Qin Shi Huang (秦始皇, 259–210 BC) is comparable, in terms of his influence on the history of philosophy, to Alexander the Great: his unification of the center of the Eastern world opened the way for the Confucian-Taoist East. At the same time, he might be compared as a statesman to

Julius Caesar, since both marked a new period in the history of an empire: the latter became the first Caesar in the West and the former became the first emperor in the East. Alexander was not only a great conqueror but an enlightened leader. Aristotle was his teacher, and during his campaign, he took along philosophers, scholars, and scientists. Julius Caesar was a brilliant orator and writer, composing *The Gallic War* and other works, although he is better known, of course, for his military prowess—that is, as a man of the sword. Qin Shi Huang was equally ruthless and brilliant in his military conquest of China, as attested to by his famous terracotta army. But at the same time he was a man of the pen, bequeathing the image of a civilian emperor of all people under Heaven.

These contrasting images should be attributed more to posterity than to the men themselves: despite their common ground as men of the sword and the pen, the West privileged the military image of Alexander and Caesar, whereas the East privileged a cultural image of Qin Shi Huang. This is what we would expect: while the West continued to value the military hero above all, the East soon changed its preference from the sword to the pen. From the very first Han emperor, Gaozu (漢高祖, 247–195 BC), all Chinese emperors wanted to be remembered as men of the pen. Motivated in part by literary vanity as well as political needs, most emperors in the East left poems and calligraphies to posterity. Mao Zedong, who has often been compared to Qin Shi Huang, also left a similar literary legacy.

Charlemagne vs. Taizong of Tang

Charlemagne (742–814) was arguably the most pivotal ruler of the medieval West. In the East, during this period, the Emperor Taizong (唐太宗, 599–649) of the Tang dynasty stands out.

Although Charlemagne was also a renowned cultivator of letters, bringing together scholars from all over Europe to teach his citizens—producing what has been called the Carolingian Renaissance—he is principally remembered for his military successes. This heroic image is demonstrated, for example, in Figure 5-1—the king receiving the pledge of fealty from his paladin Roland. He is known to have become the master of the West "by the sword and the cross." By contrast, even though he was a formidable general and empire builder, the image of Taizong favored by the East was not of a warrior, but of a civilian scholar, Junzi, as in Figure 5-2.

Fig. 5-1. Charlemagne (742–814): the pledges of fealty from Roland.
(http://en.wikipedia.org/wiki/ Charlemagne)

Fig. 5-2. Emperor Taizong (唐太宗, 599–649) of Tang Dynasty
(http://en.wikipedia.org/ wiki/Emperor_Taizong_of_ Tang)

Since the history and character of Charlemagne is well known, let us instead examine those of Emperor Taizong. The establishment of the Tang dynasty owes more to Taizong than to his father, who became the first Tang emperor. His judicious governance of the empire was regarded as the example against which all other emperors should be measured.[3] Consequently he established his reputation as one of the greatest emperors in history. Providing peace and prosperity to the nation, he was as effective as he was magnanimous, a quality common to all the great leaders of the East and the West. Three characteristics stand out above all: he openly laughed at the superstitions and omens to which most of his advisers still clung; he allowed criticism against the abuse of his absolute power; and he showed universal affection to the people, often even breaking the customs of his time: "One of the first actions that Taizong carried out as emperor was releasing a number of the ladies in waiting from the palace and returning them to their homes, so that they could be married."[4]

Taizong personally led many military campaigns, but he wanted to be remembered as Junzi, a model scholar-official, rather than as a conquering hero, due to the Eastern view of the sword as inauspicious. Military weapons were expressly condemned both by Confucianism and Taoism as bringing bad luck. Taizong was also a man of letters, leaving many calligraphic manuscripts. Charlemagne, by contrast, is known to have been illiterate, despite his consolidation of the Western Church. This stark contrast between the two personalities is due to the West's reliance on the Hero, and the East's preference instead for Junzi.

Enlightenment: Rule by Law vs. Rule by Ethics

This contrast between Hero and Junzi proved to be an enduring one. If we compare the most prominent figures of East and

West during the seventeenth century, Emperor Kangxi (康熙) of China, and King Louis XIV of France, we will find a similar contrast.

These two figures have one thing in common: longevity and glory. Louis XIV remains the longest-reigning sovereign in Western history, and Kangxi the longest-reigning emperor in the East.[5] Both reigns were considered glorious, and both embodied "enlightened despotism," as defined by the thinkers of the Enlightenment. Like Louis XIV, Kangxi actively promoted literature. Kangxi ordered the compilation of the most complete dictionary of Chinese characters ever put together, the Kangxi Dictionary. Apparently, in an attempt to win over the Chinese literati to his Manchu rule, he actively pursued and wooed the Chinese scholar-officials: he enhanced the role of Chinese literati and gave them greater responsibility. His policy of assimilation succeeded brilliantly, contributing to the peace and stability of the empire.

Thus, like Louis XIV, who laid the foundation for France's later glory, Kangxi prepared China for long-term peace and prosperity—a period called the Kang-Qian Period of Prosperity, lasting from 1661 until 1799.[6] But the similarities between the Sun King and Kangxi end there. The difference between them is crucial: the Sun King wanted to be remembered as a victor and conquering hero, whereas Kangxi preferred to be memorialized as a Junzi, as Figures 5-3 and 5-4 demonstrate. The difference, to be clear, is not absolute; Louis XIV contributed enormously to French culture, while Kangxi personally led many military campaigns—but the majority of their respective portraits are military and civilian. The Western Enlightenment remained based on the sword and on law, whereas that of the East was centered on the pen and on ethics: Hero vs. Junzi.

Fig. 5-3. Louis XIV (1638–1715) King of France (http://en.wikipedia.org/wiki/Louis_XIV_of_France)	**Fig. 5-4. Emperor Kangxi** (康熙帝1654–1722), **Qing Dynasty** (http://en.wikipedia.org/wiki/Kangxi_Emperor)

The reign of the pen provided the East with an ethical system of enduring depth. For example, such values and principles as Humanity, Tao-Virtue, integrity, propriety, frugality, sincerity, loyalty, and filial duty were accepted universally, comparable to religious doctrines in the medieval West. The absence of anthropomorphic religion in the East enabled these principles and values to become the sole guiding principles for human conduct and behavior.

It was only in the twentieth century, with the paradigm shift in the West from warfare to commerce, that the world finally agreed on preferring the pen to the sword, as the sword had exhausted its role in the expansive world. Western history and culture has dominated that of the East in the world since the

Industrial Revolution; this is why mankind faces such a challenge in its attempt to absorb the Yin values of pen, ethics. A preference for the pen did not free the East from internal struggles and competitions; until the East received the West's input, it experienced rule *by* ethics rather than the rule *of* ethics. In other words, rulers not infrequently used ethics for the benefit of their rule instead of their rule being firmly bound by ethics themselves. Indeed, the East was plagued by incessant non-military conspiracies and schemes within its governments. But aside from these schemes, the East generally favored harmony among men, producing yin culture and ethics, which can and should serve as reference points in our present circumscribed world. Junzi, at the center of Eastern ethics, will adapt himself to the prevailing Western paradigms.

The Philosophy of Junzi

The opening chapter of the Confucian *Analects* begins with the importance of inner conviction: "To be unperturbed when not appreciated by others is of Junzi, is it not?" Understanding this concept is crucial in understanding Eastern culture since it epitomizes the ethical principles on which that culture is founded. We have examined four fundamental aspects of Junzi—nature, human nature, ethics, and politics—and concluded that he is deistic, rejecting mythology, theology, metaphysics, and ideologies, which are cultural manifestations at most, not the sources of solutions. We have also concluded that Junzi has a specific understanding of human nature: self-interest as the neutral expression of self-preservation, although more often greedy than altruistic. His ethics is universal, making no distinction between citizens and barbarians, nobility and commoners, masters and slaves, believers and infidels—only between himself and Xiaoren. Junzi's ultimate aim is political, since the state, or even the world, is the farthest limit of his capacity.

Junzi vs. Xiaoren I: Division of Labor

Junzi and Xiaoren are best construed as two sides of one coin, since the one cannot exist without the other, and both can coexist within a single individual. This duality well illustrates Eastern culture in general. In most cases, a Chinese character, being an ideogram rather than an alphabetic letter, represents a concept instead of a single word or meaning. In a similar vein, some Eastern expressions stand for a philosophy rather than a mere notion or idea. The Junzi-Xiaoren pairing is a good example, since it represents the whole Eastern philosophy, with all its ethical, political, and even economic connotations.

Junzi-Xiaoren was not the monopoly of Confucianism. The same concept is so widely used in Eastern culture that one can safely assume it represents the entire ethical system of the East. Taoteking also uses Junzi to represent its ethical ideal, although the term "Sage" (聖人) is more frequently used than Junzi. Sage and Junzi share the same ethics. With the same ethics, Taoist Sage defines the relationship between Nature and Man, and Confucian Junzi defines the relationship between Man and Man. One interesting aspect is that Taoist Sage is also concerned with the economic ethics of a nation, whereas Junzi is more exclusively concerned with ethics and politics.

The Junzi-Xiaoren duality was studied in the East as intensely as the Western study of the Spirit and Body dichotomy. Eastern thinkers dealt with human *nature*—both mind and body— whereas the West focused on the mind, excluding the body. Although in later Confucianism the same terminology evolved to mean "evil" in a more distinctive way, we must recall that during the time of Confucius the terms good (善) and evil (惡) were almost equivalent to liking (好) and disliking (不好). The pairing of good/liking and evil/disliking can be understood more easily if one considers that the religious connotations of virtue and sin, heaven and hell, were absent in the East. This is an important distinction, as Junzi considers Xiaoren not as an evil being to be eliminated, but simply as a person not to his liking.

"Junzi assists the poor; he does not add wealth to the rich."[7] As we pointed out, Junzi, in his compassion, accepts human desire and avarice as inevitable, to which emotions Xiaoren remains prisoner—his aim is not to eradicate these impediments, but simply to educate and guide his fellow man. But he must also guard against acquiring such negative traits—and most notably that of profit-seeking. An important result of this premise with respect to economics is that greed, while deplorable, must be accepted as a matter of fact. Junzi does urge Xiaoren to control himself, but not to sacrifice his interests and desires for the sake of others or God, which is, Junzi knows, impossible. Altruism is possible but very rare, and reserved for Junzi alone; the multitude will always remain as Xiaoren, seeking their self-interest. This shall be examined in more depth, along with the philosophy of Wuwei, in chapter 9.

Because Junzi repudiates profit-seeking, he will tend to adopt a laissez-faire approach to economics. Indeed, throughout the history of the East, commercial enterprises were discouraged by scholar-officials as the concern of Xiaoren. These officials were far from the philosophy of Adam Smith, but their practice had much in common with the "invisible hand" he proposed in theory. The concept of Junzi, then, encouraged Eastern governments to implement laissez-faire as the default approach to economics; they relied heavily on private investments even in building schools, except for the central schools built in the capital, which they managed directly. Schools were supposed to be financed, built, and run by local groups of literati, who devoted themselves to education, as they had not qualified for positions in the government.

Such an economic system naturally prevented any statism or tribalism from emerging in the East. This tradition was also indirectly linked to the recognition of the impracticability of altruism. Since self-interest is common to all human beings, Junzi perceives that altruism at the governmental level is bound to be altered and distorted by Xiaoren for the purposes of turning a profit. This principle is inherent in the Taoist philosophy of Wuwei: the State should limit, as far as possible, the extent of its laws and regulations, for no matter how good its intentions, a State's laws are bound to be misused to seek profit.

For example, the Eastern tendency to reject the thirst for profits in either personal or national matters became dogmatic—almost religious. As we shall see in the case of Admiral Cheng Ho, this principle was to be upheld even when dealing with neighboring counties. He resolved to treat foreigners not with aggression but with kindness, not out of altruism, but simply as an extension of the Eastern practices he took for granted. The notion of exploiting other countries was simply unthinkable, just as it would have been unthinkable to a contemporary Western captain to sail for a year only to treat other cultures with kindness.

Junzi vs. Xiaoren II: Leadership and Enlightened Self-Interest

Junzi is well aware of the difficulties involved in action by default—such a strategy demands a clear understanding of human nature. Spinoza explains with astonishing perspicacity: "But human power is extremely limited, and is infinitely surpassed by the power of external causes; we have not, therefore, an absolute power of shaping to our use those things which are without us. Nevertheless, we shall bear with an equal mind all that happens to us in contravention to the claims of our own advantage, so long as we are conscious, that we have done our duty, and that the power which we possess is not sufficient to enable us to protect ourselves completely; remembering that we are a part of universal nature, and that we follow her order. If we have a clear and distinct understanding of this, that part of our nature which is defined by intelligence, in other words the better part of ourselves, will assuredly acquiesce in what befalls us, and in such acquiescence will endeavour to persist."[8]

Compare the Taoist doctrine: "Following Tao, one diminishes his doing every day until one arrives at doing nothing. Having arrived at this point of Wuwei, there is nothing one cannot do."[9] Most humans, being Xiaoren, act unwisely—contrary to Tao—most of the time, due to their desires, passions, jealousies, and profit-seeking. One can find an almost perfect explanation of this principle in Spinoza's *Ethics*: "Hence, men who are governed by reason—that is, who seek what is useful to them in accordance with reason—desire for themselves nothing, which they do not also desire for the rest of mankind, and, consequently, are just, faithful, and honorable in their conduct."[10] Consequently, Junzi is characterized more by circumspection than by action. Laissez-faire, ultimately, brings less misfortune.

In this context, we can understand Junzi's profound misgivings over metaphysical subtleties, as expounded in Taoism: "The more one advances, the more ignorant one becomes." If the anthropomorphic monotheism that thrived in an expansive world has proved to be unnatural and irrelevant to today's circumscribed world, then its numerous theologies and ideologies must also be considered relics of an obsolete environment. Taoism warns: "When knowledge and intelligence appears, great hypocrisy begins."[11] This has been amply demonstrated by the havoc wreaked on Western society by such extremist ideologies as communism and fascism, which grew inevitably out of the West's intellectual heritage.

Junzi acts only out of genuine altruism, aiming at "enlightened" self-preservation, which requires striking a balance between self-preservation and the preservation of others. This is achieved primarily through education, enlightenment, and life-experience. The difficulty of such a process is acknowledged by Spinoza in his *Ethics*: "If the way which, as I have shown, leads hither seems very difficult, it can nevertheless be found. It must indeed be difficult since it is so seldom discovered; for if salvation lay ready to hand and could be discovered without great labour, how could it be possible that it should be neglected by almost everybody? But all noble things are as difficult as they are rare."

Junzi considers that it is neither possible nor desirable to abolish or suppress desire, passion, and drives, as this can be achieved only by extinguishing life. And because it is difficult, men tend to look for salvation via shortcuts, that is to say, via doctrines and dogmas. Yet, in a way, devotion to doctrines means abandoning efforts toward self-fulfillment. Ideology may bring about temporary respite. In the end, though, eventual disillusionment is unavoidable because absolute truth is beyond human reach. What Junzi can do, however, is channel his drive toward self-preservation by judiciously employing reason. As previously noted, self-preservation can best be achieved by preserving others at the same time (i.e., by altruism). Culture itself is largely conditioned by biological necessity. But, as we see in the case of the relationship between the neocortex (new brain) and limbic system (old brain), some degree of freedom has been achieved by integrating the two disparate elements. This "enlightened" self-interest lies precisely in the realm of human action and achievement. As Spinoza asserted in *Of the Power of the Intellect, or Of Human Liberty*, it is up to the individual to make a choice: Junzi follows his intellect and finds liberty, whereas Xiaoren follows his desires and finds only bondage.

Junzi follows the Way, according to which Nature achieves self-preservation by Wuwei; thus also Confucius, recommending the preservation of others for one's own benefit: "If you seek to establish yourself, establish others"; "If you want profit for yourself, profit others—pursue mutual profitability"; "Self-interest is altruism, pursue self-interested altruism."[12] Thus, Junzi must make the interest of his society his own interest. On the other hand, the Western Hero operates with a different mechanism. He assumes that he is chosen by the Spirit for a specific purpose or goal and that he must lead the multitude in that direction. The interests of the multitude must be identical to following his goal; it goes without saying that the Hero usually assures the multitude that their interests would be safeguarded in the end. Making the interests of others his own is tantamount to altruism. Thus, altruism is central to the ethics of Junzi.

The most important distinction between Junzi and Xiaoren is greed. For the former, greed is the fundamental cause of social problems. Xiaoren, by contrast, follows the path of greed and egoism. Since most people would act as Xiaoren, given free rein, self-interest tends to cause conflict and chaos. Ethics, therefore, must protect self-interest from greed, both within society and within the individual; greed cannot be eliminated, but must be managed. Here perhaps lies the most rational ethical value pertaining to the post-industrial political economy: how to define and deal with individual economic activities that are given a quantum leap of productivity thanks to industrialization.

For Junzi, the need for ethics comes from the biological necessity for self-preservation. This can best be called "enlightened self-interest," and Confucian Benevolence is aligned with this behavior. The same can be said for other great teachings, such as Compassion in Buddhism, Neighborly Love in Christianity, and Brotherly Love in Islam. Spinoza recognizes the power of passion as a basic motivation, as well as the role of reason, which guides us toward enlightened self-preservation: "But no one, to my knowledge, has determined the nature and powers of the affects, nor what, on the other hand, the mind can do to moderate them."[13] Junzi rejects the distinction between mind and body, on which most theologians and metaphysicians, including Kant, relied. Spinoza explains, "An idea that excludes the existence of our body cannot be in our mind, but is contrary to it.... The mind, as far as it can, strives to imagine those things that increase or aid the body's power of acting."[14]

The philosophy of Junzi was remarkably successful in promoting harmony and peace within its own society. One of the most distinct characteristics of Junzi ethics is that it is universal, while Western ethics works only within the boundaries of a particular religion or nation. We admit that Jesus Christ expanded the applicability of "neighborly love" from Judaism to all mankind, and therein lies his greatness and significance. But it is undeniable that Christianity as a religion and as an institution naturally implies the division between "us" and "them." We have seen that classical ethics, both Greek and Roman, were founded on a system of slavery. The East makes no such divisions along religious, racial, or national lines. The lack of both religious dogma and slavery may have facilitated the sense of universality in Junzi ethics.

Neglect of Law in Junzi Philosophy

The weakness of the philosophy of Junzi is its neglect of law in favor of ethics. Legal professions have existed in the West for over two millennia, since the classical period. No lawyers existed in the East until it imported the West's legal systems in the nineteenth century. Since Junzi regarded laws as the instrument of rulers according to the teachings of Confucianism and Taoism, the East relied heavily on ethics.

But law also is essential in protecting individual freedoms and initiatives—an indispensable aspect of the Western heroic ideal. The spirit of enterprise and personal profit existed in the maritime West long before the advent of monotheistic religion, which perhaps benefited from the fertile climate in which it arose.

Relevance of Hero and Junzi to the Twenty-First Century

In the Preface, I hinted that traditional Eastern behavior with its Yin traits may constitute the most relevant experience for our present circumscribed environment—both in terms of its successes and its failures. It is not that the East will prevail in this century—rather that our environment now matches that with which the East historically developed, and so all of us must adapt our behavior to fit the model made successful in the East for so long.

The eight sub-paradigms that we shall examine in chapter 10 are all Yin attributes, which will prevail in a circumscribed Yin world. Any attempt to introduce Yang attributes and paradigms into such a world will lead to conflict and failure. There is nothing intrinsically "good" about Yin, or "bad" about Yang—the only issue is relevance to our present situation.

The journey of the Western Heroes toward rule of law was far more dramatic and religious than Junzi's path toward the rule of ethics. From its mystifying and beautiful Judaic and Greco-Roman birth to its tragic and grotesque Hegelian Communist and Nietzschian Fascist demise, the Western spirit travelled many thousand years and around the world. It relied on law and force to impose its will. The West prevailed in the realm of law and the non-West in the domain of force. In the end, the Western spirit conquered the world, and with this, it died, having fulfilled its role. It could live only in an open-expanding world, not in a closed world where spirit must be united with body. The old Western spirit may be resurrected if mankind embarks on a new journey into the unknown universe, which will prompt us again to believe in myths, legends, miracles, and doctrines—this is essentially what science fiction is about. Until then, we can safely assume that the history of the Western spirit, and of rule by law and force, has ended. But a new commercial paradigm has arisen—and one no less exciting or dangerous than that which preceded it.

Hero vs. Junzi

Let us now compare the fundamentals of Junzi to those of the Western ideal, the Hero. To this end, we will mostly use quotations from Confucius and the Taoist canons. In our comparison, we shall resort to our old categories of Nature (Man-Nature relationship), Human Nature (Mind-Body relationship), and Ethics (Man-Man relationship), as well as Politics (including Nation-Nation relationship).

Hero vs. Junzi I: Nature

In their attitude toward Nature, Junzi and Hero show a clear contrast: Junzi does not recognize supernatural interference in the affairs of man; Hero welcomes and often prays for divine assistance. Consequently, Junzi is a man of "common sense," whereas Hero is a man of charisma, ready to cloak himself with a special aura or divine blessing. From this perspective, one can discern that the role of theology and metaphysics was, in part, to support the image of the Western Hero.

In his acceptance of common sense over dogma, Benjamin Franklin could have passed as a model Junzi. Indeed, one can find a very similar process in his rejection of metaphysics, of which he had been aware since his early years. By contrast to many of his peers, the pragmatic Franklin soon realized the trap of metaphysics. He writes in his autobiography: "I began to suspect that this doctrine, tho' it might be true, was not very useful. My London pamphlet, which had for its motto these lines of Dryden:

> *Whatever is, is right. Though purblind man*
> *Sees but a part o' the chain, the nearest link:*
> *His eyes not carrying to the equal beam,*
> *That poises all above;*

and from the attributes of God, His infinite wisdom, goodness, and power, concluded that nothing could possibly be wrong in the world, and that vice and virtue were empty distinctions, no such things existing, appeared now not so clever a performance as I once thought it; and I doubted whether some error had not insinuated itself unperceived into my argument, so as to infect all that followed, as is common in metaphysical reasonings. I grew convinced that *truth, sincerity,* and *integrity,* in dealings between man and man, were of the utmost importance to the felicity of life; and I formed written resolutions, which still remain in my journal-book, to practise them ever while I lived."[15]

In his rejection of metaphysics in favor of common sense, and of simple but solid values like sincerity, integrity, honesty, humility, and frugality, Junzi remains uncompromising. "Man expands Tao; Tao does not expand Man." "On Humanity, no concession is to be made even to one's master."[16] "Junzi has true faith but is not a partisan; Xiaoren is a partisan but has no true faith."[17] For more than one and a half millennia, Junzi could preserve his rejection of metaphysics and religious doctrine thanks to the secular nature of Eastern culture. Although there were numerous Western philosophers who expressed doubts on religious matters, they were not safe in these opinions, since the mainstream promoted religious dogma and discouraged skepticism. The first British empiricists, such as Thomas Hobbes (1588–1679) and David Hume (1711–1766), among others, were cases in point. Britain during this period was arguably more tolerant than other Western countries in religious matters, perhaps due to its physical and intellectual distance from Rome. Nonetheless, both thinkers were censured for impiety by the Church of England: "From the time of the Restoration [Hobbes] acquired a new prominence; 'Hobbism' became a fashionable creed which it was the duty of 'every lover of true morality and religion' to denounce.... His denial of incorporeal entities led him to write, for example, that Heaven and Hell were places on Earth, and to take other positions out of sync with church teachings of his time.... The king was important in protecting Hobbes when, in 1666, the House of Commons introduced a bill against atheism and profaneness. That same year, on 17 October 1666, it was ordered that the committee to which the bill was referred 'should be empowered to receive information touching such books as tend to atheism, blasphemy, and profaneness ... in particular ... the book of Mr. Hobbes called the Leviathan.' Hobbes was terrified at the prospect of being labeled a heretic, and proceeded to burn some of his compromising papers. At the same time, he examined the actual state of the law of heresy."[18]

Dogma is an important phenomenon in the West. In religion and in ideology as well, as the realm of faith is involved, dogma cannot be explained rationally. But such doctrines existed for the sake of self-preservation; in an expansive environment, one needed any effective means to supports one's own survival and prosperity. This is precisely what Junzi, the product of a circumscribed world, would reject to preserve personal ethical integrity. Now that the West itself has become a circumscribed world like the East, some prominent Western thinkers have been free to question the values of the doctrines that have long constituted the core of Western ethics.

Let us listen, for instance, to Einstein: "We know nothing about God and the world at all. All our knowledge is but the knowledge of schoolchildren. Possibly we shall know a little more than we do now, but the real nature of things, that we shall never know, never."[19] "I do not believe in immortality of the individual, and I consider ethics to be an exclusively human concern with no superhuman authority behind it." "During the youthful period of mankind's spiritual evolution, human fantasy created gods in man's own image, who, by the operations of their will, were supposed to determine, or at any rate to influence, the phenomenal world. Man sought to alter the disposition of these gods in his own favour by means of magic and prayer. The idea of God in the religions taught at present is a sublimation of that old concept of the gods. Its anthropomorphic character is shown, for instance, by the fact that men appeal to the Divine Being in prayers and plead for the fulfillment of their wishes."[20]

With Hobbes, Hume, and Einstein as our background, we can understand more clearly the fundamental tenets of Junzi regarding religious and ideological doctrines. Junzi argues that those doctrines were invented by men for their own interests and were reinforced by the use of the sword. It also warns that the Confucian value of Humanity will eventually be usurped by man for his own benefit. Indeed, many Eastern rulers who were closer to Xiaoren than to Junzi used Confucianism to legitimize their own despotism.[21] More fundamentally, Taoism perceives virtually all cultural concepts, doctrines, and philosophies as constructs to satisfy greed, self-interest, and self-preservation, or else turned later to such ends: "Keep people without knowledge and without desire, and where there are those who have knowledge, keep them from presuming to act. When there is this abstinence from action, good order is universal."[22] Thus Junzi supports the Yin values of flexibility, inertia, and nothingness. Molded in this frame of mind for almost two millennia, Junzi could not possibly be tempted by religious or ideological dogma. Like Franklin, who valued *truth, sincerity*, and *integrity*, Junzi will always focus on how best to put into practice those commonsense values as truth, sincerity, integrity, frugality, humility, friendship, and service to others in life.

Hero vs. Junzi II: Human Nature

As Hero readily accepts divine intervention as the product of Spirit, he acts, consciously or unconsciously, on the premise of Spirit-Body separation; Junzi does not accept such a separation, and he does not recognize the Spirit as an entity separate from the Body. This contrast between the two has a profound impact on their interpretation of human nature. Junzi considers that men would naturally pursue their self-interest and expects that most of them, like Xiaoren, tend to be greedy rather than altruistic.

Self-preservation is usually interpreted very narrowly: that is, in an egoistic sense. But man is a social animal, and in society cooperation is as important as profit-seeking for self-preservation. Similarly, "self-interest" in a narrow sense means pursuing one's own interest against another's. Altruism is ultimately more a biological than moral necessity. As Antonio Damasio observes in *Looking for Spinoza*, "The biological reality of self-preservation leads to virtue, because in our inalienable need to maintain ourselves we must, of necessity, help preserve other selves. If we fail to do so, we perish and are thus violating the foundational principle, and relinquishing the virtue that lies in self-preservation."[23] One finds a similar argument in the classic statement of this in Richard Dawkins's *The Selfish Gene*. Indeed, altruism may have a biological origin: "Our selfish and aggressive urges may have evolved by the Darwinian route of individual advantage, but our altruistic tendencies need not represent a unique overlay imposed by the demands of civilization. These tendencies may have arisen by the same Darwinian route via kin selection. Basic human kindness may be as *animal* as human nastiness."[24]

All great teachers instruct us to follow the same human necessity—altruism—that we find in the *humanity* of Confucius, the *compassion* of Buddha, the *agape* of Christ, and the *brotherly love* of Mohammed. Western democracy implemented enlightened self-interest, by which one looked after the interests of others while tending to one's own, thereby ensuring the long-term interests of all. Again, mere parochial self-interest is harmful to the community and consequently to one's own preservation. The best way to ensure long-term survival is an "enlightened" self-preservation (i.e., altruism).

One essential aspect of altruism is that there is no distinction between us and them. But for religions and ideologies, the "us vs. them" division is paramount—if you accept the doctrines, you are one of us; if you refuse, you are against us. Neither in Taoism nor in Confucianism is there any reference to the pagan, the atheist, the foreigner, or the Other. As we noted in chapter 1, "all within the four seas" and "all under the heavens" includes all of mankind. As the following shows, Confucianism addresses all men without distinction: "Knowing how to cultivate his own character, he knows how to govern other men. Knowing how to govern other men, he knows how to govern the universe with all its states and families."[25] Taoism also embraces the universe beyond a particular nation: "Cultivate virtue in yourself, and it will become a seed; Cultivate it in the family, and it will germinate; Cultivate it in the village, and it will grow; Cultivate it in the nation, and it will prosper; Cultivate it in the universe, and it will be ubiquitous."[26]

If one accepts that self-interest is value neutral (i.e., another expression of self-preservation), then one understands that all the following expressions are identical: "No one wishes to preserve his being for the sake of anything else." "The first and only foundation of virtue, or the rule of right living, is seeking one's own true interest." "Self-interest is altruism." "Men who are governed by reason desire for themselves nothing, which they do not also desire for the rest of mankind." "If you seek to establish yourself, establish others." "If you want profit for yourself, profit others."

Thus, the contrast between East and West lies in their respective notions of human nature, and of the role of altruism. In the East, altruism remains in the realm of ethics as something considered to be attainable only by a few persons of impeccable ethics (i.e., Junzi). Altruism is not to enter the realm of law and institutions, as it is bound to be distorted and usurped by Xiaoren to legitimize his greed. On the contrary, in the West, altruism exists largely in the legal domain: it is attainable by all men, and it is to be applied equally to all men, through laws and institutions.

Hero vs. Junzi III: Ethics

Since Western heroism presupposed the existence of barbarians (the Greco-Roman period) or pagans (the Middle Ages and the modern era), it ultimately reflected a Master ethics. The exploitation and enslavement of weaker groups was the Western norm, which in large measure constituted the *raison d'être* of the Hero. Junzi, on the other hand, was taught to abide by a Universal ethics as expounded in Confucianism and Taoism. We shall examine the characteristics of Cheng Ho and Vasco da Gama, who represented the ideals of Junzi and Hero, respectively.

The Hero thrives on law and force, whereas Junzi operates with ethics. Law requires the sword more than the pen for its enforcement, whereas ethics relies more on the persuasion of the pen. It is clear from history that the expansive West has preferred the sword for its self-preservation, while the circumscribed East has preferred the pen. From this perspective, the Hero represents the sword and Junzi, the pen. It is said in the West that the pen is mightier than the sword. This famous phrase was coined by the English writer Edward Bulwer-Lytton in 1839 for his play

Richelieu; On the Conspiracy.[27] But it must be taken into account that by this time the ancient Western preference for warfare was already being replaced by a new interest in trade—a shift we shall examine in our final chapter. A similar sentiment has been attributed to Euripides, the Old and New Testaments, William Shakespeare, Thomas Jefferson, Napoleon, and so on. Again, they demonstrated the truth that men are swayed more by ideas than by violence, in contrast to the prevailing mainstream trend—with its conspicuous hero worship and preference of the sword to the pen. In the East, since the pen has obviously and always been mightier than the sword, it has gone without saying.

Both Confucianism and Taoism emphasize the primacy of moral force over physical force: the state is to be governed by ethics rather than coercive laws. Both unequivocally stress their preference of the pen to the sword. Here are several quotations: "Those who serve the prince with Tao do not seek to employ force of arms to manage the world, as such employment will certainly be returned in kind." "In the wake of a great army, bad years are sure to follow."[28] "However tempting they appear, weapons are inauspicious instruments. They bring evil to all men. Men of Tao would not employ them." "Swords are inauspicious; Junzi makes no use of them."[29] "There are no righteous wars.... Conquest means nothing but the exploitation by the powerful of the weak."[30] "Junzi is dignified, but not quarrelsome; he is sociable, but not a partisan."[31] "Lying low creates a great nation into which all things flow; thus, a great nation demonstrates humility towards small nations."[32]

Admittedly, the history of China demonstrates periods of trial and tribulation when the sword reigned: the Spring and Autumn Period (722–481 BC), the Warring States Period (481–221 BC), the Disunity Period (200–589), the Mongol rule of the Yuan dynasty

(1271–1368), and the Manchu rule of the Qing dynasty (1644–1911). This constitutes about half of China's history. On the other hand, the remaining half was a time of peace and prosperity ruled by the pen. As China was living in a circumscribed environment, imperial expansion was not an option, which explains the lateness of its conquest of Taiwan in 1683, over seventeen centuries later than Caesar's conquest of Britain. Under these circumstances, it is no wonder that China should prefer the pen to the sword, and that Junzi should be a man of ethics, not of force.

In the West, there were of course many thinkers who preferred persuasion and ethics to the sword, but they had less impact on history than generals, kings, and conquerors. By contrast, Eastern military heroes had less impact on their history than scholars and thinkers like Confucius, or the scholar-officials of the official government. While Western culture revered its warriors, officers in the East had less prestige than scholar-officials. As the sword was considered inauspicious, the military class was not even represented in the traditional four occupations: scholar, farmer, craftsman, and merchant. Eventually, the military class had to learn not only the arts of the sword, but those of the pen in order to be respected in society. Thus, most military commanders were well versed in the Confucian canons.

The non-militarism of Confucianism was reinforced by the non-interventionism of Taoism. Taoism counsels the value of a laissez-faire attitude—that is, making most of the present situation rather than actively trying to change it, which was the philosophy of Wuwei. We have already examined Eastern Yin vs. Western Yang characteristics. In a culture where Yin values were actively pursued, the sword naturally lost its significance. Taoism counsels man to follow nonviolent paths: "Giving birth and nourishing, bearing yet not possessing, working yet not taking credit, leading yet not dominating—this is the Virtue."[33] On the other hand, the West could not afford to value Yin attitudes, as it had to use the "rule of force," especially in regard to other nations. It is interesting to observe that the West now increasingly stresses the importance of "soft power," like the traditional Eastern Yin power, as opposed to its own military force, which projects national as well as individual power and prestige.

The following are ethical examples in the *Taoteking* that characterize Junzi's soft power: "In caring for others and serving Heaven, there is nothing like using restraint; restraint begins with giving up one's own desires"[34]; "Why is the sea the mother of a hundred streams? Because it lies below them ... When a sage guides the people, he serves with humility ... As he does not compete, he does not meet competition"[35]; "Three treasures I hold and keep. The first is benevolence; the second is frugality; the third is humility. From benevolence comes courage; from frugality comes generosity; from humility comes leadership"[36]; "A man is born gentle and weak. At his death he is hard and stiff. Green plants are tender and filled with sap. At their death they are withered and dry. Therefore the stiff and unbending is the disciple of death. The gentle and yielding is the disciple of life. Thus an army without flexibility never wins a battle. A tree that is unbending is easily broken. The hard and strong will fall. The soft and weak will prevail."[37]

One problem now facing the West is the lack of a role model to replace the Hero. As the West no longer believes in barbarians or pagans, there is little room for heroism in the traditional sense. One ancient ideal that may suffice is that of the Good Samaritan, which is grounded in Universal ethics—but the West may demand a more active role model, and this it may find in the Rich Man or Celebrity. It seems that the West is now readier to accept wealth and fame than universal charity as goals. In fact, it is not altogether an exaggeration to argue that today in the West, the young generation is conditioned to become rich and famous as opposed to Good Samaritans on the Christian model, or what we may call Junzi. Is the East different? Can it maintain Junzi as the role model in our era of a largely free market political economy?

Hero vs. Junzi IV: Politics

Let us pick up where Junzi assumed that the multitudes, as Xiaoren, would pursue greed. Under the circumstances, Junzi realizes that he must act altruistically if he intends to become the leader. And Junzi does not consider his altruism as a sacrifice; he does it for his own self-interest as a pleasure. In sum, altruism becomes self-interest for Junzi and sacrifice for Xiaoren. On the other hand, for the Western Hero to sacrifice his self-interest for self-preservation is regarded as sinful in the West.

Confucius established the primacy of virtue over blood nobility: this revolutionary concept was incarnated in Junzi. Even a person of noble birth is Xiaoren if he lacks virtue; likewise, even a poor or ignoble person is Junzi if he attains virtue. Junzi is to aim solely for self-fulfillment without expecting any other recognition or reward. Albert Einstein remarked: "If people are good only because they fear punishment, and hope for reward, then we are a sorry lot indeed."[38] So in the East: "Junzi is distressed by his want of ability; he is not distressed by his lack of recognition by others."[39] "What Junzi seeks is in himself; what Xiaoren seeks is in others."[40] "Junzi makes overcoming the difficulty his first priority; he makes success only a secondary consideration."[41] "To good, I respond with good; to evil, I also respond with good; this way, goodness prevails. To sincerity, I respond with sincerity; to insincerity, I also respond with sincerity; this way, sincerity prevails."[42] "The sage does not have his own mind; he makes the mind of the people his mind."[43] "Therefore the sage acts without claiming results as his; he achieves merit but does not dwell on it: he does not wish to display his superiority."[44]

As we have seen, the Western duality between Charity and Faith constituted a practical ethical dilemma, but since Love was the single ultimate value in the East, there was no such dilemma. According to Confucius, faith did not rule man, but rather man ruled faith. This was a very different conclusion from that of Christianity; Man is justified by his Faith and not by his deeds. Although this is specifically a Protestant position, not so much a Catholic one, where "good works" count, religion as an institution generally tends to emphasize faith as much as, if not more than, good works. Faith expects divine recognition, if not the reward of Heaven. But Junzi, who believes in no anthropomorphic God but rather in a Tao or Nature indifferent to human affairs, cannot possibly act in the hope of divine reward or recognition. He may receive recognition from others, but at the same time he knows that this recognition is not important, lest his virtue be conditional.

Thus, for Junzi, Love and Faith become one and the same ethical standard. The perplexity of Western enlightenment thinkers—whether an ethical system is possible without divine revelation—is thus resolved and clarified by the secular ethics of Junzi. The same question had been asked by Plato in his *Euthyphro*: is something good because God wills it, or does God will it because it is good? Yet already with Plato, the concept of God had become the sine qua non of Western thought. Indeed, this constitutes the cardinal difference between Junzi and Hero. The true question for Junzi must rather be whether a Universal ethics is compatible with religious or ideological dogma: Junzi would readily accept that the true teaching of Jesus was a Universal ethics, rather than a dogma. For Junzi, such responsive Eastern values as Humanity, Tao, Virtue, sincerity, and propriety held the same place as Western religious doctrines like the Trinity, Biblical inerrancy, heaven and hell, and the Creation. Violating humanity, Tao, or sincerity was just as grave in the East as doubting the Trinity was in the West—although the retribution in the East was one of moral condemnation rather than excommunication or inquisition.

International Politics: Hegemon-King vs. Hero-Conqueror

We briefly introduced Xun Zi's concept of the Hegemon-king in chapter 3. When Xun Zi argued for the potential benefit of a Hegemon-king, it was based on historical reality in contrast to the Confucian ideal of the benevolent king. During the Spring and Autumn Period, five Hegemon-kings had emerged.[45] To the two kinds of Confucian kings, "ordinary" and "benevolent," Xun Zi added a third—the "Hegemon-king"—between the two. This Hegemon-king is often compared to what we might call a "Machiavellian" king. Let us examine the differences between these.

The Confucian Benevolent-king is different from Plato's philosopher-king in that his aim is simply to rule with benevolence. Plato's concept of the philosopher-king embodies an ideal that most ordinary people cannot see or understand. Once freed from the darkness of ignorance and illusion—symbolized in his famous parable of the cave—the philosopher can glimpse the truth of the world and act accordingly. He thus becomes qualitatively different from the multitude. He then returns to the cave—to the world of ordinary men, albeit reluctantly, in order to govern them. But according to Confucius, the people do not see illusions. What they see is as true as what the king sees. It is only that they are not in control of what he sees. This is what makes the Benevolent-king a leader. The Confucian king already has a goal to attain, whereas Plato's king establishes his own goal. Confucius therefore denies the personal transformation inherent in Plato's model.

Although Xun Zi emphatically stressed the importance of the Benevolent-king, it is evident that this concept remained an ideal for him. His aim in presenting three types of kings was to demonstrate the realistic benefit that people and nations could draw from the Hegemon-king, rather than pursuing the illusive concept of the Benevolent-king.

Xun Zi's Hegemon-king was different from Hobbes's *Leviathan*: the latter was presented as the best possible ruler under social contract with his subjects with a view to avoiding a "war of all against all" in which human life would be "solitary, poor, nasty, brutish, and short." Xun Zi's Hegemon-king was far from being absolute, since he was bound by the ethical norms laid out by Confucianism. Although the Hegemon-king would replace a Benevolent-king for practical purposes, he was simply the second best model, as Xun Zi reiterates. The Hegemon-king is supposed to be bound to his subject by ethical norms, like a father to his family, and more importantly for us, he is to abide by certain cardinal ethical rules, such as trustworthiness, in dealing with other kings.

Xun Zi's third class of king is comparable to Cesare Borgia, who served as model for Machiavelli. Both value military force, trickery, and deception, with a view to ensuring victory, and pay little attention to ethics, since they view it as an impediment to effectiveness. But there is an important difference. Xun Zi's model has more to do with international politics than with national security. For Xun Zi, the third king was to the second as Xiaoren was to Junzi, since the third had to impose his will by force and deceit. This kind of king, according to Xun Zi, may succeed at first, but would ultimately fail to secure the respect of other kings and consequently lose his kingdom. It was a mistake, Xun Zi reasoned, to ignore ethics for the purpose of short-term victory. Such an approach would work in an expansive environment, as victory produces leadership, but fails in a circumscribed environment, since leadership also depends on ethics and mutual respect.

The Hegemon-king may be usefully compared to the West's hero-conqueror. The two differ in that the former was supposed to lead other nations by example, the latter by physical domination. There was only room in the West for a Master ethics: as a result, the older West has little in common with today's circumscribed world in which nations must coexist peacefully under a Universal ethics. The difference between the Eastern Hegemon-king and the Western Hero-Conqueror lies in whether an explicit consent of others is necessary for his leadership. This contrast was manifest in the international congresses between East and West. During the five Hegemon-kings period, a Hegemon-king did regularly convene international congresses. The objective was to secure the consent of the other kings for his leadership, which he was committed to exercise with circumspection for the benefit of all nations involved. He loses his mandate when he no longer enjoys their explicit consent. The Western international congresses, such as Westphalia, Utrecht, Vienna, and Paris, on the other hand, were convened to ensure post-war peace and stability with a treaty in which the participating nations were bound on equal terms. They did not aim for the consecration of an international leadership for a nation.

Today's world needs a leadership among nations, and so the Hegemon-king concept is worth reviewing. Inherent in this Eastern concept is the provision of assistance to other nations crucially lacking in the traditional Western treaty system, which is geared more toward exploitation. The concept of the Eastern tribute system was inherent in Xun Zi's theory of the Hegemon-king, in that both suzerain and king were supposed to "buy" allegiance from their client states (i.e., offer material incentives in exchange for allegiance). The relevance of these two concepts to the contemporary world is evident in the case of the Soviet alliance system, in which Moscow offered material incentives to its satellite states in exchange for their adherence to communism. The current economic assistance given by developed countries to the developing world follows a similar concept: aid is given more generously to those countries that accept such Western paradigms as democracy, human rights, good governance, and so forth.

Characters: Western Yang vs. Eastern Yin

It will be helpful here to expand our two core concepts—unity-harmony, embodied in Eastern Junzi, and separation-liberty, embodied in the Western Hero—into a broader range of attributes, attitudes, and behaviors. In the expansive, maritime Western environment, such Yang attributes as assertiveness, exclusivity, activism, dynamism, dialectic, instruction, extroversion, and analytical prevailed. In the West, Yang characteristics dominate the relationship between Man and Man, leading to the assertion of self, that is, of individuality over the group. These traits dominate the foundations of Western law and represent the Hero as ideal.

By contrast, in the circumscribed, continental East, the predominant qualities are such Yin attributes as receptivity, inclusivity, laissez-faire, equanimity, integration, suggestion, introversion, and synthetic. Here, relationships with others take precedence over the assertion of self and lay the foundations for a society built on ethics rather than law. We shall compare Junzi and Hero from an ethical point of view in chapter 7. In this chapter, we shall focus on a contrast of cultural traits. Indeed, our comparison between Junzi and Hero can also be applied to other pairings—Universal ethics vs. Master ethics; Good Samaritan vs. Crusader; Sage vs. Prophet; ethics vs. law; Harmony vs. Freedom; Yin vs. Yang. The last of these is perhaps the best pair, since the terms are value-neutral and universal in application.

1. Receptivity vs. Assertiveness

Junzi is receptive; Hero is assertive. Junzi is a man of ethics, whereas Hero is man of law and force, which requires him to be assertive. A culture of ethics naturally recommends receptivity, whereas a culture of law encourages assertiveness. Indeed, both

Taoism and Confucianism extol the former quality, while Western religion prizes assertiveness and ordains aggressive proselytism. Western thought stresses the importance of being assertive: "You are the light of the world ... you give light to everyone in the house" and "You are the salt; if the salt loses its taste, how can you make your food seasoned?" We find the exact opposite in the Taoist emphasis on receptivity: "Mud is used to make celadon, but it is the emptiness of the celadon that becomes useful" and "Doors and windows are used to make rooms, but it is the emptiness of the room that becomes useful."[46]

Receptivity gives rise to societies that are flexible but not proactive: "Under heaven nothing is more soft and yielding than water. Yet for attacking the solid and strong, it has no equal. The weak can overcome the strong; the supple can overcome the stiff."[47] Again, these two attitudes exist in contrast as Yin to Yang; as such, one is no better or worse than the other. They are simply relevant or irrelevant according to the environmental context in which a given population lives and acts.

This receptive vs. assertive contrast manifests itself even in everyday dialogue. In the East, the capacity to listen to others is stressed and valued, whereas in the West, the right to speak and express oneself is emphasized and prized.

2. Inclusivity vs. Exclusivity

There are exceptions among Western heroes—for example, Winston Churchill and the American leadership after World Wars I and II—who demonstrated magnanimity toward those they defeated. But, in general, one can say that Western heroes acted to exclude their opponents, whereas Junzi was inclusive, abiding by Universal ethics. In a circumscribed context, exclusion of others makes no sense, as it would lead to unproductive conflicts and frictions. It is necessary to maintain an inclusive attitude toward others for one's own self-preservation and self-interest. But in an expansive context, one must constantly venture into the unknown. For self-preservation, a division between us and them is inevitable. While the East has usually found it easy to accept and absorb foreign teachings, the West, especially with respect to religion, has shown a consistent tendency toward exclusion.

To reiterate a point already made, Taoism plays a Yin role and Confucianism a Yang role in life. When one engages in public life, one follows Confucianism; in private life, one tends to follow Taoism. Buddhism became the Tang dynasty's (ca. AD 618–907) official religion, but this in no way impeded the dynasty's introduction of an examination system based on the Confucian canon. Thus, H.G. Wells depicted the characteristic Eastern tolerance: "Muhammad sent an embassy by sea to Tang in 628 with 'The Prophet of God' message, which was most probably identical to the ones sent to the Byzantine Emperor Heraclius and to Kavadh in Ctesiphon.… But the Chinese monarch neither neglected the message as Heraclius did, nor insulted the envoys after the fashion of the parricide Kavadh. He received them well, expressed great interest in their theological views, and helped them, it is said, to build a mosque for the Arab traders in Canton—a mosque which survives to this day. It is one of the oldest mosques in the world."[48]

3. Laissez-Faire vs. Activism

It is obvious that a laissez-faire attitude will never lead to heroism, for the hero must be active. On the other hand, Junzi's first principle of action is non-intervention, unless faced with a violation against humanity. The starting point for Eastern ethics was the identification of desire as the main cause of trouble in society. Man acts most of the time to fulfill his own desires; these actions necessarily clash with those of others. Therefore, being non-interventionist and patient contributes more effectively to an Eastern ethics than being active. But in the expansionist world of rule by law, activism prevails. The Western golden rule encourages an active stance—"Act as ye would that men should do to you, do ye also to them likewise."[49] The Eastern version of this rule is weighted toward passivity. In the words of Confucius: "Do not do unto others what you do not want others to do unto you."[50] Taoism and Confucianism both constantly warn against excessive action or aggression. Lao Tzu wrote, "Yield and overcome; bend and be straight; empty and be full; wear out and be new; have little and gain; have much and be confused."[51] He also wrote, "The brave and passionate will kill or be killed; the brave and calm will always preserve life.... Tao does not strive, and yet it overcomes. It does not speak and yet is answered; it does not ask and yet is supplied with all its needs; it seems to have no aim and yet its purpose is fulfilled."[52]

Certainly, both the Bible and Taoism recommend humility as well as concession, and also offer consolation. The Bible preaches: "Blessed are the poor in spirit.... Blessed are they that mourn.... Blessed are the meek.... Blessed are ye, when men shall revile you, and persecute you."[53] Taoism proposes, "Accept disgrace with grace; do not be concerned with loss or gain. Accept misfortune as the human condition, misfortune comes from being human.... Surrender yourself humbly; then you can be trusted to care for all things. Love the world as your own self; then you can truly care for all things."[54] In the West, however, along with humility and concession, an active attitude is frequently stressed. The Bible, for instance, emphasizes activism by the parables of the seed and the leaven: to be and act like a seed yielding crops a hundredfold and like the leaven that is enough for three measures of meal.[55]

Again, both Taoism and the Bible recommend wariness of material wealth. But the Bible goes one step further in counseling an active attitude. Taoism suggests simple passivism: "Amass gold and jade, and no one can protect it: Claim wealth and titles, and disaster will follow."[56] The Bible emphasizes activism: "Lay not up for yourselves treasures upon earth, where moth and rust doth corrupt, and where thieves break through and steal: But lay up for yourselves treasures in heaven, where neither moth nor rust doth corrupt, and where thieves do not break through nor steal."[57]

4. Equanimity vs. Dynamism

Junzi is equanimous; Hero is dynamic. Eastern culture promotes reflection, caution, consideration of others, long-term consequences, inner peace, and group harmony rather than individual liberty. On the other hand, Western culture promotes action, audacity, self-assertion, short-term results, tangible achievements, and liberty over harmony. These promote individual and national dynamism.

Separation produces competitive dynamism between individuals; unity promotes holism, which in turn gives rise to equanimity. Both God and Tao are eternal, but whereas God is absolute, Tao is not. Tao remains ineffable and refuses any absolute definition. God, by contrast, makes his vicar the one who lays down acceptable definitions. As a consequence, assertion and absolutism, along with a sense of mission, underpin Western civilization, while harmony and inertia, along with a sense of equanimity, underpin Eastern civilization.

Taoism encouraged equanimity, whereas Christianity cultivated activism and absolutism. Consider the words of the Bible: "Whosoever therefore shall confess me before men, him will I confess also before my Father which is in heaven. But whosoever shall deny me before men, him will I also deny before my Father which is in heaven"[58]; "And if thy right eye offend thee, pluck it out, and cast it from thee.... And if thy right hand offend thee, cut if off, and cast it from thee: for it is profitable for thee that one of thy members should perish, and not that thy whole body should be cast into hell."[59] Consequently, in the West, all religious sects and ideologies claim to be the custodians of absolute truth.

Indeed, religious tolerance in the East stands in striking contrast to Western intolerance. For example, the religious war between Catholics and Protestants consumed much of Europe in the sixteenth century, culminating in the Thirty Years' War. But it was precisely during this period of savage sectarian conflict in the West that the Chinese Emperor Kangxi (康熙) proclaimed his "Toleration Edict" (1692), which allowed incoming Europeans to practice Christianity freely.[60]

5. Integral vs. Dialectic

Heroic action reflects a dialectic evolution and progress, whereas Junzi's action is based on integral transformation. As we have seen, the Eastern world was physically circumscribed within a central plain, and so an integral attitude was naturally accepted without alternative: "If Tao is just, to what does the unjust belong? If Tao is good, to what does the bad belong? Tao is the blessing of the just and the protection of the unjust."[61] Since Tao is essentially Nature, it must be all-inclusive. Again, the Western God followed a different path; since He is proclaimed exclusivity as the God of Justice, much time and energy has been spent in the West attempting to solve the intractable problems of injustice and evil. On the other hand, the dynamism generated by Western dialectics was instrumental in the growth of law, personal liberty, and eventually the institution of democracy.

The cardinal Confucian teaching is "to love mankind," and that of Christianity is "to love thy neighbor as thyself." In essence, they are identical, yet because of the Western tendency toward individuation, the Christian lesson is also fractionalized: *Love thy neighbor* versus *Love thy self.* During the Reformation, for example, the Calvinists put such an emphasis on "love thy neighbor" that "loving oneself" was regarded as a sin. The Calvinists forbade laughing, having fun, singing anything other than religious songs, and wearing anything other than dark clothes. Kant also believed that loving oneself had no ethical value and advocated loving only one's neighbor. But an Eastern mind would question whether one could truly love one's neighbor without loving oneself. Each culture, ultimately, got what it wanted: the East, social harmony; the West, individual freedom. What outcome will follow from the interaction between the two?

The attitude of integration encourages human relationships, whereas that of dialectics emphasizes personal individuality. The East normally moves from the general to the individual case, whereas the West moves from the specific to the general. In the West, for instance, one is taught to write one's name first, then the street, city, and finally the state where one lives. In the East, one starts with the state, followed by the city, street, and finally one's name. Even in writing one's name, the West gives priority to the given name, and then writes the family name; in the East, one writes one's family name first, then the given name. In reference to chronology, the West starts with the day or month, then the year; the East starts with year, then month, and finally the day.

6. Suggestion vs. Instruction

Junzi prefers suggestive manners; Hero instructs and orders. Universal ethics operates better with persuasion, whereas a Master ethics prefers instruction. Taoism recommends: "Cultivate virtue in yourself, and it will become a seed; Cultivate it in the family, and it will germinate; Cultivate it in the village, and it will grow; Cultivate it in the nation, and it will prosper; Cultivate it in the universe, and it will be ubiquitous."[62]

By contrast, Christianity proselytizes in an emphatic way: "Think not that I am come to send peace on earth: I came not to send peace, but a sword. For I am come to set a man at variance against his father, and the daughter against her mother, and the daughter-in-law against her mother-in-law. And a man's foes shall be they of his own household. He that loveth father or mother more than me is not worthy of me: and he that loveth son or daughter more than me is not worthy of me. And he that taketh not his cross, and followeth after me, is not worthy of me."[63]

The tension and urgency behind these statements stand in evident contrast to the relaxed manner of Confucianism. Consider the start of *The Analects*: "Isn't it a delight to learn and put into practice; isn't it a pleasure to have a friend come from afar?"[64] To emphasize its teachings, the West does not hesitate to issue extreme warnings: "So shall it be in the end of this world. The Son of man shall send forth his angels, and they shall gather out of his kingdom all things that offend, and them which do iniquity; and shall cast them into a furnace of fire: there shall be wailing and gnashing of teeth."[65] Because the East's way of teaching is by suggestion and persuasion, warnings and threats are conspicuously absent in both Taoism and Confucianism.

7. Introversion vs. Extroversion

Junzi focuses on domestic management; Hero focuses on outward actions. Extroversion is one of the essential characteristics of the expansive West. With its faith in progress, the West expanded into unknown territories, ceaselessly moving outwards. By contrast, Eastern culture always looks for causes within and praises introversion as a virtue. Taoism suggests, "Knowing others is wisdom; knowing oneself is enlightenment. Mastering others requires force; mastering oneself requires confidence."[66] Also, when encountering problems or difficulties, an Easterner first tries to find the cause within, whereas a Westerner first tries to find the cause without. The patterns of expansion shown by today's corporations generally demonstrate the same contrast, which is evidence of the pervasive differences between the two cultures—a Western corporation first becomes a multinational by doing the same business in many countries, whereas an Eastern corporation first becomes a multi-business inside one's own country, encompassing diverse manufacturing and services. As we know, much American industry followed a vertical integration strategy at the turn of the century; "robber-barons" were typical examples of such a Western mode of expansion.

We can describe the same pair in different terms as centripetal (Eastern) and centrifugal (Western); these two motions are manifested even in small, everyday settings. Let us analyze, for instance, how the two cultures use a spoon to eat soup: in the West, one is taught to move one's spoon from inside the bowl to the outside of the rim, whereas an Easterner will do the reverse. Another example is found when we use our fingers to count: an Easterner will fold his fingers in sequence when counting from one to five, while a Westerner is taught to count by unfolding his fingers one after another. These are not simple differences of etiquette; rather, they denote deeper cultural contrasts. Eastern countries achieved self-preservation by centripetal motion while the West achieved success by centrifugal movement (e.g., expansion and conquest). Few Eastern countries sought expansion or conquest, and consequently most remain where they have always been. Admittedly, the early Tang dynasty and twentieth-century Imperial Japan—leaving aside the ill-fated Japanese misadventure under Toyotomi Hideyoshi in the late sixteenth century—are exceptions. China's aggrandizement is more the result of centripetal attraction than centrifugal expansion. To give two prime examples, both the Mongols and Manchus conquered China but were finally absorbed by it, resulting in an expansion of Chinese territory. Taoism says: "He who acts defeats his own purpose; he who grasps loses. The sage does not act; so is not defeated. He does not grasp; therefore does not lose.... This is called marching without appearing to move; rolling up your sleeves without showing your arm; capturing the enemy without attacking; being armed without weapons."[67]

This introversion vs. extroversion contrast manifests itself in sports. All the Eastern martial arts, such as Judo, Taekwondo, and Kungfu aim at promoting self-control, self-discipline, and self-defense, whereas the Western sports from the "Greek-Roman gladiator fighting" to later sports like boxing and wrestling all aim at victory and showing superiority or winning over the adversary.

8. Synthetic vs. Analytical

This Yin-Yang contrast is more pertinent to the comparison between Junzi and Western non-military heroes (e.g., theologians, metaphysicians, and prophets), than to that between Junzi and military heroes. As Eastern culture is grounded in unity, it tends to retain a synthetic perspective with regard to nature and within the self. The books of Taoism and Confucianism are essentially collections of aphorisms and therefore lack logic and analytical reasoning. But wisdom is transmitted more effectively by synthesis than by analysis. Thus, although Eastern aphorisms may seem vague, ambivalent, or even contradictory, they nonetheless function effectively within their cultural context. Analysis, by contrast, focuses on individual facts or concepts, but runs the risk of lacking perspective and a sense of the whole. The Western separation of Nature, Mind, and Body is an excellent example of these habits.

Eastern culture relies on intuition as much as reasoning. Given its attempts to find interconnectedness in everything, it focuses on the bonds that exist between individuals. Thus, in Eastern society, human relationships are governed by tacit understanding rather than explicit explanations. What one has to learn in handling such human relationships is not so much knowledge as wisdom. Unlike knowledge, which can be taught gradually, wisdom can only be learned by a personal process of understanding. Generally, wisdom is not fully expressible in words, but is gained through enlightenment, which occurs with a "leap" in mental processing, not by a steady accumulation of facts. Such learning requires intuition.

Since Eastern education focuses on wisdom, its pedagogical methods are those of indirect suggestion, leaving it up to the students to reach their own understanding. Likewise, aphorisms are the preferred way of transmitting wisdom, which makes the translation of Eastern classics so difficult for Westerners, who are accustomed to analytical language. One can *teach* knowledge; one can only *learn* wisdom. Confucianism claims that "I can only instruct the eager and enlighten the fervent. If I hold up one corner and a student cannot come back to me with the other three, I cannot go on with the lesson." Intuition does not come gradually, but rather follows the mechanism of "critical mass." One accumulates facts, concepts, and knowledge; this accumulation goes through a process of internal reflection; this reflection, in combination with observations and feelings, reaches a critical mass, which, in a flash of insight, leads one to understanding and enlightenment. On the other hand, the West relies on the intellect to accumulate knowledge, which will enable the student to achieve progress or attain victory. Once again, knowledge is more useful for self-preservation in an expansive world, whereas wisdom is valued as the path to self-preservation in a circumscribed one.

Science: Yin and Yang Traits

We have examined eight pairs of Yin-Yang traits. What does science say about these traits? For two millennia, Western science adhered strictly to Yang, with the absolutism and certainty embodied in the work of Euclid and Newton. Mankind appeared to be on the verge of breakthrough, thanks to its God-given capacity for reason. Such Yang traits as certainty, activism, absolutism, and assertiveness were at their heights.

But in the twentieth century, Western scientists found the older models incomplete: Euclidean geometry was only appropriate to local areas of a curving space-time, and Newtonian physics only applicable to objects of an everyday scale, or moving at a limited velocity. Albert Einstein (1879–1955) introduced the notion of relativity, bringing together Time and Space as relative, not absolute phenomena, and demonstrating the equivalence of matter and energy in his famous equation, $E = mc^2$.

Likewise, quantum physicists disproved the ancient maxim that "Nature does not make leaps," since they discovered "quantum leaps," for instance in the energy levels of bound electrons. Before the quantum breakthrough, scientists and metaphysicians took for granted the principle *Natura non facit saltum*, meaning "nature does not make leaps." But modern scientists abandoned this doctrine when they discovered that electrons do actually make "quantum leaps" between a "ground state" and an "excited state." The development of a new form of light, the laser, was made possible by this new discovery.

Fig. 5-5. Coat-of-Arms of Niels Bohr (1885–1962)
http://en.wikipedia.org/wiki/File:Coat_of_Arms_of_Niels_Bohr.svg

Niels Bohr's complementarity principle (Niels Henrik David Bohr, 1885–1962) rejects conflict and exclusion, and instead embraces harmony and inclusion. Likewise, Heisenberg's uncertainty principle (Werner Karl Heisenberg, 1901–1976) accepts probability, randomness, and chance. Bohr employed the Eastern Yin-Yang diagram in his personal coat of arms, with the motto *Contraria sunt complementa*, meaning "Opposites are complementary." The West has long interpreted opposites as contradictory, but now its leading scientists believe that they are complementary.

The journey of science over the last two centuries appears as tumultuous and revolutionary as the journey of Western philosophy through the crucible of the Age of Ideologies. Now, as science and technology progress at breakneck speed, we find that the domain of our uncertainty is only increasing. We therefore must accept both Yin and Yang traits—Euclidian geometry and Newtonian physics, as well as relativity and quantum uncertainty.

CHAPTER 6

Culture:
Western Religion vs. Eastern Education

"Destruction of the enemy forces is always the superior, more effective means, with which others cannot compete."[1]

Carl von Clausewitz

"Taking the enemy nation intact is best; destroying it is only second best.... To subjugate the enemy's army without engaging in battle is the highest excellence."[2]

Sun Tzu

272 • Y. J. Choi

Religion vs. Education

In the formation of Western and Eastern ideals, religion and education were pivotal. Even though Western religion produced the model of the good Christian, it also contributed to hero worship in the West. Let us compare the character and philosophy of Christian and Hero in the West with those of Junzi in the East.

AD 380 in the West vs. AD 608 in the East

The historic importance of the year 380 for the West is well known to most of us, for this was the year when the Roman Emperor Theodosius proclaimed Christianity as the state religion. Since then, for more than one and a half millennia, the West has been under the overwhelming influence of the Christian religion: "Nor was the influence of Christianity confined to the period or to the limits of the Roman Empire. After a revolution of thirteen or fourteen centuries, that religion is still professed by the nations of Europe, the most distinguished portion of human kind in arts and learning as well as in arms. By the industry and zeal of the Europeans, it has been widely diffused to the most distant shores of Asia and Africa; and by the means of their colonies has been firmly established from Canada to Chile, in a world unknown to the ancients."[3]

It was only with the Enlightenment that Western culture began to lose its deeply religious nature, turning instead toward secularity. During this period, the Western ideal was the good Christian, and his opposite was the pagan or heathen, whom Western explorers encountered and conquered in their global expansions.

The significance of AD 605 in the East is quite comparable to that of AD 380 in the West. This was the year when the Imperial

Examination System (Keju, 科ㄷ) was formally established by Emperor Yang (隋煬帝, 569–618) of the Sui dynasty. Ever since, the meritocratic examination system, with its extraordinary emphasis on education, has undergirded Eastern civilization.

The Imperial Examination does not consist of simple tests to select government officials. Rather, it comprises a complex cultural, social, and political phenomenon unique to the East; it became the de facto education system for the entire nation. Anyone who completed the examination, regardless of birth or rank, could become a high government official and attain honor and wealth for himself and his family. As we shall see, the entire Eastern intellectual world revolved around this enduring institution in the same way that the West revolved around Christianity.

Fig. 6-1. Saint Ambrose and Emperor Theodosius (346–395)
(http://en.wikipedia.org/wiki/
File:Anthonis_van_Dyck_005.jpg)

Fig. 6-2. Emperor Yang of Sui Dynasty (隋煬帝, 569–618)
(http://en.wikipedia.org/wiki/
File:Sui-yangdi.jpg)

Imperial Examination System

The rudiments of the system are dated as early as 165 BC during the Han dynasty (206 BC–AD 220), when certain candidates for public office were called to the examination by the emperor.[4] From this period on, for many centuries, the imperial examinations continued, intermittently, to evolve and be refined. By the second century AD, the first formal curriculum had been adopted. This system took a dramatic step forward in the year 605, thanks to Emperor Yang; it became an official state examination system for the entire Chinese population. These Sui examinations are regarded by most historians as the first standardized tests of merit in human history.[5]

The need for this epoch-making decision was self-evident, given the inward-looking and centrifugal nature of state management. Lacking any motivation or ambition for territorial expansion, domestic administration was the ruler's primary concern. For this task, he required a vast number of literate civil servants; this marked the origin of the mandarins. Something very similar can be seen in the development of European universities around AD 1200, when the bureaucracies of the Papacy and state governments became far stronger and more formalized, and literacy rapidly increased. The crucial difference is that bureaucracy coexisted with nobility in the West, whereas in the East, the one replaced the other. This Imperial Examination System spread to other Eastern countries in the tenth century.[6] The Eastern examination system was introduced to India during the eighteenth century, and even to the West during the nineteenth century, although its application was limited.

After many changes and adaptations, the practice has continued to flourish in the East, even today. The imperial examinations have now become state examinations, as they are no longer conducted in the emperor's presence. But the system's essential basis in merit has remained intact. The system went through many different stages and changes, and so it can be defined by no single template. However, a typical Imperial Examination System would consist of two groups of tests: the preliminaries were open to all and offered at the local level each year; the main exams, open to those who passed the preliminaries, and administered every three years, consisted in turn of three stages.

As the system was consolidated, each degree of accomplishment was given a distinctive title. One who passed the preliminaries was called "Talented Person" (Xiucai, 秀才 or Shengyuan, 生員); one who passed the first stage of the main exams was titled "Recommended Person" (Juren, 舉人); anyone who passed the second was a "Consigned Scholar" (Gongshi, 貢士); and a person who passed the final stage became a "Presented Scholar" (Jinshi, 進士).

The final stage was conducted in the presence of the emperor himself. Among those who completed the final exam, there were a further three degrees of achievement, each titled according to his state position: the first was only awarded to three individuals, the very highest of whom was named "Exemplar of the Empire" (Zhuangyuan, 狀元), and upon whom was bestowed many honors, including an imperial banquet. He became a national hero and achieved great glory and fortune for himself, his family, and home town. But even those achieving second and third degrees at the final exam were guaranteed a high post in the imperial government. Many went on to become ministers and even prime ministers.

Eastern Literati vs. Western Gentry

Printing technology spread books and curricular materials to an ever-wider population: "The enhancement of widespread printing and print culture in the Song period was thus a direct catalyst in the rise of social mobility and expansion of the educated class of scholar elites, the latter which expanded dramatically in size from the eleventh to thirteenth centuries."[7] By this time the examination system became virtually the only means of recruiting government officials. Officials were classified according to nine hierarchical grades, with each grade divided into two degrees. This classification survived for centuries. Their remuneration was measured in rice.

Fig. 6-3. Western Gentry	**Fig. 6-4. Eastern Literati**
Richard Brathwait's *The Complete English Gentleman* (1630) showing the exemplary qualities of a gentleman (http://en.wikipedia.org/wiki/Gentlemen)	The Imperial Examinations Candidates gathering around the wall where the results are posted, 1540 (http://en.wikipedia.org/wiki/Qiu_Ying)

During the Ming dynasty, which lasted 276 years, ninety palace examinations took place; these produced over 24,000 Presented Scholars—around 300 per exam, or 3,000 per generation, that is, about one in ten thousand candidates. In the same period there were 100,000 Talented Scholars, or one in 300 candidates.[8] This system created the network of scholar-officials who finally replaced the traditional aristocracy. These officials, along with the other candidates, tutors, and retired officials, comprised the vast intellectual foundation of Eastern society. A group of literati was thus formed, supporting the empire with its own system of ethics, quite different from the Western basis of law. This core scholarly group has invariably been translated as "gentry," apparently to facilitate understanding in the West. But the word "literati" is more accurate, since these men were honored more for their grades than for their ownership of land. Many remained poor but upheld their pride and dignity by their scholarly accomplishments. However, this group replaced the land-owning nobility and so can be compared to the Western aristocracy in terms of its function within society.

Once secured, an individual retained his title of Talented Person, Recommended Person, Consigned Scholar, or Presented Scholar for life. This is completely different from the Western class system, being much more like qualifications of academic merit, with the additional premium of a high office in the national government. By ensuring that the examinations were based solely on merit, the government could select the best and brightest talents in its service, ensure the loyalty of the local elites, whose sons all competed for success, and maintain cultural and social unity throughout the country. Although only a small fraction of candidates were successful, the great reward encouraged all to apply.[9] In other words, the entire population was involved in the system. Even today, in the East, the year revolves around the entrance examinations to high schools and colleges, and the state examinations. It is now the same in the West.

Figure 6-4 depicts a scene in which a multitude of candidates are gathered to learn the result of their examination. For thousands of years, the results were published in the form of a roll unfolded and attached to a wall. This scene was arguably the most important national event—annually for the preliminary and triennially for the main examinations. A provincial examination place would have a permanent building with a capacity of 7,500 individual cells for the preliminaries. This image helps us to imagine the significance of the examination system for Eastern civilization.

Christian vs. Junzi

All of this education in the East was geared toward an ideal: Junzi. This concept is crucial to our overall comparison of East and West, not only for its own sake, but because we are going to use this concept as the principal expression of the fundamentals of Eastern culture, and of its adaptation to a post-industrial and globalized environment.

As we have briefly examined in chapter 3 with our study of human nature, Junzi has no equivalent in the West. To some, Junzi may appear equivalent to Plato's philosopher-king or other exemplary religious figures of the medieval or modern periods, but these do not truly grasp the essence of the Eastern term, due to the profound conceptual differences between the respective cultures.

In many ways, Junzi is quite comparable to Christianity as originally envisioned by Jesus. Junzi's basic attitude is loving humankind just like a Christian: Junzi's Humanity, as we have seen, is not different from Christian neighborly love. Junzi's true strength is inside of him just as a Christian's is. Just like a Christian, Junzi's nobility is not that of blood but of virtue. The concept of Junzi was employed by most schools, but most extensively studied and refined by Confucianism. Just as it must have been with early Christianity, that virtue might replace nobility of birth was a revolutionary idea in Confucius's time, and particularly the idea of virtue as directed inwardly: "Junzi demands of himself, Xiaoren demands of others"[10]; "Junzi is distressed by his own inability; he is not distressed by others not appreciating him"[11]; "Junzi has great pride but does not compete with others. Junzi associates with others roundly but does not form factions."[12] Junzi and the examination system were symbiotic: the one reinforced the other. Thus, all in all, this image of Junzi is quite similar to the Christian of Universal ethics (e.g., the Good Samaritan).

Christians: Good Samaritans vs. Crusaders
The similarity between Junzi and the Christian ideal ends, however, when the concept of Heathen is introduced. The Good Samaritan, by definition, loves all of mankind, and so he does not conceive of non-Christians as heathens. But once Christianity began to expand, such a notion was necessary to distinguish friend from foe. The new Christian ideal, then, was no longer the Good Samaritan, but the Christian hero—that is, the Crusader. The heathen plays the same part in relation to this ideal that the "barbarian" played in relation to the ancient Greeks: both were to be eliminated or enslaved. Just as a Universal ethics produced the Good Samaritan, a Master ethics or a rule by law produced heroes and heathens.

It was the latter model—Hero and Barbarian, Crusader and Heathen—that dominated Western history until the present, thanks to the ideological and metaphysical support offered by Western philosophers. In today's circumscribed world, however, the notion of a heathen is obsolete: likewise, Christians will increasingly aspire not to military heroism, but to the ideal of the Good Samaritan, just as the East has always aspired to the similar ideal of Junzi.

Heathen vs. Xiaoren

Junzi's most distinctive feature, by contrast to his Western counterpart, is best understood by reference to his antithesis, Xiaoren or Petty Man. Xiaoren seeks only immediate gains without respecting the fundamental Confucian values of benevolence, sincerity, loyalty, propriety, righteousness, and so on. Despite constant and pervasive famine, drought, and floods, it was important for Junzi to maintain his inner strength: "Junzi worries about the Tao, not about poverty."[13] Because the values associated with Junzi were so widely known and used, they carried a weight comparable to the Christian ideal in the West. Equally, Xiaoren would have been equivalent to the atheist, idolater, or heathen in Western culture with one fundamental difference: Xiaoren is not a religious category. From a Western perspective, most Easterners are pagans because they do not believe in the Christian God, whereas an Easterner would class a Western man as Junzi or Xiaoren by his actions alone, regardless of faith. Thus, from the perspective of Universal ethics, the Good Samaritan is comparable to Junzi, but the Crusader, with his Master ethics, is far different from Junzi.

Here lies the crucial difference between the values of Junzi and those of the Christian West: the secularity of the former, with all its ethical implications. For the Easterner there is no godliness, no pure spirit, no heaven or hell, no religiously grounded good or evil, piety or sin—only a man composed of both Xiaoren and Junzi, to be guided with education toward the latter. Consequently, Junzi's virtue is his own reward; he expects no compensation other than his own satisfaction and pleasure. Xiaoren, likewise, has only to fear moral humiliation while he lives and acts in this world.

By the same logic, Junzi would not automatically qualify for paradise in the West. As Western civilization is predicated upon Christianity, being virtuous is not sufficient condition to be granted heaven—one must also be a Christian. Faith can be more important than good works, as Luther in particular emphasized. Ethics is provided by God and must be followed as a law, in the form of the Commandments. By contrast, ethics in the East derives from man and lacks the character of commandment or law. No Eastern ruler was above the ethical standard of Junzi. This is the ethical implication of the distinction between Junzi and Xiaoren, which sets the East apart from the West: the rule of humanist ethics as against rule by the law of God.

Unlike the Junzi-Xiaoren pairing, the Western pairing of Christian and Heathen is grounded in the more fundamental distinction between Spirit and Body. Christians are supposed to belong to the Holy Spirit, while non-Christians are alien to it: this image is not unlike Aristotle's master-citizens who, uniquely, have soul. From the fourth to the nineteenth century, when secularism took hold in the West, all non-Christians were treated as heathens, deserving neither law nor ethics, but only control through force. This was in perfect tune with Aristotle's Master ethics, as he considered that barbarians must become slaves since they do not have soul. (We have already examined this point in chapter 4.) The division was that simple.

Unlike Confucianism, founded on a secular ethics, Christianity was supported by two pillars: law and ethics—the first more important than the second. Although many Christians, following the Good Samaritan (Luke 10:25–37), privileged ethics or good actions over faith, these remained outside the mainstream as long as Christianity was the state religion and operated more with Master ethics than with Universal ethics. The essential dilemma for Christianity, therefore, was that, as an *institution*, it had to sacrifice the ethical teachings of Christ to support the rule of law. The Church acted according to the principle: "apply law whenever one can, and apply ethics when one must." As we will recall, this is the same pattern adopted by the first sailors who plundered whenever they could and traded when they had to. As Christianity diminished in political power, it had to shift its emphasis from law to ethics, but despite this, its underlying directive has remained the same—self-preservation.

The paradox of the Christian-Heathen dichotomy became conspicuous when the West finally repudiated its distinction between Spirit and Body. What pair might replace that of Christian and Heathen? What ideal represents the West now? With the advent of the free market and affluent society, has the divide between rich and poor replaced that between Christian and Heathen?

Good Samaritans vs. Conquering Heroes

As we have equated Junzi with the Good Samaritan, we still have to deal with the Crusader (i.e., those Christians whose activities were centered on defeating heathen enemies). They can be grouped under the broader category of heroes. The image of Crusade Christians was Heroic in theme. In this group is also included all those Western heroes of Greece and Rome before Christianity became the religion of the West. From this perspective, the real East-West comparison in terms of role models can be made between Junzi and Heroes.

Western heroes, who served as role models for their society, can be divided into two groups: military and nonmilitary. Military heroes include Leonidas, Themistocles, Alexander the Great, Marius, Sulla, Julius Caesar, Charlemagne, Hernán Cortés, Napoleon Bonaparte, Christopher Columbus, Vasco da Gama, and Magellan; nonmilitary heroes include Socrates, Plato,

Aristotle, Cato, Cicero, Seneca, Saint Paul, Saint Augustine, Saint Francis, Saint Bernard, Thomas Aquinas, and Luther. Military heroes are uncommon in Eastern history, since they have far less relevance to a world that repudiated military rule in favor of ethics. Even non-military heroes are quite rare. The East's role models were instead Junzi (as an ideal) and its successful scholar-officials (in practice).

Exceptions: Western Sages vs. Eastern Prophets

The contrasting fundamentals between education and religion engendered two types of dominant personalities: in the East, Junzi and sages; in the West, heroes and prophets. The dominant figures of the Eastern world, Lao Tzu, Confucius, Buddha, and all the Eastern leaders arising from the Imperial Examination System, were sages (i.e., men of harmony, wisdom, balance, and moderation). Even military heroes, such as Sun Tzu mostly followed this pattern. As sages and benevolent administrators, they were bent on reflection, management of the status quo, ensuring social harmony, and maintaining peace in the world.

On the other hand, the dominant figures of the Western world, the spiritual leaders as non-military heroes—Moses, Christ's Apostles, the medieval founders of spiritual orders, Martin Luther, and Ignatius Loyola—were all prophets (i.e., men who reveal and interpret the divine). The conquering Western heroes from Caesar to Napoleon, as well as the courageous explorers like Columbus and Vasco da Gama, were all men of action, but they shared with the prophets the characteristic of being pioneers, or at least charismatic individuals. Western history has been shaped by such personalities whose extraordinary individual initiatives ventured into the unknown, both spiritual and physical.

Thus, the sages in the East and the prophets in the West shaped their respective histories and civilizations. Of course, there were exceptions—Eastern prophets who valued individual initiatives and Western sages who valued social harmony. The latter group we shall now examine.

Western Sages: Heraclitus, Carneades, and Spinoza

Although we have referred to the West as a Yang civilization, notable exceptions included Heraclitus, Carneades, and Spinoza, who advocated Yin thoughts in a Yang world. The philosophies of these figures shared such Yin traits as complementarity, uncertainty, chance, and probability. Heraclitus (ca. 535–475 BC), for one, remarked, "Everything follows cyclical change; the way up and down is one and the same; God is day/night, winter/summer, war/peace, and satiety/hunger; ease gives rise to difficulty." He would surely have been welcomed in the Eastern Yin-Yang school. The similarity of his approach to that of Taoism becomes clear when we examine his writings: "Having and not having arise together. Difficult and easy complement each other. Long and short contrast each other. High and low rest upon each other. Void and solid harmonize with each other." His *Logos* is quite similar to Tao: "The Logos holds always but humans always prove unable to understand it, both before hearing it and when they have first heard it.... All things come to be in accordance with the Logos." "Although the Logos is common, most people live as if they had their own private understanding." If Logos is replaced with Tao, these sentences would fit perfectly into Taoteking. Heraclitus, besides his theory of the unity of opposites, also believed that the universe is in constant flux—"you cannot step twice into the same river"—just as the East believes in change and transformation. Hence he is called a philosopher of becoming as opposed to a philosopher of being. He did not believe that humanity is the image of God: "To God all things are fair and good and just, but people hold some things wrong and some right."[14] He recommended people follow the common view and not have their own judgment—a very similar attitude to Taoism. Heraclitus is a rare example of a Western thinker who interpreted contrasts in complementary terms; most others of his time regarded contrasting pairs in terms of conflict. No wonder the Greeks nicknamed him the "Riddler." Nor is it surprising that he was heavily criticized by Plato and Aristotle. Later, Heraclitus was labeled a pantheist by mainstream Western thinkers.

Among post-Platonic philosophers, Carneades (ca. 214-129 BC) would easily pass as a Taoist. He served as head of the later Platonic Academy, but shared little of Plato's philosophy. Unlike Plato, Carneades did not believe in absolute knowledge: "All knowledge is impossible." Carneades was the first Greek philosopher to pronounce the failure of metaphysics, refuting the doctrines of the Stoics and Epicureans. The basis of his doubt was his conviction that neither the senses nor reason could acquire truth—equivalent to the Taoist principle that truth is beyond human reach. Yet Carneades thought that relative or "probable" truth *could* be discerned by man, and that this enabled us to live and act correctly—equivalent to the Taoist attitude that one can discern relative truth from Tao's manifestations. He denied determinism, recognizing the importance of chance and probability. He did not recognize the conformity of morality with nature, maintaining instead that our ideas of justice were purely artificial and expedient[15]—equivalent to the Taoist warning against regulations and government policies. Carneades was later labeled a skeptic and an atheist by mainstream Western thinkers.

Given these countervailing arguments against Plato and Aristotle, one wonders why modern Western philosophers, such as those of the Enlightenment, did not take the views of Heraclitus and Carneades more seriously. One reason is that, unlike Plato and Aristotle, their works were lost. It was the rediscovery of Plato's works after almost a millennium that rekindled the West's interest in him. Heraclitus had no such luck, and it is chiefly through later writers, such as Diogenes Laertius and Plutarch, that we know his ideas. Carneades left no writing; his successor, Clitomachus, did write on his ideas, just as Plato had done with Socrates, but these works were also lost. Their inaccessibility, then, contributed to their obscurity, but another reason is that their Yin philosophy did not mix well with the West's generally Yang attitude. The labeling of Heraclitus as pantheist and Carneades as atheist attest to this.

The Copernican Revolution in Philosophy: Kant vs. Spinoza

The mainstream historiography of Western philosophy has considered Immanuel Kant as a thinker who provoked a paradigmatic, "Copernican" revolution in the discipline. Kant did criticize the organizations and practices of Christianity, but ultimately he defended the core principle of Christianity. As such, Kant denied miracles but he defended the separation of the soul from the body. According to the pre-Kantian Western theology and metaphysics, Man, whose essence is Spirit, was created by God, whose essence is also Spirit—as opposed to Body—and this Spirit performed miracles for Man. Consequently, if miracles are denied, the immortality of Spirit must also be denied, as well as anthropomorphic God. This was the predicament facing the pre-Kantian Western philosophy. But Kant succeeded in stripping away the fanciful, miraculous elements of Western religion, while retaining its core. He based his transcendental idealism and moral philosophy on theism while taking an ambiguous attitude toward the supernatural. This he achieved by placing the human mind, not an independent and absolute point of reference, such as God, at the center of his epistemology. Man, he argued, should be treated as an end—that is, as a moral agent in his own right—rather than as the means to an end: this marked a great contribution to Western thought. But from an Eastern perspective, Kant's revolution was less radical than that of, say, Spinoza, who denied the duality of mind and body, and of God and nature.

As we have seen, Spinoza thought that God and Nature were one and the same, that Mind and Body were one and the same, and that Intellect and Will were one and the same. He also argued that religion should stop being divisive between men. He denied both the concept of substance and the existence of atoms. Thus, had it been widely accepted, Spinoza's new system might have provided a genuinely "Copernican" revolution within Western philosophy. But his radicalism could not be supported by many others. Kant's revolution proved more acceptable, since it was only partly deistic and could incorporate the theism still embraced by the majority of Western thinkers. But for any Westerner who wants to understand the East, Spinoza provides a useful point of reference, since his ideas closely harmonize with those of Junzi and Wuwei. It is no wonder that a Cartesian philosopher of his period, Nicolas Malebranche, identified the "impious" Spinoza with the Eastern philosophers.

But Western sages like Heraclitus, Carneades, and Spinoza advocated their philosophical theories outside the mainstream of Western thought and were subsequently marginalized. After his death, Spinoza had a profound influence on many Western philosophers. Fichte's "*Ich*," Nietzsche's "will to power," and Bergson's "*élan vital*" are all variations on Spinoza's "self-preservation." But, probably under the influence of Kant, none accepted Spinoza's essential monism, and consequently they produced more aggressive and extreme conclusions than those he had advanced. Hegel was correct when he wrote that "to be a philosopher, one must first be a Spinozist." But most post-

Spinozist thinkers, including Hegel, were more metaphysicians (or "anti-metaphysicians") than philosophers. As Nietzsche said, philosophy reveals the philosopher's own life more than some abstract truths. All profound utterances represent the varied facets of diverse minds.

Legalists: Eastern Prophets

There were also Yang thinkers in the East, such as the Legalists or School of Law, during the sixth to third century BC. Like Machiavelli, Hobbes, and Nietzsche in the West, the Legalists rejected ethical values and emphasized the ruler's absolute leadership. As a logical corollary, they placed efficiency before wisdom, shunning both Tao and the concept of Benevolence. The Legalists played a pivotal role in achieving the first Chinese Empire in the third century BC—this was an unusual period of expansion in Chinese history.

Despite almost two thousand years between them, there are clear parallels between Machiavelli and Han Fei (韓非, 280–233 BC), one of the most prominent Legalists. According to Han Fei, "A prince must not depend on the loyalty of his vassals not to betray him, but depend on his own preparedness that will not allow his vassals to betray him; a prince must not depend on the integrity of his vassals not to deceive him, but depend on his own shrewdness that will not allow his vassals to deceive him."[16] He writes about royal subjects: "Subjects will serve the prince with loyalty when he is perspicacious; subjects will abuse the prince with cunning when the prince is foolish."

One finds almost exactly the same vision of human nature in *The Prince* by Machiavelli: "This is to be asserted in general of men, that they are ungrateful, fickle, false, cowardly, covetous, and as long as you succeed they are yours entirely; they will offer you their blood, property, life and children, as is said above, when the need is far distant; but when it approaches they turn against you. And that prince who, relying entirely on their promises, has neglected other precautions, is ruined…. A wise prince should establish himself on that which is in his own control and not in that of others."[17] On the loyalty of the subjects toward a prince, Machiavelli writes: "Men will always prove untrue to you unless they are kept honest by constraint."[18]

Fig. 6-5. Han Fei (韓非, 280–233 BC) Chinese Legalist Philosopher (http://german.cri.cn/chinaabc/ chapter17/chapter170201.htm.)	Fig. 6-6. Niccolò Machiavelli (1469–1527) (http://commons.wikimedia.org/ wiki/Image:Santi.)

Han Fei, Machiavelli, and Hobbes

Hen Fei resembles Machiavelli in his analysis of human nature, and Thomas Hobbes in his theory of sovereign authority. All advocated rule by law and provided an intellectual framework for the application of such a rule. Since the Legalist school developed in the wake of intense turmoil, the Legalists longed for order and found it in a powerful monarch. Hobbes, likewise, formulated his theory in the wake of an intense Civil War, which predisposed him to seek order in the establishment of a strong monarch. Naturally, both Han Fei and Hobbes thought that giving men total freedom would result in the perpetuation of warfare, which could only be ended by an uncontested central authority.[19] Both were materialistic, rejecting supernatural authorities and the worship of saints, images, and relics as superstitions. Both considered those who claim supernatural authority dangerous to the order of the state, and both advocated censorship of free speech for the sake of stability.

Han Fei could not develop his ideas in the form of a social contract as Hobbes did, but Hobbes could not fully reject supernatural phenomena, as he admitted the truth of Biblical miracles while rejecting the validity of Revelation and the doctrine of Heaven and Hell.[20] But these limitations were the product of their times rather than their own characters. It is particularly regrettable that the seed of law in the Eastern Legal school could not come to fruition. The geopolitical condition of the East explains this failure; unlike Hobbes, who could develop his ideas in Paris, Han Fei and his followers had no other countries in which their ideas could flourish.

Typical of Yang behavior, the Legalists also urged burning the books of rival schools, especially those of Confucianism. When in power, they made it a capital crime to discuss Taoism or Confucianism. Consequently, this school stands out in Eastern history as the only one to advocate exclusion. But the Legalists soon lost their influence, again becoming a relatively minor school, although Han Fei's realism and emphasis on law continued to find eager ears, albeit in private, just as Spinoza later found many secret admirers.

We can regard the Legalists as prophets whose role was to achieve the first unified empire in the East. By contrast, Spinoza was a Western sage whose role was to provide an entirely new framework for philosophy. Whereas Spinoza lived as a sage, the Legalists behaved like prophets. Voltaire describes the modus operandi of a prophet: "If you are desirous of obtaining a great name, of becoming the founder of a sect or establishment, be completely mad; but, be sure that your madness corresponds with the turn and temper of your age. Have in your madness reason enough to guide your extravagancies; and, forget not to be excessively opinionated and obstinate. It is certainly possible that you may get hanged; but if you escape hanging, you will have altars erected for you."[21] The Legalists ended up either dead or brilliantly successful, as did the Western prophets, but Spinoza lived a life of reflection and peace, like an Eastern sage.

Looking back, one cannot help but recognize an ever-contracting intellectual context in the East; with the Han Empire in the second century BC, the Legalist school lost its influence in favor of Confucianism and Taoism. With the Song Empire of the eleventh century, Xun Zi's branch of Confucianism yielded to that of Mencius. The schools of both Han Fei and Xun Zi had the potential to enrich Eastern culture with their new perspectives on human nature and statecraft; their recognition of the role of law might have offered a balance to the exclusively ethical perspective of Taoism and Confucianism.

Legalism and Plato

The Socratic faith in knowledge, "man errs by ignorance," constituted an important leitmotif of Western civilization. In a fundamental way, this attitude was shared by the Eastern Legalists. Socrates famously said, "I know that I know nothing";

his ultimate aim for life was wisdom, not wealth. And Socrates, Plato, and Aristotle did maintain balance between their quest for logos and sense of moderation, Sophrosyne. Plato himself was very much aware of this balancing act as he discussed the dangers of technology and civilization (specifically of *writing*) in the parable of Thamus and Theuth, in his *Phaedrus*. Plato's dialogues often deal with the problem of knowledge—and often reach an ambiguous and skeptical conclusion about the possibility of knowing absolutely. But Western philosophy later disregarded Plato's skepticism about knowledge, acquiring instead an unwavering faith in man's ability to discover the truth: "Virtue is knowledge." The West, with its élan for expansion, privileged the quest for knowledge to the detriment of moderation, as demonstrated by its support for heroism throughout its history.

This attitude also forms the background of the legend of Faust, which concerns man's search for ultimate knowledge. The West found in ancient Greece the motivation and inspiration for its millennia-long search for knowledge and truth. The intellectual heroism of the ancient Greeks spurred the West to an incredible accumulation of knowledge and technology. At the same time, they started the West on its search for theological, metaphysical, and ideological certainty. From this perspective, Socratic faith in knowledge constituted the antithesis of ethics; its faith aimed at resolving existential questions by discoveries obtained through knowledge, whereas ethics aims at management.[22]

Socratic belief in logos, possibility of human spirit, and ultimate truth served the West well in its pursuit of theologies, metaphysics, and ideologies. On the other hand, Eastern thinkers did not believe in absolute knowledge, reason, or progress; instead of trying to attain this, they advocated a realistic management of the situation at hand. Hence, they regarded ethics as an essential counterbalance to man's natural greed—that is, as a means of maintaining equilibrium.

Science and Knowledge

The greater our faith that scientific progress can resolve our problems, the less do we need to rely on management. The West's belief in salvation by absolute truth is nowhere more evident than in its quest for scientific knowledge. Indeed, the wondrous progress of science was such that by the nineteenth century, the West believed itself to be on the verge of mastering nature completely. For more than a millennium, Euclidian geometry provided solid ground and guidance to the West's scientific confidence. Modern Western metaphysicians believed that Euclidian geometry contained absolute truth and built their dreams on it. Furthermore, Newtonian physics offered a seemingly infallible mechanical model, with its faith in strict and regular causality. This belief in absolute causality, which is easily within the reach of most humans' understanding, postulated that mankind's problems were material and hence readily solvable by technology or, more to the point, by applied reason. The Enlightenment emancipated reason from religious dogma but in so doing led ultimately to an overreliance on rationalism. The combination of Newtonian physics and an absolute faith in human reason spawned the unique European atmosphere of the nineteenth century: one that passionately aspired to engineer Utopian perfection.

But in the twentieth century, this confidence was shaken by discoveries in physics and mathematics. Euclidian geometry was proved incomplete by Einstein. Regular causality was shown not to hold at a subatomic level. Fritjof Kapra summed up: "Two separate developments—that of relativity theory and of atomic physics—shattered all the principal concepts of the Newtonian world view: the notion of absolute space and time, the elementary solid particles, the strictly causal nature of physical phenomena, and the ideal of an objective description of nature. None of these concepts could be extended to the new domains into which physics was now penetrating."[23] Contemporary quantum physics has destroyed "absolute" faith in causality.

Regular causation is still accepted at a macroscopic scale, but we have also discovered probability and uncertainty at the microscopic scale. Metaphysical systems founded on absolute causality have thus been abandoned. Meanwhile, discoveries of sub-atomic mass-less particles, such as neutrinos have undermined our Newtonian notions of substance and mass—and of the indivisible "atom" itself. Our search for a single key to the universe remains inconclusive. Absolutism and extremism—the staples of Western prophets and metaphysics—have lost their "scientific" basis.

Can our scientific advances keep pace with advances in our civilization? To solve the international problems facing all of us at the dawn of the third millennium, it will be necessary to harness our mental abilities for the collective good. This is the problem we address in the final chapter.

Military Paradigm: Clausewitz vs. Sun Tzu

As we shall examine in chapter 10, the third millennium has been marked by a paradigm shift from the military to commerce. Within the ancient military paradigm, nothing reveals a civilization's view of its "enemy" more clearly than its theory of warfare. But it is difficult to find two treatises that discuss the same kind of war on the same terms in the East and West. As earlier noted, China's essential tenets of unity and harmony were largely enforced by a single leader on the Central Plain. Indeed, the closest analogue to the nationalist "total" wars of nineteenth-century Europe can only be found in the China of the fifth century BC: "The period in Chinese history which most closely corresponds to the stage in Western Europe state formation ... was that of the Warring States—all of a millennium and a half earlier than the corresponding phase in Europe."[24]

As a curious parallel, this is precisely when each civilization produced its most venerated tracts on war: Carl von Clausewitz's *On War* (1832) and Sun Tzu's *Art of War* (fifth century BC).

Context: Sun Tzu vs. Clausewitz

Sun Tzu's work is counted as the most important of the Seven Military Classics that were canonized during the eleventh century. China experienced another age of protracted warfare during the Period of Disunity from 220 (the end of the Han dynasty) to 589 (the start of the Sui dynasty). During this period, treatises on war, including the Seven Military Classics, were examined and put into practice, and Sun Tzu's *Art of War* came out invariably as the most influential work.[25] Even though the *Art of War* is attributed to Sun Tzu as an individual, most consider it, in fact, a collection of theories and observations on warfare belonging to the Warring States Period.

In a closed environment, such as Sun Tzu's, war could hardly be glorified, since it brought more hardships than benefits. Raids and warfare could not be used, as they were in the ancient and medieval West, to plunder and take slaves. So while Clausewitz insisted on victory in war, Sun Tzu advocated avoidance of war as far as possible: even victories were often Pyrrhic. In the same vein, Sun Tzu has proven his relevance to modern times, which is characterized by a circumscribed environment. Many articles have compared the military strategy used by Mao Zedong during his historic Long March to those propounded by Sun Tzu. Mao wrote: "The enemy advances, we retreat; the enemy camps, we harass; the enemy tires, we attack; the enemy retreats, we pursue."[26] Sun Tzu had written: "When near, make it appear that you are far away; when far away, that you are near. Offer the enemy bait to lure him; feign disorder and strike him. When he concentrates, prepare against him; where he is strong, avoid him."[27] Sun Tzu's contemporary relevance arises from the fact that our present environment is much like his—that is, circumscribed.

It is critical to understand that Sun Tzu stands for the paradigm of a circumscribed environment in the East whereas Clausewitz represents the culmination of the traditional paradigm of an expansive environment in the West.

Clausewitz's *On War* is perhaps the closest Western counterpart to *The Art of War*. Although the West had long experienced warfare, and produced many manuals of battle, from Vegetius' *De re militari* to Machiavelli's own *Art of War*, it did not produce a treatise of comparable scope to that of Sun Tzu. Just as the latter ranks as the greatest of the Seven Military Classics in the East, so Clausewitz's work, written at a time of comparable strife, stands above its peers. Clausewitz's military experience was in the Napoleonic Wars of the early nineteenth century; his work remained unfinished at his death in 1831 and has been criticized for apparent internal contradictions, but nonetheless proved highly influential for the remainder of the century. The "total" character of the First and Second World Wars, in fact, bear the unmistakable legacy of Clausewitz.

The Enemy: Eastern Assimilation vs. Western Annihilation

A comparison between the two treatises' cultural and sociopolitical contexts will help us better understand their contrasting views: Sun Tzu advocates assimilation of one's enemies, while Clausewitz advises annihilation of them. If assimilation now appears more virtuous than annihilation, it is because we live today in a circumscribed world in which the former is more practical than the latter. In the earlier expansive environment of the West, the physical elimination of one's enemy, either by death or enslavement, invariably constituted the most effective means for lasting victory and peace. In sum, Clausewitz applied to military theory the traditional Master ethics of the West from the Greco-Roman period to modernity, whereas Sun Tzu based his own theory on the Universal ethics of the East. The Clausewitzian principle of annihilation can be interpreted as the logical outcome and continuation of a Master ethics based on the Aristotelian justification of subjugating barbarians and the Christian justification of eliminating Heathens.

In the West, the necessary precedes the ethical—slavery is a case in point. For a thousand years, the West accepted slavery, including capturing slaves through warfare and profiting from their trade. In the nineteenth century, the social and political environment became such that the West had no choice but to abandon the practice; moral condemnation of slavery by mainstream society only came after the need for it declined. On the other hand, the absence of slave markets and, consequently, of slave taking by raid/war in Eastern history greatly diminished the appetite for warfare.

Ever faithful to the Eastern emphasis on harmony and assimilation, Sun Tzu regards the enemy as a possible later ally, remarking: "To gain a hundred victories in a hundred battles is not the highest excellence; to subjugate the enemy's army without engaging in battle is the highest excellence." Clausewitz, on the other hand, faithful to Western exclusionary dialectics, treats the enemy as a permanent opponent to be utterly annihilated. For him, "The destruction of the enemy is what always matters most." How did the East seek to prevent warfare? All means, including diplomacy, bribery, espionage, and stratagem, were to be exhausted prior to the engagement of physical forces. The enemy's assimilation or persuasion is always retained as the first priority. A similar view was advanced by Hobbes: force and fraud are the two cardinal virtues in war.[28]

Fig. 6-7. Sun Tzu (孫子 400–320 BC) (http://commons.wikimedia.org/ wiki/Image:Suntzu2.jpg.)	Fig. 6-8. Carl von Clausewitz (1780–1831) (http://en.wikipedia.org/wiki/ File:Clausewitz.jpg)

Sun Tzu considered stratagem an integral part of military strategy. But such stratagem carried little significance for Clausewitz, who described it as mere "cunning." Likewise, Sun Tzu's advice on espionage is clear and concise: "What enables the enlightened rulers and good generals to conquer the enemy at every move and achieve extraordinary success is foreknowledge. Foreknowledge cannot be elicited from ghosts and spirits; it cannot be inferred from comparisons of previous events, or from the calculations of the heavens, but must be obtained from people who have knowledge of the enemy's situation."[29] Clausewitz, by contrast, sees non-violent means as a last resort, preferring direct collision with the enemy: "The weaker the forces that are at the disposal of the supreme commander, the more appealing the use of cunning becomes. In a state of weakness and insignificance, when prudence, judgment, and ability no longer suffice, cunning may well appear the only hope."[30]

Clausewitz preferred a decisive war of annihilation, whereas Sun Tzu always preferred a war of strategy. The latter wrote, "Therefore, the best strategy in warfare is to attack the enemy's plans, next is to attack alliances, next is to attack the army, and the worst is to attack a walled city."[31] Clausewitz states, "The fighting forces of the enemy must be *destroyed*.... The country must be occupied.... Yet both of these things may be done and the war ... cannot be considered to have ended as long as the enemy's *will* has not been broken."[32] Victory constituted the ultimate aim of war for Clausewitz, whereas self-preservation was the ultimate objective for Sun Tzu.

This complete reversal of priorities between Clausewitz and Sun Tzu springs from different perspectives on the nature of the enemy. For Sun Tzu, yesterday's enemy can be tomorrow's ally; for Clausewitz, an enemy is always an enemy, and always to be annihilated. In Sun Tzu's circumscribed world, founded almost exclusively on an agrarian economy, enemy soldiers and people were potentially irreplaceable resources, ideally to be assimilated. But in Clausewitz's expansive world, enemy soldiers constituted obstacles to be annihilated or enslaved for the sake of wealth and glory.

Strategy vs. Tactics

The most striking difference between the two treatises is Clausewitz's total neglect of "the day after." Instead he is concerned exclusively with the actual engagement and its directions. "Though strategy in itself is concerned only with engagements, the theory of strategy must also consider its chief means of execution, the fighting forces.... Strategy is the use of the engagement for the purpose of the war."[33] When Clausewitz defines war as a continuation of policy by other means, his emphasis, contrary to popular belief, is not on policy at all: "The conduct of war, in its great outlines, is therefore policy itself, which takes up the sword in place of the pen, but does not on that account cease to think according to its own laws."[34] Thus, *On War* remains at the tactical level: it focuses exclusively on military engagement on the field of battle.

This contrast appears with respect to the issue of profit in warfare. If profit is possible, victory justifies the war and can overcome most of the difficulties involved. This allows Clausewitz to focus on war itself without regard for its aftermath. On the other hand, if there is no chance of profit, utmost caution on the situations before and after is necessary. This forces one to adopt a strategic perspective.

Neither Clausewitz nor Machiavelli showed any inclination to discuss management before or after a war. But for Sun Tzu, war remained an integral part of state affairs. Clausewitz's exclusive focus on battle would have been anathema to him, as he was constantly aware of the broader implications of war in politics. For example, Sun Tzu repeatedly warned against protracted warfare: "I have heard of military campaigns that were clumsy but swift, but I have never seen military campaigns that were skilled but protracted. No nation has ever benefited from protracted warfare."[35]

The three Indochinese Wars of the twentieth century succinctly illustrate the question of protracted war raised here by Sun Tzu. The first and second of these were both protracted. The first, which ended in 1954 with the defeat of France, was in essence a colonial war. A century earlier, France had been successful in colonizing Vietnam; nonetheless, this colony was lost in 1954. The old exploitation was no longer possible; France made a mistake in trying to use nation-state politics in a newly circumscribed world.

The Second Indochinese War involved the United States and ended in 1973 after more than ten years. Two years later, the unification of Vietnam was achieved. The United States, with its deep moralistic idealism, started the Vietnam War with the aim not of colonial gain but of containing the spread of communism in East Asia. Initially, the American public supported the war. As combat dragged on, however, popular opinion became increasingly critical, to the point of dividing the nation. Without tangible benefits or concrete results, no protracted war can enjoy public support. And in a circumscribed world, no tangible benefit is possible from a prolonged war—even the victor loses.

The Third Indochinese War involved China and Vietnam, with the situation in Cambodia as its backdrop. It began with China's attack in February 1979 and ended one month later, with apparently inconclusive results. While preparing for the war, China repeatedly declared that it would be of limited duration, intended simply as a "lesson" to Vietnam. It ended with both countries claiming victory; here was a case of limited, not protracted, warfare, with a clear objective applied in a circumscribed world.

Why this difference between East and West? In an expansive world where the logic of "winner takes all" prevails, protracted warfare can be justified because war can bring slaves and resources, and is therefore worth enduring for the good of the nation and its people. The reward is so great that post-war management becomes secondary. However, in a circumscribed world, post-war management becomes a crucial concern because victory does not necessarily reap spoils. Quite the contrary—a military victory and occupation of foreign land and people often increases the victor's burdens. War is therefore treated as the means to achieve a larger political or strategic objective.

Glorious Victory vs. Pyrrhic Victory

So as better to serve his nation, Sun Tzu insists on the alleviation of economic and social burdens for ordinary people. He highly recommends using intelligence and spies to diminish the preparatory costs of war, and even criticizes the inhumanity of leaders who neglect intelligence and espionage. His concern for the economy and for ordinary people stemmed not so much from high-minded morals as from practical financial considerations. Unlike Western wars of conquest and expansion, wars in the East did not result in amassing spoils, in the Western sense of the word, or in wholesale slavery. "To the victor belong the spoils" has no counterpart in the East.

Piracy and raiding cannot flourish in a circumscribed environment because "hit and run" tactics are physically impossible. This also explains the absence of slavery in the East. Again, we should not fall into the trap of anachronistic moral judgment. Rather, let us remember that reason cannot be the source of morality, but only provides a later justification of moral actions. We have already examined this when we compared Aristotelian Master ethics with Confucian Universal ethics in chapter 4. Because wars were rarely profitable in the East, leaders considered their costs and benefits carefully. Spoils and booty often failed to compensate for the cost of war, so that victories were frequently Pyrrhic. Thus, wars were much less common in the East than in the West.

Sun Tzu's thought shares the core principles enshrined in Taoist and Confucian thinking, just as his various strategic recommendations reflect the exigencies of the East's circumscribed environment. He accepts Nature and Tao, and employs natural phenomena as the key models for military strategy: "The army's formation is like water. The water's formation avoids the high and rushes to the low. So an army's formation avoids the strong and rushes to the weak. Water's formation adapts to the ground when flowing. So then an army's formation adapts to the enemy to achieve victory."[36]

In the same vein, Sun Tzu's abhorrence of inhumanity, and his warning against drawn-out warfare, relate to Confucian Benevolence and Tao. In the East, Universal ethics were ultimately inevitable, no matter how much generals preferred to follow Master ethics during periods of warfare. Taoism advises: "Weapons are instruments of fear; they are not a wise man's tools. He uses them only when he has no choice. Peace and quiet are dear to his heart, and victory no cause for rejoicing. If you rejoice in victory, then you delight in killing; if you delight in killing, you cannot fulfill yourself."[37] This strategic insight emanates from the concept of harmony among men, which pervades all aspects of Eastern civilization.

On the other hand, ever faithful to Western Master ethics, Clausewitz advances the opposite view: "Kind-hearted people might of course think there was some ingenious way to disarm or defeat an enemy without too much bloodshed, and might imagine this is the true goal of the art of war. Pleasant as it sounds, it is a fallacy that must be exposed: war is such a dangerous business that the mistakes that come from kindness are the very worst."[38] The inhuman trench warfare of World War I was one outcome of this attitude. Clausewitz continues, "The maximum use of force is in no way incompatible with the simultaneous use of the intellect. If one side uses force without compunction, undeterred by the bloodshed it involves, while the other side refrains, the first will gain the upper hand. That side will force the other to follow suit; each will drive its opponent toward extremes, and the only limiting factors are the counterpoises inherent in war."[39] The concept of total war is already present here; it can only be justified by the prospect of enormous spoils, which has long constituted the basis of the West's expansion. Since victory was usually accompanied with benefit in the West, it was invariably glorious. On the other hand, as even victory did not usually make up the cost of war in the East, it was quite often Pyrrhic in nature.

In short, this important contrast leads Sun Tzu and Clausewitz to different definitions of war, namely in terms of strategy and tactics. The following quotations clearly illustrate this difference. Sun Tzu: "War is a matter of cardinal importance to the nation. It will decide the fate of it; either prosperity or death. The matter should be reviewed with all the necessary circumspection."[40] Clausewitz: "War is nothing but a duel on a larger scale.... War is thus an act of force to compel our enemy to do our will."[41] In a duel, one does not need much strategy; tactical decisiveness counts more.

In the Eastern world, war was "a matter of cardinal importance to the nation" because it was usually the last resort in deciding the nation's fate. On the other hand, in the West, where war has frequently been used for the purpose of expansion and conquest, it resembles a pastime of kings. The definition of war as a "duel" sums up Clausewitz's logic as a whole, just as Sun Tzu's definition of war as a matter of "prosperity or death" accurately reflects his own philosophy.

We must stress again that neither attitude is right or superior; each simply grows out of its environment. In the expansive West, the promise of profit made viable the concept of total war. In the circumscribed East, annihilation of an enemy represented a Pyrrhic victory, since it left fewer people to work the land, and so represented a danger to agriculture.

Go vs. Chess

The contrast between Sun Tzu and Clausewitz is reflected in the war games of Western chess and Eastern Go. Chess matches are fought on a board of 64 squares compared to the 361 points of Go. But the latter game is also qualitatively different in that it involves the incalculable: feeling, intuition, and instinct. Chess computers have been beating the best human masters since the mid-1990s, whereas in Go, machines remain only at the level of medium amateurs, since they lack the instincts that mark true Go masters. Chess is a matter of strict calculations in sequence; the player who makes the fewest mistakes wins. The game is like a fierce duel, in which destroying the enemy king is the ultimate objective. Just as in Clausewitz's war of annihilation, there is in chess relatively little distinction between the battle and the entire war.

On the other hand, the game of Go, probably developed in China 3,000 to 4,000 years ago, more closely resembles a great war consisting of numerous smaller battles. The chief aim is to secure and maintain overall strategic advantage, rather than immediate tactical gains. As such, it requires global and long-term thinking much more than short-term conflict.

Beginners at the game are invariably preoccupied with immediate tactical gains, losing sight of the larger strategic plan, and so playing into the hands of more experienced players. The outcome is more often decided by blunders and mistakes arising from short-sighted greed than by proactive and brilliant moves. This aspect may arise from the crucial difference between chess and Go—the role of the king. In chess, the aim is to take or block the enemy king, which wins the game. It is therefore a game of relentless attack, whether direct or indirect, on the king. But in Go, the aim is to secure as much land as possible. Go rewards self-control, long-term perspective, and a sense of proportion; aggression is less relevant than in chess since it has no ultimate purpose.

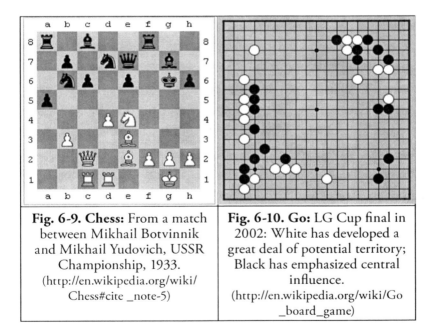

Fig. 6-9. Chess: From a match between Mikhail Botvinnik and Mikhail Yudovich, USSR Championship, 1933. (http://en.wikipedia.org/wiki/ Chess#cite _note-5)

Fig. 6-10. Go: LG Cup final in 2002: White has developed a great deal of potential territory; Black has emphasized central influence. (http://en.wikipedia.org/wiki/Go _board_game)

One wonders whether these contrasting views of war in East and West also apply to their respective business models. As the

East has learned from Western business, it has begun to produce a number of successful corporations, several of which have become multinational companies as powerful as their Western counterparts. But Eastern business plans and strategies, as well as corporate behavior, exhibit quite a contrast to their Western counterparts. It has often been observed that Eastern corporations prefer, and can afford, a long-term perspective and investment plans. On the other hand, Western corporations tend to focus on immediate return and profit, such as stock-price fluctuation and dividends. Figuratively, Eastern businessmen behave as if playing Go, whereas Western businessmen behave as if playing chess.

The East-West contrast also concerns business management, or the preservation of what one has already achieved. Such preservation is a skill that the East was disposed to hone; Eastern Junzi can therefore be understood as a benevolent administrator. But business is not only about management; it is also about creation and innovation—and these are fostered by the attitudes of Western business practices. Almost all technological inventions, as well as new business initiatives, have originated in the West. This also fits the image of the Western hero who dares and wins. Although such important inventions as paper, printing, gunpowder, and the magnetic compass emerged from the East, it was the West that put these to the greatest practical use. We therefore posit a contrast between Eastern management and Western creativity—at least until now.

Sun Tzu in the Twenty-First Century

Henry Kissinger, who pioneered the Sino-American rapprochement, makes a similar evaluation: "In chess, the objective of the game is absolute advantage. Its outcome is total victory or defeat. The game is conducted head-on, in the center of the board. The aim of Go is relative advantage; the game is played all over the board, and the objective is to increase one's options and reduce those of the adversary. The goal is less victory than persistent strategic progress."[42] To secure "persistent strategic progress" is the best way to "win a war without attacking," advises Sun Tzu. Clausewitz, who aimed at conquest in an expansive Western environment, only theorized about war from a Western perspective and thus conceived it as a direct clash. But the results of his extremist logic, for which he is not to be blamed, have been grim—the West experienced the meaningless carnage of trench warfare during World War I and of "total war" in World War II. The movement toward this state of "total war" was inevitable; only the lessons learned from these wars, combined with the advent of atomic weapons, have prevented a headlong rush toward annihilation.

The advent of weapons of mass destruction makes emphatically clear the suicidal tendency of Clausewitzian logic. In a nuclear age, the annihilation of the enemy means our own annihilation, too. The nuclear strategy of the cold war, mutually assured destruction (MAD), was the end result of the kind of reasoning espoused by Clausewitz. Since the world has become circumscribed, the relationship between nations has shifted from independence to interdependence. This new situation also supports our argument that the Master ethics inherent in Clausewitz's theory have become obsolete.

Today, therefore, the practice of subjugating weaker nations, with its attendant poverty and isolation, has given way to a prosperity and stability founded on interdependence and global cooperation. Economic globalization intensifies these new features. Consequently, Sun Tzu, with his older, circumscribed perspective, has decidedly more relevance to today's world than Clausewitz, whose logic developed within the context of an expansive Western environment.

CHAPTER 7

Civilization:
Vasco Da Gama vs. Cheng Ho

"Neither the King nor his people ever think of waging a war of aggression. They are quite content with what they have and are not ambitious of conquest. In this respect they are much different from the people of Europe."

Matteo Ricci (1552–1610) on China

"Treat distant people kindly."

Instruction of Emperor Yongle (永樂, 1360–1424) to Admiral Cheng Ho (鄭和)

Admiral Cheng Ho: Ethics

The first sustained contact between East and West was finally established via the Indian Ocean in the early sixteenth century. Prior to this, however, there was a narrow miss between two extraordinary maritime adventures: that of Admiral Cheng Ho in the early fifteenth century, and that of Vasco da Gama at the end. By contrasting these two expeditions in terms of their size, characteristics, intentions, and legacies, we can grasp fundamental differences between their respective civilizations in their approaches to life.

East and West in the Fifteenth Century

The Chinese Admiral Cheng Ho (鄭和, 1371–1433) sailed as far as Somalia during his seven epic expeditions between 1405 and 1433; in 1498, the Portuguese explorer Vasco da Gama (ca.1460–1524) arrived in Calicut, India, which had been the destination of Cheng Ho's first expedition as well. Vasco da Gama was given the title "Admiral of the Indian Seas" by his king. Cheng Ho, likewise, had been given the title "Admiral of the Western Ocean," that is, the Indian Ocean.

The size and technological sophistication of Cheng Ho's fleet would have astonished Vasco da Gama. Each of his seven missions were said to be of comparable size. The first consisted of around 300 ships—including troop ships, equine ships, in which he later transported giraffes from Somalia to China, and water tankers, carrying one month's supply of fresh water—and a crew of 28,000, including navigators, sailors, doctors, soldiers, civil servants, and scholars. By contrast, Vasco da Gama's fleet consisted of only four ships with 170 sailors. The vastness of Cheng Ho's flagship would have astounded a Western contemporary. Figure 7-1 compares the famous *Santa Maria* of Christopher Columbus—similar in size to Vasco da Gama's ship—to the flagship of Cheng Ho.

The well-known maritime history of the West from Ancient Greece to the Age of Discovery may suggest that the West was well in advance of other civilizations in its sailing techniques, but the study of Eastern seafaring demonstrates a different reality: until the Industrial Revolution, which enabled the West to make a great leap in seafaring, the East was in fact more advanced: "It could probably be safely said that the Chinese were the greatest sailors in history. For nearly two millennia, they had ships and sailing techniques so far advanced of the rest of the world that the comparison was embarrassing. When the West finally did catch up with them, it was only by adapting their inventions in one way or another. For most of history the Europeans used ships far inferior in every respect imaginable even as late as 1800."[1]

East and West in the Fifteenth Century

Fig: 7-1. Cheng Ho's treasure ship and Columbus's Santa Maria illustration by Jan Adkins
(source: copyright authorized by the author)

Using its sailing technologies, Song dynasty China was actively involved in the maritime world known to it: "It was the first government in world history to issue banknotes or paper money, and the first Chinese government to establish a permanent standing navy. This dynasty also saw the first known use of gunpowder, as well as first discernment of true north using a compass. To protect and support the multitudes of ships sailing for maritime interests into the waters of the East China Sea and Yellow Sea (to Korea and Japan), Southeast Asia, the Indian Ocean, and the Red Sea, it was a necessity to establish an official standing navy. The Song dynasty therefore established China's first permanent navy in 1132, with a headquarters at Dinghai."[2]

For centuries the level of Eastern civilization was on a par with, if not ahead of, that of the West; why is this fact so little known today? Marco Polo's story helps to explain this. Marco Polo (1254–1324) was the first Westerner to leave a detailed report of the East, which, while arousing great curiosity, was promptly ignored and dismissed in the West. Many simply disbelieved him: for centuries, Westerners referred to liars as "Marco Polos." On his deathbed, he received a priest who encouraged him to disavow the "lies" he had propagated.[3] Marco Polo sighed deeply and responded that he had told only a part of what he had seen in the East.[4] When other sailors finally circumnavigated the African continent and arrived in the East, they discovered the truth of this: Marco's account was not only true, but incomplete. The East was even more amazing than he had suggested.

But the balance between East and West was already beginning to shift in favor of the West during the Age of Discovery. Indeed, in our comparison between Cheng Ho and Vasco da Gama, there is more to the case than meets the eye. The size of the two operations tells us nothing of their character. Although small, da

Gama's fleet was driven by individual initiative, determination to find a direct sea route to the Spice Islands, greed for goods and slaves, and a secret plan for colonization and exploitation. These Western characteristics of initiative and exploitation were totally absent from Cheng Ho's much larger fleet. Cheng Ho's aim was to demonstrate the power and prestige of the emperor, who had ordered him to spread his goodwill far and wide and to treat other people with kindness. His undertaking can best be characterized as a goodwill mission. This comparison between the aims of each mission reveals the essential characteristics of Eastern and Western civilizations of the time.

Cheng Ho and His Diplomatic Mission

Cheng Ho was a Muslim eunuch and a trusted commander of the third Emperor Yongle (永樂 r. 1403–1424) of the Chinese Ming dynasty. His name, Cheng Ho, was given by the emperor; his birth name was Ma Sanbao (馬三寶), a Muslim name, "Ma" referring to either Muhammad or Mansur. During his seven missions, Cheng Ho paid several visits to Persia and other Arab nations; as a Muslim leading a fantastical armada, he must have left a deep impression on the local people. It has been claimed that Sinbad the Sailor of *The Arabian Nights* was actually based on Sanbao.[5] The coincidences are too great to be dismissed.[6]

Well before the adventures of Ma Sanbao, an Arab geographer recorded the Chinese marine merchants visiting Yemen: "The economic power of Song China heavily influenced foreign economies abroad. The Moroccan geographer al-Idrisi wrote in 1154 of the prowess of Chinese merchant ships in the Indian Ocean and of their annual voyages that brought iron, swords, silk, velvet, porcelain, and various textiles to places, such as Aden (Yemen), the Indus River, and the Euphrates in modern-day

Iraq."[7] Given the active trade already established between China and the outside world, and given that marine commerce was not under the jurisdiction of the Scholar-Officials, foreigners, including Muslims, must have constituted an important force in Chinese trade.

Fig. 7-2. Cheng Ho (1371–1433) : "Admiral of the Western Ocean" (http://www.es.flinders. edu.au/~mattom/ science+society/lectures/ illustrations/lecture15/ chengho.html)	Fig. 7-3. Vasco da Gama (1460–1524): "Admiral of the Indian Seas" (http://commons.wikimedia.org/wiki/ Image:Vascodagama.JPG.)

Cheng Ho's expeditions thus covered only the areas known to the East. By contrast, his Western counterparts ventured into the unknown. When, eleven years earlier than Vasco da Gama, Bartholomew Diaz rounded the southern tip of the African continent in 1487, giving it the name "Cape of Good Hope," he found Muslim merchants active along the eastern coast of Africa; neither he nor Vasco da Gama had any affiliation or common ground with the locals. Da Gama's expedition covered areas unknown to Europe at that time: beyond the Cape of Good Hope, the course was completely uncharted in the West. He would pay for his lack of local knowledge: on his first voyage, he spent only 23 days crossing the Indian Ocean to Calicut, but on the return trip he spent 132 days sailing against the wind. Cheng Ho would not have suffered such difficulty since he must have been assisted by his fellow Muslim navigators.

Besides the fact that Cheng Ho was less trailblazing than Vasco da Gama, his expeditions were neither commercial trips nor pirate raids. They were purely diplomatic missions, undertaken for the purposes of demonstration, in conformity with the prevailing Eastern tribute system of the time. According to the norms and practices reserved for the suzerain within this system, the admiral carried cultural superiority, scholars, books, and gifts from the emperor to foreign kings and rulers; in return, he was to accept their allegiance and token tributes. As an essential principle of his mission, he was to give more than he received. Consequently, he brought back neither gold or spices nor slaves. Instead, he returned with foreign plants and animals, as well as kings, ambassadors, and repentant pirate captains, all desiring to pay their respects to the emperor. Cheng Ho's fleet harbored no aggressive or exploitative design; it was simply a mission to display the grandeur of the Middle Kingdom and magnanimity of its emperor. "Soft power" had already replaced military might as the foreign policy of the East.[8]

At one point, a detachment of the admiral's fleet reportedly sailed to northern Australia, but because his aim was neither conquest nor colonization, this largely uninhabited land did not interest him. Cheng Ho took great care to bring back giraffes from Africa; his reason for this was that a legendary Chinese animal, similar to the giraffe, was supposed to appear only when an emperor received the Mandate of Heaven. Naturally, the Ming emperor did everything to capitalize on this: he received dignitaries in Beijing from all over China to show them the giraffe as living proof of his gaining the Mandate of Heaven.

Cheng Ho's instruction from the emperor was to "treat distant people with kindness." This aspect constitutes the most striking difference from his Western counterpart's mission: Vasco da Gama had agreed with his investors to maximize profit by all means, including piracy, trade, and expropriation. Indeed, the East's culture of "treating distant people kindly," or its absence of war and conquest, greatly puzzled an early Western visitor, the Jesuit Matteo Ricci (1552–1610). Upon reaching China, Ricci noted: "Neither the King nor his people ever think of waging a war of aggression. They are quite content with what they have and are not ambitious of conquest. In this respect they are much different from the people of Europe."[9] Indeed, what Matteo Ricci witnessed was the application of Universal ethics in the East, as opposed to the Master ethics that were familiar to him.

Tribute System: West vs. East

In order to grasp the true nature of Cheng Ho's maritime expeditions, we must understand the Eastern tribute system (朝貢). This was a complex managerial method employed for international relations; complex because it involved a two-way traffic, with honor belonging to the strong but reward to the weak.

Crucially, this system lacked the West's exploitative approach, not necessarily because of any high moral standard but because it better suited the interests of the nations involved. The essential motive was self-interest, not altruism. The Ming dynasty, in particular, reinforced two principles of the tribute system: "the tributary state pays respect to the suzerain state and the latter takes care of the former with benevolence,"[10] and "the tributary state pays a small tribute to the suzerain state and the latter returns generous gifts to the former."[11] The emperor instructed Cheng Ho to treat the people he encountered with kindness, not out of fear or altruism, but because the emperor was supposed to reign over the entire world with benevolence according to the tribute system. Neither the emperor nor Cheng Ho could do otherwise.

The tribute system lasted for thousands of years in the East. Despite this, it is frequently misunderstood, due to a misuse of the word "tribute." The West also had a system of tribute, which was one-way traffic and extortion of the vanquished. "Tribute," when understood in this sense, badly misrepresents Eastern practice. The fundamental principle of mutual benefit defies Western logic. How could a Westerner of the fifteenth century have understood that a tribute system can be beneficial, in terms of material reward, to the one who pays tribute?

The Eastern system developed during the Han dynasty, which was roughly contemporary with the Roman Empire. Unlike the Roman Empire, which grew outward from a single city to cover a large landmass, the Han dynasty succeeded the Qin Empire (the first unified Empire in China) and retained control of the same territory without expanding it. The importance of the Han Empire, in terms of its landmass, population, resources, and culture, was so overwhelming to its neighbors that its foreign policy required a different approach than that of the West. No conquest was necessary, since China was thought to possess everything under the heavens. Consequently, all it wanted was a peaceful environment in order to concentrate on its own internal affairs, which remained daunting.

For this reason, the Han dynasty developed its unique tribute system to maintain order within its surroundings. China imposed submission on its neighbors, requiring their rulers to recognize the Chinese sovereign as the one emperor and to present him regular tribute, but also giving them more than it received. There was to be neither exploitation nor direct interference in internal matters, prompting some experts to describe the relationship as one of "benign neglect." Furthermore, when a country paid China tribute, a trade mission was allowed to accompany the officials, and so an official "international" trade could develop. Through such trade missions, China's superior culture and technology were transmitted to its vassal countries.

Because the tribute system provided a net benefit, materially speaking, for the vassal states, most preferred to send frequent envoys, often once every year. During the early sixteenth century, the Ming dynasty tried to limit tributes because of the costs involved. Having pledged allegiance to China, vassal states could only benefit from more frequent missions; they would bring more gifts in exchange for token tributes, permitting access to the rich cultural resources of China, and opening up the possibility of an official trade mission, especially since the Ming dynasty had forbidden maritime trading. The tribute countries took advantage of every possible occasion, such as royal births and coronations, to send envoys. At times, diplomatic negotiations were required to resolve the differences. This contrasts sharply with tributary relations as they existed in the West, from Greco-Roman times until the modern era; there, vassal states tried to avoid paying tribute because these payments were one-sided.

Client states of Rome and Persia also greatly benefited from their position, including increased peace, security, and religious freedom. Yet in terms of material benefit, the client states always paid tributes in a one-sided manner. It was like buying peace and security from Rome with money. It was the other way around in the East, where it was more like the suzerain state buying allegiance from client states with money. The Chinese tribute system was actively managed by all the succeeding dynasties, and especially by the Tang, Song, Ming, and Qing dynasties, until the nineteenth century; it only ended when China ceased to be the Middle Kingdom. With the arrival of the West, the East was forced to deal with a new expansive environment and ceased to be circumscribed. It remains to be seen how the ancient tribute system will manifest itself, if at all, in the twenty-first century, in a world dominated by Western paradigms of individual freedom, democracy, science, and commerce.

There is no question that the archaic system should perish with the opening of the Eastern world. But cultural heritage cannot be extinguished so easily. The question arises: Will the East simply discard the core concept of its tribute system, based on ethics, simply by replacing it with the Western treaty system, grounded in law and force? Or will the East be able to develop an international system combining ethics and law? We shall explore this issue in our final chapter.

Eastern Tribute System vs. Western Treaty System
To regulate its relations with other nations, the West had two systems, tributary and treaty. The tributary system was based on its Master ethics (i.e., the exploitation of the weak by the strong); the treaty system, meanwhile, was developed in the West with the rise of nation-states. Unlike the East, where China's importance was an undeniable reality, in the West there were multiple powers of comparable magnitude, allowing for competition and contention, and eventually giving rise to a treaty system. Alliances

and counteralliances were formed by open as well as secret treaties. Peace-time treaties, such as the Treaty of Tordesillas (1494), which divided the New World between Portugal and Spain, as well as wartime treaties, such as the Treaty of Westphalia (1648), ending the Thirty Years' War and marking a new era of nation-states, were already solidly in place within the Western system.

The treaty system involves contracts and promises to be honored by both parties. The violation of a treaty is sufficient cause for war. In this respect, the Western system is not so different from that of the East: both are based on formal contracts. The principal difference is in the respective roles of their participants. The treaty system is between equals, whereas the tribute system is between a suzerain and his vassals.

The Western treaty system involved a dynamic set of relationships between equals, standing as a distinct contrast to the static and hierarchical model of the Eastern tribute system. But this is only the outward appearance. In substantive terms, the principal difference is between ethics and law. If the Eastern tribute system is based upon ethics, the Western treaty system is based on law; only with this in mind can we understand why the Eastern tribute system lacks an exploitative aspect, and why the East in general did not favor the individual initiative characteristic of Vasco da Gama's expeditions.

Vasco Da Gama: Law and Force

While Cheng Ho's mission displayed all the characteristics of a Yin civilization, based on the concept of Harmony, Vasco da Gama's venture demonstrated all the characteristics of a Yang civilization, founded on the concept of Liberty, which enabled individual initiative to blossom to its full extent.

Vasco da Gama: In Search of Asian Spice

Vasco Da Gama's principal aim was to discover, at any cost, a direct maritime spice route between Europe and Asia. For this purpose, he had to venture into an unknown world, risking his life and relying only on his courage, wits, and soundness of judgment. His expeditions had little in common with the leisurely diplomatic missions of Cheng Ho. Da Gama's adventures embodied the Western drive to explore for profit. Confronted with stronger nations, he entered into trade agreements, but confronted with weaker ones, he plundered or colonized. The latter activities were particularly pronounced during his second expedition.[12] Following his epoch-making first expedition of 1497, in 1502 Vasco da Gama sailed with twenty warships to the Indian Ocean. His fleet attacked and extracted tribute from the Muslim ports of East Africa and engaged in privateering against Muslim merchant ships: "Once he had reached the northern parts of the Indian Ocean, Gama waited for a ship to return from Mecca and seized all the merchandise on it. He then ordered that the hundreds of passengers be locked in the hold and the ship—which was named *Mîrî*, and which contained many wealthy Muslim merchants—to be set on fire."[13] Once he arrived in Calicut port, Vasco da Gama destroyed all the ships there and succeeded in extracting favorable trade concessions.

More importantly, Vasco da Gama's profiteering was not an isolated event, as in the case of Cheng Ho's goodwill mission. Not only did it continue the long Western tradition of exploration and exploitation, but it embodied the spirit of its time. Before Vasco da Gama, other Portuguese captains, such as Bartholomew Diaz in 1487, explored the Indian Ocean around the southern tip of Africa. Following the route taken by Diaz, Vasco da Gama reached India in 1498; six years earlier, Columbus had reached the American continent. Another Portuguese sea captain, Ferdinand Magellan (1480–1521), reached Asia in 1519 via the Pacific for the first time in history. The maritime expeditions of the sixteenth century emphatically illustrate the West's desire for exploration, expansion, exploitation, and expropriation, in stark contrast to the Eastern focus on harmony and self-preservation. In a nutshell, the West was reactivating in the Atlantic and Indian Ocean the exploitative activities that it inherited from antiquity.

Legacy: Empire vs. Giraffe

As different as the admirals were in motive, their legacies were even more distinct. After the deaths of the Yongle Emperor and Cheng Ho, the Ming dynasty mandarins forbade any further maritime adventures, and even went further by destroying records of these extraordinary voyages. The reason for this policy may have been, at least in part, that maritime expeditions were unnecessarily expanding the Middle Kingdom's "tribute system," which would incur greater economic burdens. Indeed, the voyages brought the imperial treasury no profit; instead, they put the imperial finances under severe strain, without tangible political gain. Cheng Ho's expeditions were exclusively supported by the treasury and were used to demonstrate the ruler's prestige—no private investment or profit was possible. It was therefore only a matter of time before Cheng Ho's grandiose demonstrations had to come to an end, having exacted a monumental expenditure without recompense.

By contrast, Vasco da Gama's lucrative voyages were imitated and repeated for centuries by other captains and rulers as sources of enormous profit. Consequently, the most intriguing question arising from Beijing's suppression of Cheng Ho's maritime adventures was not, as is commonly thought by Western scholars, why they happened, but rather, why the Ming mandarins, or leaders, did not think of turning China's seafaring capability and experience, which was far superior to that of the West, into a profitable business, by piracy, colonization, or international commerce. It seems that the answer must boil down to the characteristics of the culture in this era.

In Cheng Ho's time, Eastern people simply did not possess the necessary concept of individual liberty or profit-seeking, foreign adventure, conquest, or exploitation—that is, the products of a Master ethics. Thus, the crucial institutional drives for Western-style expansion—the possibility of individual risk and reward—did not exist. Its own tradition of Universal ethics, deriving from the canons of Confucianism and Taoism, would have frowned on any suggestion of such profit-seeking schemes.

Thus, even just as diplomatic expeditions, Cheng Ho's ventures were an aberration in the history of China. His grand expeditions were a passing episode, the most important legacy of which was perhaps his transport of a giraffe—the symbol of the "Mandate of Heaven" for the emperor—all the way from Somalia to Beijing.

Legacy: Empire vs. Giraffe

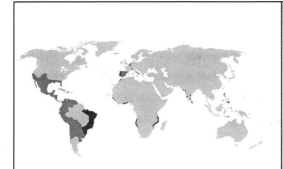

The Iberian Empires: Showing the result of Treaty of Tordesillas in 1494

Fig. 7-4. The Iberian, Portuguese-Spanish, Empires in the 16th Century (http://en.wikipedia.org/wiki/File:Iberian_Union_Empires.png)	Fig. 7-5. Giraffe brought from Somalia by Cheng Ho in 1415 (http://en.wikipedia.org/wiki/Zheng_He)

By contrast, Vasco da Gama's legacy was truly historic. His intrepid explorations opened up a whole new perspective for Western expansion into, and exploitation of, India and East Asia. In stark contrast to Cheng Ho's obscured legacy in China, Vasco da Gama became a national hero. When he returned to Portugal as the first captain to reach India from Europe, he was bestowed with all sorts of honors, including his appointment as Admiral of the Indian Seas. The whole nation watched and awaited his success. His maritime explorations opened up the possibility of vast profit for the entire nation and its citizens. As such, the Western expeditions were an enterprise in which the whole nation—kings, nobles, and private merchants alike—participated, and which were often financed by private citizens, as well as by monarchs seeking profit. Vasco da Gama's enterprise, for instance, was directly supported by the kings of Portugal at that time, John II and Manuel I.[14]

In the year 1500, three years after Vasco da Gama's first voyage to the Indian Ocean, the Portuguese crown sent another captain, Pedro Cabral, to the Indian Ocean to replicate his route. Cabral, before finally reaching Calicut, India, accidentally discovered and colonized Brazil, when his thirteen-ship fleet was blown westward to its shores. Only four of his ships returned to Portugal in 1501, but these were laden with pepper and other spices. The success of the two explorers led Portugal to establish a fortress at Goa in 1510. Several decades later, Portuguese ships reached China. Vasco da Gama's voyage ultimately resulted in the Portuguese Empire.[15]

The clear contrast in legacies between the Eastern and Western maritime expeditions originates from their differences in character. The imposing size of Cheng Ho's fleet embodied the Eastern ethical and political tradition as a manifestation of its rulers' omnipotence. On the other hand, the small but sturdy fleet of Vasco da Gama, brimming with infinite promise, symbolized dynamism, expansion, and exploitation characteristic of the Western Master ethics.

Western Empires: Plundering and Piracy, Spice and Slave Trade
The driving force behind Vasco da Gama's expedition and the ultimate success of Western empires over the next 400 years was the motive of individual profit. Doubtless, his voyages and the emergence of the Western empires were also motivated by irresistible curiosity for the unknown world and by a strong

proselytism on behalf of Christianity. Matteo Ricci's presence in China demonstrates the exploratory and evangelical character of the Christian faith, which went hand in hand with European expansion.

Profit, however, remained the most prominent motivation for the West's maritime expeditions. Vasco da Gama's adventures followed the long Western tradition of seeking profit and plunder where possible, but trade only where necessary. In this and all other Western voyages until the nineteenth century, plunder and colonization, and the trade in spices and slaves, were the strongest motivations. In examining an often-vilified aspect of Western civilization, we must try to do so without moral prejudice. We remain convinced that if Easterners had had the same environment, chance, and opportunities, they would have developed the same culture with the same exploitative habits and practices. With this in mind, let us see how piracy, plundering, and the spice and slave trades played a crucial role in Western expansion during the early part of the Age of Discovery.[16]

Plundering, Piracy, Privateering, and Colonization: From Greece to Modern Europe

Piracy, plunder, and conquest were common features of human affairs in the ancient and medieval West—from Greece and Rome to the Vikings[17]—and modern civilizations.[18] This is because, unlike the confined East, the West enjoyed an open and expansive environment, which gave birth to a Master ethics. The Viking raiders terrorized the entirety of Europe from the ninth to the twelfth centuries. "The raiding business was so profitable that the taste for it spread throughout Scandinavia ... The Vikings sailed every year in greatly increasing numbers upon their forays and returned triumphant and enriched. And their example inspired all audacious spirits and younger sons. Other fleets ranged more widely. They broke into the Mediterranean. Charlemagne gazing through a window in a town near Narbonne saw these sinister ships haunting the coast and uttered an impressive warning of the wrath to come. It was not until 835 that the storm broke in fury and fleets sometimes of three or four hundred vessels rowed up to the rivers of England, France, and Russia in predatory enterprises on the great scale."[19]

Let us note that piracy was not the monopoly of the West. Muslim pirates were active in the Mediterranean from the end of the seventh century until the fifteenth century, systematically attacking the northern Mediterranean settlements, especially in Sicily and Italy. The countless *Torri Saracene* now converted for use as tourist sites attest to this. Similarly, from the sixteenth to the nineteenth centuries, while European explorers were rapidly transformed into national navies, the Barbary pirates and corsairs from Morocco, Algeria, Tunisia, and Libya remained active in the Western Mediterranean as well as on the European Atlantic coast. The influence and activities of Barbary pirates were so common that one can find them in such stories as *Robinson Crusoe* and *Candide.* Cervantes himself lived for five years as slave in Algeria after his capture by corsairs; he was finally ransomed by his parents. It was only with the Industrial Revolution, which gave the West an overwhelming advantage over the Barbary pirates, that the West could terminate their activities.

Pirates existed in the East as well. Japanese pirates, known as Wokou (倭寇), were active in East Asia for almost four centuries. During the thirteenth century, Japanese pirates began raiding the coast of the Korean peninsula and later spread across the Yellow Sea to China. As the Ming dynasty implemented a closed-door policy forbidding maritime trade, those affected in China began to collude with Japanese pirates. This led to the second phase of Eastern piracy in the sixteenth century, characterized by a joint Sino-Japanese piracy, still known as Wokou. Their activities covered the entire East Asian sea, often making the most of rivers, just as the Vikings had done in the West.[20] Wokou were comparable to Viking or Muslim pirates, roaming the western coast of the Pacific in search of booty. Their exploits undoubtedly shared more with the Viking and Muslim pirates than with those of Admiral Cheng Ho, as they were driven by the self-interest and profit-making impulses of both captain and crew. However, there is one fundamental difference: piracy never became a national enterprise in the East, including Japan, nor were there Japanese privateers or corsairs. These latter practices did not exist in the East, and they have no exact translation in Eastern languages. Indeed, when Japan had a strong central government, the activities of pirates declined. The only exception to this was when the Japanese government actively engaged in overseas expansion and conquest during its invasion of Korea toward the end of the sixteenth century.[21] Compared to Western maritime history, however, this invasion could easily be treated as an historic aberration. The fundamental point is that piracy never reached mainstream legitimacy as an acceptable pursuit in the East. As such, with the consolidation of central authority by Toyotomi and Tokugawa during the late sixteenth and early seventeenth century, Wokou activities began to decline and soon disappeared entirely.

On the other hand, the ubiquity and profitability of piracy in the West soon brought about its legitimized pursuit at a national level. The phenomenon of the privateer—a private warship authorized by a national sovereign to attack foreign commercial vessels—is not unique to Western countries. There were similar instances of state-sanctioned piracy in the Muslim world. Yet in terms of its magnitude and systematic use, they were no match for their Western counterparts. From the plunder and piracy of the ancient Mediterranean, through the privateers of the Renaissance, and finally to the participation of national navies in the colonization of remote territories, the West was most active as it continued to operate in an expansive environment. Privateers were not only officially sanctioned by the state, they also formed a kind of national enterprise; the costs of these ventures were borne by private investors, including the royal families themselves. The very first examples of such ventures at the national level occurred thanks to the spice trade.

Spice Trade: From Venice to Portugal-Spain

One of the fundamental motivations for the Age of Discovery was the pursuit of spice. For example, even after the discovery of the Americas, Columbus made his fourth voyage, at least nominally, in search of the Strait of Malacca to the Indian Ocean. Asian spices followed the introduction of Chinese silk into Europe. To the Romans, the East was represented by silk; they called the Chinese the "*Seres*," "the people of silk." During the Middle Ages, Arabs and Persians, using the Silk Road as well as sea routes, acted as middlemen between East and West. Already in the Middle Ages, spices had replaced silk as the most important item even in the Silk Road trade. The rise of Venice—lasting nearly a millennium—was driven largely by its monopoly of the Mediterranean spice trade, and its subsequent fall was due to its loss of control to the Ottoman Empire. For centuries, Venice monopolized the spice trade; ships arrived into the Gulf ports from South and South East Asia via the sea route dominated by Muslim marine merchants. From the Gulf to the Mediterranean seaports, such as Alexandria, they were carried by Muslim caravans; then it was Venice that transported them from Alexandria to Europe for enormous profits. It is estimated that Venice dealt with one thousand tons of spices a year; this was enough to ensure its wealth and glory, and it long maintained its status as the richest and most populous city in Europe.

With this backdrop, one can imagine the stakes involved in exploring the direct sea route from Europe to Asia. When Vasco da Gama successfully linked Portugal to the Indian Ocean, he created just such a route to the Spice Islands, irrevocably eclipsing the Mediterranean's centrality in trade with the East. Venice's power was thus decisively compromised. Spain was subsequently in hot pursuit of a direct spice trade route; this ambition was achieved by Magellan. On September 6, 1522, his original fleet returned to Spain after a three-year epic voyage around the globe, the first in history; the fleet had been reduced to only one ship, *Victoria*, with a crew of eighteen. Magellan himself had been killed in the Philippines, but the remaining crew succeeded in bringing home twenty-six tons of spices, mostly cloves and cinnamon. The original objective of the voyage had not been to circumnavigate the globe, but to find a secure and independent route to the Spice Islands for Spain, since the eastern route had been monopolized by Portugal; Magellan therefore had to take a westward route, and so, in the end, his fleet circumnavigated the globe. Upon their return, the crew was greatly puzzled by the discrepancy of a day between the date registered by their ship's log, and that accepted in Spain: they had unwittingly discovered the need for an international date line.[22]

Thus, the combination of national and individual profit-seeking was a unique development in the West, one that allowed it to achieve new success in exploration and exploitation.[23] But in addition to the quest for spice, European sailors and pirates were interested in the burgeoning slave trade.[24]

Slave Trade: From Greece to America

Since antiquity, slavery had been an indispensable element in the socio-economic structure in the West. All Greek city-states were founded on the practice—these were comprised of citizens, freemen, and slaves: citizens for politics, freemen for commerce, and slaves for agriculture. In the case of Sparta, for example, agricultural production was left entirely in the hands of slaves, called helots, taken in war from other city-states. War, piracy, and trade were the main sources of slaves, who formed an integral part of the Greek socio-economic structure. In Rome, meanwhile, slaves made up, at least, about a quarter of the city's population. As the Roman Republic expanded outward, entire populations were enslaved from conquered territories, much as the Spartans had done. During the empire, the annual required provision of slaves was calculated at around several hundred thousand. In Rome, it was said that "slaves were either born or made."[25] Wherever the Roman legions went, they were accompanied by slave merchants: *Homo hominis lupus*—man is the predator of man.

After the Greco-Roman period, the Vikings, as maritime explorers and exploiters, naturally engaged in slavery: "The slave trade was one of the pillars of Norse commerce during the sixth through the eleventh century. One of the primary profit centers of Viking trade was slavery. The Church took a position that Christians should not own fellow Christians as slaves. This took much of the economic incentive out of raiding, as the Vikings became Christianized."[26] During the Middle Ages, slaves were acquired mostly through Islamic traders of the Mediterranean. But such trade remained low, partly because of the general economic stagnation in Europe, and partly because the Mediterranean trade was increasingly closed to the West by Muslim navies and pirates.[27]

Slavery was revived with the Age of Discovery.[28] Portugal's ascent as the first great Western maritime power began with Henry the Navigator (1394–1460), whose maritime expeditions received a great boost when his captains captured slaves on the east coast of sub-Saharan Africa, indicating that the West was no longer dependent on Muslim traders.[29] For Columbus, slavery was an important source of profit.[30] After indigenous Americans had been decimated by disease and exploitation, the colonists began transporting slaves from Africa to the New World. With the blessing of the Church,[31] most Western nations eventually participated in this lucrative business. In the Mediterranean, slavery continued to thrive with piracy until the nineteenth century.[32]

By contrast, there was no slavery as institution in the East in terms of slave raid and slave trade. To be sure, exploitation existed: lifelong servants, bond servants, serfs, and so on, but not an institutionalized system of slavery. Most contemporary articles casually mention the same existence of slaves in the East. But they miss the essential aspect of the issue: the absence of slave taking and slave trade. Slave markets could only exist in an expansive environment that operated according to a Master ethics. The Universal ethics of Confucius was the result, not the cause, of an absent slave market. The evidence is undeniable; unlike the West of Plato and Aristotle, there is no reference either before or during the period of Confucius to any practice of slavery. On the contrary, the East, especially China, was actively engaged in liberating slaves captured by neighboring "barbarian" nomads: "On June 11, 631, Emperor Taizong sent envoys to the Xueyantuo bearing gold and silk in order to persuade the release of enslaved Chinese prisoners who were captured from the northern frontier during the transition from Sui to Tang; this embassy succeeded in freeing 80,000 Chinese men and women who were then returned to China."[33]

In addition to its circumscribed environment, we may adduce the East's agrarian economy as a reason for its lack of slavery: food, and the land needed to produce it, was always in short supply. Feeding the people thus remained the most important task for any Eastern ruler. Just as conflict and war dominated the West, so famine and drought were the most pressing problems of the East. Where food is scarce, a slave is simply another mouth to feed—the cost of slavery therefore outweighs its benefit.

As Western powers began to arrive with more frequency in the East during the sixteenth century, there arose a concern about slavery. When the first Portuguese navigators arrived in the East in the early sixteenth century, they attempted to capture slaves; they were thwarted only by superior local forces in China. In Japan, the Christian Daimyos traded local women with the Portuguese for gunpowder. This affected Japan's reaction to Christianity: in 1588, the ruler of Japan, Toyotomi Hideyoshi (1536–1598), abolished slavery. His motivation must have been more political than ethical, but the ban remained effective and was maintained by his successors. The absence of slavery in the East cannot be ascribed to moral virtue—the ethical rejection of this practice dates only from the nineteenth century. To repeat, this absence was a corollary of the East's environment, just as its practice was a natural corollary of the West's situation, which remained expansive until the nineteenth century. In the West, even before the nineteenth century, there had been strong abolitionist movements and individuals whose foundations were religious and moral. For example, two of the Founding Fathers of America—Benjamin Franklin and Alexander Hamilton—were wholly against slavery, well before the geographical divisions of

North and South. Nonetheless, it was only in the nineteenth century that the West abolished the slave system and prohibited the slave trade.

Us vs. Them Division

One crucial contrast between East and West is the distinction between Us and Them, absent from the East, but essential to the West. Confucius implored his disciples to "Teach without discrimination."[34] His one and only distinction was that between Junzi and Xiaoren. But in the West, a division between us and them legitimized plundering, slavery, and colonization. Many mechanisms, and especially religion, were used to justify and amplify profit margins and the abuse of others' natural resources. Absent morality, the West was simply applying the same Master ethics as laid out by Aristotle: his theory of enslavement of barbarians by Greeks was copied by the Church: "Reduce any Saracens, pagans, and any other unbelievers to hereditary slavery."[35]

It goes without saying that Westerners were not wholly blind to the double standards of Christian morality. Immanuel Kant lamented the exploitative aspects of conquest and trade in his work *Perpetual Peace*: "Let us look now, for the sake of comparison, at the inhospitable behavior of the civilized nations, especially the commercial states of our continent. The injustice that they exhibit on visiting foreign lands and races—this being equivalent in their eyes to conquest—is such as to fill us with horror.... America ... the Spice Islands ..., etc., were on being discovered, looked upon as countries which belonged to nobody; for the native inhabitants were reckoned as nothing.... Oppression of the natives followed, famine, insurrections, perfidy, and all the rest of the litany of evils which can afflict mankind.... And this has been done by nations who make a great ado about their piety, and who, while they are quite ready to commit injustice, would like, in their orthodoxy, to be considered among the elect."[36]

Thus, the early modern West was naturally ambivalent in its attitude toward outsiders: it engaged in both trade and plunder according to its balance of power. But since most foreign nations were weaker, the West predominantly engaged in plunder rather than trade. It was only with the transformation of the world environment from an expansive to a circumscribed one in the course of the nineteenth century that the West began to take a clear stand in favor of trade, making a clean break with its long tradition of plunder—in other words, with its division between Us and Them. This important change coincided with the historic paradigm shift from war to trade. This point will be further explored in our final chapter.

Western Initiative vs. Eastern Meritocracy

Plunder and piracy, spice and slave trades, and the "us vs. them" division were all essential ingredients in the making of Western empires. Yet these were also common in many other civilizations. As Nietzsche succinctly observed, exploitation as the basis of self-preservation is one of the most fundamental features of human nature.

These ingredients, however, constitute only the external manifestations of Western imperialism. At the heart of the phenomenon was the concept of personal liberty, unique to the West. This concept of liberty gave birth to the rule and system of law, and the practice of legal compacts guaranteeing individual initiatives.

In the East, the essential principle behind its tribute system, and behind Cheng Ho's diplomatic missions, was the concept of Universal ethics of humanity and harmony, which was nurtured and inculcated by thousands of years of education throughout the population. From the perspective of an early modern Westerner, Cheng Ho's mission must have sounded like a fairy tale: how could harmony possibly be a basis for foreign policy? Little known is the two-thousand-year-old tradition of Eastern meritocracy, promoted by the Imperial Examination System. Over time, this meritocratic examination system oriented the entire population toward education, since only by this means could social mobility be achieved.

From this perspective, we can conclude that education became, like religion in the West, the most pervasive social structure in the East. Likewise, ethics based on meritocracy constituted the backbone of Eastern civilization, just as the rule of law, enabling individual initiative, provided the foundation for Western civilization.

Western Initiative Guaranteed by Law

The Western drive to profit and exploitation is only part of its history. Why did Easterners, who are, after all, members of the same species as Westerners, not acquire the same tendencies? The answer lies in the personal liberty and initiative of Western explorers, unknown to the East. Crucial to this initiative was the idea of contracts, respected by subject and sovereign alike; this enabled legal technology—unlocking entrepreneurship and risk-taking—and so constituted the key to the West's success at conquest. The West owed its concept of law to its Greco-Roman ancestry as well as to the Judeo-Christian belief in God's decree.

While other civilizations knew of trade and plunder, science and navigational technology, without the West's legal system guaranteeing individual profit, these innovations could not have flourished and remained inert.

In other civilizations, including that of the East, successful generals and other public individuals stood in danger of royal jealousy: close advisers of kings would effect their downfall or demise. In the West, where even kings were bound by law to respect the rights of individuals, such political machinations were much less frequent—legal compacts thus protected personal ambitions.

For example, Christopher Columbus negotiated with the Spanish monarchs and obtained the following contractual rights and benefits: "He would be given the rank of Admiral of the Ocean Sea and appointed Viceroy and Governor of all the new lands. He had the right to nominate three persons, from whom the sovereigns would choose one, for any office in the new lands. He would be entitled to 10 percent of all the revenues from the new lands in perpetuity ... he would also have the option of buying one-eighth interest in any commercial venture with the new lands and receive one-eighth of the profits."[37]

Fig. 7-6. Columbus and Queen Isabella (http://en.wikipedia.org/wiki/ Christopher_Columbus)	Fig. 7-7. Emperor attending the Imperial Examination (http://www.chinatourguide. net/12_14.htm)

Figure 7-7 shows a scene of the final stage of the Imperial Examination attended by the emperor himself. In terms of the significance and weight it carried in the Eastern world, this picture is equivalent to Figure 7-6, which shows Columbus negotiating with Queen Isabella: those who succeeded in the Examination became leaders of the country in the East in the same way as those with successful contract arrangements became leaders in the West.

The concept of the legally binding contract was crucially lacking in the East. Even adventurous captains like Cheng Ho had to depend entirely on imperial benevolence. Nobody would have had the audacity to request a share of the profits from his discoveries, all of which, if any, would flow by right to the emperor. Columbus also adopted and used his own coat of arms, in the Western tradition of individual assertion.[38] Cheng Ho would never have imagined adopting his own arms, which would have been regarded as a sign of independence from his sovereign and, hence, of grave disrespect.[39]

Both the bulwark of individualism and its contractual mechanism were outgrowths of a long tradition and cultural heritage in the West. It is therefore incorrect to argue that the East missed its chance to become a maritime power like the West by suppressing Cheng Ho's ventures; these were rather aberrations. Given the lack of legal support for individual profit, profiteering maritime expeditions were simply not a reality in the East.

The contract system in the West guaranteed profit sharing for the individual even with respect to monarchs. But while the East did not have such a system, it did have a comprehensive system of education. Although the West first introduced mandatory universal education, this only arrived later with industrialization. Prior to this, education was far more widespread in the East.

Eastern Meritocracy Undergirding the Imperial Examination System

In the previous chapter, we discussed the genesis of the Imperial Examination System in the East; let us now examine its characteristics. The indispensable mechanism for its success was its principle of meritocracy, which enabled any individual with determination and competence to improve his social status The Eastern tradition of meritocracy was as unique as the Western legal compact, and the East's extraordinary emphasis on education was its natural outgrowth.

With a view to ensuring meritocracy, various mechanisms in favor of transparency were developed early on: "In order to ensure transparency in the process of the examinations, candidates were identified by number rather than name, and examination answers were recopied by a third person before being evaluated to prevent the candidate's handwriting from being recognized."[40] These measures are still maintained.

Figure 7-9 shows a government official, most probably a high scorer in the examination: the two cranes embroidered in his outfit attest to this. These symbols were equivalent to Columbus's coat of arms (Figure 7-8), but instead of being chosen by the individual, such symbols were strictly regulated by the imperial court.

Fig. 7-8. Individual Arms of Columbus (http://en.wikipedia.org/wiki/ Christopher_Columbus)	Fig. 7-9. A Scholar-Official with Insignia of Ranking (http://en.wikipedia.org/wiki/ Imperial_examination)

The Imperial Examination System was open to all. In reality, as the preparation for it was long and costly, wealthy and powerful families could more easily produce candidates. When the system became corrupt (i.e., when the principle of the meritocracy was broken—which usually coincided with a period of dynastic decline), the examinations were useless and official posts were sold. Despite this, the principle of meritocracy held firm all through Eastern history. Success stories of those who rose through the ranks throughout the East inspired the population to educate themselves for millennia.[41]

Eastern rulers had personal incentives to maintain a meritocratic system. During the Han, Sui, and Tang dynasties, rulers still struggled with the powerful legacy of the hereditary regional aristocracy. Confucian meritocracy appealed to the emperors, who alone could claim exemption from such a rule. For this the rulers needed well-organized scholar-official elites to counterbalance the aristocrats. Rulers also distorted Confucian teachings to promote respect for their own authority: "This competitive procedure was designed to draw the best talent into government. But perhaps an even greater consideration for the Tang rulers, aware that imperial dependence on powerful aristocratic families and warlords would have destabilizing consequences, was to create a body of career officials having no autonomous territorial or functional power base."[42] "The examination system, used only on a small scale in Sui and Tang times, played a central role in the fashioning of these new elite. The early Song emperors, concerned above all to avoid domination of the government by military men, greatly expanded the civil service examination system and the government school system."[43]

Whatever the political motivations are, the fact that the East had introduced so early on a mechanism that ensured social mobility must be viewed as the defining factor for Eastern civilization. William Manchester describes the lack of social mobility in Great Britain during the Victorian era of the nineteenth century: "Social mobility, as we understand it today, was not only unpursued by the vast majority, it had never existed. For centuries the Englishmen's fate had been determined at birth. The caste system was almost as rigid as India's. Obedience to the master had been bred in childhood. And those who left the land for the mills as the agricultural class seeped into the cities were kept in line by custom and the example of all around them. Successful merchants were an exception and a significant one;

they built mansions, bought coaches, and hired servants. Yet they were never fully accepted by the patriciate."[44]

Individual Initiative vs. Meritocracy

As we have seen with Vasco da Gama, the West relied heavily on individual initiative for its imperialism. In the East, management of empire, not expansion, was the primary concern; management required education, and so mandated a meritocracy. Current statistics speak volumes about the extraordinary focus on education by Eastern peoples: they represent around 2.4 percent of the total population of the United States, but around 17 percent in Harvard and MIT, and 27 percent at UC Berkeley. This discrepancy demonstrates the stronger commitment of Asian parents to the education of their children and their focus on hard work.

By contrast, Western culture put more emphasis on initiative than on education. Consequently, Western history can be read as a history of heroes who succeeded on their own terms: conquerors, prophets, explorers, adventurers, trailblazers in science and literature, and so on. The very first line of the most important book of Eastern civilization, *The Analects of Confucius*, concerns education: "To learn and to practice what is learned time and again is a pleasure, is it not?" This opening may seem almost banal compared to the first lines of Genesis or John's Gospel, but it encapsulates the Eastern attitude toward the world. Likewise, all Eastern parents know the famous story of Mencius' mother moving three times to find him suitable education.[45] A Western counterpart was the father of Horace, who accompanied the boy to Rome for his basic education and then sent him to Athens for advanced studies. The poet left a moving tribute to his father: "If my character is flawed by a few minor faults, but is otherwise decent and moral, if you can point out only a few scattered blemishes on an otherwise immaculate surface, if no one can accuse me of greed, or of prurience, or of profligacy, if I live a virtuous life, free of defilement (pardon, for a moment, my self-praise), and if I am to my friends a good friend, my father deserves all the credit."[46]

Again, Eastern children are repeatedly indoctrinated with the idea of "studying with the glow of fireflies during summer and with the glimmer of snow during winter," that is, allowing no excuses not to study, not even an inability to afford lamplight. Common folk in the East despised those who did not study diligently, comparing them to "animals with human clothing." The emphasis on education is often cited as one of the most conspicuous aspects of Eastern civilization and an important factor in its rapid economic and sociopolitical development. But this is only half the story. All other peoples value education and have developed examination systems: what they have lacked is the Eastern insistence on meritocracy, without which there is little motivation for education.

As the West entered the Dark Ages after the demise of the Roman Empire, the East established its meritocratic and impartial examination system. It was realized that security and stability were best guaranteed by attracting talented persons and securing their loyalty to the regime. The principle of meritocracy was contained in Confucianism as well as in Taoism, but it was Mohism (墨家) that stressed it most emphatically. This school, founded by Mozi (墨子, 470–ca. 391 BC), developed contemporaneously with Confucianism, Taoism, and Legalism, and remained a strong rival to Confucianism until the Han dynasty adopted the latter as its official state philosophy. Mohism is notable for its advocacy of universal love, as well as thrift and non-aggression. Its doctrine of impartial concern was criticized by Confucians as impractical, and the Confucian practice of three years' mourning was criticized by Mohists as extravagant.

Here are some examples of the Mohist focus on meritocracy as the key to state administration: "In ruling the state, the sage-king valued moral excellence and recognized ability without fail. If capable, even a farmer or an artisan would be employed: commissioned with high rank, remunerated with liberal emoluments, trusted with important charges, and empowered to issue final orders."[47] "When the virtuous and capable run the government, the ignorant and humble remain orderly; when the ignorant and humble run the government, the virtuous and capable become rebellious: therefore, recognition of the virtuous and capable is the foundation of government."[48] "In good governance, there are three rules—rank, emolument, and delegation of authority: when the rank of the virtuous and capable is not high, people do not show them respect; when their emoluments are not adequate, people do not place confidence in them; when their orders are not final, people do not stand in awe before them. So the sage-king placed them high in rank, gave them liberal emoluments, trusted them with important charges, and decreed their orders to be final."[49] "The sage-king in honouring the virtuous and employing the capable in government followed the ways of Heaven: Heaven does not discriminate among the poor and the rich, the honourable and the humble, the distant and the near, and the related and the unrelated. The capable were promoted and honoured; the incapable were kept back and chased away."[50] "In governing the state, the sage-king honoured those who were capable: he did not honour his relatives; he did not honour the rich without merit; he did not honour the good-looking without ability."[51]

Western Diversity vs. Eastern Conformity

What individual initiatives and the legal system did for the West was done by education and meritocratic examination in the East. One crucial outcome of the extraordinary focus on education was the spread of a uniform ethics in the East. This uniformity is quite comparable to that of religion in the West, especially in terms of the degree of faith attached to its principles and values. This feat was made possible by a uniform curriculum among all the examinees (i.e., by the entire population in the education of their children).

When West met East during the nineteenth century, the West had already become largely secular and was no longer suffocated by intellectual uniformity, as it had been in the Middle Ages. This process gave rise to dynamic diversity in the West. By this time, the East had lost almost all of the intellectual curiosity and diversity it had possessed during the time of Confucius, confining itself to a very limited number of Confucian classics. Thus, Western diversity contrasted strongly with Eastern conformity—a contrast that remains evident even today.

Prior to the maturity of the Imperial Examination System, civil servants were chosen by the recommendation of other officials and aristocrats, both central and local. But already, the quality of one's education, as well as one's grasp of the Eastern classics, constituted more important factors than the nobility of one's birth. This tendency was more firmly established with the examination system, by which, for almost two thousand years, the Confucian and Taoist canons spread the core concepts of Tao and Humanity and so firmly infused Eastern civilization with its Universal ethics.

Since the early seventh century, Easterners have invested great fortunes in education, since success in this field brings them great honor and wealth. Since the same examinations are offered across the land, the same textbooks are used in teaching; thus the East has attained a profound cultural conformity. Since the early fifteenth century, the system has been grounded in the Four Books and Five Classics, the Confucian canon selected by the scholar Zhu Xi.[52] For more than five centuries, anyone who claimed to be educated has had to be well versed in these texts.

Within such a system, regional or sectarian diversities were simply not possible. This lack of variety was compensated for by social harmony across the nation. The East's cultural conformity has often been misconstrued as a result of authoritarian rule, but it is, in fact, the natural outgrowth of its ancient system of education, which shaped and propagated a distinct culture, and a set of values, throughout the East. The system did not promote individual initiative and creativity, and so produced neither democracy nor a native capitalist economy. But such conformity must be distinguished from ideological or religious *uniformity*, for it was mostly non-dogmatic in these areas.

Neo-Confucianism never dominated the East in the way that Christianity did in the medieval West, or ideology in parts of the modern West—it was always counterbalanced, not only by Taoism and Buddhism, but also from within by differing interpretations. Lu Jiuyuan (陸九淵, 1139–1192), Zhu Xi's principal contemporary rival, argued against any separation between Mind and Principle, while Zhu Xi emphasized the importance of Principle; Wang Yangming (王陽明, 1472–1529) established a new brand of neo-Confucianism, reviving Lu's philosophy and emphasizing the importance of Mind. Some consider Wang one of the four most important Confucian thinkers, along with Confucius himself, Mencius, and Zhu Xi. Wang's teaching was particularly influential in Japan and produced many followers there. These included Togo Heihachiro, the heroic admiral of the 1904–1905 Russo-Japanese war. Dai Zhen (戴震, 1724–1777) was another outstanding example. He tried to revive Han Confucianism, as opposed to Song neo-Confucianism, arguing that the truth was to be found in an active life, not in contemplation. Dai's pragmatism and hostility to metaphysics struck a chord with the Eastern character. When the Chinese responded well to Deng Xiaoping's reclamation of traditional Chinese pragmatism—the "white cat, black cat" principle—Deng knew that he could rely on this cultural heritage.

The East as Seen by Preindustrial West

Eastern philosophy was first introduced to the West during the sixteenth century. Thus, the West's image of the East during the Enlightenment was one of pristine nature, revealing much of the fundamental contrast between the two cultures. Fresh impressions were expressed and points were discussed by the Western thinkers of this era.

Let us examine some of these views, as collected by Walter Demel in his article, "China in the Political Thought of Western and Central Europe, 1570–1750": "The West found the Chinese to be kind and industrious but ultimately heathen and superstitious. They were surprised by many things: that an Eastern candidate for magistracy was chosen for his knowledge and virtue, disregarding his nobility and wealth; that scholarship was held in singular esteem in the East, and that statistics was much advanced; that China enjoyed abundance even without God's blessing. The West thought the Chinese pagan people, even though ethical, most polite and ingenious, with no religious judgment, with no knowledge of the Bible and Aristotle. Western thinkers were annoyed that China did not fit into their system … a cultural configuration different from those found elsewhere in the world.

They were impressed by the emperor's interest in agriculture; he advised European monarchs of the time to follow his ceremony of tilling the soil, and several took his advice, including Louis XV, Louis XVI, and Joseph II. Voltaire believed that China's ruling class was wise and deistic, while all other countries appeared rife with superstition. The absence of an intermediary power, an aristocracy, with a title of its own was foreign to the West. Every able man worked, and there was no idle aristocracy; the 1692 edict of tolerance was criticized by certain Western thinkers as excessive. Many of them thought that China was governed by philosophers and delighted that it lasted and was dominant so long, promoting officials by grade, paying well, and forbidding them to accept gifts or bribes on pain of severe punishment. The West was surprised that the monarch, time and again, was himself a philosopher or at least employed philosophers as his permanent counselors. Thus, the monarch ruled on the advice of a literate ruling class composed of serious thinkers; this was the realization of a perfectly enlightened despotism; virtue was the leading idea as well as the good. Virtue was not only an attainable ideal but a practical aim which could be achieved by a normal man who did not have to be a pious Christian."[53]

Let us now examine other impressions collected by D.E. Mungello in his work on "Confucianism in the Enlightenment": "Voltaire and other Enlightenment thinkers argued that China was a model enlightened monarchy in which the emperor ruled by the rational values of Confucianism. In other words, the monarch was required to consult with the scholar-official class. François Quesnay, the author of *Le despotisme de la Chine* (1767), venerated the leading sage of China to such a degree that he was called the 'Confucius of Europe.' The Five Classics were presented not as particular to any sect, but rather as universal among all

Easterners. The teachings of Confucius contained a rational ethics which was both logically consistent and of great practical benefit. Confucianism was capable of establishing an ideal form of government, and thus it represented a historical confirmation that morality was possible without religion. The Enlightenment rejected neo-Confucian cosmology and metaphysics on the grounds that it was materialistic and even atheistic. Confucianism was translated and introduced into eighteenth-century England; Samuel Johnson praised Chinese nobility and knowledge, a marked contrast with his own country, where the London financiers were buying political offices. Many cultivated country gentlemen of England saw affinities between themselves and the land-based scholar-officials of China, since neither they nor the Chinese literati were narrowly specialized. China was thus vaunted as a living confirmation of a learned meritocracy. The examination system was praised for the way it rewarded intellectual achievement with official rank."[54]

Many of these favorable impressions and points were undoubtedly motivated by a critique of religious fanaticism in the West. Through their introduction and comment, Eastern ideas may have played a role in the modernization of Western intellectuals in the early stages of the Enlightenment. But the image was a narrow one, for Westerners had no direct knowledge of Eastern culture, but only as it was mediated by their own missionaries. Taoism and pre-Song Confucianism remained completely unknown to the West. As suggested above, the Eastern characteristics that were viewed as surprising and so different from the West were embodied in the concept of Junzi—but direct Western knowledge of this concept has had to wait till comparatively recently.

Such important concepts as Junzi or Wuwei were not introduced by the Jesuit missionaries to the West during the Age of Enlightenment. The West subsequently lost interest in Eastern philosophy; after the West's discovery of its own overwhelming power in the wake of the Industrial Revolution, the East diminished, once again, in its eyes.

Part III: Adaptations

CHAPTER 8

Industrial Revolution:
Western Paradigm and Eastern Fundamental

"*Homo homini lupus*—Man is the predator of man."

Plautus

"Black cat, white cat, the good cat is the one that catches mice."

Deng Xiaoping

Industrial Revolution: The Culmination of Western Expansion

In our first four chapters, we examined the fundamentals of Eastern and Western civilizations in terms of their environmental contexts, and of the three cardinal relationships of Man. In the second part of this book—chapters 5 to 7—we examined how these fundamentals actually played out in each culture: law in the West, and ethics in the East. Both law and ethics, we argued, were developed to serve man's most basic purpose: self-preservation.

In the present and final part, we shall study the huge impact the Industrial Revolution had on the two civilizations and their adaptation to it. This phenomenon helped complete the West's expansion over the entire globe and brought with it a paradigm shift from warfare to commerce. As the world has become circumscribed, capitalism and democracy have become the norm in economics and politics. Both East and West appear to have adapted successfully to their new situation. But beyond this immediate transition, industrialization challenges the very future of mankind, since our own mental capacities, which produced both law and ethics, are now called into question: are they a blessing or a curse?

Western Expansion: Pre-Industrial Equilibrium to Post-Industrial Domination

Despite the legacy of Vasco da Gama, Western imperialism and colonialism did not penetrate the East until the nineteenth century. Although poverty tended to be prevalent and rulers tended to be despotic, Easterners continued to enjoy social harmony and to focus on self-fulfillment, frugality, modesty, and humility, as well as a deep love of nature. Their civilization, grounded in the meritocratic examination system, contrasted with that of the West, which was founded instead on individual initiative and was guaranteed by a contractual legal system.

But this contrast ended abruptly with the advent of industrialization in the West, by which—following liberation movements that allowed a greater range of individual initiatives in science and commerce—the West conquered the rest of the world.

The irony is that by conquering the world, the West transformed it from an expansive environment into a circumscribed one, thus bringing to an end its ancient paradigm of military expansionism. In the Age of Discovery, expansion had been a natural consequence of the Western character. No other civilization had demonstrated so consistent a profile: neither nomadic nor agricultural civilizations were supported by an élan for expansion. Although nomadic cultures also showed a tendency toward expansion when led by leaders like Attila the Hun, Genghis Khan, and Timur, this followed no consistent pattern. Their occasional expansionist policies can be interpreted within the larger historical framework of the waxing and waning of their power, rather than as the inevitable expression of an expansionist character. Instead, Eastern agricultural civilizations demonstrated an introverted and centripetal nature, with a focus not on expansion, but on managing the status quo.

During the period of Western discovery, competition between national powers played an essential part; it ended with the emergence of nation-states, fostering intense competition and ultimately provoking imperialism. The competition between Portugal and Spain, to take one example, is well known and was discussed in the previous chapter.

But the industrialists of the late eighteenth century went further than the explorers of the fifteenth: they provided a quantum leap in mobility and military firepower, and so enabled Western expansion to conquer the remotest parts of the globe, including the East. Equipped with its new technology, the West expanded with a sense of invincibility; the East, on the other hand, had long been stagnating and was at its lowest ebb. Thus, when Westerners finally arrived in the East in the mid-nineteenth century, the local populations proved no match for the invaders. It is commonly asked, "Why did other civilizations besides the West fail to industrialize?" But this is not the right question; we should ask instead why the Industrial Revolution succeeded in the West. The answer may be found in the West's combination of science and commerce; immense were the imperialist incentives of scientific and technological innovation, as well as for commercial activity and territorial expansion. Furthermore, as we have claimed, its unique legal and political framework, favoring individual initiative, provided the foundation for the West's advancement.

Industrial Revolution: Quantum Leap

Portuguese captains, following Vasco da Gama's voyages, began to approach the East in search of commerce and economic advantage in the sixteenth century. The East, meanwhile, sought to regulate such commerce and the Western presence according to its traditional tribute system. Until the beginning of the nineteenth century, the East remained too powerful for the West to conquer and could therefore define the terms of the West's participation. The first Opium War (1839–1842), and the subsequent Treaty of Nanjing in 1842, ended three centuries of coexistence between the two civilizations. These events were the results of the Industrial Revolution.

The West's combination of science and commerce, embodied in its steam-powered gunboats and its insatiable appetite for trade and goods, led to its defeat of the East. The comparison we have been making in this book between East and West suddenly lost its relevance at this period, as Eastern nations were forced, one by one, to open themselves to the West by a series of unequal treaties: "The Industrial Revolution, which gave Europe the decided economic and military edge over all other nations in the world, did much to suggest that Christian civilization was inherently superior to all others. Was this not a Divine Blessing? Weren't all other nations and all other religions now obviously inferior?"[1]

This process would not have succeeded had the West not used its new industries to dramatically increase its military capacities.[2] Unlike the East's traditional laissez-faire approach to commerce, the West actively pursued the practice with uncommon zeal. Technological innovation further enhanced its commercial activities and the volume of its trade—and the culmination of this process came with the Industrial Revolution, which enabled mass production, demanding vast amounts of resources, and thereby ultimately creating the free market economy. As we examine the exponential growth of resources used during the Industrial Revolution, we see that the textile and cloth industries were at its forefront. In 1760, just before the Revolution began, Britain imported around 1,000 tons of raw cotton; in less than a hundred years, imports rose over two hundredfold. Capitalism, international trade, and the exponentially growing use of natural resources inevitably followed. How can a society control such an explosion of resources and markets, with all its environmental, developmental, and ethical implications? We shall examine this question in the final chapter.

The impact of industrialization has been economic, social, political, ideological, and even evolutionary. Its most important result must be the emergence of political economy, a phenomenon the implications of which we have not yet fully grasped.

Opium War: Elliot vs. Lin

The Industrial Revolution enabled the West to send powerful fleets to the East to enforce its own business practices. This resulted in the Opium Wars—a classic conflict between force and ethics. China was exporting large amounts of tea, silk, and porcelain to Britain, but since it deemed itself self-supporting, it did not purchase any British products, preferring to accept silver in exchange for its own products. As time passed, with China hoarding enormous quantities of silver, Britain's silver reserves dwindled to unacceptable levels. To solve this problem, opium was cultivated on a massive scale in British India and its neighbors, and exported to the Chinese for silver. Opium dens multiplied in China like "bamboo shoots after the rain." The Chinese government naturally declared the opium trade illegal, and so the British government declared war on China. This, in brief, was the background to the wars.[3]

At that time, the Chinese drug trade was a significant enterprise that Britain could hardly do without. Sir Charles Elliot (Figure 8-2), Chief Superintendent of Trade and British minister in China, stationed in Macao, put pressure on China to legalize opium. The annual export of the drug to China amounted to about 40,000 chests, each containing about 100 pounds. Beijing sent Lin Zexu (林則徐, 1785–1850, Figure 8-1) as a commissioner to control the situation. Lin confiscated over 20,000 chests and expelled foreign drug traders.[4]

Fig. 8-1. Lin Zexu (林則徐, **1785–1850**) Chinese Imperial Commissioner in charge of the British Opium Trade. (http://en.wikipedia.org/wiki/ Lin_Zexu)	**Fig. 8-2. Sir Charles Elliot** **(1801–1875)** Chief Superintendent of Trade and British Minister to China in 1835. (http://upload.wikimedia.org/ wikipedia/commons/6/66/ SirCharlesElliot.jpg)

In 1839, with the goal of stopping the trade completely, Lin published an open letter to Queen Victoria. He asked whether she would promote opium to her own subjects, arguing that, if not, she must halt the forced drug trade to the Chinese people: "Suppose there were people from another country who carried opium for sale to England and seduced your people into buying and smoking it; certainly your honorable ruler would deeply hate it and be bitterly aroused. We have heard heretofore that your honorable ruler is kind and benevolent. Naturally you would not wish to give unto others what you yourself do not want."[5] Lin's logic reminds us of one of the fundamental ethical principles of Confucianism: "Do not do unto others what you do not want others to do unto you."

As we have seen, this Eastern tenet stands in contrast to the Western credo of "Do unto others as you would have them do unto you." For the East, such a value was more worthy of defense than the profit-seeking of Western mercantilism. Thus, the Opium War represented a fundamental clash between East and West. There is no evidence that his letter ever reached Queen Victoria. However, William Gladstone, a newly elected Member of Parliament, and the future prime minister of Great Britain, severely criticized the Opium War: "a war more unjust in its origin, a war more calculated to cover this country with permanent disgrace, I do not know."[6]

But Lin's taking the moral high ground could not prevail without being supported by force. His forceful measures against the opium trade acted as the major catalyst of the first Opium War (1839–1842). The Chinese military, however, was no match for Western gunships. After a humiliating defeat, Lin was dismissed from office and sent into exile. In the aftermath of the wars, China and other Eastern nations were forced to open their ports and markets to Western trade on Western terms. The equilibrium between West and East, which had lasted since the sixteenth century, was thus decisively broken in the West's favor. The Industrial Revolution was the key factor.

East vs. West in the Nineteenth Century

The West's triumph over the East was made possible by its steamships and guns, which in turn were ultimately the product of its promotion of individual initiative by law. Eastern ships of the nineteenth century were virtually identical to those of Cheng Ho's time, whereas Western ships had evolved in size, operation, and weaponry. For example, Elliot's flagship *Melville* carried seventy-four guns, while HMS *Nemesis* (Figure 8-3) had forty-six guns. The Eastern junk ships were no match for these Western vessels.

The earlier interaction between East and West had reflected a successful compromise. This period represented coexistence between the two civilizations, each living on its own strengths and merits. But the precariousness inherent in the Eastern tribute system eventually became apparent, and Western nations increasing challenged it.[7] Eventually, the West replaced the system with its own system of unequal treaties, which reflected the imbalance of power between the two civilizations.[8]

East and West in the Nineteenth Century:
After the Industrial Revolution

**Fig. 8-3. *Destroying Chinese war junks, by E. Duncan*
First Opium War, 1839–42**
The steamship HMS Nemesis, commanded by Lieutenant W. H.
Hall, with boats from the 'Sulphur', 'Calliope', 'Larne' and 'Starling',
destroying the Chinese War Junks in Anson's Bay, on 7 January 1841.
(http://www.portcities.org.uk/london/server/show/conMediaFile.6440/
Destroying-Chinese-war-junks-by-E-Duncan.html)

During this period, the East sank deeper into stagnation, inertia, and poverty. The West exulted in the omnipotence of its own "Spirit." Sensing that the balance of power had tilted in its favor, the West started to push the tribute system toward its own treaty system, on unequal terms. Trade began to give way to plunder. Britain, followed by other Western powers, forced its own administration on Eastern activities. In the second half of the nineteenth century, the West used military force to occupy Eastern lands and force treaties advantageous to itself, ironically titled "Treaties of Amity and Commerce."[9] China accepted a humiliating treaty recognizing Britain as an "equal" to China and conceding Hong Kong to British rule.

Subsequently, China was forced to recognize the extraterritorial privileges of British citizens in its own ports. In 1844, the United States and France signed a similar treaty with China. After China, it was Japan's turn; Commodore Matthew Perry opened Japan to the West in 1854. Other Eastern countries followed: French troops landed in Vietnam in 1858; in 1882, Korea signed a trade treaty with the United States. Korea, Vietnam, and Japan, like China, were no match for the West's gunboats. The East's earlier naval superiority had evaporated, and Western ships annihilated its wooden boats like toys.

Industrial Revolution and the Culmination of Western Expansion

The global importance of the Industrial Revolution is also evident in the West's relationship to the Barbary corsairs. Despite its successful expansion elsewhere, the West remained powerless against these pirates during the Age of Discovery. They plundered at will and captured slaves throughout Europe: "In the first half of the 1600s, Barbary corsairs—pirates from the Barbary Coast of North Africa, authorized by their governments to attack the shipping of Christian countries—ranged all around Britain's shores. In their lanteen-rigged xebecs (a type of ship) and oared galleys, they grabbed ships and sailors, and sold the sailors into slavery. Admiralty records show that during this time the corsairs plundered British shipping pretty much at will, taking no fewer than 466 vessels between 1609 and 1616, and 27 more vessels from near Plymouth in 1625."[10]

The Mediterranean states, lacking any better solutions to the problem, simply advised their people not to live in the coastal regions, as China and Korea had previously done in response to Japanese pirates: "The widespread depopulation of coastal areas from Malaga to Venice, the impoverishment caused by the kidnapping of many breadwinners, the millions paid by the already poor inhabitants of villages and towns to get their own people back—all this is only just beginning to be understood by modern-day historians."[11]

Likewise, just as some Chinese sailors joined Japanese pirates in search of plunder and profit, so many Western sailors joined the Barbary corsairs, voluntarily or through conversion during captivity: "The Sack of Baltimore took place on June 20, 1631, when the village of Baltimore, West Cork, Ireland, was attacked by Algerian pirates from the North African Barbary Coast, led by a Dutch captain turned pirate.... They captured 108 English planters and local Irish people, but not much in terms of valuable treasure. Almost all of the villagers were put in irons and taken to a life of slavery in North Africa."[12]

From Pre-Industrial Equilibrium to Post-Industrial Domination

Fig. 8-4. 1669, Battle between the English frigate HMS *Mary Rose* and seven Algerian pirate ships (http://en.wikipedia.org/wiki/File:HMS_Mary_Rose_and_pirates.jpg)	Fig. 8-5. 1816, Bombardment of Algiers by Lord Exmouth by Thomas Luny (http://en.wikipedia.org/wiki/File:Sm_Bombardment_of_Algiers,_August_1816-Luny.jpg)

As we observed in chapter 7, there were two significant differences between Japanese pirates and the Barbary corsairs or the Western privateers: the former were private, not sponsored by monarchs like the latter, and they took only food and valuables, rather than slaves, since there was no market for slavery. But since slavery was one of the main activities of the Barbary corsairs, the West developed a system to ransom its victims: "Europeans sometimes attempted to buy their people out of slavery, but no real system emerged before around 1640. Then the attempts became more systematic and were sometimes state subsidized, as in Spain and France. Almost all the actual work, however—from collecting the funds, to voyaging to Barbary, to negotiating with the slave owners there—was carried out by clergy, mostly members of the Trinitarian or Mercedarian orders."[13]

Just as there had been a preindustrial equilibrium between the East and West, the balance between the West and the Barbary corsairs was maintained (as Figure 8-4 illustrates) until the eighteenth century. But in the wake of the Industrial Revolution, the West successfully attacked (as Figure 8-5 demonstrates) and occupied the Barbary States known today as Morocco, Algeria, Tunisia, and Libya, bringing an end to the corsairs.

The question arises as to why the Barbary States remained content with piracy for centuries, when they possessed the ability to expand and colonize, as the West continued to do. But that remains for another book to answer.

Eastern Isolationism: Closing of the Mind

Why had the East adopted a "closed door" policy for four centuries—from the time of Cheng Ho to that of the Opium Wars? Although its attempts to curb the West's military and commercial inroads were sensible, the same cannot be said of its neglect of Western learning. There was no Eastern Matteo Ricci or William Adams until the nineteenth century.

The West: Bill of Rights vs. Colonialism

The East's isolation was of its own making, a deliberate decision following its cultural closure in the Song dynasty. It did not approve of the military and commercial colonialism of the West, since this stood in opposition to its own cultural tenets. When the West first arrived in the East, it had two aspects, one visible and the other invisible. The visible aspect was its aggressive colonialism, represented by Vasco da Gama—the East perceived this and found nothing in it to admire or adopt.

Several thinkers of the Western Enlightenment were sympathetic to the East's attitude: they "found the Eastern isolationism justified by reason of state but inimical to the West's commercial interests and tradition."[14] Voltaire praised its expulsion of the Western missionary who insisted on the exclusive acceptance of his own religious doctrines.[15] Immanuel Kant, in his work *Perpetual Peace*, praised the East's approach to the West after having criticized the latter's unscrupulous exploitations in other regions: "China and Japan, which had made an attempt at receiving guests of this kind, have now taken a prudent step. Only a single European people, the Dutch, has been given the right of access to their shores."[16] Adam Smith, meanwhile, in his *The Wealth of Nations*, denounced the West's colonial and imperial exploitation: "the savage injustice of the Europeans ... Superiority of force was so great on the side of the Europeans, that they were enabled to commit with impunity every sort of injustice in those remote countries."[17]

This was how the West appeared to the men of the East at the time, but unknown to them was its other aspect—the West of the Magna Carta, nation-states, the Reformation, the Age of Discovery and of the Legal Compact, the Bill of Rights, the Enlightenment, the Industrial Revolution, the rule of law, and finally, capitalism and democracy. The East was unaware of these phenomena and of the West's great sacrifices for them. The Magna Carta of 1215 was a landmark achievement as the very first document of compromise between a king and his barons, but it was bought with endless struggle, with the Roman Catholic Church playing an indispensable part. The Reformation had its antecedents in the execution of Jan Hus of Prague (burned to death in 1415 in spite of a promise of safe-conduct) and John Wycliffe of Oxford (burned posthumously as a heretic in 1428). It was launched by the courage of Martin Luther, John Calvin, and Ulrich Zwingli in the sixteenth century. Its legacy persisted through the Thirty Years' War, which ended only in 1648. The Age of Discovery was made possible by the Western program of legal compacts enabling individual initiative. The ground for the Bill of Rights of 1688 was prepared by the sacrifices of the English Civil War and made possible by the "Glorious Revolution." All of these events contributed to the eventual emergence of the Enlightenment in the eighteenth century and of capitalism, industrialism, and democracy in the century after. The East remained ignorant of these crucial developments in the story of the West.

The early modern East was complacent enough to take the colonialism that it saw for the sole reality of the West, failing to grasp the meaningful evolution behind it. Its decision to close its doors to the West was therefore misguided, and indeed, it paid a dear price for this.

Haijin and Sakoku

This complacent and introverted attitude of the East stood in stark contrast to the West's active and extroverted character, as seen, for instance, in Elizabethan Britain: "Trade and diplomatic relations developed between England and the Barbary States during the rule of Elizabeth. England established a trading relationship with Morocco in opposition to Spain, in spite of a Papal ban.... Diplomatic relations were also established with the Ottoman Empire.... A Treaty of Commerce was signed in 1580."[18] Nor did intrepid Englishmen shy away from visiting the East: "The first Englishman to reach Japan, William Adams ... would play a key role as a counselor to the Japanese Shogun, and helped establish the first diplomatic contacts and commercial treaties between England and Japan."[19]

Strong minds treat challenges as opportunities and go outward to meet them; weak minds treat them as dangers and shrink away from them. The latter occurred in China, Korea, and Japan. Emperors of the Song, Ming, and Qing dynasties restricted their subjects' reading to a small collection of Confucian classics and, in so doing, diminished the intellectual diversity of earlier periods. In Korea and Japan, the closed-door policy equally meant the closing of the mind. Quite the reverse was happening at the same time in the West, as intellectuals broadened their horizons immeasurably.

Beginning around 1370, the Ming authorities, with a policy known as Ocean Prohibition (Haijin, 海禁), forbade all maritime trade except official tribute-related missions. One of its principal motivations was to curb the activities of the Japanese pirates, the

Wokou (倭寇). However, this measure in fact only strengthened the pirates, as the outlawed Chinese merchants made alliances with them, and the leadership of Wokou became as much Chinese as Japanese.[20] As the pirates' activities multiplied, the Eastern tribute system was severely damaged in the sixteenth century. The Ocean Prohibition policy also provoked widespread emigration of the Chinese coastal population to the countries of Southeast Asia, the consequences of which are still felt today. The Portuguese became active as intermediary traders between China and Japan. Furthermore, as a measure to reinforce control, specific ports were designated for trade purposes—one with Japan, one with the Philippines, and one with Indonesia.

In 1479, the Ming War Ministry burned the court records of Cheng Ho's seven maritime expeditions, signaling China's reinforcement of its isolationist policies. Maritime commerce with foreign countries and large-scale shipbuilding was restricted, resulting in the weakening of the Ming navy. Meanwhile, the Yi dynasty of Korea generally complied with the Chinese Haijin policy. Japan also began to adopt a similar closed-door policy, known as Sakoku (鎖国), with the emergence of the Tokugawa regime in the early seventeenth century: "The Jesuits, in a phase of ascendancy, persecuted and insulted the Buddhists with great acrimony. These troubles interwove with the feudal conflicts of the time. In the end the Japanese came to the conclusion that the Europeans and their Christianity were an intolerable nuisance, and that Catholic Christianity in particular was a mere cloak for the political dreams of the Pope and the Spanish monarchy—already in possession of the Philippine Islands."[21] But Japan managed this policy more effectively than China or Korea—its door remained "ajar," using a process called "Dutch studies" to acquire Western knowledge and technology. In the end, this subtle and wise attitude paid off; it prepared Japan better than China or Korea to cope with Western influence when the entire East was forced to open its doors to the West in the nineteenth century. The brilliant Meiji Restoration owed its success to this preparation.

The Qing dynasty inherited and reinforced the closed-door policy with a temporary respite during the Kangxi reign. The closing of the Eastern mind reached its zenith with Emperor Qianlong (乾隆帝, 1711–1799) and Empress Dowager Cixi (慈禧太后, 1835–1908).[22] They failed to comprehend the significance of the increasing number of Western ships and visitors, and of their superior arts and technologies, clearly evident in their medicines, firearms, clocks, pianos, paintings, and so on. Instead, they continued to believe that China was the center of the world, lacking in nothing and so requiring nothing from the West. They called the Western envoys and merchants barbarians and, ignoring traditional courtesy, humiliated them by forcing them to kneel and kowtow to empty thrones.

After its humbling defeat during the Opium Wars, China could no longer continue this pretense, and it launched an imperial program of "learning from foreigners." But this timid attempt was again hindered during the reign of Cixi. She had no idea what to do with the new liberal ideas and shut the country's door to foreigners even more tightly.

Literary Inquisition vs. Religious Inquisition

With its horizons so narrowed, the East inevitably became submerged in factional struggles, which had begun in the Song dynasty. These struggles evolved around academic schools that had spread across the country:[23] "From the Song on, a tension arose between private academies, such as Donglin, devoted Confucian moral and philosophic instruction, and officially sponsored academies and schools, such as the Hanlin, oriented toward 'official studies,' that is, the mechanical training required to master the state orthodoxy."[24] The first well-known schism of this sort occurred between conservatives and reformers, the former represented by Chancellor Sima Guang (司馬光, 1019–1086) and the latter by Chancellor Wang Anshi (王安石, 1021–1086). Even though the two sides fought bitterly, the struggle remained within prescribed boundaries and involved no loss of life. The Confucian spirit of criticizing bureaucracy and corruption prevailed: "The canon served also as an ideology by which the ruling class rationalized the political order or curbed despotic power, anti-establishment scholars censured bureaucratic corruption, censors impeached the ruler and his officials, reformers advocated their cause, and Confucian martyrs vindicated their innocence."[25]

The situation deteriorated during the Ming dynasty, at which time the most famous and drawn-out schism involved conservatives and liberals within the neo-Confucian framework. In 1579, the conservative Zhang Juzheng (張居正), grand secretary to the emperor, took severe measures against liberals: "Academy grounds were ordered to be returned to their local communities, and the buildings of the academies were to be turned into government offices. Gatherings for political discussion were forbidden, and regional censors were commanded to supervise local education more carefully."[26] Zhang's persecution failed to quell the popular aspiration for reform and liberalism. In 1603, Gu Xiancheng (顧憲成) succeeded in rebuilding the Donglin Academy and restoring it to its earlier level of cultural prominence. The revival of private academies enjoyed the financial support of local literati and merchants, who became the powerhouse of liberalism during the Ming and early Qing periods. This revival of liberalism provoked an equally powerful reaction from the conservatives. The schism between the two factions became so bitter that defeat began to entail death and exile: "In the summer of 1625, the purge of Donglin partisans reached its climax. Arrests and deaths by torture of Donglin leaders were accompanied by imperial denunciations of private academies as politically subversive organizations. Private academies throughout the empire were ordered destroyed."[27] This may perhaps be compared to the Western religious schism between Catholicism and Protestantism, which resulted in the Thirty Years' War, as well as the Saint Bartholomew's Day massacre. The crucial difference is this: while the Eastern struggles were confined to the imperial court, repeating the same pattern of impeachments with increased violence, the Western conflicts were accompanied by a Reformation movement involving nation-states, which in the end opened a new future for the West.

The Chinese court worsened still further in the Qing period—even the pretense of a factional struggle yielded to the outright persecution of any unorthodox opinion. This gave rise to the gruesome Literary Inquisition and Literary Censors, who were mobilized to eliminate any sign of heretical thinking.[28] The Literary Inquisition had occasionally been practiced during the Ming and early Qing periods, but developed into a pattern during the later Qing dynasty. In some ways it resembled the religious inquisition of the West, only it preferred slicing and mutilation to burning at the stake and the thumbscrew: "The authority would judge any single character or any single sentence's neutrality; if the authority ... decided these words, or sentence[s] were derogative or cynic[al] toward the rulers, then persecution would begin. In Emperor Qianlong's time, there were 53 cases of literary inquisition, resulting in the victims being beheaded, or corpses being mutilated, or victims being slowly sliced into pieces until death, which could take a few days."[29]

It is interesting to note that the West tended toward enlightenment in the period between the Renaissance and modernity, whereas in the East, between the Song and Qing dynasties, the opposite happened—a closing of mind, with schisms and persecutions that became increasingly barbaric.

Gender: Theory vs. Practice

During the Qing dynasty, the closed-mindedness and pettiness of the Eastern mind hit its nadir. This was especially conspicuous in the treatment of women. Beginning in the Song dynasty, and continuing in the Ming, Yuan, and Qing dynasties, women endured a much lower status than men in society. Many neo-Confucians tended to reinforce this discrimination with suffocatingly conservative attitudes. While Xun Zi did not mention women, Mencius was explicitly in favor of a woman's subordination to her father in her youth, her husband in her maturity, and her son in her old age. As we know, neo-Confucianism supported Mencius against Xun Zi.

During the Qing dynasty, women led thoroughly submissive lives and suffered harmful practices like foot-binding for the sake of conformity to the period's bizarre standards of beauty. Unfortunately, this situation remained common in the East for several centuries. Arguably, the Yi dynasty in Korea held the record among Eastern countries in terms of its gender discrimination: conservative Yi Confucians had even conceptualized seven justifiable reasons for a man to divorce his wife, including her jealousy of his concubine. Gender discrimination came to be regarded as an integral part of culture in the East. But this had not always been the case. In fact, before the Song dynasty, Eastern women enjoyed an open social life and an elevated social status. The Tang period had been characterized by a very liberal attitude toward women, who, for instance, pursued outdoor sports. Glazed earthenware figurines of the era depict women playing polo, a sport imported from Persia.

With the arrival of the Western paradigm, including gender equality, the East is now rapidly and successfully assimilating this new concept. Again, the easy assimilation of gender equality is due to the absence of any cultural theories and doctrines that function as obstacles to change, as was the case with the East's absorption of free market economics and political democracy. This was not the case in the West. As we have seen in chapter 4, Aristotelian Master ethics placed slaves, barbarians, and women at the same level as animals, with little or no soul. Aristotle deemed that only men had a soul; what a woman provided for her child was matter while a man gave it soul or form. Aristotle must have learned from his teacher Plato. Although Plato's views about women were more nuanced than that of Aristotle, as he advocated for women's enhanced position in society and their equal education, he was very clear in his belief that only a man had a soul. In his words: "It is only males who are created directly by the gods and are given souls. Those who live rightly return to the stars, but those who are 'cowards or lead unrighteous lives may with reason be supposed to have changed into the nature of women in the second generation.' This downward progress may continue through successive reincarnations unless reversed. In this situation, obviously it is only men who are complete human beings and can hope for ultimate fulfillment; the best a woman can hope for is to become a man."[30]

However, the West has had a better record on women's status than the East, despite its theoretical gender discrimination. Western history is full of stories emphasizing the value of personal freedom, as well as women's rights. For instance, military campaigns in the ancient and medieval worlds ensured long absences for large numbers of the male aristocracy, thus contributing to the empowerment of the women left behind—such a situation was unknown in the East.

By contrast, one can hardly find any theory supporting gender discrimination in Taoism or Confucianism. In *The Analects*, Confucius made no particular mention of women except for the following sentence: "Woman and Xiaoren are most difficult to behave to. If you are familiar with them, they lose their humility. If you take distance from them, they become resentful."[31] There is no mention of women in the Taoteking. Taoism is intended to be of universal application. The only distinction it made was between Sage and Multitude, which is almost identical to Junzi vs. Xiaoren. But the fundamental tenet of Taoism is the superiority of Yin (feminine) over Yang (masculine): "All things under the Heaven have a beginning; at the beginning there was a mother. When the mother is discerned, it is possible to understand her offspring; protecting one's mother, one is never in peril" (Taoteking, 52). "At birth, all is soft and supple; at death, all is hard and firm. The place of being hard and firm is below; the place of being soft and supple is above" (Taoteking, 76). "Nothing in the world is softer and suppler than water; yet it tames all that is firm and hard" (Taoteking, 78).

These notions in Taoteking and the absence of reference to gender in Confucius suggest that there was no theoretical barrier against gender equality in the East. The West, by contrast, was hampered by the views of classical philosophy, as well as the Bible's depiction of Woman as being created second and responsible for the downfall of Man. This was why the process of women's empowerment in the West began only with the Enlightenment. The gender issue has come to the fore in earnest only with the paradigm shift from warfare to commerce, which privileges intellectual over muscular power. The point to be made here is that, despite severe practices of gender discrimination in the East, the East could rapidly and successfully assimilate the Western paradigm of women's empowerment thanks to the absence of any theoretical or philosophical barriers.

Wu Zetian vs. Catherine the Great

The high status of women in pre-Song China was epitomized in the person of Empress Wu Zetian (武則天, 625–705), who ruled China with an iron fist for forty years and remains the only female empress in China's history. There were, however, around fifteen empress dowagers in China, many of whom completely eclipsed their sons in the actual exercise of power. The first was the redoubtable Lu (呂太后, 241–180 BC) of the Han dynasty, who reigned as the most powerful person in China for around fifteen years after the death of her husband: "Empress Lu proved herself to be an able administrator, and quickly built a strong working relationship with the emperor's officials, who admired her for her capability and feared her for her ruthlessness."[32] But during the Song and Ming dynasties there was not a single empress dowager. China had to await the Qing dynasty, established by the Manchu tribe, for the reemergence of the empress dowagers. Of these, Cixi (1835–1908) was the most prominent figure.

Wu Zetian stands out as the only woman who ruled China as a genuine empress, having acquired and maintained power thanks to her sheer will, ruthlessness, cunning, and intellect. Appropriately, she promoted gender equality, a revolutionary idea in the seventh century. She ruled China through her husband and sons for twenty-five years, from 665 to 690, and as empress in her own right for fifteen years thereafter, until her death in 705. She even attempted to establish her own dynasty by changing the name of the dynasty from Tang to Zhu during the years 690–705.

Wu began her extraordinary life at the age of thirteen, as one of the numerous imperial concubines. But she quickly rose to an influential position through her charm, luck, and good decisions. At the age of twenty-five, in the year 650, she became Consort Wu and outwitted Empress Wang to gradually become as influential as the emperor himself, without incurring his resentment. At the age of thirty-one, she became empress and, with her allies, began purging those who had opposed her ascendancy, with the aim of consolidating her power. In 665, she began to "sit behind the screen" at imperial political meetings—hence giving birth to the phenomenon of "ruling behind screens" in subsequent Eastern history—and became more influential than the chancellors, princes, and even the emperor himself, on whose behalf she started making important decisions. At the age of forty-one, Empress Wu felt secure enough to sacrifice to her ancestors at an official ceremony after the emperor but before the Crown Prince—an unprecedented order in Chinese history. At the age of fifty, Empress Wu persuaded the emperor to adopt two measures (among others): the inclusion of Taoteking (the Taoist canon) in the imperial curriculum, and an observance of three years of mourning for a mother's death, even if the father was still alive. She also employed scholars to compile a number of works, including the *Biographies of Notable Women*. In 683, at her husband's death, Wu became Empress Dowager and regent. As the subsequent emperor, who was her first son, showed signs of asserting himself, she deposed him in favor of her second son, whom she appointed instead.

In 690, Wu took an unprecedented action, defying the traditional Chinese order of succession and successfully quelling opposition, to become Empress Regnant, the first and only woman to rule China. She even changed the name of the state from Tang to Zhou and ruled China for the next fifteen years in an absolute capacity. It was during this time that she actively promoted the Imperial Examination System with a view to firmly establishing scholar-officials as a countervailing force against the aristocracy. Her rule was considered benign and effective: "Since Wu Zetian was declared emperor of China, in spite of her ruthless climb to power, her rule proved to be benign. She found the best people she could to run the government, and treated those she trusted fairly. She reduced the army's size and stopped the influence of aristocratic military men on government by replacing them with scholars. Everyone had to compete for government positions by taking exams, thus setting the practice of government run by scholars. Wu also was fair to peasants, lowering oppressive taxes, raising agricultural production, and strengthening public works."[33] It goes without saying that the conservative neo-Confucians hated her for her defying the tradition of male rule, and consequently offered many unfavorable opinions of her.

Whatever our evaluation of this remarkable woman, one cannot deny that she made an enormous contribution to gender equality during the Tang dynasty. Perhaps this aspect of her legacy helped to encourage later thinkers like Li Zhi (李贄, 1527–1602), who argued that women were intellectually equal to men and that women should be given a better education.[34] This novel idea did not please the gruesome Qing literary censors; Li was imprisoned for propagating "dangerous ideas" and committed suicide while in prison. It should also be noted that the imperial examinations began to accept female candidates in the late nineteenth century.

One can find Empress Wu's Western counterpart in Catherine the Great of Russia. There have been several female rulers in the West, including Empress Maria Theresa (1717–1780), who, reigning for forty years, was the only female ruler of the Habsburg Empire; Queen Elizabeth I (1533–1603), who ruled England for forty-four years; and Queen Victoria (1819–1901), who reigned over Great Britain for over sixty-three years. But all three of them had acceded to the throne by succession. Among important regents in the West was also Catherine de Medici (1519–1589), who was granted real power for thirty years after the death of her husband, Henri II of France, in 1559. No real female ruler was produced in the West during the Roman Empire or the Middle Ages.[35] Thus, Catherine the Great appears to be the only empress in the West who took power not by blood succession but rather by her own resources.

Fig. 8-6. Empress Wu Zetian (武則天, 625–705) (http://en.wikipedia.org/wiki/ File:A_Tang_Dynasty_Empress_ Wu_Zetian.jpg)	Fig. 8-7. Empress Catherine the Great (1729–1796) (http://en.wikipedia.org/wiki/ File:Empress_Catherine_The_ Great_1787_(Mikhail_Shibanov).jpg)

As Catherine's life is well known, this section will not focus on her to the same extent as Empress Wu. Although more than a millennium separates her from Wu, these two extraordinary women share many interesting characteristics as effective rulers. Catherine had, like Wu, a weak husband as emperor. This provided the occasion for both to rise to power; both showed ruthlessness in maintaining power and, at the same time, enlightened rulership; both had a keen grasp of human nature and an eye for talent; both inspired loyalty; both had a number of lovers many years their junior, disposing of them for disloyalty or as politics demanded; both left offspring who became emperors after them; perhaps most importantly, both had an acute sense of their monarchical responsibilities, putting all personal matters behind those of the state; "whatever Catherine's other activities, she emphatically functioned as a sovereign and as a politician, guided in the last resort by *reasons of state*."[36] We find a very similar evaluation of Wu by a Song dynasty historian: "Even though the Empress Dowager excessively used official titles to cause people to submit to her, if she saw that someone was incompetent, she would immediately depose or even execute him. She grasped the powers of punishment and reward, controlled the state, and made her own judgments as to policy decisions. She was observant and had good judgment, so the talented people of the time also were willing to be used by her."[37]

Democracy-Free Market and Junzi-Wuwei

In the wake of the West's conquest of the world, the East seems to have been the greatest beneficiary of Western advances. Thanks to European values and institutions, which it has assimilated for the past one and a half centuries, the East can resolve its ancient problems of hunger and authoritarianism. Are we witnessing a new Eastern Renaissance, thanks to the stimulation of Western industrialization, science, commerce, democracy, sports, arts, music, and so on? If so, we may compare it to the East's stimulation of the Western Renaissance in the fifteenth century: paper making, printing, gunpowder, and the magnetic compass.

Domination vs. Opportunity

Although the "Scramble for Africa" occurred after the opening of the East, the East nonetheless constituted the last frontier of Western conquest. The completion of this process marked the closing of the world—that is, its transformation from an expansive to a circumscribed environment. The complete victory of the West ushered in over a century of great tumult and tribulation in the East, testing the validity of its ancient Yin civilization. But in addition to its shock, the East began to reexamine its cultural legacy. How relevant could its own culture be to the third millennium?

For the last 150 years, the Yin attributes of this culture have interacted with the Yang attributes of the West; most intriguingly, perhaps, is the fact that despite the West's initial domination, Yin aspects began to assert themselves again in the second half of the twentieth century. The reason for this may be that the Western conquest of the world has transformed it into a Yin environment. The East is entitled, therefore, to view the prevailing Western paradigms of capitalism and democracy not as an imposed yoke, but as an offered opportunity.

The East appears to be a greater beneficiary of Western paradigms than other cultures, because, unlike the others, it eventually understood these as opportunities to be welcomed—opportunities, specifically, to overcome poverty and despotism. The East has been largely successful in this enterprise; most of its countries now enjoy material prosperity and individual freedom on an unprecedented scale.

In his book *Culture Matters*, Lawrence E. Harrison offers a succinct explanation of the relationship between culture and social progress, including economic development.[38] He observes that Confucian values lacking in other regions that fail to make a similar economic advance—such as an emphasis on the future, education, meritocracy, hard work, and frugality—in fact constitute the force behind Eastern economic success. This culture, he surmises, has allowed the Chinese, Japanese, and Koreans to flourish wherever they emigrate. In fact, with the rise of the East, the West has coined phrases like "the Confucian work ethic," similar to the Protestant ethos of hard work, personal savings, and harmonious relations between management and labor. Some observers have praised other Eastern cultural elements as well: a strong emphasis on education evidenced by a high literacy rate; drug-free societies with low crime; cost-effective governments; and more efficient legal and welfare systems. Some analysts have gone even further by predicting that the Eastern world will surpass the West in the twenty-first century in terms of economic power and technological achievement.

Leaving aside such immature competition, it suffices for us to accept that the East has been most successful in assimilating Western assets, such as science, commerce, and democracy, which have allowed it to realize material wealth and a cultural blossoming. This rare feat would have been impossible without the fundamentals embedded in its culture and civilization: the revamping of its Imperial Examination System into a meritocratic state system, although it maintained its extraordinary focus on education, as well as its core values of frugality, propriety, sincerity, and self-fulfillment. The overall cultural background of the East has thus been more important than the politics and economics at any given point in its history.

But this period has also been one of great conflict; Eastern countries fought both the West and each other. It seems as if the West's old military paradigm engulfed the East, propelling it toward endless confrontation. The East accepted and even emulated Western ideologies, but it seems that it has not lost much of its own identity in the process of absorption, as was once feared.

Western Paradigms: Science and Commerce, Free Market and Democracy

Since opening up to the West, the East has had to acknowledge its moral weaknesses—complacency, fatalism, inertia, and inaction. The East regarded the West with admiration. There, military power and material wealth seemed to enable everything to flourish: art, literature, architecture, science, music, and sport. The East lagged far behind in all of these brilliant achievements. It was only natural that most post-industrial Western thinkers, as epitomized by Hegel, regarded the East as a spent cultural force.

The East even criticized itself, lamenting the impotence of its rigid Confucian social order and its pitiable willingness to endure despotic rule. A yearning for Yang culture was expressed, undermining its own self-confidence.[39]

Soon after its initial confusion, the East began to understand the real forces—personal liberty and initiative—behind the Industrial Revolution. With this new understanding, the East could finally see beyond the West's imperialist façade, discovering the true value of its science and commerce as well as its free market and democracy. Those paradigms are important Western contributions to humanity, and they will enrich other civilizations when successfully assimilated. As the current world is managed by those Western paradigms, it is inevitable that they should dominate the talk of the "global village" in which we live. The East is thus applying these assets into its own civilization—the consequences of which have not yet become fully clear.

Eastern Fundamentals: Junzi and Wuwei

Two Eastern fundamentals were of particular importance in its assimilation of Western paradigms—Junzi and Wuwei. The former, as the basic building block of Eastern civilization, would be tested against Western paradigms in ethics and politics; the latter against the free market and political economy.

As we have seen, the philosophy of Junzi is already post-Enlightenment. If Western Enlightenment meant secularization, anti-irrationalist doctrines, and liberalism, Junzi philosophy was already beyond this, since it was fundamentally nonreligious. Junzi, perhaps more than Enlightenment thought, provides an ethical role model for man. In the same vein, as we shall see, the philosophy of Wuwei already represents a version of laissez-faire liberalism. If Western free market theory, as expounded by Adam Smith, aimed to protect the market's invisible hand from statism, Wuwei has no need of such measures, since Eastern economy was almost never under the state's control. Wuwei, more than the free market, provides ethical protection to the invisible hand. By confounding self-interest with greed, Western laissez-faire policies overlooked the menace posed to the invisible hand by greed. Wuwei proposes to protect the invisible hand from both statism and greed.

Junzi was unable to prevent despotism in the East. But he had not advocated it, and one of his principal roles was to advise the emperor against despotism, and even to impeach those who had become totalitarian. The first Westerners in the East were surprised to find imperial employees whose responsibility was to criticize and correct the emperor's behavior: "The West was astonished by the power of censors and historians in the imperial court. They surmised that even though the rule of law was lacking, the education of the emperor and scholar-officials was a warrant that there would never be abuse of power, like father ruling a household who is responsible for the happiness and prosperity of the family members."[40] They also served to record all the acts of the emperor, and especially his errors, for the benefit of his successor. No emperor was permitted to read his own record.

As we shall see, from the perspective of the Eastern philosophy of Junzi and Wuwei, free market democracy is the most successful mechanism for managing human self-interest. We can therefore see why the free market has been embraced so successfully and so efficiently in the East. There remain many doubts about the nature of Eastern regimes in terms of democracy. But if one accepts that economic freedom is inseparable from political freedom, one must also accept that the free market East must eventually become democratic. Nobody now questions Japan's successful assimilation of the free market and democracy. Until a few years ago, doubts abounded about whether Korea's assimilation of democracy was genuine, but these have now been laid to rest. China is a more difficult case since it seems to experiment with the assimilation of democracy and, at the same time, with a sinicized communism. It is not implausible to suggest that China may eventually produce a political system different from that of the West in certain respects, as we have seen in chapter 4. Yet no Eastern country will succeed on a global stage without valuing individual liberty and initiative (e.g., the free market and democracy). I remain confident that Junzi, working according to the principle of Wuwei, will prevail in assimilating the free market and democracy throughout the East, including China.

The Eastern Assimilation of Western Science

History shows that geometry and commerce could fully develop only in a seafaring civilization. The discovery of causal relationships in the West was made possible by "the systematic experimentation of the Renaissance," which was in turn made possible by a profit-seeking culture of commerce. The developments of science and commerce thus go hand-in-hand in Western history.

It also appears that, although rudimentary scientific discoveries and inventions of great potential had been made in the East, they could not fully blossom, since they did not have the incentive of profit. The East, as we have seen, produced many inventions before the West, even in seafaring, but these did not provoke a culture of systematic research and theory—that is, a scientific culture—nor did they result in widespread practical use. Instead, they remained isolated phenomena; discoveries occurred on an occasional basis. The development of weaponry is a particularly clear case. The Eastern world discovered iron casting more than a thousand years before the West. It also invented gunpowder in the ninth century and used these to make rudimentary bombs, cannons, and rockets. But without a strong commitment to commerce and warfare, it lacked the urge or opportunity to develop further the combination of iron

EAST AND WEST   • 389

casting and gunpowder into effective weapons. It was therefore the West that first developed the iron-barrel cannon, probably in the early fourteenth century. The pace of refinement was rapid due to the prevalence of warfare in the West.

As we have already remarked, many have often asked why the East failed to make scientific advances like the West. But now that the East is finally competing with the West in this field, it has become apparent that such a question was not the correct one.[41] As Einstein famously pointed out, the real question is why science developed at all in the West:[42] "In my opinion one need not be astonished that the Chinese sages did not make these steps. The astonishing thing is that these discoveries were made at all."[43] Einstein believed that geometry and causality were the foundations of Western science: "The development of Western science has been based on two great achievements, the invention of the formal logical system (in Euclidean geometry) by the Greek philosophers, and the discovery of the possibility of finding out causal relationships by systematic experiment (at the Renaissance)."[44]

The implications of this approach are decisive for non-Western civilizations. If this tells us why they did not develop science, one must begin by identifying the obstacles inherent in them and eliminating them. On the other hand, if the approach is why science was developed in the West, the other civilizations have only to assimilate those identified elements with a view to absorbing science from the West. Precisely from this perspective, the East presents no intrinsic barrier to Western science. The East owes such an absence to its philosophy of Wuwei, which prevented most mythical, theological, metaphysical, and ideological doctrines to take root in Eastern culture—and which might not be in harmony with scientific principles.

The Eastern Assimilation of Western Commerce

According to conventional wisdom, the East suppressed both domestic and international commerce as it clung to its fundamental Confucian and Taoist proscription of profit-seeking, and so suffered inevitable humiliation in the nineteenth century. It is argued that, instead of stifling commerce, the East should have sought to unlock the immense potential in active commercial exchange. It is true that merchants in the East had the lowest socio-economic status of the four hierarchical categories: literati, peasants, artisans, and merchants. They were often discriminated against and treated by literati as profit-seeking parasites of society. But the reality is more complex.

Before its modern suppression of maritime trade, the East had a strong record of active international trade. More importantly, it never promoted government intervention in commerce. Its default attitude was Wuwei (e.g., non-interventionism or laissez-faire), a position of great importance when it came to adopt Western capitalism. While the West languished following the fall of the Roman Empire, the East enjoyed an orderly and prosperous international trade. In the fifth century AD, Korean marine merchants dominated the Yellow Sea trade with China, Japan, and Balhai (a powerful dynasty occupying the Manchu area). As the relationship between Korea and Japan deteriorated in the late seventh century, Japanese trade ships were forced to explore routes further south, via Yangzi River ports, so as to avoid Korean ships. When relations improved again, maritime trade between the three countries expanded to cover the entire East China Sea: "In order to sail back to Japan in 838, the Japanese embassy to China procured nine ships and sixty Korean sailors from the Korean wards of Chuzhou and Lianshui cities along the Huai River. It is also known that Chinese trade ships traveling to Japan set sail from the various ports along the coasts of Zhejiang and Fujian provinces."[45]

This practice of free trade blossomed during the Tang and Song periods. The name of Korea derives from this era: since the trade between Song China and the dynasty of Koryo in Korea was very animated, those traders who came from India, Southeast Asia, and the Middle East started to use the name of Koryo (Korea). We have abundant records of China's foreign trade. Thousands of foreigners from Korea, Japan, Southeast Asia, Persia, the Arabian Peninsula, and Central Asia came to live in China to promote trade. The presence and activities of those from other regions were welcomed and facilitated, partly because of the aversion of the Eastern literati who formed and represented the government. As their Confucian teaching did not allow them to engage in commerce and profit-making, they instead left it to others, including foreigners. Tang traders sailed as far as the East African coast and competed with Arabs for business. The active trade between East Asia and the Arab world has been demonstrated by the discovery of a shipwrecked Arab vessel preserved in silt, containing 63,000 pieces of Tang gold, silver, and ceramics.[46] In 1154, the Arabic geographer and traveler al-Idrisi recorded the activities of Chinese traders importing various items, including iron, swords, silk, and porcelain to Arabic ports, such as Aden in Yemen.[47]

Thus, until the Ming dynasty, which closed its doors to maritime trade, commerce prospered throughout the East's history without government intervention. This spirit of entrepreneurship, even though it did not enjoy government sanction and limited itself to the merchant class, remained alive even under the repression of the Ming and Qing periods. This indomitable spirit was expressed in a proverb: "It is up to the government to make the policies; it is up to the people to develop alternatives." It is much like the Italian proverb, *Fatta la legge, trovato l'inganno*: as soon as the law is made, the loophole is discovered. Western commerce, then, is unlikely to pose major obstacles to the East, given the latter's long entrepreneurial history.

Two important points must be made before we proceed: Eastern entrepreneurial history was based on Wuwei (i.e., non-intervention from the government), whereas Western commerce was actively promoted by the state. Secondly, there is a crucial difference between Eastern Wuwei and Western laissez-faire, in that the former is a default mechanism, while the latter is an action against statism.

It is true that the East did not traditionally promote commerce. It is also true that, unlike in the West, the Eastern ruling class and government showed little interest in commercial investment. But the East did take numerous important measures to facilitate commerce, such as building roads, bridges, and canals. More importantly, the state did not intervene in commercial activities of individuals, and the tax rate was low compared to that in the West. As the state and its scholar-officials remained preoccupied with the management of an agricultural economy, they were not interested in a state monopoly on such items as salt, iron, or rice. Unlike the West, Eastern governments very rarely exercised state monopolies on commodities. As we shall see, this laissez-faire economic policy proved to be one of the reasons that enabled the East to quickly and successfully digest and adopt a Western market economy. As we have seen, the preindustrial economic policies of the East were in fact more liberal and laissez-faire than those of the West. And this Eastern laissez-faire was embedded in the philosophy of Wuwei.

Confucianism and Democracy

Two obvious deficiencies of the East were its lack of personal liberty and the absence of democracy. As the East has, in recent times, actively assimilated these Western developments, it is crucial for us to examine whether they are incompatible with, or even antithetical to, the fundamental tenets of Eastern culture, as represented by, for example, Confucianism. It cannot be denied that the Confucian emphasis on filial duty, revived by the neo-Confucians, helped to shape Eastern society into a very rigid and conservative environment.

Such an attitude fundamentally differs from that of Christianity, as exemplified by the following story of Jesus: "While he yet talked to the people, behold, his mother and his brethren stood without, desiring to speak with him. Then one said unto him, 'Behold, thy mother and thy brethren stand without, desiring to speak with thee.' But he answered and said unto him that told him, 'Who is my mother? and who are my brethren?' And he stretched forth his hand toward his disciples, and said, 'Behold my mother and my brethren! For whosoever shall do the will of my Father which is in heaven, the same is my brother, and sister, and mother.'"[48] This aspect of Western culture—its emphasis on expanding beyond the framework of the family—must have helped the West to enrich Roman law and eventually develop the "rule of law," since it made the West enlarge its perspective beyond family and ethics.

The strict hierarchical order often attributed to Confucius should be more accurately attributed to his neo-Confucian successors. By the eleventh and twelfth centuries, this new movement stressed the unilateral obligation of the subject to his ruler, the son to his father, the wife to her husband, and the younger brother to his elder brother. Song neo-Confucianism had forgotten Confucius' explicit injunction that understanding the real meaning of filial devotion would lead one to overcome the family context, by reaching out to all sons and fathers beyond one's family. Consequently, neo-Confucianism made no serious effort to move beyond a narrow application of its theoretical doctrines.

The East made several unsuccessful attempts to enlarge its intellectual horizons by relying on Han learning, which embraced all schools of thought. Despite the East's non-interventionist attitude toward individual freedom, it failed to institutionalize its principles: it remained passive and unable to limit despotism. This trajectory stands in contrast to the West's, where personal freedom was translated into the institution of liberal democracy. Although the West inherited its legal system from the polytheistic Romans, subsequent monotheism has probably reinforced the status of Law in the Western world by placing the Law above all men. Many subsequent developments, as we have seen, aided the process of institutionalizing liberty as democracy in the West; the East lacked any such developments.

Still more importantly, the conflict between religious and secular powers eventually led to the foundation of democratic institutions. While the modern East still suffered from despotism, rigid social hierarchies, unproductive ancestor-worship, and gender discrimination, the modern West fought for the full blossoming of individual freedom, which it achieved via the successful establishment of democratic institutions.

The lack of democracy in the East should be interpreted as a deficiency rather than as an impediment, since the situation may easily be repaired. From this perspective, we should note that the East has no experience of theocracy, military dictatorship with ideological justification, or totalitarianism—nothing, in other words, that would intrinsically hamper the introduction of democracy. Mancur Olson has emphasized this point: "The key to an explanation of the spontaneous emergence of democracy is the *absence* of the conditions that generate autocracy. The task is to explain why a leader who organized the overthrow of an autocrat would not make himself the next dictator or why any group of conspirators who overthrew an autocrat would not form a governing junta."[49]

The East had no experience of, for example, such regimes as the "oriental despotisms" described by Karl August Wittfogel. As rightly pointed out by Joseph Needham, East Asia lacked divine rulers supported by a priestly or military caste; its monarchs were bound by ethical norms upheld by the influential literati and accepted by the entire society. Not infrequently, an Eastern ruler's despotism led to public criticism, and finally downfall. But there has never been any official mechanism to replace that of hereditary succession. Bad leaders therefore represented a disaster for the people, for whom revolt and revolution were the only solutions, and these methods had a meager chance of success in a circumscribed world. Eastern men thus depended on the benevolence of their rulers.

But it would be too hasty to conclude, as some do, that civilizations without the necessary history and social structures are incompatible with genuine democracy. Likewise, attempting to pit Confucianism against Western democracy would be misguided and erroneous. As demonstrated by the rapid and successful assimilation of democracy by the East, there does not appear to be any issue of compatibility. Professor William Theodore de Bary, for one, correctly situates Confucian values: "It is clear that Confucius, as recorded in *The Analects*, would have nothing to do with mindless conformism or coercive measures to enforce filial duty."[50] Moreover, Confucius' central teaching of self-fulfillment, which advocates "learning for oneself" as opposed to "learning for the sake of others' approval," is quite compatible with human rights and democracy.[51]

It would therefore be just as erroneous for Easterners themselves, as for Westerners, to suggest that Western democracy is incompatible with Eastern values. There is no middle ground— either the East accepts democracy, with which it is quite compatible, or it remains, as it has been, under the perpetual threat of despotism.

Democracy and Political Parties

Leadership no longer involves a single ruler, but a party instead. We must therefore assess the role and validity of political parties in a free market democracy. Democratic leaders are often criticized for being too concerned with maintaining short-term power to give due attention to long-term safeguards of the free market or of democracy itself; how does the presence of a party system affect this state of affairs?

In the West, contrary to conventional wisdom, political parties are a rather recent phenomenon; they were not welcomed until the nineteenth century, as they were deemed to be against the public interest. The significant exception to this is England, where parliamentary power began to assert itself after the Glorious Revolution of 1688, although its seeds had already been sown by the Magna Carta of 1215. As the power of the parliament grew, it naturally gave rise to the consolidation of political parties. The party system reached its full glory during the Victorian era, as the Liberals and Conservatives managed the burgeoning empire between them. Now, with the spread of Western democracy across the globe, political parties are accepted as the principal rallying point for democratic rule. At the same time, parties are supposed to ensure that their private interest is the same as (or at least harmonious with) the public interest of their nation, as they commonly claim. This may be tested by their success at managing their nation's democratic free-market economy.

In terms of its misgivings about political party formation, the East had the same attitude as the West, without the breakthrough that the West experienced in the nineteenth century. The East has struggled unsuccessfully with party formation since the eleventh century. The problem derived from one of the core tenets of Confucianism—that Junzi would not form factions: "Junzi is encompassing and forms no factions; Xiaoren forms factions and is not encompassing."[52] This warning against party formation was reinforced by another warning against doctrines and ideologies: "The study of strange doctrines is injurious indeed!"[53]

The first attempt to form a political party was that of Ouyang Xiu (歐陽修, 1007–1072), who led a reform movement, pressing for increased official salaries, law enforcement, reduced favoritism, and the addition of practical statecraft to the civil examinations.[54] In 1045, he submitted a memorandum to the emperor entitled "On Factions," presenting the view that "Junzi forms factions for his principles; Xiaoren forms factions for his profit." This attempt was quelled by Zhu Xi (朱熹, 1130–1200), who strongly condemned the formation of parties, as they would pursue their own profit to the detriment of the common good—that is, the public interest. Wang Yangming (王陽明, 1472–1529), with his emphasis on the role of the individual mind in finding the true teaching of Confucius, brought not only a major contribution to neo-Confucianism, but a great boost to liberalism against the strict state monopoly on education. Gu Xiancheng, by reviving the Donglin Academy in 1603, rekindled the attempt to legitimize party formation. Naturally, the Academy argued that their party was grounded in principle and public interest, and denied any factionalism pursuing private interest. Gu's initiative received wide support from the literati and powerful merchants outside of the capital.[55] But this attempt was also eventually quelled by Qing dynasty officials, who naturally tried to keep their central power stronger than any regional centers of power.

With the advent of political economy, the political party system seems to have been accepted as an integral part of capitalist democracy. It may be true that there is no alternative to party formation in such a system, but the qualms and misgivings experienced by both East and West on the matter have not been sufficiently elucidated.

CHAPTER 9

Political Economy:
Western Invisible Hand and Eastern Wuwei

"Led by an Invisible Hand … by pursuing his own interest he frequently promotes that of the society more effectually than when he really intends to promote it."

Adam Smith

"The Sage has no plan of his own; he uses the plan of the people.… Governing with Wuwei, people will take action; governing without decrees, people will enjoy abundance."

Taoteking

Free Market: Adam Smith and Deng Xiaoping

The Industrial Revolution ultimately enabled the rise of the free market, which has become the leitmotif of the twenty-first century. If Adam Smith is its foremost theoretician, Deng Xiaoping is the foremost practitioner of the free market in the East. The West has Smith's Invisible Hand theory to explain the free market; the East has its philosophy of Wuwei to assimilate this Western paradigm. Let us compare the Western invisible hand with Eastern Wuwei.

Adam Smith: Invisible Hand vs. Mercantilist Statism

As we know, Adam Smith (1723–1790) proposed his laissez-faire economic principle as a response to the prevailing mercantilist interventionism: protectionism, state monopolies, and the accumulation of bullion. Even to this day, the West reveals its characteristic dialectic between state interventionism and laissez-faire, as embodied in the debates between big and small government, or the welfare state vs. private sector policies. Smith's insight was to realize the incompatibility of mercantilism—the product of the exploratory Renaissance—with the Industrial Revolution. Although overseas trade had grown rapidly, the mode of production was largely based on preindustrial methods, which limited our imagination within a zero-sum game framework. For the theorists of mercantilism, exports must exceed imports for the nation, and gold and silver must be accumulated as a direct consequence. The accumulated precious metals would constitute the nation's wealth and, therefore, its strength.

By extension, all sorts of state controls, interventions, subsidies, and protective tariffs were considered necessary, good, and justified measures: "Adam Smith's attack on mercantilism and his reasoning for 'the system of natural liberty' in *The Wealth of Nations* (1776) are usually taken as the beginning of classical political economy. Smith devised a set of concepts that remain strongly associated with capitalism today, particularly his theory of the 'invisible hand' of the market, through which the pursuit of individual self-interest unintentionally produces a collective good for society. It was necessary for Smith to be so forceful in his argument in favor of free markets because he had to overcome the popular mercantilist sentiment of the time period. He criticized monopolies, tariffs, duties, and other state-enforced restrictions of his time and believed that the market is the most fair and efficient arbitrator of resources."[1]

The state had been the principal agent in the emerging pre-industrial political economy; it was in this context that Adam Smith saw the possibility of prosperity for individuals as well as the nation by doing away with statism. And the key to this process was the Industrial Revolution—as long as goods were produced by human muscle power, they would remain scarce, and exploitation of the weak by the strong would remain inevitable. But as soon as goods are machine-produced, they become plentiful and exploitation becomes unnecessary, or even harmful, to optimal production.

Deng Xiaoping: Wuwei vs. Communism

If Mao Zedong embodied imported communism as an ideologue and radical, Deng Xiaoping embodied traditional China as a pragmatist and scholar-official. Mao's life can be neatly divided into two segments: the period between the Long March and the establishment of the new Chinese Republic in 1949, and that from 1949 until his death in 1976. The first of these was an extraordinary success, while the second was full of disasters and failures. During the first half of his life, Mao began from almost nothing and succeeded in reunifying the deeply fractured Chinese nation. This feat is often compared to the establishment of the first empire by Qin Shi Huang in 221 BC. But the radical experiments of his later life—the Hundred Flowers Campaign during early 1950s, the Great Leap Forward in 1958, and the Cultural Revolution launched in 1966—were all catastrophic, since they were founded on an incorrect concept of human nature.

Figures 9-1 and 9-2 illustrate Adam Smith and Deng Xiaoping, respectively the most important theorist and the most important Eastern practitioner of free market economics. As early as the 1980s, an astute Western mind had already anticipated the rapprochement between communism and capitalism. An advertisement by the company Mobil reads: "Karl Marx, meet Adam Smith. Chinese pragmatists under Deng Xiaoping have begun to energize the population. Can it be that these doctrinaire Communists have finally seen the light? Hardly. Nobody expects them to disavow communism. But they are redefining it, so that their latter-day interpretation of Karl Marx sounds more and more like the free-market economist Adam Smith. Many now believe that this economic revolution has grown too large to be snuffed out. For the good of capitalists and Communists alike who share this planet, we hope history proves this to be correct."

It was Deng Xiaoping who, in the years after 1978, rescued China from the chaotic experiments set in motion by Mao Zedong, introducing free market economics into the country. As we have seen in chapter 4, he had already struck a chord with the core element of Chinese culture and people when he advocated pragmatism with his "black cat-white cat" speech in 1961, amid the growing disenchantment with Mao's Great Leap Forward by the Chinese people and political parties. After assuming China's helm in 1978,

Deng reintroduced the philosophy of "seeking truth from facts," which had prevailed in China during the eighteenth century, with a view to justifying "Socialism with Chinese Characteristics."[2] This was a politically masterful move, since the new philosophy allowed him to introduce the market economy without alienating the still-powerful Communist ideologues in the party.

Fig. 9-1. Adam Smith (1723–1790) (http://en.wikipedia.org/wiki/File:AdamSmith.jpg)	Fig. 9-2. Deng Xiaoping (鄧小平, 1904–1997) (http://en.wikipedia.org/wiki/File:DengXiaoping.jpg)

When China was confronted with what was arguably the most serious danger since its establishment in 1949—the Tiananmen Square protest of 1989—it was again Deng Xiaoping who steered China through the dangerous storm. In a speech given in September of that year, Deng advised China to be "calm, calm and again calm," focusing on economic modernization, which he believed to be most important for China at that time.[3] He also helped initiate the crucial modernization of the Communist party. The leadership was selected in three crucial stages: the party's members were largely chosen from those who had graduated from good schools, with entrance examinations as competitive as the imperial system; its cadres were chosen by promotion within the party, subject to cross-checking and peer review; and its highest leaders were selected from those who had been successful as regional governors and mayors. In short, Deng was relying on the traditional core principle of the Imperial Examination System (e.g., meritocracy).

Ever the pragmatist, Deng left his options open for a compromise with Communist ideology: "While the state retained ownership of large enterprises, it does not use this ownership to intervene to change prices, which are set by the market"; "But if we adhere to socialism and apply the principle of distribution to each according to his work, there will not be excessive disparities in wealth"; "One important reason for China's backwardness after the industrial revolution in Western countries was its closed-door policy"; "Socialism means eliminating poverty. Pauperism is not socialism, still less communism."[4]

Deng Xiaoping, far from being a Communist, was a quintessential Junzi. In chapter 5 we examined four distinct characteristics of Junzi: of these, the most important distinction from the Western ideal is altruism vs. greed, which carries deep implications for the issue of political economy. And this aspect is explained as Wuwei, a principle pertaining more to Taoism than to any other individual school, but permeating all schools.

The Philosophy of Wuwei

We examined the basic aspects of Wuwei (無爲, non-interventionism) in chapter 2: "The Sage has no plan of his own; he uses the plan of the people.... Governing with Wuwei, people will take action; governing without decrees, people will enjoy abundance."[5] Although Taoteking did not use the term "invisible hand," it accepted a similar principle. Here are some quotations from Taoteking with this sense: "The Sage manages affairs with Wuwei.… All things spring up … they grow … they go through their processes … the work is done, but no one can see it" (Taoteking 2); "The Sage, in management, empties the minds of people from knowledge and actions.… With the abstinence from action, good order prevails" (Taoteking 3); "Tao produces all things and nourishes them.… It presides over all, and yet does not control them.… This is what is called the 'invisibility' of Tao" (Taoteking 10); "Tao takes the Form of the Formless and the Semblance of the Invisible.… We meet it and do not see its Front; we follow it, and do not see its Back" (Taoteking 14); "Profound and invisible, the essence is there. From this essence, truth unfolds itself. And from truth, trust can be found" (Taoteking 21); "Tao is omnipresent. It is on the left and it is on the right; All things depend on it for their being.… When its work is accomplished, it does not make any claim" (Taoteking 34); "Tao is invisible, it has no name. Yet Tao imparts and enables" (Taoteking 41); "Having no possession of its own, it passes everywhere; Therefore nothing is more useful than Wuwei. Imparting lessons without instructing, Wuwei attains the highest usefulness" (Taoteking 43); "He who devotes himself to learning increases his knowledge every day; he who devotes himself to the Tao diminishes his action every day. He diminishes it and again diminishes it, till he arrives at Wuwei. Having arrived at this point of Wuwei, there is nothing that he cannot achieve" (Taoteking 48); "Tao produces things, nourishes them, brings them to their full growth, nurses them, completes them, matures them, maintains them, and reproduces them. Yet it makes no claim, no control. This is called the invisible way of

Tao's operation" (Taoteking 51); "The Sage governs with Wuwei; people act by themselves" (Taoteking 57); "He who forces to govern by his plans is a curse to the state; he who does not force his plan is a blessing to state" (Taoteking 65).

We have concluded that Wuwei is more than a single concept: rather, it is an entire philosophy, and it is the modus operandi of Junzi and Eastern civilization. Wuwei is based on an understanding of Nature, on human nature, on the desirable form of government, and on international affairs. Thus, Wuwei shares with Junzi philosophy the four fundamental aspects that we have examined in the latter. But Junzi is practical; Wuwei is theoretical.

Wuwei, in terms of political economy, is quite comparable to the Western idea of the "invisible hand." Although they share their central aspect (e.g., noninterventionism or antistatism), they have subtle but crucial differences, as we shall illustrate. And these differences may have a great bearing on how we deal with political economy in the twenty-first century, including the role of political parties.

Invisible Hand: Mandeville, Smith, and Wuwei

Smith's concept of the invisible hand is the key to his justification of the laissez-faire principle. The invisible hand, he asserted, will guide selfish individual interests toward the common good: "By directing that industry in such a manner as its produce may be of the greatest value, he intends only his own gain, and he is in this, as in many other cases, led by an invisible hand to promote an end which was no part of his intention. Nor is it always the worse for society that it was no part of his intention. By pursuing his own interest he frequently promotes that of the society more effectually than when he really intends to promote it."[6] The concept first appears in Smith's *Theory of Moral Sentiments*, which opens with this description: "In spite of their natural selfishness and rapacity, though they mean only their own convenience, though the sole end which they propose ... be the gratification of their own vain and insatiable desires, they divide with the poor the produce of all their improvements. They are led by an invisible hand to make nearly the same distribution of the necessaries of life, which would have been made, had the earth been divided into equal portions among all its inhabitants, and thus without intending it, without knowing it, advance the interest of the society."[7]

The concept was implicit in the works of several thinkers who influenced his philosophy, including Bernard Mandeville, Bishop Butler, Lord Shaftesbury, and Francis Hutcheson. Bernard Mandeville (1670–1733) had the insight to recognize self-interest as the driving force for civilization—an idea contrary to the prevailing ethics of Christianity. Mandeville's masterpiece, *The Fable of the Bees*, therefore, became both famous and infamous throughout Europe. This text had been worked up from an earlier poem, *The Grumbling Hive: or, Knaves turned Honest*, in which he had written:

"The 'hive' is corrupt but prosperous, yet it grumbles about lack of virtue. A higher power decides to give them what they ask for:

But Jove, with Indignation moved,
At last in Anger swore, he'd rid the bawling
Hive of Fraud, and did.

The very Moment it departs, and Honesty fills all their Hearts; this results in a rapid loss of prosperity."[8]

In the later *Fable*, Mandeville wrote: "Civilized man has stigmatized his private appetites and the result is the retardation of the common good … the Vileness of the Ingredients that all together compose the wholesome Mixture of a well-ordered Society; in order to extol the wonderful Power of Political Wisdom, by the help of which so beautiful a Machine is raised from the most contemptible Branches."[9] Both the concept of the invisible hand and the paradox of thrift—that a community which forsakes luxury for savings achieves neither—are evident in Mandeville's philosophy.

Joseph Butler (1692–1752), in his *Sermons on Human Nature*, argued that "pursuing the public good was the best way of advancing one's own good since the two were necessarily identical."[10] His epigram, "Everything is what it is, and not another thing," better captures his similarity to Mandeville. Likewise, but in reverse order, Lord Shaftesbury argued that "acting in accordance with one's self-interest will produce socially beneficial results. An underlying unifying force that Shaftesbury called the 'Will of Nature' maintains equilibrium, congruency, and harmony. This force, if it is to operate freely, requires the individual pursuit of rational self-interest, and the preservation and advancement of the self."[11] Francis Hutcheson, while accepting the convergence between public and private interests, attributed the mechanism, not to rational self-interest, but to personal intuition, which he called a moral sense.[12] Darwinian natural selection can also be construed to support the concept of invisible hand and the convergence of personal interest and the common good.

Now we have arrived at the core principle that underlines the theory of invisible hand—the convergence of private and public interest, which must be automatic, natural, and inevitable. Western thinkers later discovered several supplementary mechanisms and attenuating concepts in support of this principle, including the tragedy of the commons and positive or negative externalities. But the basic tenets remained unchanged: "the invisible hand of the market must be protected from statism *as private and public interests converge.*" On this essential point, Wuwei differs from the Western invisible hand. Wuwei would argue that "the invisible hand of the market must be protected from statism *as private and public interests diverge.*"

Wuwei philosophy believes that private and public interests diverge since private interest is an expression of greed, whereas public interest is an expression of altruism. Wuwei philosophy can be summed up as following: *Self-interest, the driving force of civilization, although value neutral per se, tends to be greedy rather than altruistic.* The concepts of laissez-faire, the invisible hand, and the convergence of private and public interests are all crucially important to the free market and democracy. But from the Wuwei perspective, based on ethics, there is one critical element that has been overlooked in the Western theory, and that is the issue of greed. Mandeville and Smith make no distinction between self-interest and greed. If they praised these two together, it was in conscious opposition to Christian values.

But for whatever reason, the problem of greed has not been addressed by the Western theorists of the free market, but simply subsumed within self-interest. Smith argues that man's "own gain, his own interest, his natural selfishness, rapacity, and the gratification of his own vain and insatiable desires" will be led by the market's invisible hand to advance the interest of society. The same is true for Mandeville: "private appetite, vileness, the most contemptible Branches" contribute to a well-ordered society. Greed, then, is either praised or condoned as an appendix to self-interest. As with Mandeville and Smith, the theories of Butler,

Shaftesbury, and Hutcheson hold only when greed is subsumed in self-interest.

Here Wuwei sees contradiction: why should an individual's self-interest be good but the state's self-interest bad? According to Wuwei, both are bad. But statism must be prevented because its greed poses a much greater threat to the invisible hand than that of the individual—the Soviet Union is one good example.

Greed: Statism, Tribalism, and Individualism

Individual self-interest is less bad than that of the group, which necessarily embodies greed disguised as regulations and state interventions. So laissez-faire (i.e., the free market) is best for society. Wuwei's difference from Western laissez-faire lies in its attempt to guide the individual toward altruism. The East's rational and holistic approach is possible because it is grounded in ethics. By contrast, Western ambivalence about individual self-interest stems from its Mind-Body dichotomy.

The invisible hand is the central concept of the free market, in the sense that government intervention is considered harmful to the functioning of the market, except in the production and construction of common goods. Given human nature, no society or political system prohibiting by law the pursuit of self-interest can stand the test of time. Communism is a case in point: the entire population was prevented from seeking profit while a small clan monopolized profits. In the end, the strain became too great and the system collapsed. On the other hand, if the political system permits everyone to pursue individual profit, it cannot legally prevent greed from being socially acceptable and even desirable; this can only be prevented by strong social ethics. Thus, a society needs both law for the free market to flourish and ethics to remain healthy.

There is no denying that, according to Adam Smith, greed is in the end good, even if we cannot simply say that "greed is good." Here lies the fundamental problem: is greed really good? Was Adam Smith trying to say that man is selfish but that selfishness is good or unimportant? Is this so because selfishness is led by the invisible hand to the common good, or because man's other nature, benevolence, would make selfishness rational? Whatever our answers to these questions, Adam Smith appears to have left his theory incomplete and bequeathed great confusion to his readers.

Wuwei warns against all state intervention. Some may argue that opposing state intervention is not the same as permitting laissez-faire. Nonetheless, the two follow the same underlying logic. From this perspective, Adam Smith's theory may be considered incomplete, although it promotes a less unjust result of man's commercial activities than any other vision. Of all political institutions, democracy is the best (or the least bad) for the invisible hand, since it prevents private interventions in the market through the mechanism of checks and balances.

The incompleteness of Adam Smith's laissez-faire appears to be due to his ambiguous interpretation of human nature, which was the mirror image of his ambiguous description of the invisible hand. To repeat, the fundamental tenet of Adam Smith remains valid: interventions are bad as they are bound to distort the logic of the market, and despite their professed goal of the common good, they almost always cater to the special interests of one group. At the same time, however, he never explained with any clarity the problem of greed.

In its negative sense, the Invisible Hand theory is crystal clear: statism is bad and must give way to the free market. What is not clear with Adam Smith is the positive sense of the invisible hand.

He appears to be indicating what he called "the nature of moral sentiment (i.e., benevolence and other propriety). Benevolence, or altruism, may be present in human nature as a possibility but, given his acceptance of self-interest as a basic feature of human nature, how could one expect altruism to become the prevailing principle of the invisible hand? In contrast, Wuwei is without ambiguity in either its negative or positive senses; statism is bad and must be replaced by self-interest of individuals; the invisible hand can never become the prevailing principle of altruism. Rather, self-interest must be guided by ethics, not by laws. Wuwei's fundamental distrust of law is based on its uncompromisingly realistic understanding of human nature. Law is established by men motivated by self-interest and will always end up as another instrument of statism. This problem remained unsolved by Adam Smith and law-based Western civilization.

Wuwei appears to suggest an answer—albeit far from a satisfactory one—to this problem facing the West. Simply put, it goes as follows: the self-interest of individuals, while much less harmful than statism, nonetheless remains problematic, since it cannot be expected to be guided by altruism. Because this self-interest cannot be regulated by law, it must be guided by ethics. And Junzi must show leadership by example as best he can, otherwise Xiaoren's greed will have free run. In the end, it all depends on leadership—this is why the Eastern solution is imperfect. If Junzi is in charge, then society has a better chance of success, since sound ethics will prevail; if Xiaoren, society will suffer.

Individual greed poses fewer problems in an expansive environment, since all nations and individuals share the same objective and survive collectively. But in a circumscribed environment, such as that of our present world, the incompleteness of the invisible hand is magnified, and so it begins to create global problems. The invisible hand cannot be augmented with legal mechanisms—this would be a contradiction in terms; we therefore need an ethical framework to check individual and national greed. History shows that, sooner or later, greed disguised as self-interest always asserts itself, remaining the greatest challenge to the free market: "In the late nineteenth century, the control and direction of large areas of industry came into the hands of trusts, financiers, and holding companies. This period was dominated by an increasing number of oligopolistic firms earning supernormal profits. Major characteristics of capitalism in this period included the establishment of large industrial cartels or monopolies; the ownership and management of industry by financiers divorced from the production process; and the development of a complex system of banking, an equity market, and corporate holdings of capital through stock ownership. The petroleum, telecommunication, railroad, shipping, banking, and financial industries are characterized by its monopolistic domination."[13] As we know, the American government played the key role in passing antitrust laws. But we are ultimately left with the question of group greed, whether that of businesses or political parties. Can Wuwei regulate greed?

Invisible Hand and Wuwei

The crucial difference between the invisible hand and Wuwei lies in their conceptions of nature and human nature, which have critical implications for the free market and for democracy.

Invisible Hand vs. Wuwei I: Nature

"Tao is infinite, Tao is eternal; Tao has no purpose; Tao has no desire; this makes Tao eternal and infinite" (Taoteking, 7). Like the theory of the invisible hand, Wuwei accepts self-preservation as the driving force of civilization. Human actions are founded on self-interest. A laissez-faire attitude is therefore accepted without dissent.

Wuwei is predicated on an objective observation of nature, so there is no sin, evil, punishment, or reward in its philosophy. It treats mind and body together, in a holistic unity. Consequently, self-interest is considered not sinful, but rather a human necessity, for man is part of nature, and so unless nature is not considered sinful, neither should man be. It may develop either into a beneficial altruism, or into a harmful greed. Junzi (or Sage) will attain altruism; Xiaoren will remain greedy.[14] Since Xiaoren is more common than Junzi, it is likely that government interventions will "tend" to be initiated by Xiaoren and therefore serve greed instead of altruism. Wuwei favors small government, understanding that bureaucracy is wasteful and tends to be inclined to fraud or theft. For this reason, welfare could not easily be accepted in the East.

As Wuwei is predicated on a unity of man and nature, and of mind and body, it accepts no unnecessary factionalism. It also addresses economics as well as politics, and so its noninterventionist policy applies both to democracy and to the free market. The two necessarily went together: no viable market economy was possible without political freedom, and no political freedom could be genuine if it interfered with free-market principles.

The free market can only flourish fully when a society or nation provides a legal mechanism to protect and promote individual initiatives. This is best enabled in a democracy, which limits the ruling body's natural but harmful inclination to interfere in the market. It would therefore be incorrect to categorize the traditional Eastern economy as controlled. In fact, few dynasties exercised any sort of control, except for their constant attempts to lower taxes. Their isolationism can be understood better as a political act of shielding the empire from outside influence than as a control of trade; the empire, indeed, was hardly interested in foreign trade at all. The same can be said of political freedom; the East was not democratic, nor was it *anti*-democratic, since its empires did not impose any particular doctrine on their peoples. Confucianism was brought to the population by education and examination rather than imposed upon it with the threat of punishment.

Unlike the West, no Eastern economy practiced either mercantilism or protectionism. Some may mention the Japanese economy under the military regime or the Chinese Communist economy as examples of such cases—but these had been imported from the West, during a brief period of cultural turbulence, and fit ill with the local character. It would also be wrong to assume that the introduction of capitalism into China succeeded because it separated market economics in the Special Economic Zones (SEZ) of the South East Coast from the political authority of Beijing; in fact, both economic and political freedom were permitted in the South East Coast, and both were limited in Beijing. The two kinds of freedom were inseparable.

This also explains the predicament facing North Korea in its experiment with the Kaesong Industrial Park project. As North

Korea does not enjoy the strategic depth that allowed China to place the SEZ far from Beijing, it had no choice but to deprive the project workers both economic and political freedom. Had these two freedoms been separable, the Pyongyang government would have permitted economic freedom to SEZ while strictly controlling political freedom; the project would have succeeded, opening valuable international exchange with the regime, without entailing political risk. The fact that both the free market and political freedom have been absorbed by the East is proof that the philosophy of Wuwei embraces both together.

Adam Smith had little to say about political freedom in connection with his free-market theory. But since the two go hand in hand, Smith indirectly promoted political freedom, guided by his favorite concept of the invisible hand. Both democracy and the free market, ultimately, are predicated on and promote freedom of the individual. This is what we are witnessing in the East in the wake of its assimilation of Western paradigms.

Invisible Hand vs. Wuwei II: Human Nature

The problem of human nature has fascinated East and West alike from the dawn of philosophy. The debate is still going on, and thus the issue remains unresolved. If human nature is malleable or fundamentally altruistic, then state intervention may be justified. The demise of communism indicates that human nature is fundamentally neither altruistic nor malleable.[15] Rather, it tends toward avarice and so must be guided by law and ethics.

The human nature espoused by Adam Smith was greatly influenced by David Hume (1711–1776): "Smith is reported to have complained to friends that Oxford officials once detected him reading a copy of David Hume's *Treatise on Human Nature*, and they subsequently confiscated his book and punished him severely for reading it.… Smith's close friend and colleague David Hume, with whom he agreed on most matters, was described by contemporaries as an atheist."[16] What, then, was the human nature understood by Hume? Hume's views on the subject were new to the point of heterodoxy: "Morals excite passions, and produce or prevent actions. Reason itself is utterly impotent in this particular. The rules of morality, therefore, are not conclusions of our reason.… Given that one cannot be motivated by reason alone, requiring the input of the passions, Hume argued that reason cannot be behind morality."[17]

Judging from Hume's description, Adam Smith seems to have accepted that human nature was based on self-interest. It is unclear, however, if this was also the origin of his "invisible hand." But what was the nature of the self-interest propounded by Smith? This concept was illustrated in his book, *The Theory of Moral Sentiments*, which he considered much superior to his *Wealth of Nations*, revising it constantly. In this work, Smith explains that human nature is based on self-interest, but capable also of benevolence: "How selfish soever man may be supposed, there are evidently some principles in his nature, which interest him in the fortunes of others, and render their happiness necessary to him, though he derives nothing from it, except the pleasure of seeing it."[18]

This double nature—selfish or benevolent, greedy or altruistic—has proved ambiguous to Smith's readers, who have debated this aspect without conclusive agreement. Insofar as he commended self-interest, Smith stood in harmony with the traditional religious interpretation; insofar as he praised self-interest, Smith stood as the hero of free market. Smith's invisible hand was necessarily grounded in this ambiguous interpretation of human nature. The upshot is that current free-market philosophy remains extremely unclear with regard to the question of greed: does it condemn or promote greed? Indeed, the contemporary debate over human nature remains with this dichotomous ambiguity to become dangerously moralistic, involving religious and ideological dogmas, as well as metaphysical speculation.

Eastern Wuwei philosophy, by contrast, was founded on a holistic, as opposed to a dialectic, conception of human nature, with self-preservation at its core. "Tao is not benevolent; it is indifferent to all things in the world; Sage is not benevolent; he is indifferent to all people in the world" (Taoteking, 5). "Tao applies to all equally; it is blessing for the good; it is protection for the bad" (Taoteking, 67). Tao is present in human nature as the fundamental principle of self-preservation—a value-neutral fact simply to be accepted and upon which the philosophy of Wuwei is based. Both the Invisible Hand theorists and Wuwei, then, recognized self-interest as the basic drive of the free market as well as of political freedom: "The first and only foundation of virtue, or the rule of right living, is seeking one's own true interest."

The difference is that Wuwei takes self-interest (or self-preservation) as a natural and value-neutral principle. Here we find the most important contrast between Wuwei and the invisible hand: the latter praises greed as well as self-interest, while the former condemns greed as the negative expression of self-interest. As one's interpretation of self-interest has a direct bearing on one's understanding of human nature, the West either condemns human nature as sinful or praises it as the source of civilization. This attitude has given birth to a dichotomous view of Man in the West, which persists even today: Christianity is hostile to wealth, while capitalism promotes it. As secularization has weakened the influence of religion, wealth and fame is now the goal of younger generations.

Western proponents of laissez-faire rightly argued that greed cannot be regulated by law, within the framework of Western civilization. Regulating greed by law would be tantamount to regulating self-interest, which is equivalent to statism or mercantilism. Thus, laissez-faire is the right approach to greed as well as self-interest within the Western context. But this conclusion would not have suited the Eastern mind, which operates within the framework of ethics. According to the Western cultural framework based on law, the invisible hand must ignore greed lest self-interest be interrupted by the state. But according to the East, self-interest can be given free run by law, while greed is condemned by ethics.

As Wuwei and the invisible hand differed in their understanding of greed, they also differed in their attitude toward benevolence or altruism: Smith assumed that self-interest would ultimately lead to benevolent actions, while the Taoists, like Spinoza, expressed a different opinion: "Most people seem to believe that they are free, in so far as they may obey their lusts ... they would return to their own inclinations, controlling everything in accordance with their lusts, and desiring to obey fortune rather than themselves." Only a minority can be Junzi, whose self-interest leads to benevolent actions. Now we better understand the limits of the argument advanced by Butler, Shaftesbury, and Hutcheson—"the convergence of private interest and public interest." According to Wuwei, the convergence is not a given; it can be achieved only by a minority. This leads us to the domain of ethics.

Invisible Hand vs. Wuwei III: Ethics

The difference between Wuwei and the invisible hand is nowhere as conspicuous as in ethics. Since the nature of greed has an immense bearing on free-market practices, especially in regard to the irresponsible trading known as "casino capitalism," let us revisit the origin of the Invisible Hand theory. If one compares Mandeville's assertion that "civilized man has stigmatized his private appetites and the result is the retardation of common good" to Smith's arguments that "man's own gain, his own interest, his natural selfishness, rapacity, and the gratification of his own vain and insatiable desires will be led by the invisible hand to advance the interest of society," one cannot but arrive at the conclusion that "greed is good."

We must ask why such great minds as Mandeville, Butler, Shaftesbury, Hutcheson, and Smith saw a natural convergence between self-interest and public interest, and judged self-interest itself as good. One possible explanation can be found in the dialectic evolution between mind and body of Western philosophy—since the Christian West had long considered self-interest to be sinful, and since this theory no longer fit their observations, they proposed the opposite: that self-interest is fundamentally good. Perhaps for those Western thinkers, proposing a third way—by declaring something sinful to be value-neutral—was not relevant in a cultural environment characterized by dialectic dynamics between opposites. As an afterthought, "praising altruism and condemning greed" in human society-as-allegory would have done more justice to the amoral world of bees, as they cancel each other out at least; bees would not be happy if they knew that Man described their society simply as greedy.

How could these Western thinkers arrive at such a conclusion? It seems that two mistakes have been made, both regarding ethics: one simple and the other complicated. The simple mistake is their confounding of animal society with human society. Bees' self-interest is instinctive and natural, and does not involve greed. They collect pollen and honey for their colony—they do not invade and conquer other colonies to expand their kingdom. Animals do not kill for greed; they kill only to eat. Once they have eaten enough, the killing stops. They do not colonize and enslave other animals; they do not have "rapacity or insatiable desires." There is no opportunity for greed, and so no need for ethics in their society. But human greed is insatiable, and so an ethical distinction between self-interest and ethics is essential in human society. Unlike animal society, if equilibrium is to be maintained in human society, it is a result of the emphatic role ethics plays in condemning greed, not at all ensuring free rein to human greed. This is a fundamental difference between animal economic activity and human economic activity. Mandeville and, by extension, Smith appeared to have missed this point.

The second, more complicated mistake, appears from the context in which Mandeville and Smith worked. It cannot be overemphasized that the social force of Christianity, which condemned greed, was still overwhelming during their time. And that religion had defined for more than one and a half millennia that man's self-interest is sinful. If man did not repent his sin, he would go to hell. To contradict Christian teachings on anthropological grounds required insight and courage. It is not difficult to imagine the exultation that must have filled the hearts of Mandeville and Smith when they discovered the truth against millennium-old doctrine, which in their minds would open a new world for the entire good of humanity. But Mandeville and Smith, like Christianity, continued to conflate self-interest and greed.

From the perspective of Wuwei, Mandeville made a crucial theoretical contribution in preparing the ground for the free market with his insight that self-interest constitutes the drive of civilization, but at the same time an Easterner would be puzzled by Mandeville's confusion between animal and human society.

If one sees no difference between the invisible hand observed by Mandeville and Smith, then the latter's theory seems to overlook a crucial element of man's economic activity.[19]

In the West, religion has played a pivotal role in promoting both altruism and egoism. Thus, the pairing of altruism and egoism played a key role both in medieval theology and in modern metaphysics. In the East, this pair played no role of importance, since it was simply assumed that Xiaoren would act egoistically, while Junzi would act altruistically. Instead of requiring altruism of everyone, which is unrealistic, or praising egoism, which is cynical, the East focuses on self-development and fulfillment as a lifetime's commitment.

This difference in life purpose is manifested in differing attitudes toward reward and punishment: the Western Heaven and Hell, as against the Eastern focus on inner satisfaction. Junzi's goal is at the same time self-interest and altruistic (i.e., an attainment of well-being for himself and service to others). There is no external punishment or reward. Western society, by contrast, was deeply imbued with such a system of judgment after death—from Dante in the fourteenth century, who believed in the literal existence of Hell beneath Jerusalem, to Isaac Newton in the seventeenth century, who recalculated the age of the world since creation as around five millennia.

Given man's natural tendency to greed, society must praise altruism for the sake of equilibrium. In no Eastern school can one find any argument defending greed—rather, it is perceived as one of the cardinal problems, if not the central problem, of civilization. As such, greed is identified as one of the most conspicuous characteristics of Xiaoren. "The Way of Heaven diminishes abundance and supplements deficiency; the Way of Man supplements abundance and diminishes deficiency; who among men can diminish abundance to serve all under the heaven? Only those who understand the Way of Heaven" (Taoteking, 77). "The sage does not accumulate possessions; the more he works for others, the happier the sage is; the more he distributes to others, the more the sage has" (Taoteking, 81). The Wuwei position on public and private interests can be summed up as follows: the invisible hand of the market, which is as natural as Tao when unperturbed, will restore balance and equilibrium, but individual men will always act to promote private interest or greed more than public interest or altruism. As a counterweight, the society needs Junzi, since he alone can help the invisible hand to work for the sake of public interest, using Wuwei—the indirect, ethical method to discourage and counteract greed.

Traditionally, it was the same in the West: greed was condemned as one of the seven deadly sins. But no distinction was made between greed and self-interest. The eighteenth century, likewise, supported both. Only Wuwei praises one and condemns the other. This leads us to the political aspect of the Wuwei-invisible hand contrast. Whatever the reason, mainstream Western philosophy made a crucial shift from the preindustrial to the postindustrial epoch in its treatment of man's self-interest: the shift was from condemnation to praise. Even though innumerable tracts and arguments condemning greed exist in the West, virtually none really made a distinction between greed and self-interest in condemning greed. The upshot is in the West, both greed and self-interest have been condemned (preindustrial) or praised (postindustrial). The most plausible explanation for this can again be found in its expansive environment—as heroes and expansion always brought along spoils and slaves (preindustrial) and commercial benefits (postindustrial), the West did not feel acutely the need to differentiate greed from self-interest. Wuwei arose in a context of endless warfare, in which greed had to be delineated from self-interest: the former to be condemned, the latter to be tolerated. Such a distinction, following the global financial collapse of 2008, is more important than ever. Can Wuwei, then, provide an answer to the problem of greed without jeopardizing self-interest?

Invisible Hand vs. Wuwei IV: Politics

Wuwei, as we have seen, proposes ethics rather than law as a remedy to greed. But both are necessary—safeguarding the free market requires constant observation and adjustment. This may be compared to the homeostasis of an organism, which relies on both positive and negative feedback, just as society requires positive feedback from law, to protect it from interference, and negative feedback from ethics, to protect it from greed.

At the crux of this homeostasis is individual freedom (i.e., self-interest). "The more prohibition you have, the less virtuous people will be; the more weapons you have, the less secure people will be; the more subsidies you have, the less self-reliant people will be" (Taoteking, 57).[20] Wuwei addresses ethics, politics, and economics as a single entity. When Eastern culture was first introduced to European thinkers of the Enlightenment, they were particularly struck by two things. First, there was little tax, and that was levied entirely by the emperor, although the local infrastructures were well-maintained, facilitating transportation and promoting industry and commerce. Second, while personal liberty was not yet the norm in the West, it was more common in the tolerant East. They also noticed the lack of distinction between moral and political principles.[21] Since they were only familiar with Confucianism, they failed to realize that these phenomena derived more from the Taoist principle of Wuwei—equivalent to the doctrine of laissez-faire in both economic and political life.

On the other hand, the invisible hand of Smith pertains only to economic phenomena, although it has made an invaluable contribution to the promotion of democracy, since, in the final analysis, political freedom and economic freedom are inseparable. The role of the invisible hand in the political domain is explained by Mancur Olson as the "left" invisible hand. We shall examine this in the next section. Olson's conclusion is the same as ours— political freedom is inseparable from economic freedom.

Political Invisible Hand: Olson and Smith

Mancur Olson, in his book *Power and Prosperity*, persuasively describes the origin of government with the metaphor of a bandit. At some point in history, according to the model, roving bandits realized that they could increase their power and revenue by remaining stationary within villages sited on fertile lands. By staying still, these bandits could monopolize theft within their domains and eventually impose a rate of regular theft, which they called tax. Furthermore, they realized that a thriving (and tax-paying) population was in their interest, so they funded public services, such as schools, police, and hospitals. Religion was used to instruct the population that theft, violence, murder, and suicide were immoral, further aiding the growth and prosperity of the people—and so of the "stationary bandits," who called themselves kings. The key point is that the common good is also that of the ruler. The system amounts to a political version of Adam Smith's "invisible hand"—Olson calls it an "invisible left hand," in comparison to the "invisible right hand" of the free market. One can also characterize Olson's invisible left hand as the "political" invisible hand in contrast to Smith's "economic" invisible hand.

Olson's theory has much in common with the philosophy of Wuwei, which also suggested that taxes are basically a form of theft by rulers, and so he advocated low taxes and small government: "If the people suffer from famine, it is because rulers impose too many taxes. Taxes cause the famine which the people suffer; if the people appear difficult to govern, it is because the rulers impose too many policies. Policies pose difficulties to the governance of the people."[22] Nor does Wuwei advocate the welfare state. "The simpler and plainer rules and regulations, the greater the benefits to the people; the more extensive and sophisticated the rules and regulations, the lesser the benefits to the people."[23] Given the similarity, we are interested to discover that Olson formulated his theory when he read about the bandits of 1920s Manchuria: roving bandits like White Wolf (Bai Lang) were defeated by the warlord (stationary bandit) Feng Yuxiang with the support of the local population.[24] The affinity of his ideas to those of Taoism therefore derived from his understanding of a similar situation—Wuwei had been formulated in the chaotic eras of early China, which had much in common with Manchuria of the 1920s. Olson's account succinctly explains the trajectory of Western history, in which "stationary bandits," or kings, made innumerable contributions to the progress of civilization for over four millennia, interrupted only by occasional episodes of roving banditry.[25]

Prima facie, one may find similarities between Hobbes's *Leviathan* and Olson's political invisible hand. Yet their theories are in fact quite different. For Hobbes, the monarch should exercise absolute power so that his people may escape chaos; for Olson, stationary bandits ruled the population without their consent or contract, but managed to secure support by offering protection from roving bandits in exchange for taxes. For Hobbes, the monarch is a divinely sanctioned solution to human problems. For Olson, the monarch remains a stationary bandit who would lose legitimacy if he could not ensure mutual benefit. On this score, the Eastern concept of the Mandate of Heaven is closer to the theory of Olson than to that of Hobbes. The Mandate of Heaven, unlike the divine right of kings in the West, was invariably used in the East to depose tyrants.[26] As such, the legitimacy of tyrannicide was firmly established in the East by the fifth century BC: "We call those who violate benevolence 'bandits'; we call those who violate righteousness 'villains.' The ruler who violates benevolence and righteousness is no sovereign, but a mere man. Eliminating such a tyrant is a rightful act, not a regicide."[27] Since then, other than short-lived attempts by the Legalists in the third century BC, the East produced no theory in support of a ruler's unconditional authority.

The theory of political economy expounded by Mancur Olson appears to be based on the same understanding of human nature as the Eastern philosophy of Wuwei.

Democracy and the Invisible Hand

The political invisible hand therefore came to existence with stationary bandits in the West and the Mandate of Heaven in the East. The difference was that the Western invisible hand was protected by law while the Eastern one was protected by ethics. The stationary bandits' desire to act like roving bandits was loosely checked by law in the West, while the emperor's caprice was restrained by ethics in the East. Both were periodically broken by episodes of warfare and roving banditry.

The West then made the "improbable" transition to democracy (to borrow Olson's word), which consolidated the political invisible hand to an unprecedented degree: the encompassing interest of the stationary bandits that gave birth to the invisible hand has come to be solidly institutionalized as democratic leaders are bound by checks and balances. Once consolidated, the political invisible hand struck an alliance with the economic invisible hand of Adam Smith to produce the democratic free market, which has proved to be the most efficient system of production in history, as it enabled individual freedom to flourish both politically and economically.

By assimilating Western democracy and the free market, the Eastern Mandate of Heaven appears to have all but disappeared. Nonetheless, the concept reflected precisely the ethical aspect of the political invisible hand in the East. Successive Eastern dynasties, by contrast, relied on ethics to produce their "invisible hand."

The chief point of difference between Olson and Wuwei is that Olson's theory is based not on ethics, like that of Wuwei, but on a legal system—as one would expect from a Western thinker. Also, Olson focuses on the menace from without—anarchy, uncertainty, and monopoly—and identifies checks and balances as the necessary remedy to prevent reversion to roving banditry. Wuwei, by contrast, emphasized the menace from within—chiefly greed—and identified ethics as the solution. We can find a parallel between Smith's economic invisible hand and Olson's political invisible hand: both focus on law and menace from without, and consequently both invisible hands could be better safeguarded with the addition of ethical protections from greed.

In fact, both Smith and Olson expressed a strong distrust of group interests. Smith warned against monopoly.[28] Olson, likewise, is very specific in his warning against special interest groups: "The awesome difficulties in keeping narrow special interests from dominating economic policy making in the long-stable democracy ... although democracies have the great advantage of preventing significant extraction of social surplus by their leaders."[29] Olson assumes that "individuals will act collectively to provide private goods, but not to provide public goods," and consequently the policies made by and for narrow special interests would harm the public interest: "These policies will tend to be protectionist and antitechnology, and will therefore hurt economic growth; but since the benefits of these policies are selective incentives concentrated amongst the few coalitions members, while the costs are diffused throughout the whole population, the 'Logic' dictates that there will be little public resistance to them. Hence, as time goes on, and these distributional coalitions accumulate in greater and greater numbers, the nation burdened by them will fall into economic decline."[30]

These misgivings of Smith and Olson are expressed as problems accompanying the overarching principle of the invisible hand. By contrast, Wuwei takes them as seriously as the invisible hand itself because all of them arise from the same source: greed. According to Wuwei, the political powers of today, if left to their own devices—or restrained only within legal limits—will behave just like the stationary bandits who preceded them, or like any privately motivated individual; human nature will tempt them to pursue short-term private interest over public interest. Whatever is not prohibited by law is protected by law.

In this process, however, ethics has not been fully taken into account, since the West relied more on law than on ethics. The stake of Smith's invisible hand is more of an economic nature, whereas Olson's deals more with politics. But fundamentally, they are one and the same: both economic and political invisible hands protect individual freedoms from statism. Both are self-regulating mechanisms. But eventually people found better, nonviolent means to achieve their goals (e.g., democracy). Democratic checks and balances have proved to be the best means to dissuade rulers from resorting to their natural inclination to self-interest. This was the historic process of democratization: the stationary bandit became

430 • *Y. J. Choi*

king, the king conceded his power to parliament, and the parliament was dominated by political leaders elected by the people.

Although much civilized, the fundamental struggle between rulers and their subjects remains intact, since each wish to pursue their own interests. History shows that only occasionally did exceptionally enlightened rulers appear who identified their interests with those of the populations they ruled. It is the same with political party leaders: only occasionally do we see the emergence of exceptional leaders who identify their interests with those of the populations they are elected to lead; most of the time, most leaders seek their own party's interests (e.g., greed). That is precisely the reason why democracy needs checks and balances and why democracy remains, to quote Churchill, "the worst form of government, except for all those other forms that have been tried from time to time."

We can say the same thing about Olson's political invisible hand; it needs protection by checks and balances as well as by ethics. From the Eastern point of view, leadership must be entrusted to those who would honor the public interest on the basis of ethical values. For this reason, Olson's insightful theory may also need to be complemented by ethics, just like Smith's economic invisible hand. Relying on laws alone to contain the self-interest of rulers has proven insufficient. Rather, *enlightened* self-interest must be engrained in the minds of rulers as a moral principle.

Altruism or Enlightened Interest: Junzi vs. Xiaoren

Rational leadership realizes that only an enlightened or altruistic self-interest leads to success in government: this is crucial for guidance by the left invisible hand. The philosophy of enlightened interest is a formidable safeguard against statism, as statism invariably claims the common good, on which every totalitarian economy has relied. Eastern ethics would not easily allow a state to succumb to the temptation of a controlled economy. However, because of the spirit-body dichotomy, the West insisted on the vice of self-interest and the virtue of altruism. And in the end, the pretense of altruism was used as a tool by those who disguised their self-interest as the common good, which was possible when they acted as the incarnation of the Western spirit or force of history. The East, on the other hand, was far more wary of those who claimed the common good, as in the East, altruism was considered attainable only by Junzi, who would then apply it to the management of economics.

Eastern market economies have one clear critical advantage over their Western counterparts: their frugality and thriftiness. One of the important principles of the free market—or capitalism, for that matter—is to save current capital for future investment. The West seems to have lost sight of this valuable principle and has fallen prey to the illusion that a greedy consumer society can be sustained indefinitely. From an Eastern perspective, this is a classic Xiaoren mistake.

Political Economy: Profit-Making vs. Greed

With the rise of free markets and democracy, it has become almost meaningless to discuss politics without referring to economics, or vice versa. Let us, then, examine the ethical dimensions of political economy.

Impact of Ethics on Political Economy:
Thriftiness vs. Consumerism

The role of ethics in political economy is not well recognized, since Western thinkers, from Adam Smith to contemporary free-market proponents, have focused instead on law in formulating their theories. But under scrutiny, the impact of ethics on the free market is not to be underestimated. Figures 9-3 and 9-4 tell us more about culture than it does about economics or regulations relying on laws; it demonstrates a culture of saving in the East against a culture of consumption in the West. We have already seen that thrift is deeply ingrained in Eastern culture. This virtue has been praised in innumerable Eastern poems, novels, and anecdotes; it is virtually impossible to find any Eastern literature that praises personal or conspicuous wealth. Self-fulfillment being the ultimate goal of life for Junzi, material wealth is considered to be an impediment rather than a boon.

The West, on the other hand, has exhibited a tendency toward dialectic evolution between thrift and consumerism. Greco-Roman culture did not shun luxury and consumption, as was natural in a master-slave society, although Greece had schools of thought, such as that of the Stoics, preaching temperance and moderation. More important than these was perhaps their ultimate inspiration—the culture of Sparta, which was founded on frugality and discipline. Yet we should also remember that the decline of Sparta was brought about by the spoils it acquired from its successful campaign in the Eastern Mediterranean in the wake of its victory over Athens during the Peloponnesian War. Despite the Christian praise of frugality over wealth, Western nobility tended toward luxury at the expense of the peasant class. The Protestant work ethic, grounded on savings and investment, contributed to the rise of capitalism, but at the same time, the growing bourgeois class came to accept consumerism and luxury. This equilibrium seems to have been lost in the process of secularization. The upshot is that the West now clearly favors consumption over frugality, whereas the East has maintained its culture of thrift, as shown in Figures 9-3 and 9-4.

In line with this trend, Western economists have even proposed the paradox of thrift—that a community which forsakes luxury for savings achieves neither. Has the ancient virtue of thriftiness become anachronistic with the advent of the free market? It remains alive and well in the East, even after the incorporation of capitalism into Eastern economies. China, Japan, South Korea, Taiwan, Hong Kong, and Singapore now constitute the bulk of world savings in terms of foreign exchange, totaling over three trillion dollars, as shown in Figure 9-3. And this reserve is growing rapidly. For instance, China's foreign reserve was only $146 billion in 1999; ten years later, it is $2,273 billion. Over 1.6 billion Eastern people are working hard and saving for the education and future of their children, as they have been taught by the ethics of their culture. Indeed, many government policies have contributed to this phenomenon. But the most crucial factor is a culture of thrift. Where there is no cultural foundation for frugality, no policies will work to produce such significant reserves. Culture, as we have seen again and again, precedes politics.

Culture Table: Saving vs. Consuming

China	2,273 (Sep 2009)	United States	-731.214
Japan	1,019 (Jun 2009)	Spain	-145.141
Russia	434 (Nov 2009)	United Kingdom	-105.224
Taiwan	321 (Apr 2009)	Australia	-56.342
India	285 (Oct 2009)	Italy	-52.725
South Korea	264 (Oct 2009)	Greece	-44.218
Hong Kong	240 (Nov 2009)	Turkey	-37.684
Brazil	235 (Nov 2009)	France	-30.588
Germany	184 (Sep 2009)	Romania	-23.234
Singapore	182 (Sep 2009)	Portugal	-21.987
	Billions of dollars		Billions of dollars

Fig. 9-3. Top 10 Countries with most Foreign Exchange Reserves (http://en.wikipedia.org/wiki/ Foreign_exchange_reserves)	**Fig. 9-4. Top 10 countries with most Current Account Balance in Deficit** IMF Data for 2007. (http://en.wikipedia.org/wiki/ List_of_countries_by_current_ account_balance)

Despite this, Westerners, without a doubt, have a far higher standard of living, with welfare benefits and a wide variety of consumer goods. Perhaps the paradox of thrift is correct. The only problem is that Western debt, both personal and national, increases every year. In other words, part of Westerners' better life is borrowed from their children. If this trend can sustain itself, then we need not worry about the ethics of thrift. "Black cat, white cat, the one that catches the mouse is a good cat." Some theories, indeed, support the sustainability of such a consumption economy; although the absolute amount of debt is increasing, its ratio to GDP remains stable at around 100 percent. But if this trend proves unsustainable, then we may have to pay closer attention to the ethics of the economy. The moment of truth for the Western consumer is fast approaching.

But at the international level, ever-growing national savings can become hoarding, which the East treats as a form of greed.

Rather, savings must be spent on younger generations or transnational issues. Eastern leaders need to show the initiative in broadening their perspective beyond a national framework, to bring stability to the world. We risk returning to the causes of the nineteenth-century Opium Wars, which we discussed earlier in this chapter—consumption in the West, and hoarding in the East. The larger the Eastern foreign exchange reserves become, the larger the moral problem facing the East. From this perspective, the East's economic concerns are as serious as those of the West.

Political Economy I: Profit-Making and Greed

The question of thrift vs. consumption is intimately linked to the problem of profit-making. Is profit-making to be encouraged as an important social and national goal? Because the free market is rapidly making nations interdependent, the issue of profit-making has come to the fore in the field of political economy. Multinational financial management corporations are a clear case in point, as evidenced by the worldwide financial crisis of 2008, but, as we shall see in the final chapter, global issues like climate change and nuclear weapons also boil down to the same question. Our dilemma is that we can neither condemn profit-making, since it is the driving force of civilization, nor praise it, since it amounts to greed.

In the contemporary West, especially in America, one finds individuals who advocate profit-making and greed: Ivan Boesky as a practitioner, and Ayn Rand as a theorist. Ivan Boesky, in his May 18, 1986, commencement address to the University of California's Berkeley School of Business Administration, said, "Greed is all right, by the way. I want you to know that. I think greed is healthy. You can be greedy and still feel good about yourself."[31] Ultimately, in a world managed by law, once self-interest is justified and praised, greed cannot be regulated by law. There are thousands of smarter Boeskys, who were not so clumsy as to break the law in a conspicuous way. As Balzac remarked: "The secret of a great fortune without apparent reason is a crime forgotten because it was done properly."[32]

It is true that Boesky was eventually "regulated" by the law—but he was condemned only by the law, not by ethics. In the long term, greed can be regulated only by ethics, and for this to happen, society must condemn greed as a whole. Some might argue that Western society does condemn, and has always condemned, greed: "It is easier for a camel to go through the eye of a needle than for a rich man to enter the kingdom of heaven."[33] Some might argue that Boesky said what he did as a paradox. Actually, the West did condemn greed throughout its history, which is full of ethical teachings on the virtues of frugality and modesty. But we also find that this ethical trend exists more in theory than in practice. Indeed, ethical warnings against wealth or greed have long coexisted with the glorification of wealth inherent in war, victory, conquest, and exploitation. Ethical qualms about greed have either been overwhelmed by political reality—"To the victor belongs the spoils"—or condoned by a legal conscience. Thus, the coexistence in the West of condoning and condemning greed illustrates yet again its diversity, in contrast to the conformity of the East.

This precarious balance appears to have been further tilted in favor of greed by the Invisible Hand theory, since this theory freed the pursuit of self-interest from traditional religious condemnation. This liberalizing tendency has been pushed further by such thinkers as Ayn Rand. Rand has become influential in the West for her vigorous defense of self-interest from state interference, without the ambiguity still present in Smith (as we have examined above). Ayn Rand, who immigrated to America from early Bolshevik

Russia, understood the monstrosity of statism more clearly than Western thinkers. In reaction to this, she advocated unalloyed self-interest as embodied in pure capitalism, although she occasionally used the term "rational" self-interest.

On the other hand, the East's repudiation of greed did not provide a panacea. Although the East, with its tendency to conformism, universally condemned greed, this condemnation created its own problems, since it shunned useful profit-making as well. The East has always questioned the ethical value of profit-seeking: "Mencius went to see King Hui. The king said, 'Master, since you have not counted it far to come here, a distance of a thousand miles, may I presume that you are provided with counsels to profit my kingdom?' Mencius replied, 'Why must your Majesty use that word "profit"? What I am provided with, are counsels to benevolence and righteousness, and these are my only topics. If your Majesty says, "What is to be done to profit my kingdom?" the great officers will say, "What is to be done to profit our families?" and the inferior officers and the common people will say, "What is to be done to profit our persons?" Superiors and inferiors will try to snatch this profit the one from the other, and the kingdom will be endangered.'"[34]

But how can a free market thrive without profit-seeking? Can one seek profit without being greedy? Where is the dividing line? This is the predicament that faced the East and that faces today's free market.

Political Economy II: Leadership vs. Profit-Making
"The only asset he had when he died was the house he lived in.... When he retired from office in 1952, his only income was the army pension of $112 a month.... When offered corporate positions at large salaries, he declined, stating: 'You don't want me. You

want the office of the President, and that doesn't belong to me. It belongs to the American people and it's not for sale.'" This is a portrait of President Harry Truman. This image strongly reminds us of Cincinnatus, the Roman consul and dictator, renowned for his modesty, simplicity, and civic spirit. In economic terms, both rulers embodied a leadership that transcended profit-seeking.

But just as many Western leaders have shown these virtues, many others have concerned themselves with profit—from Sulla and Caesar among the Romans, through the aristocracies of the Middle Ages, to the war heroes, robber barons, and tycoons of today. Leadership sets an example, good or bad, to the populace; a leader who boasts of his wealth encourages his people to do the same, to his own cost, and to theirs. The rise of the bourgeoisie in the West led to the increase and legitimization of profit-seeking; as the bourgeois succeeded the aristocracy in positions of power, profit-seeking became even more socially acceptable. We can no longer expect our leaders to ignore profits; this would be anachronistic. Wealthy tycoons and financial wizards seem to have replaced military conquerors as the role models of our society. The stakes are high for both cultures. The East, swamped by Western capitalism and by the consumerist desire to be "rich and famous," stands to lose the ethics at the heart of its civilization; the West, equally, may lose its wealth and power if its culture becomes wholly abandoned to unfettered greed, with most of the population in pursuit of rich and famous.

The best mechanism found by the East was to divide these roles: Junzi, in his position of leadership, shall not seek profit; the job of profit-making, which is necessary for society, would be left to Xiaoren. Consequently, Junzi is supposed to behave altruistically: "Junzi, seeking to establish himself, establishes others; seeking to expand himself, expands others";[35] "Junzi is anxious to acquire truth; he is not anxious to acquire wealth."[36] Thus, Junzi accepts altruism as his enlightened self-interest. Taoism also counsels "enlightened self-interest" for Junzi: "The Sage never tries to store things up; the more he does for others, the more he has; the more he gives to others, the greater his abundance."[37] Consequently, the concept of altruism or enlightened self-interest is deeply ingrained in Eastern culture as the center of its ethics. The importance of altruism for Junzi is found again in the Eastern concept of leadership by example. And this altruism is considered to be incompatible with profit-making.

Both ethics and law serve, in a rational manner, the ultimate purpose of self-preservation, whether for an individual or those in positions of leadership. In reality, however, both are invariably influenced by special interests; this is why some argue that the invisible hand is *too often* invisible. The issue of greed is as acute with Olson as it is with Smith. And since greed cannot be regulated by law, ethics is needed as an indispensable complement to support the invisible hand.

Should leadership be excluded from profit-making? Legally, the answer is yes, but ethically, the matter is more ambiguous. All countries now have legal sanctions against the involvement of political leaders with commercial activities. The concept of "conflict of interest" is a case in point. But from an ethical perspective, these sanctions have proven insufficient, and many leaders have found ways to become rich in one way or another. This question becomes more serious when applied to political parties whose *raison d'être* is inextricably linked to special interest groups.

Political Economy III: Political Parties vs. Profit-Making

As most democratic countries have now accepted that laws are to be made by the legislative branch of the government, the role of political parties has come to the fore in terms of political economy: shall they be able to put long-term public interests before their own private interests? The question is an ancient one. As Juvenal asked: *Quis custodiet ipsos custodes?*[38] Who will watch the watchers? Who, ultimately, can be trusted with power?

The Western philosophy of laissez-faire seems to have neglected the notion that an individual without greed could protect the market from political interference. Wuwei, by contrast, is predicated on just such an idea. This individual is embodied in Junzi. The cardinal distinction between Junzi and Xiaoren gives rise to the possibility that Junzi, who has transcended greed, may indeed guard a free market against statism: "Sage desires what others do not desire, he does not seek treasures sought by others; Sage learns what other do not learn, he does not seek knowledge sought by ordinary people; Sage does not act for himself, he only endeavors to preserve and restore balance in nature";[39] "Only the learned leaders have the ability to maintain principle amid poverty; the people in poverty do not maintain principle";[40] "When law governs and punishment rules, people forget ethics in avoiding them; when virtue governs and propriety rules, people maintain ethics in following them."[41]

In a multiparty system, power will be compromised by the interests of opposition parties, which can lead to an impasse or paralysis. This is something explicitly advocated by the American Founding Fathers, hence the slowness of the American political process. Yet checks and balances between political parties are different from the bad deal that political parties tend to make in conjunction with special interest groups. This kind of compromise sacrifices the long-term public benefits; Mancur Olson raised precisely this point.

A political party will oppose a good government initiative if such an initiative will hinder its own future chances of attaining power. The party, of course, will bring forward all sorts of objections to justify its decision as beneficial to the common good, but the struggle for power is the root cause of dissent. The West assumes that legal instruments, established one by one over a long period of struggle for democracy, will force political parties to honor the public interest. The East disagrees: Wuwei is founded on the premise that leaders and political parties in the end tend to seek profit by bending laws and regulations wherever possible. Consequently, these laws must be reinforced by ethics. In the West, we do have teachings and insights, and the incompatibility between wealth and leadership is frequently repeated. Yet, on this point, the East is clearer than the West. Wuwei emphasizes the importance of guarding oneself against greed. In principle, a wealthy person cannot become Junzi, since wealth entails greed. As Taoteking puts it: "If I were suddenly to be called to manage a nation, what I should be most afraid of would be a boastful display of luxury.... In such a nation, the court appears to be well kept but the granary is actually empty; they shall wear elegant and ornamented robes, carry a sharp sword at their girdle, pamper themselves in eating and drinking, and display luxury of property and wealth; this is a nation of robbers and boasters. This is certainly against Tao."[42]

Political Economy IV: Business vs. Greed

Can a line be drawn between profit-making and greed? At the close of the American Constitutional Convention of 1787, a lady asked Benjamin Franklin what the convention had given to the American people. Franklin allegedly responded, "A Republic, madam, if you can keep it." Adam Smith has given us the free market; can we keep it? Only if we can prevent greed from distorting it. The financial crisis of 2008, which almost paralyzed the global economy, may be construed as a result of greed: "casino capitalism." Nor have we since established any mechanism to regulate greed, and so the root cause of the crisis remains intact.

Adam Smith was not completely unaware of this problem, and here and there he left indications of his concern. He wrote against the monopoly of business barons as well as statism. But the question remained as to who would set the rule or laws against greed, and who would implement, manage, and adapt the rules and laws once they were formulated? Wuwei does not believe in the legal basis of altruism; likewise, greed cannot be prohibited by law. However good government's intentions may be, its economic interventions will sooner or later be usurped by a greedy individual or group. This was precisely what happened under Communist regimes, propagated with good intentions like those of Marx and Engels, but eventually corrupted in practice by political machinations.[43] It is clear to a Wuwei thinker, then, that greed can be guided only by ethics. Our condemnation of greed has become all the more urgent since the world has entered into its circumscribed state, for in this condition, as we have recently seen, the greed of individuals can induce a collapse of the system, and so tragedy for all.

The issue of profit-making and greed leads us again to the contrast between Wuwei and Western laissez-faire. In the East, even after the introduction of the free market, greed has remained the subject of moral condemnation. Business tycoons and politicians are expected to demonstrate frugality and modesty; if they do not, they will incur the censure of the press and the people. If they continue, they may be subject to political action not strictly within the purview of the law. As the Western press has remarked, not without justice, such measures may contravene the spirit of the free market. But it is believed in the East that such measures ultimately benefit the common people, and so promote democracy and the free market within a broader perspective. This radical Eastern experiment has gone largely unnoticed, and its outcome remains uncertain. If successful, the East will have contributed meaningfully to the global free market.

As we have seen, the eighty-one chapters of the Taoteking were written in such a way that different interpretations can be drawn not only by different readers but even by the same reader at different times. The same is true of commerce and science—does man control them, or do they control him? Perhaps we have blind faith in the virtue of profit-seeking as expounded by Adam Smith and his invisible hand, at the expense of our own spiritual or moral development.

One of the most serious challenges of transnational problems is that no one individual or nation can control them. The vertiginous speed with which commerce multiplies and science advances makes many of us uncomfortable. We are still unable to grasp the true significance of the Industrial Revolution, remaining only vaguely aware of its impact on our future.

Invisible Hand vs. Grasping Hand

As Smith's invisible hand needs protection from statism, the invisible hand of Olson also needs protection from the "grasping hand" of rulers in order for it to function. The "encompassing" interest perceived by autocrats makes a state well run (i.e., prosperous and strong). Not all autocrats wisely perceive the value of the encompassing interest; even the same autocrat can change his mind. Given human nature, even benevolent autocrats will never be free from the temptation of becoming arbitrary about taxation and increasing their discretion on the use of revenues. This explains the ups and downs of the fate of nations and the suffering of people in history: "There is no lack of historical examples in which autocrats for their own political and warfare purposes collected as much revenue as they possibly could. Consider the largest autocratic jurisdictions in Western history. The Bourbon kings of France were (especially on the eve of the French Revolution) collecting all they could in taxes. The Habsburg kings of Spain did the same. The Roman Empire ultimately pushed its tax rates at least to the revenue-maximizing level."[44]

So, for Olson's invisible hand to function properly, it needs a checks-and-balances mechanism against the autocrat's natural penchant to behave like a roving bandit: "The theory suggests that the key to an explanation of the spontaneous emergence of democracy is the *absence* of the conditions that generate autocracy. The task is to explain why a leader who organized the overthrow of an autocrat would not make himself the next dictator or why any group of conspirators who overthrew an autocrat would not form a governing junta."[45] In the final analysis, it all boils down, again, to a power struggle between the interest of rulers and that of the people.

Wuwei recommends that the checks-and-balances mechanism be supplemented with ethics for the rulers. The idea of a political invisible hand, buttressed by both law and ethics, has become all the more pertinent in our present era of globalization, when international matters directly affect the fate of individuals. To protect the free market and democracy, Enlightened National Interest (ENI) and leadership by example are essential. For this, Wuwei points out that profit is antithetical to leadership: If the leadership emphasizes profit, then everybody in the nation will seek profit. This will eventually endanger the nation. Consequently, the leadership must emphasize such values as benevolence and righteousness instead of profit.[46] The precepts of Wuwei against party formation are based precisely on this interpretation of human nature. As man tends to seek his own interest rather than that of the public, those who form political parties tend to seek their own party's interest. And since the greed of a group is more powerful than that of the individual, parties post a greater risk than individuals to the public interest. Likewise, the greed of an absolute ruler is greater than that of a group, and so factions and parties are still preferable to an absolute monarchy.

The free market will test the soundness of political party ethics. Will political parties succeed in keeping the free market alive while preserving their natural tendency to pursue their own interests over those of the people? Will political parties be able to protect the invisible hand from their own interests? Even if the answer is yes, what is to be done about the grasping hand of business? Will law—for instance, antitrust laws—be able to do this job? Or will ethics prove its validity by safeguarding free markets while recommending frugality and altruism to political parties amid apparent social affluence?

Global industrialization in a circumscribed world has begun to pose a threat to the common interests of mankind. Where is the third "invisible hand" (that is supposed to check the wanton pursuit of parochial national interests in favor of a common international good)? A third invisible hand presupposes the emergence of international leadership or global governance, which can only be based on the concept of Enlightened National Interest. This point shall be further explored in the final chapter.

Science and Commerce: Is Greed in Control?

Commerce and science, the backbone of the Industrial Revolution, soon produced serious ethical problems for mankind: commerce raised the issue of insatiable greed for wealth, and widening gaps between rich and poor; science raised the specter of self-destruction—weapons of mass destruction and environmental degradation. The commerce-related issues touch directly on the Man-Man relation; the science-related problems concern the Man-Nature relation. This, in turn, is linked to the Mind-Body relation—in other words, how to deal with humankind's mental or intellectual capacities.

We appear to have found a conceptual solution to our problems of both commerce and science: sustainable development. Yet we are also well aware that this method is far from being substantiated by practical and effective measures. Measures to this end remain timid and tentative due to the lack of a commonly accepted system of ethics. In many developed and wealthy societies, frugality and thrift are considered archaic virtues that can now be discarded. Commercialism may lead to a society's material abundance, but this abundance, without the guidance of an ethical system, will never be accompanied by spiritual satisfaction, equitable distribution, or future sustainability. Given the obvious limitation of worldly resources, this abundance cannot go on forever. For the spiritual well-being and long-term viability of a society, thrift must regain its traditional status and be reinstated among our core ethical values.

Blind faith that knowledge will lead humanity to ultimate truth has allowed science to run its course unchecked by moral considerations. From an ethical point of view, environmental degradation is the ultimate consequence of separating Man from Nature. And according to some experts, this fundamental new situation has given birth to an alarming premise in the West: "human beings and the natural world are on a collision course." The same is true of the separation of Man from Man. If we follow the logic of this separation to its conclusion, the proliferation of nuclear weapons is inherent in the philosophy of separating Man from Man.

Despite the successes of science, we are in danger of letting it control us, rather than the other way around. If we cannot control nuclear energy, and especially nuclear weapons, then we must admit that the Promethean fire was a curse rather than a blessing and the Industrial Revolution was something of a Faustian bargain, which will lead humanity to its ultimate demise.

What clearer proof could there be that science and commerce need ethics? In an expansive world, we could enjoy their growth without concern for the consequences, but today, we must guide their progress with law and ethics. The role of law in controlling commerce and science is ambivalent, for it always leaves loopholes. In the past, it gave a free hand to the crudest exploitations, and it required time to refine the law to serve the common interests of all. The central problem for a capitalist democracy, then, is to check greed; this can be solved by subjecting a democratic ruler to his own laws and ethical system, and by safeguarding an invisible hand within a free market. The latter's room to maneuver is inversely proportional to the number of regulations and laws that ultimately represent the interest of only a single group of individuals.

The Third Invisible Hand: Political Economy among Nations

If the second invisible hand has been discovered in domestic politics, can one discover a third invisible hand in international politics? Would this international invisible hand require ethical as well as legal protection for the benefit of all the nations? As we shall examine in the next chapter, nations became organized to an unprecedented degree when they attained the commercial paradigm. Olson argues that the ruler's enlightened interest would be guided by the political invisible hand for the benefit of the population. Can the same enlightened interest of the leading nation or nations be guided by the international invisible hand for the benefit of all nations?

We have concluded that, in addition to legal protection, invisible hands need ethical protection: the *economic* invisible hand needs to be protected from individual greed to the same degree as the *political* invisible hand needs to be protected from a ruler's greed. The same is true of the *international* invisible hand under the commercial paradigm: it needs to be protected from the greed of nations, as these also tend to satisfy their own national interests above that of the world as a whole, insofar as they can do so legitimately within the regulations of international law. This is so because, as with the first two invisible hands, the legal mechanisms in international trade do not prevent unethical behavior. It is thus self-evident that law should be complemented by ethics in the international arena.

At least at the cultural level, the East appears better positioned than the West to accept the idea of Enlightened National Interest. In the East, leaders were traditionally discouraged from commerce and profit-making. Nothing is to be gained by returning to a short-sighted closed-door policy; we may, however, question the validity of our present obsession with ever-greater profits, on both the individual and the national level. Globally, this has led to a greater divide between the North and South, rich and poor. Under the warfare paradigm, it was unrealistic to expect strong nations to establish laws in favor of weak nations. But the commercial paradigm urges rich nations to do so for the poor nations. For this to become genuine, it would require a commonly accepted ethics, premised on ENI and leadership by example.

Thus, one can see the emergence of the third invisible hand in the international arena as nations are increasingly engaged in a political economy. In the new global era, one can apply Olson's model to the world as a whole: crude exploitation is in nobody's best interest. Just as regulated taxation by a monarch or state is preferable to chaotic plunder by raiders and pirates, so commerce is preferable to warfare—in each case, both sides benefit. The necessity of ENI is acutely felt in international affairs, although the third invisible hand remains obscured by greedy, short-term national interests. The degree of disturbance posed by greed to the invisible hand—be it economic, political, or international— was limited when the world remained expansive, since the force of expansion absorbed greedy impulses. But now, with industrialization and our shift to a circumscribed world, greed can cause irreversible damage—ultimately, the demise of humanity. Of course, the third invisible hand of international trade must be subject to checks and balances, like national markets and government based on ENI. Consequently, at the outset of the third millennium, humanity is once again facing the same old questions of greed and civilization. This time, however, we face it not as individuals or nations but as an international community.

CHAPTER 10

The Twenty-First Century:
Paradigm Shift and Global Governance

"From what we know of mankind, we are bound to conclude that the first sailors plundered when they could, and traded when they had to."

H.G. Wells

"All the great dangers threatening humanity with extinction are direct consequences of conceptual thought and verbal speech, the greatest gift of man."[1]

Konrad Lorenz

"Heaven and Earth are not benevolent: they treat all things like ceremonial straw puppets, which are to be thrown away with indifference at the end of the day."

Taoteking 5

Paradigm Shift: From Warfare to Commerce

We are now at the dawn of the third millennium. At this juncture, one distinctly feels that the historical warfare paradigm is over—its era of heroes, crusaders, theologians, metaphysicians, and ideologues has been consigned to the past. Under the new paradigm of commerce, the Good Samaritan, Universal ethics, and the rule of law will become increasingly relevant. Their relevance may be due not so much to these values being right or inevitable as to the fact that the West's exploration and conquest of the world has been completed with the consequence of turning the world from an expansive to a circumscribed one.

The End of the Warfare Paradigm

Montesquieu believed that the first sailors were pirates. Kant echoed: "The state of peace among men living side by side is not the natural state; the natural state is one of war." H.G. Wells summarized: "From what we know of mankind, we are bound to conclude that the first sailors plundered when they could, and traded when they had to."

Piracy and war have long been man's most profitable activities: conquerors and raiders were once revered for bringing their nations plunder and spoils—Alexander, Julius Caesar, Attila, Charlemagne, Genghis Khan, Mehmed II, Hernán Cortés, and Napoleon, among many others. The colonial "Scramble for Africa" and the First World War might be described as the culmination of this time-honored model. The Nazi Third Reich may have been the last attempted raid on a grand scale, and thankfully it soon failed.

But World War II proved to be a turning point. In its aftermath, war ceased to be profitable for the first time in human history. For example, the Soviet Union, despite its military power, was unable to exploit or subjugate its neighbors during the cold war. From an economic point of view, it cost Moscow dearly to maintain these "allies." Ultimately, unable to sustain the expense, the Soviet Union let its neighbors go. The same happened in Vietnam after unification. Following its ancient impulse to expand into the Indochinese Peninsula, Hanoi invaded Cambodia. But no sooner had it established itself in Phnom Penh than it decided to withdraw; Hanoi quickly realized that occupation was not profitable. Similarly, the West, instead of committing its own troops, uses the United Nations peacekeeping mechanism in Africa, the continent into which they raced little more than a century ago.

It appears that we are now in the midst of a historic paradigm shift from *warfare* to *commerce* in international relations. Countries now compete with each other in predominantly commercial, rather than military, arenas. Paradigm shifts of equal historical importance can perhaps be found in the change from hunter-gatherer to agricultural-animal husbandry societies some 10,000 years ago and, in the natural sciences, in the change from the Ptolemaic to the Copernican theory of the universe in the sixteenth century.

Circumscription of the World

There may be many explanations for this event—the advent of democracy; the revolution in communications and transport, which made slavery and piracy more difficult because they were easier to publicly reveal; or the scientific advances making these practices less necessary and war more dangerous. From this perspective, the Industrial Revolution appears to have been one prerequisite for the shift, even though it occurred over two centuries ago. Yet the single most important cause of all is the circumscription of the world following the West's relentless expansion and conquest: there is simply no more space to discover.

One cannot exaggerate the importance of this change. The old paradigm prevailed in the expansive world where unknown and new territories abounded, and limitless possibilities—both physical and intellectual—appeared everywhere. Since the world has become circumscribed, mankind has had to turn from piracy and warfare to trade and commerce. In doing so, it has made the world still more interconnected and interdependent.

Eight Examples of Sub-Paradigm Change

Whatever its causes, this paradigm shift will bring about a sea-change in every aspect of our present life. Following are eight examples of such changes; I here focus on international affairs, but even these are by no means exhaustive.

1. From *Independence* to *Interdependence*: Independence between states was a prerequisite for piracy, raid, plunder, and war. But in commerce, interdependence is crucial—and so old isolationist policies will not prosper. The former Soviet Union was a case in point—focusing on independence and military supremacy at the expense of other available resources, ultimately resulting in its demise. China, by contrast, has embraced its interdependence with other nations through trade and investment, ultimately resulting in its survival and renewal. East and West Germany, and North and South Korea, are similar examples: East Germany perished because it insisted on independence; West Germany has thrived by welcoming interdependence. Likewise, North Korea's current predicament can mostly be attributed to its self-isolation, whereas South Korea's prosperity was made possible by its policies of interdependence. In the new commercial paradigm, independence entails isolation,

poverty, and insecurity, while interdependence produces prosperity and stability. Military strength remains crucial, less as a means to expand or invade, than as a safeguard of economic wealth.

A corollary is the change from *Competition* to *Cooperation*: warfare is essentially predicated on a zero-sum game that promotes competition between nations. The new commercial paradigm, by contrast, benefits both sides, and so it encourages cooperation more than competition. The rise of transnational problems will drive nations further toward consultation, cooperation, coordination, and multilateralism to safeguard their own interests. The North-South Divide, which is increasingly shaping the twenty-first century (instead of the old East-West Divide), has been paralyzing much international negotiation because countries cling to an older, parochial notion of their own interests.[2] The present century requires all nations of the world to make short-term sacrifices for the sake of long-term survival and prosperity.

2. From *Power* to *Wealth*: Raid and warfare were predicated on a distinction between strong and weak tribes or nations. Commerce has replaced this with the distinction between rich and poor states. The new distinction has produced a divide between North and South in the world, corresponding to developed and developing economies. Almost all international issues are now dealt with according to this new divide, producing stalemates in trade negotiations, human rights issues, and debates over nuclear weapons and climate change. The emerging fault line lies not along national or civilization borders, but along the North-South Divide, roughly speaking between the "haves" and the "have-nots." This divide, with its attendant transnational problems, will constitute major concerns for humanity in the twenty-first century—much more than the classic and traditional question of

war and peace. Turning a blind eye to such a division is not an option, as its problems will not go away.

A corollary of this is the shift from conceiving of lesser nations as *prey*, to seeing them as a *burden*. Formerly, weak nations used to be the prey of strong nations, but rich nations now try to turn a blind eye to poor ones. In the old paradigm of raiding for profit, strong nations "took care of" weaker ones. But within the new paradigm of trading for economic profit and stability, poor nations are left behind and become a burden to the international community. The advent of "failed states" is explained by this paradigm shift. The new concept of human security and the "responsibility to protect" arise from it. The slogan of the old raiding paradigm (e.g., "to the victor belong the spoils") is being replaced by one that references the new trading paradigm: "to the international community belong the burdens."

3. From *International* to *Intranational Conflicts*: Under the new commercial paradigm, nations avoid wars, seeing no profit in them. They also tend to ignore failed states, seeing no profit in intervening in their affairs. The situation of such states is inherently unstable, as they are prone to civil conflict within their borders, as we have witnessed since the end of the cold war. These conflicts, caused by ethnic, religious, and cultural differences, have emerged as major security concerns—Cambodia, Somalia, Bosnia, Rwanda, Angola, Kosovo, East Timor, Sierra Leone, Liberia, Haiti, the Democratic Republic of Congo, Côte d'Ivoire, Chad, and Darfur, to name the most prominent, are cases in point. Richer nations are reluctant to intervene in these affairs unless they are located in strategically sensitive regions. Consequently, the international community depends on the United Nations peacekeeping operations to deal with them.

4. From *Geopolitics* (*War and Peace*) to *Transnational Problems*: Geopolitics, which deals with war and peace, remains important for the global strategy of any nation, just as military force remains an essential element of its security. But as commerce replaces war as the chief activity of the international community, geopolitics assumes less significance and will cease to play such a prominent role. The military is used increasingly for deterrence rather than aggression. With the advent of the new commercial paradigm in a circumscribed world, humanity faces emerging transnational problems, such as terrorism, weapons of mass destruction, climate change, overpopulation, and pandemic disease. These have begun to replace geopolitical concerns as the most urgent issues of the present century.

Under the commercial paradigm, national problems are in fact international—they have become truly global in nature. The emergence of such problems naturally entails a shift in concerns from military conflicts to other problems, such as global warming, human rights issues, overpopulation in the developing countries, and depletion of natural resources.

5. From *Male Dominance* to *Gender Equality*: Under the old paradigm of raid, war, and conquest, men dominated the world by virtue of their superior physical power. Intelligence, of course, is more important than such power, but could previously operate only within the framework of physical competition, from which women had been excluded. In today's world, intelligence is gaining more and more traction over strength, and women have consequently improved their social standing and abilities; this looks set to continue until they attain equality. Just as other aspects of our new paradigm cannot be resisted, so this process is ineluctable. Women's rights should not be understood as granted for ethical reasons: for ethics, as we have seen, follow sociopolitical developments, not

vice versa; it is not something to be permitted, or given as a gift or concession, because it is advocated from the viewpoint of human rights or overcoming entrenched prejudice. As we have seen, moral exhortation or standards do not precede social or political changes. Although at a later stage, moral exhortations do accelerate social change, at the start it is social or political change that begets moral exhortations or fresh ethical standards.

Likewise, the twenty-first century will witness a shift from the *Monopoly of Nations* to the *Rise of Non-State Actors*. The emergence of global issues, along with the paradigm shift outlined above, has led naturally to an enhancement of the role of non-state actors, such as civil society organizations and multinational corporations. These groups are set to play an expanding role even in the domain of international affairs, which was formerly the exclusive province of state governments. Nations will remain the principal actors, but their monopoly will diminish in proportion to the rise of transnational problems—managing the latter needs the continued involvement of the former. This will be even more conspicuous if nations continue to cling to their own interests in a parochial manner, rather than showing leadership by example, as we have recommended. Commensurate with the inability of nations to adapt to the new paradigm, such global leadership would increasingly be forfeited by civil societies, since they are freer within the new paradigm than the nations remaining prisoner of the old paradigm and as they are more conscious than the nations of the imperatives of new ways of thinking, which is sine qua non, after all, for the survival and thriving of humanity, not necessarily nations.

6. From *Rule by Law and Force* to *Rule of Law*: This change may be counted as among the most critical of those accompanying the paradigm shift from war to commerce. Until the triumph of

democracy and the free market, based upon the rule of law, the world was run according to "rule *by* law inside" and "rule by force outside" of a nation: in other words, the ruler used law as a tool to dominate others, while he remained above it. Furthermore, rule by law was applied only within a country; outside force was used to conquer and subjugate other tribes and nations. Thus, the modus operandi of the warfare paradigm was rule by law inside and rule by force outside. With the evolution of the commercial paradigm, the use of force diminished; rule *by* law gave way to the rule *of* law. I am emphatically not arguing that military force has become obsolete—on the contrary. As human nature is always looking for its self-preservation, physical force is a sine qua non for the peace and stability of a society, whether national or international. Nonetheless, the military will be used only for defense and protection, not to attack other nations, since wars no longer bring benefits in the current paradigm.

The spread of the rule of law encouraged the simultaneous development of democracy and the free market. With the advent of rule of law, we witness a shift from *Hard* to *Soft Power*; the hard power of the sword gives way, inevitably, to the soft power of the pen. Rule by law and force required military action to enforce the monarch's will; the rule of law, by contrast, forbids the use of force by definition. This does not exclude the use of physical force by law enforcement agencies; rather, it implies that the use of military force to acquire slaves and spoils is no longer feasible under our present paradigm. Consequently, the use of force—hard power—has become anachronistic. The rise of soft power also means the rise of ethics. Under the new commercial paradigm, law and ethics will begin to replace force as the major instrument of law to manage society.

It is no wonder that many scholars, following the example of Professor Joseph Nye, increasingly underline the importance of soft power as a means of projecting prestige and protecting national interests. Indeed, cooperation and interdependence can better be attained and managed by soft power than hard power; hard power is more efficient than soft power for coercion and enforcement, the realm of raid and war. From the mid-twentieth century onwards, few military operations brought material profit. Most, on the contrary, incurred a loss of both resources and prestige, in contrast to the soft power projects of commerce and cultural exports. It is intriguing to note that the adage "the pen is mightier than the sword" was coined in the nineteenth century when the paradigm shift from warfare to commerce had already been set in motion following the Industrial Revolution.

One corollary of the rule of law, in the wake of the commercial paradigm, is the shift from *Rule by Ethics* to *Rule of Ethics*. This transition is universal, but more acutely felt in the East because its civilization is based on ethics rather than law. And along with these two transitions, we see a rapprochement *between Law and Ethics*. As we have argued, Eastern ethics and Western law share a common objective of self-preservation, like all human actions, for both nations and individuals. It is important for us to remember this underlying principle so as to avoid inappropriate value judgments of Eastern or Western culture. Both law and ethics are necessary to safeguard the free market and democracy—the one to prevent statism, the other to encourage altruism—and so each culture can and must learn from the other, bringing together their contributions to work toward a common goal.

7. From *Menace from Without* to *Menace from Within*. The most crucial shift, in terms of mankind's future, may be that from "menace from without" to "menace from within." Under the warfare paradigm, the menace came from without, from one's enemies;

it was the same prior to the advent of the warfare paradigm—the menace for man came from without, either from the natural environment or from man's predators. Now, man is faced with a new situation. The menace of the third millennium comes from the transnational problems of nuclear weapons and climate change. These are man-made menaces (i.e., menaces from within).

8. From *Parochial* to *Enlightened National Interest*: Within the old paradigms of raid, independence, military power, geopolitics, and competition, nations defined their own interests in a narrow and isolated way. But under the new paradigms of commerce and interdependence, national interests are closely interrelated—taking into account the interests of other states is now understood to benefit one's own. Problems cannot be solved at the level of their creation; thus, problems and conflicts caused by individual greed can be reconciled only by the joint efforts of nations across the globe. This amounts to an "enlightened" national interest, seeking a common good. Therefore, a genuine and truly national interest within the new paradigm of commerce is one that encompasses the interests of other nations as well. It appears that this concept of Enlightened National Interest is imposed upon us by virtue of evolutionary forces if we mean to survive and thrive together, instead of marching hand in hand into our own demise by clinging to parochial national interest.

A shift from *National Leadership* to *Global Leadership* is a natural corollary of such a pursuit. By showing other nations the best way to act, rather than imposing standards artificially upon them, we will ultimately improve the condition of all. The new leadership of the twenty-first century can only lead the world by providing examples of Enlightened National Interest (i.e., by demonstrating self-sacrifice and generosity for other nations to follow, not by clinging to the old paradigm of parochial national interest). If a nation in a leadership position practices the old paradigm and takes advantage of another nation, or of other nations' interests, and other nations follow this example, the world will soon become a very ugly place to live. This is in clear contrast to the Age of Discovery, when the world was open and expanding and when the pursuit of naked national interest provided cases of leadership by example for other nations to emulate with a view to surviving and thriving.

This contrast leads us to the concept of *leadership by example.* Under the warfare paradigm, ethics had little relevance to the question of leadership. Victory was the ultimate measure of a leader's ability. Conqueror or conquering nation became the de facto global leader. But under a commercial paradigm that functions only with Enlightened National Interest, ethics has become an integral part of global leadership, since a statesman can lead the world only by providing a good example.

East and West: The End of History and the Clash of Civilizations

Our examination of the paradigm shift gives us a framework to understand other attempts to explain the post-cold war world. Let us examine, in particular, Francis Fukuyama's thesis of the End of History, and Samuel Huntington's theory of the Clash of Civilizations.

With our paradigm shift, *a* history, rather than history itself, has come to an end—that is, the history of the dialectical evolution of the Western Spirit. We examined its journey from the Greco-Roman period to modernity in chapter 3. The history of the Western Spirit concluded with the demise of the Age of Ideologies in the last century. A new history—that of the commercial paradigm—has only just begun. And the challenges brought about by this paradigm will be much greater than those faced by the Western metaphysicians, since its nature is of an evolutionary dimension.

The Clash of Civilizations theory succinctly indicates the end of tribes, nation-states, alliances, and geopolitics, which undergirded the warfare paradigm. The new century, with its new paradigm, will be quite different, since "civilizational zones" are increasingly replacing traditional nation-states. Yet nations will remain the most crucial actors on the world stage. Also, it remains to be seen whether strife, indeed, will prevail between civilizations. I am inclined to the opposite opinion; as I have already argued, cooperation, more than conflict, will define the third millennium. East Asia has no common cultural background with, and so no reason or interest to ally itself with, Islam against the West; it will cooperate with whatever forces are available, including the West and Islamic states. Warfare and military conflict, I believe, will continue to occur, but to a lesser extent, as the warfare paradigm has been replaced by the commercial one.[3]

In the meantime, transnational problems in our time require cooperation and all the wisdom and energy of every civilization. Otherwise, all of us face our end—not from each other, but from ourselves.

Future of Mankind: Menace from Within

Since its evolutionary emergence, mankind has faced continual challenges—hunger, disease, natural catastrophe, social breakdown, and war. Yet the challenges of the twenty-first century are fundamentally different. The transnational problems of our own invention are the very source of threat to our survival.

Mental Capacity I: from Extra-Specific to Intra-Specific Competition

The beginning of the warfare paradigm was closely linked with humankind's mastery of its environment. It may have started with the Stone Age around forty millennia ago, when humankind began to overcome the dangers originating from other species and the environment: "When man had reached the stage of having weapons, clothing, and social organization, so overcoming the dangers of starving, freezing, and being eaten by wild animals, and these dangers ceased to be the essential factors influencing selection, an evil intra-specific selection must have set in. The factor influencing selection was now the wars waged between hostile neighbouring tribes."[4] And it must have been firmly set in motion with the agricultural revolution of around ten millennia ago. With man's increased mastery of nature, raids and wars raged among neighboring tribes and nations. Thus, humans have become the only species to venture into intra-specific competition: all the other animals remain engaged in extra-specific competition. Man's unique mental capacity has led us toward the uncharted course of intra-specific competition.

Under a warfare paradigm, man was encouraged to exploit his fellow man as well as nature. Man could afford to rely on military means, which condoned and encouraged exploitation of Man by

Man as well as Nature by Man. Ethics is put on the back burner when the Man-Man intra-specific competition reigns: "It is self-evident that intra-specific selection is still working today in an undesirable direction ... such traits as the amassing of property, self-assertion.... [A]nd there is an almost equally high negative premium on simple goodness."[5]

Mental Capacity II: From Menace from Without to Menace from Within

Even though man made the transition from extra-specific to intra-specific competition, his principal threat remained that from outside—mostly from other tribes and nations. But under the present commercial paradigm, our greatest danger comes from within. Industrialization and free trade, which liberated us from hunger and constant warfare, contained new perils within themselves. We have therefore been burdened with a self-imposed source of danger; with this, the meaning of intra-specific competition has acquired new implications.

From this perspective, it seems that mankind has to deal with two crucial changes at the same time: from inter-specific to intra-specific competition and from menace from without to menace from within. All of these changes are due to the mental capacity unique to humankind. It appears that this intra-specific competition made a quantum leap with the Industrial Revolution, which acted as a catalyst for the paradigm shift from warfare to commerce. Now, the race between survival and self-destruction appears to constitute the major theme for humankind at the onset of the third millennium. It is our existential problem, just as the war paradigm was the central theme for our existence during past millennia.

As such, the new commercial paradigm has already proved to be a double-edged sword. On the positive side, it has put an end to the practice of crude exploitation warranted under the warfare paradigm; on the negative side, it has created unprecedented ethical problems of global dimension. The quantum leap provided by the Industrial Revolution provoked such intensity in the use of commerce and science that it brought about a qualitative evolution in terms of the impact of Man's mental capacity on his fellow humans and his environment. Postindustrial commerce has dramatically increased disparities in wealth on both the individual and national levels; postindustrial science, meanwhile, has accelerated the production of deadly weapons and caused climate change. These trends have become so alarming as to displace all other problems facing humanity. Under the commercial, post-industrial paradigm, as we have argued, competition unchecked by ethics harms all parties involved.

Mankind now enjoys the fruits of civilization amid unprecedented threats of environmental destruction and nuclear weapons. The former reflects the Man-Nature relationship and the latter the Man-Man relationship. Thus, our future depends on our ability to address, and indeed redress, these two relationships. As Richard Leakey notes, "the future of the human species depends crucially on two things: our relationships with one another, and our relationship to the world around us. The study of human origins can offer important emphasis in the way we view the two issues."[6] But how we address those two relationships is contingent on the third relationship—that between Mind and Body. The question therefore boils down to: How are we to handle our own mental capacity (i.e., our cultural evolution)?

With the Industrial Revolution, man's "mastery of nature" took a decisive turn: whereas before he had little power to harm his environment, and could therefore exploit nature with impunity, now every act has serious environmental consequences:

"The ecology of man changes much more rapidly than that of other creatures, and the speed of its change is dictated by his technological progress, which keeps accelerating in a geometrical progression. Thus man cannot avoid making fundamental changes, and all too often he causes the total breakdown of the biocoenosis, or biotic community, in which and on which he lives."[7]

As Konrad Lorenz has argued, "There are still worse consequences of intra-specific selection, and for obvious reasons man is particularly exposed to them: unlike any creature before him, he has mastered all hostile powers in his environment."[8] Just as technology has freed man from his need to plunder and wage war, we have realized that the true threat to our continued survival comes not from others but from ourselves.

But with this realization comes the opportunity for us to cast aside the old warfare paradigm once and for all, and fully embrace commerce, enlightened self-interest, and other forms of international cooperation. We need to accept the new commercial paradigm and adapt our behavior before it is too late. The end of the warfare paradigm is already with us, but it is not at all evident that we can successfully deal with transnational problems. For this to happen, humankind needs to quickly adapt itself—before it is too late—to the new commercial paradigm with all its implications. Evidently, the most important and urgent changes in man's and in national behaviors involve transitioning from the habit of competition to a habit of cooperation (against the common threat of transnational problems) and from parochial national interests to Enlightened National Interests. It is a daunting task: "intra-specific competition is the root of all evil in a more direct sense than aggression can ever be."[9] It is a race between human wisdom and the evil genius of humankind: the wisdom to rein in its own mental capacity and the evil genius that has blind confidence in and grants unbridled freedom to human intelligence and science. The latter has resulted in the spread of nuclear weapons and the speeding up of climate change.

Mental Capacity III: Prometheus, Faust, and Sisyphus

The fundamental paradox faced by our civilization is not new. Our early ancestors already anticipated the problem: both Eastern and Western myths allude to the double face of the civilizing process. According to the ancient Greeks, the Titan Prometheus stole fire from Zeus and gave it to man, thus allowing him to cook food and take his first steps toward civilization. In revenge, Zeus sent the first woman into the world, Pandora, who would be "no helpmate in poverty, but only in wealth." In German legend, the scholar Faust offers the devil his soul in exchange for knowledge—a symbol of civilization. The story can be interpreted as a deal that man makes for present gain without regard to future consequences. Sisyphus is another mythical archetype of man's quest for knowledge, but this time the quest ends in failure and eternal punishment for the defiance of god.

In Eastern mythology, the "Emperor of the Five Grains," Shennong (神農, Divine Farmer), brought agriculture to the people, so that they no longer needed to hunt and gather. Later, Huangdi (广帝, Yellow Emperor) reigned over China for a hundred years and brought social order and medicine to its people. But these two advances of civilization were perceived as problematic as well as beneficial by both Confucians and Taoists. Their seminal core tenets, Junzi and Wuwei, serve as both diagnosis and prognosis for the ills of civilization. Although there is no tragic aspect in Wuwei, it shares the basic futility of labor with the story of Sisyphus; human actions will be endless and unavailing. Even Junzi shares the mechanism of Sisyphus, since ethics is not to be passed on to posterity the same way as knowledge: every generation and every human being must start from scratch to acquire ethical values step by step, through practice and enlightenment. Yet the difference between Junzi and Sisyphus lies in that Junzi aims only at this life. From this perspective, what Junzi can do during his life for the people around him takes on all the more importance, without regard to whether his actions would have lasting, eternal meaning.

The stories of Prometheus, Sisyphus, and Faust—much more clearly than their Eastern counterparts—demonstrate an awareness of the perils inherent in knowledge and technology, and the danger of hubris. But inherent in these stories is a sense of man's yearning for knowledge and ultimate solutions, as well as heroic struggles. The West's myths thus appear to contain the usual dialectical dimension of its culture. The myths of Prometheus and Faust depict the search for ultimate knowledge, the attainment of which will set man free. In this quest for knowledge, the West has relied on revelation and law. The East, on the other hand, does not believe in revelation or law, as it makes no assumptions that man can achieve ultimate truth. Consequently, it aims at management rather than resolution.

Mental Capacity IV: Paragon of Animals vs. Parasites on Earth
Our comparison between Western and Eastern civilizations demonstrates that we are all, even in our personal beliefs, conditioned by our respective cultures. We have not changed biologically since our emergence as *Homo sapiens sapiens* fifty thousand years ago, and we are unlikely to change much over the next million years. We cannot, then, rely on genetic evolution to solve our problems—it is simply too slow, and too gradual. Instead we must rely on a cultural evolution, in which developments, once acquired, are passed on immediately.

But cultural evolution has proven a double-edged sword, bringing both unprecedented prosperity and mortal danger to mankind. Many of the extraordinary events of the past century, including the two world wars and the cold war, marked the culmination of the long history of the Western warfare paradigm. Now, at the dawn of the twenty-first century, we are faced with the specter of weapons of mass destruction capable of obliterating the globe's population several times over. Now that international terrorism has become a reality, the renewed threat of nuclear warfare places us at a critical juncture. Nuclear energy, while being harnessed to serve us, at the same time threatens the human race with extinction. The same can be said of climate change and environmental degradation.

Mankind is now groping for ways to deal with these new problems. Behind these issues lies science and technology, which have enabled machines to replace animal and human power. Admittedly, advances in science and technology, which constituted the basis of the Industrial Revolution, enabled many nations and individuals to acquire unprecedented wealth and power at a level undreamt of before. Nonetheless, it also led us with an insatiable appetite into the trap of a never-ending quest and competition for more and more wealth and power. When will this blind competition end? How can humanity control its insatiable desire for power and wealth, both at the national and individual levels? The consequences of the Industrial Revolution, as we face them now at the onset of the third millennium, are frightening. Ultimately, we shall be dealing with a question of evolutionary dimensions. Is humankind capable of controlling its own mental—that is, intellectual—capacities?

Fig. 10-1. Nuclear Explosion (http://upload.wikimedia.org/ wikipedia/commons/c/c9/ Nuclear_fireball.jpg)	Fig. 10-2. Global Warming (http://blog.lib.umn.edu/ellis271/ arch1701/2008/02/global_warming_ project_milleni.html)

Faced with these dilemmas, mankind now appears to be at a critical juncture in its evolutionary process: "To his detriment, man has learned to govern all the forces of his extra-specific environment, but he knows so little about himself that he is helplessly at the mercy of the satanic workings of intra-specific selection. *Homo homini lupus*—man is the predator of man—is an understatement."[10] "One is tempted to believe that every gift bestowed on man by his power of conceptual thought has to be paid for with a dangerous evil as the direct consequence of it."[11] Should our future be entrusted to the powers of reason alone? Will the greatest gift given Man, his intelligence, prove to be a Faustian bargain?

Man is the first species in the history of the earth to threaten its own existence. If, despite our capacity for reasoning, we prove incapable of resolving the problems of our own creation, *Homo sapiens*, the "wise man," may never fulfill his own biological potential, but instead bring about his own extinction along with that of the countless other species with which we share the planet.

In characteristically beautiful language, Shakespeare summed up the prevalent Western view of our species: "What a piece of work is man! How noble in reason! How infinite in faculty! In form and moving how express and admirable! In action how like an angel! In apprehension how like a god! The beauty of the world! The paragon of animals!"[12] But at the same time, man is, as Lessing put it, "nothing but a carnivorous ape with a megalomaniac perception of his mental capacity." One Chinese creation myth describes mankind as merely the "parasites" on the Creator's body, while Tao compares us to the straw puppets thrown away after a religious ritual. What a contrast to the teachings of Genesis, where we are made in God's own image!

Greeks stressed the importance of the sense of tragedy, and Eastern thinkers believed that a sense of awe is necessary for the balance of society: "When one loses one's sense of awe, catastrophe is not far away." This is a warning against arrogance and complacency, deriving from an astute observation of human nature. Throughout history, humanity has survived and overcome catastrophes with courage and perspicacity; it has even taken the opportunity to make historic and essential decisions. Such actions do not occur by reason alone—tragedy motivates the wise to act for the good of generations to come. A sense of awe has indeed kept humankind from arrogance and complacency.

But there's the rub—man has overcome so many catastrophes that complacency and parochial self-interest have come to prevail once more. These attitudes must be transcended if we are to escape the trap we have set ourselves. This time, there will be no turning back: nuclear or climatic catastrophe will offer no second chance. In seeking to resolve these problems, we can rely only on the same human intelligence that created the problems we seek to solve.

Global Governance: Enlightened National Interest

The need for global governance has emerged with the multiplication of transnational issues, and most of all, that of climate change. Nations cannot deal with them individually. Given the magnitude of the potential consequences, it may not be an exaggeration to say that "united we stand, divided we fall." But faced with a menace from within for the first time in history, nations are unprepared, lacking examples or precedents on which a system of global governance could be founded. Under the circumstances, it all depends on the vision and will of national leadership or of nations in positions of leadership—for example, the United States, the European Union, or China. Whichever nation it may be, its vision can be no other than that of Enlightened National Interest.

Enlightened Interest in International Relations

One of the factors enabling the paradigm shift from warfare to commerce has been economic affluence. Nations no longer need to engage in warfare to achieve their aims; trade is more efficient. But affluence has also aggravated greed to an unprecedented degree; individuals and nations alike pursue profit insatiably, as an end in itself, exacerbating transnational problems in the process. The world's problems may therefore be reduced to greed. Is it still in a nation's interests to pursue wealth independently of others? Will national leaders see the stakes involved in man's common struggle under the commercial paradigm? Since the rights of the individual constitute the foundation of this paradigm, if this commercial model is not properly managed, those rights will be imperiled: "Individual rights to property and contract enforcement were probably more secure in Britain after 1689 than anywhere else, and it was in Britain, not very long after the Glorious Revolution, that the Industrial Revolution began."[13]

Thus, the biggest problems facing our world are related to commerce and science: nuclear weapons, climate change, environmental degradation, depletion of natural resources, sustainable development, communicable diseases, and so on. It is ironic that these problems, which can be traced to two of the most significant benefits of Western culture, now present us with an ethical dilemma of the first degree. Meanwhile, traditional geopolitics has proven incapable of handling the paradigm of commerce and is rapidly being replaced by political economy, a more comprehensive tool for analyzing and interpreting the postindustrial world. At stake is this world's very survival. Will the free market and democracy hold out against the onslaught of greed? Was the Industrial Revolution humanity's Faustian bargain? Have commerce and science compelled man to face the fateful consequences of his civilization?

We have argued above that mankind has produced two basic tools to deal with his problems: law and ethics. If law alone is not enough to deal with political economy, what contribution might ethics make? The answer is the principle of Enlightened National Interest, for nations as well as for individuals. It remains to be seen if today's nations can understand the rationale of ENI for their own survival. The task is certainly difficult, given that nations have pursued their own interests at the expense of others for millennia. Such attitudes made sense under the warfare paradigm because they served the fundamental purpose of self-preservation of tribes, city-states, and nations. But they make no sense at all under the commercial paradigm, which urges nations to expand their parochial interests for the sake of survival into Enlightened National Interest.

ENI and Leadership by Example

In the twenty-first century, international affairs will increasingly have direct bearing on the lives of nations and individuals, due to their growing interdependence. However, it does not appear realistic to envision "international levees, schools, police, military, and quarantines." A world government is unlikely to come into being unless all nations were faced with common, perhaps extra-terrestrial, threats. Yet transnational problems will not wait for nations to organize the same way that individuals can organize within a nation. Within national boundaries, in practical terms, the invisible hand is constituted by small government, low taxes, and laissez-faire. But how can this work outside of national borders? There are laws and ethics, which are allies of the invisible hand within a nation. Yet nations are barely bound by international laws: ethical measures, heretofore scarcely attempted on an international level, are now acutely necessary.

However, we do have an encouraging precedent for ENI.[14] In the nineteenth century, the West successfully overcame the problem of "failing or failed" individuals—children, the poor, old, sick, and unemployed—by producing policies grounded in enlightened self-interest. Helping such citizens, Westerners realized, ultimately benefited the nation as a whole. However, a successful transition from narrow to enlightened self-interest has so far taken place only within the nation-state; in all likelihood, ENI should occur, if at all, without the benefit of an overarching global government. At best, we can hope for a regime of global governance agreed upon among sovereign nation-states. This makes the prospect of ENI rather uncertain. In the meantime, international relations will be marked more likely by a dynamic between traditional parochial national interests and new ENIs. In a globalized and interdependent twenty-first century, our central concern is for ENIs that cut across national borders.

For millennia, nations freely competed to secure the maximum national interest within the "strong/weak" paradigm. The national interest thus became the sacred credo of national leadership. Although the days for national interest are gone, this crucial change is yet to be acknowledged by national leaders. Under the circumstances, one of the important ways to spread the idea of ENI is for a leading nation to lead by example. If such a nation founded its foreign policies on such a principle, other nations would follow suit. Our leaders must now demonstrate a commitment to a long-term perspective and enlightened action on a global scale. If, on the contrary, they continue to adhere to parochial and archaic national interests, then other nations will have no incentive to act according to ENI.

Neither East nor West is unfamiliar with the concept of leadership by example: Christian and Confucian ethics are each founded on enlightened self-interest (i.e., altruism). But it would be a fantasy to expect nations to act altruistically without incentives. There was simply no incentive for nations to take others' interests into account under the warfare paradigm. Given the problems now threatening the globe, however, there has emerged a very strong incentive to do so. The adoption of ENI will require a leap of imagination on the part of our leaders, given the difficulty of understanding our present paradigm shift and the consequent need for ENI. History, especially that of the West, is full of stories and anecdotes from the warfare paradigm that encourage nationalistic and even jingoistic attitudes. We were, and still are in large measure, conditioned to venerate and emulate military heroes and conquerors of the past—but now, whatever the difficulties, we urgently require international action according to the principles of ENI and ethical leadership by example.

Rapprochement between East and West

For the principle of ENI to prevail, East and West must cooperate more than compete. Fortunately, one can observe an increasing convergence between Eastern ethics and Western law in this regard. After it opened its cultural borders in the nineteenth century, the East assimilated Western science, the free market, and democracy. The East is now rapidly acquiring the values of individual initiative and freeing itself from traditional impotence in the face of despotism. The West, likewise, has begun to cast off its extremism and absolutism. Following the terrible ideological wars of the twentieth century, the West is at last able to assimilate the Yin virtues of tolerance, relativism, and uncertainty. It no longer insists on an anthropomorphic God, or on ideological extremes; it has reduced its self-destructive exploitation of nature and now enjoys the cleanest environment in the world. Westerners are increasingly adopting the values of humility before nature, agnosticism about God or Truth, and compassion toward other men. We can discern an active rapprochement between ethics and law.[15]

The West's assimilation of Yin values has helped it complete the transition to the rule of law for everybody; likewise, the East's assimilation of Yang values has helped to complete its transition to the rule of ethics. At the end of this mutual rapprochement, we have two principal tools, ethics and law, which are the chief product of each civilization. Now, confronted with a host of new, transnational problems, East and West must present a common front to tackle them—that is, they must produce a synthesis of law and ethics. Such a synthesis will occur within a circumscribed environment that favors syncretism and cooperation. By relying on their own resources but also adding new elements, the West and the East may succeed in generating a system combining law and ethics, which we hope may guide the world's nations toward a new concept of ENI. In this section, we shall focus on the possible contribution of the East to the management of the transnational issues.

Indeed, as China's global weight in the present political economy continues growing exponentially, increasing numbers of Western experts have requested it to adopt a position of leadership. Peter Mandelson's article, "We Want China to Lead," sums up this position succinctly: "China has become the world's largest exporter, the world's largest foreign exchange reserves, and the world's biggest emitter of carbon; Europe and the United States want China to step into a leadership role; there will be no global climate change settlement without China. No Asian or global security architecture. No sustainable governance of global trade or finance without China; China needs these things as much as anyone else…. The machinery of global governance is still 'Atlantic' in its orientation and needs to be reformed to reflect China's growing influence…. China is too big, the challenges too great, and the global village too small for China to retreat into inflexibility or insularity."[16] Let us see how China's leadership role could be different from Europe and the United States in four areas of global governance: ENI, assistance, nuclear weapons, and climate change.

Global Governance I: ENI

In order to deal with the critical question of global governance and ENI, we must revisit the basis of man's economic activities with its ethical implications, a valid assessment of which can only be based on a proper understanding of human nature. The West continues to struggle with the unity between Mind and Body, and still lacks convincing terminology for such a concept.[17] The

Cartesian legacy is perhaps too strong. The significance of such a difficulty is by no means purely metaphysical—it has a direct impact on our understanding of human relations, and so on our answers to political, economic, and scientific problems. Without properly addressing this Mind-Body question, a culture remains incapable of dealing with the other two relationships, Man-Man and Man-Nature.

Any leader representing a nation that believed that God created Nature for Man to exploit would find it difficult to sell any climate change agenda based on ENI. For ENI to prevail, a proper understanding of human nature is therefore fundamental. With this in mind, let us briefly revisit our review of human nature on which this book is based.

1. Human nature works toward self-preservation, which is neither good nor evil.

2. Self-preservation naturally tends toward greed and exploitation of others rather than to altruism; this tendency, however, provides the fundamental drive of society and civilization.

3. This tendency gives rise to law or ethics in a society: the former prohibits excess of individual greed in proscribed areas only, so it has free run in all the other areas; the latter discourages greed but cannot actually prohibit it. As human nature only *tends* to be more greedy than altruistic, it should see the merits of altruism.

4. All individuals have the potential to overcome their natural greed and work instead toward altruism and self-fulfillment. Human society can maintain its equilibrium only with the constant input of law and ethics.

This rather complex and non-Manichean portrait of human nature constitutes the basis of a political realism found in the "political invisible hand" of Mancur Olson, as well as in the

Eastern philosophy of Wuwei. If we accept this portrait, we must ensure that the West begins to distinguish more clearly between greed and self-interest: the current ambiguity is harmful at both the individual and the national levels. Greed, ultimately, cannot be countered by law, but only by a Universal ethics. The conviction that altruism or ENI is the best expression of self-interest is not new. As we have seen, every great teacher arrived at this conclusion. But it had little effect on public practice under the warfare paradigm and consequently on leaders operating under this paradigm. Such teaching or conviction had been regarded as moralistic and idealistic, which was not entirely untrue when we lived in an expansive environment. Heroes and leaders of the past did not need conviction or understanding regarding ENI. What they needed was an ability to lead the nation and its people to victory for amassing spoils and material gain at the expense of other nations and people.

Today's leaders, by contrast, will not succeed unless they are truly convinced of the value of altruism as the best expression of self-interest. Nelson Mandela illustrates such a change—his greatness as a statesman is grounded precisely on his attempt to take into account even his enemies' interests. In terms of global governance, such change requires a national leadership to understand ENI as the true national interest.

Our trust in political parties and government thus becomes paramount. Is any group steadfast enough to put the public interest above its own private interests? Unlikely, according to Wuwei and thinkers like Mancur Olson. With this in mind, one better understands growing popular protest and disruptive actions against the failures of current global governance. The people of the world feel unsure that their leaders understand the crucial importance of ENI. Hence, they directly claim ENI, as illustrated by strong manifestations of world public opinion at each summit meeting regarding global governance. What these demonstrators are challenging may be far more fundamental than their leaders would imagine. They are asking: Are you serving the interests of humanity as a whole, including your own nation's citizens, or only that of your own nation, which could, at the end of the day, mean the demise of humanity, including that of your own nation's people?

Global Governance II: Assistance and Cooperation among Nations

Although it was essentially based on traditional national interest, Franklin Roosevelt's early decision to participate in World War II may be counted as a good example of the demonstration of ENI: helping others for one's own interest. And the generosity with which the West genuinely tried to assist the rest of the world after the war is another example of ENI. It was this attitude, more than military power, which gave the West the moral leadership of the world. They built a foundation of peace and prosperity for the world, with which they eventually defeated communism. East Asia has been the biggest beneficiary of this enlightened interest. It is about time for the East to share the burden of leading the world with long-term self-interest.

For this, East Asian nations and leaders must engage with the paradigm of commercial interdependence and cooperation. China can make the crucial difference in two vital areas of international cooperation and assistance: sustainable economic development and assistance to developing nations. The problem of sustainable growth is a case in point for ENI. If all nations continue to pursue their own narrow interests without concern for the earth's resources, the eventual depletion of these resources will diminish each nation's capacity for growth and profit. However, today's consumerism in the West is on a collision course with sustainable development. The insatiable desire for growth and wealth, on both an individual and a national level, would make it very difficult for any Western leader to sell the concept of sustainable development.

Already in many Western nations, an increase in taxes or a decrease in social benefits, i.e. frugality, which remains the obvious remedy to an ever-increasing public debt, has become political suicide for any national leadership. The upshot is a vicious cycle between politicians promoting continued consumerism for the purposes of reelection, and the population reelecting such politicians—at the expense of their children's future. Such a scenario cannot continue, as this represents a typical case of "*fuite en avant.*"

China seems to be at a crossroads: she can blindly copy Western consumerism with her exponential economic growth, or assert the validity of her traditional ethics of thriftiness, whose core concepts would be in harmony with sustainable development. She must be conscious of her unique position to become the very first "saving" leader instead of a global "spending" leader, and take the initiative on the sustainable development agenda. This would require China to seize global leadership at some point in the future based on ENI while preserving her culture of thrift, instead of retreating into insularity with the continued hoarding of foreign exchange reserves. She should be able to couple her ancient values with a new and broader participation in global affairs. The temptation to retreat to parochial national interest would be great, yet China does have the potential to do otherwise based on her solid cultural and philosophical heritage. Just as the West is capable of doing so, China can demonstrate a new breed of global leadership promoting sustainable economic development.

EAST AND WEST • 483

In terms of international assistance, China, at her current pace, will soon become a major donor country. She may initiate a new approach to international assistance as well, based not only on law, but also on ethics and meritocratic education. Education may require several generations to bear fruit; nonetheless, it must be done with the conviction that education is the best long-term path to peace and prosperity for any developing nation. More importantly, any successful education system must be accompanied by a social meritocracy, otherwise popular enthusiasm for education can never be fully ensured. Yet again, this new breed of assistance focusing on ethics and education may be the best complement to the current means of assistance based on law.

International assistance is obviously preferable to the old form of exploitation, since it is based on Universal ethics rather than Master ethics. But as the tenor of this assistance is determined by the West, it is predominantly focused on Western paradigms—democracy, the free market, the rule of law, human rights, good governance, and so on. These are fundamental paradigms but a rule-based approach would be incomplete: an ethical approach is required as a complementary measure. In the long run, this could be the East's contribution led by China. Given her growing economic and financial clout, China has the rare historic opportunity to complement Western initiatives by giving aid to developing countries in the form of an education system based on meritocracy.

Global Governance III: Nuclear Weapons

The issue of nuclear weapons is perhaps the best illustration of the value of ENI. International negotiations on this subject have for many years been deadlocked, since the nuclear North prefers a policy of non-proliferation, while the non-nuclear South has lobbied for disarmament. Meanwhile, the threat of nuclear weapons has continued to increase, to the detriment of all nations. It is clear that, in this respect also, nations are still pursuing their own short-term interests, attached to the older paradigm of warfare and isolation. The North has enough power not only to curb the ambitions of the South, but to exact retribution for defiance of its laws; this is very much in the old pattern and so is unacceptable in the modern commercial paradigm. An alternative must be found.

A leap of faith from short-term to long-term interests, or from parochial national interest to ENI, is necessary, but most national leaders, eager to maintain power, prefer to openly advocate the immediate interests of their nation. They may have to turn a blind eye to the paradigm shift and attendant importance of international solutions, instead adhering to obsolete ideas of national interest. The North is supposed to lead by example, simply because it possesses most of the world's nuclear weapons. As in other cases, the strong must lead the weak, since the weak can only follow the example of the strong. If the West does not demonstrate the high moral ground on this issue, then humanity as a whole is at risk from its own tools of destruction.

On nuclear weapons, the East, along with the Middle East, holds the key to our future. As non-proliferation in the Middle East may need time to get firmly on track, East Asia must stay on course. The countries of the East have the technological and financial capacity to develop nuclear weapons almost immediately; Japan, South Korea, and Taiwan are cases in point. North Korea, which lags far behind these countries in terms of its technology and financial means, has already declared itself a nuclear power. If other East Asian nations follow suit, it will spell the end of the Non-Proliferation Treaty. Japan and South Korea present a good example with their strong commitment to remaining non-nuclear despite the financial and technological clout that could make them nuclear powers very quickly. China's policy toward nuclear armament would be a telltale sign as to whether she will honor her traditional values, or whether she will simply follow the policy of the cold war nuclear superpowers.

China can choose a different path in two areas—nuclear parity and mutually assured destruction (MAD). China is quite capable of maintaining its current low number of nuclear warheads and ICBMs, since her attitude toward arms is quite different from that of the West. In retrospect, the strategy of MAD had more to do with psychological requirements than practical military needs. This policy induced the nuclear superpowers to produce thousands of nuclear warheads and rockets to be stockpiled in many different locations with a view to securing MAD. In the wake of the demise of the Soviet Union, this overproduction and spread of nuclear warheads has become the very source of nuclear menace in themselves, since those warheads may not have all been accounted for. There is great fear that one day they will fall into the hands of international terrorists whose principal targets are the old nuclear superpowers. It is also quite an irony to witness the two superpowers of the cold war now feeling threatened—not so much by each other as by the policy of MAD itself.

The policy of nuclear parity was a logical outcome of the MAD strategy. Throughout history, all military entities tended to exaggerate the strength of their opponents' arms, for obvious reasons. Under the circumstances, it was only natural that the cold war nations should continually increase their stockpiles in a competitive manner, in lieu of farsighted and courageous leadership. Such farsighted leadership could not have survived under the warfare paradigm, as it was too easy a target for its domestic political opponents. The same is true of the opinion-makers in those nations with a tradition of the warfare paradigm; they either support warfare or else prove no match for military-industrial lobbies.

China has sufficient cultural depth to maintain a different course of action. She could and should be able to see the impracticality and uselessness of nuclear parity or overkill. As a future leadership nation or superpower, she can show the world that a leadership nation has no need of nuclear parity with other nuclear superpowers. Such a realization, if it materializes, will go beyond simple nuclear politics. It goes without saying that the Western leadership nations could arrive at the same conclusion and action for the benefit of humanity provided that they overcome the legacies of the war paradigm.

Global Governance IV: Climate Change

Global leadership on the subject of climate change has so far been assumed by the West, given its economic and historical preponderance. Although the United Nations has been playing a crucial role in this area, ultimate success or failure depends on the acceptance of responsibility by leadership nations. But, as illustrated by the insufficient results of international negotiations on climate change until now, national leadership continues to be hampered by geopolitical and national interests, to which each has been accustomed for so long: "The will is even less visible outside Europe. The U.S. cap-and-trade bill, indefinitely stalled in the Senate, was already emasculated by emission permit giveaways to favored sectors. From the art of the possible, climate politics has degenerated into everyone's fight to off-load the burden of change on others."[18] The leitmotif behind this fighting is personal greed or parochial national interest.

On this account, it is quite possible that China may in the end simply emulate the pattern of Western nations' quest for parochial national interest. Yet at the same time, China is much freer than the West as she has much less historical baggage from the sacred credo of national interest. Western democracies have acted in a manner more deeply bound to cater to the immediate needs and parochial interests of their own nations. In the West, it would take extraordinary leadership to lead their populations rather than be led by them. This is so especially in terms of safeguarding parochial national interests. To begin with, how many columnists and opinion-makers would side with leaders advocating ENI rather than traditional national interests at the negotiating tables on climate change? If their numbers remain small, what would be the fate such leaders in their next election round if they did not please even the most enlightened opinion-makers? Whose leadership would risk such courageous political suicide in the West?

Chinese leadership is in a much better position than its Western counterparts to achieve ENI at the expense of parochial national interests. This freedom for Chinese leadership is due, undoubtedly, to their lacking short-term reelection concerns that consume almost all the energies of Western democratic leaders. Yet, this phenomenon goes beyond any discussion of democracy or dictatorship and deep into the cultural background of East and West. We may hope that China will soon be more forthcoming in sacrificing her parochial national interests for the sake of the long-term interests of all, including her own. In other words, China is expected to demonstrate a leap of faith at the negotiating table by absorbing greater financial burdens and leading by example. China, in contrast to Europe or the United States, remains much better prepared to do so, as it has a rich cultural heritage.

This encourages leadership by example in international affairs based on ENI, such as the history of the Eastern tribute system demonstrated in chapter 7.

Actually, such attitudes are very much present in Eastern philosophy: Taoism advises to apply Tao and Virtue progressively to oneself, family, village, the nation and the world.[19] Confucianism also advises to apply Humanity progressively to oneself, family, the nation and the world.[20] Leadership by example is a fundamental principle governing not only interpersonal relationships but also international relationships. Eastern ethics recommends humility on the part of a strong nation to attract weak nations in the same manner as a low-lying sea attracts other waters.[21] The conquest or merge of weaker nations can be justified only by the approval of that nation's people.[22] The strong nation is supposed to take care of the weak, and the weak nations are supposed to show respect to the strong.[23]

Chinese leadership appears to have another decisive advantage over its Western counterparts in terms of philosophical preparedness. Climate change is increasingly acknowledged as an issue of utmost importance. Yet it is only a manifestation of a more fundamental philosophical problem—the relationship between man and nature. Can man exploit nature with impunity? Can we continue to assume that man is superior to nature or that man is part of nature? The Industrial Revolution produced a dialectics between the free market and transnational problems. But we seem ill-prepared to deal with this complex situation. On the contrary, we are under the influence of a concept that makes us complacent about global problems. On this score, Chinese leadership is better positioned than that of Europe and the United States, as its culture is based on man-nature harmony. Properly managed, a sacrifice for the sake of man-nature harmony would be much more easily accepted by China's people than by Westerners.

Although China apparently enjoys some crucial advantages, there is no guarantee that its leadership will not shrink into psychological insularity. Western democracy may also show resilience and resourcefulness in overcoming the built-in obstacles cited above. In the end, it matters little whether China, Europe, or the United States takes the lead. But one of them must lead the world by example based on ENI. And such leaderhip, when realized, would provide not only a solution to the transnational problems but a critical contribution to the renewal of confidence in the mental capacities of mankind as a whole.

Author's note on References

The classic works of Eastern philosophy—*Taoteking, The Analects,* Xun Zi, *The Art of War,* Mencius, etc.—were consulted in the original Chinese, as well as various translations into English, French, and Korean, so as to grasp the intended meanings and to ensure the best translations.

Some quotations in this book may not have complete references. These are part of a collection that stretches back three decades. Faced with two options—to leave them out, or to put them in incomplete, for instance lacking page numbers—I chose the latter, as I believe the quotations are essential to my arguments. This book also contains references from Wikipedia, and from audio and digital books, which are more difficult to cite precisely.

---

1. This is a paraphrase of the following "Notice" of Mark Twain in *Adventures of Huckleberry Finn*: "Persons attempting to find a motive in this narrative will be prosecuted; Persons attempting to find a moral in it will be vanished; Persons attempting to find a plot in it will be shot."

2. Richard Nisbett, *The Geography of Thought, How Asians and Westerners Think Differently ... and Why* (New York: Free Press, 2004).

Chapter 1. Context: Maritime West vs. Continental East

1. Regarding Hegel, see *On Blackness Without Blacks: Essays on the Image of the Black in Germany* (Boston: C.W. Hall, 1982), 94; regarding David Hume and Immanuel Kant, see en.wikipedia.org/wiki/Racism#cite_note-EricMorton-22.

2. H.G. Wells, *The Outline of History*, Vol. I (New York: Doubleday, 1949), 304. Map by James Francis Horrabin.

3. Donald F. Lach, *Preface to Leibniz's Novissima Sinica: Commentary, translation, text* (Honolulu: University of Hawaii Press, 1957), 68.

4. Even today, East Asia sustains about twice as many people as North America and Europe combined.

5. Greek mythology has a similar creation story: Eros, Sky, and Earth came from a golden egg (www.cs.williams.edu/~lindsey/myths/myths_16.html). But otherwise, Greek culture shows a strong focus on sea and water. One of its earliest epics, *The Odyssey*, centers on one hero's struggle against Poseidon and his adventures in the Mediterranean.

6. For example, Hesiod (*Theogony*) says that Chaos was first, but then came Earth (*Gê*); Sea comes much later, after Love, Night, Day, Space, Heaven, hills, and mountains. Ovid's *Metamorphoses* describes something similar: "Chaos" is first, and he specifically notes that "Amphitrite" (i.e., the sea) has not yet encircled the earth—the earth is "unfirm" and "mixed with water and air." Finally, God separates the dry earth (*terra* in Latin, from a root meaning "dry"). The Norse *Edda* begins with fire and ice, and a giant's body being broken down into both sea and earth.

7. Other early philosophers saw fire (Heraclitus), air (Anaximenes), or a primordial mass (Anaximander) as the fundamental element of the universe. There were also atomists already in the Greek period.

8. Robert Graves, *The Greek Myths*, Vol. I (Middlesex, UK: Penguin Books, 1957), 139: "On his return to Olympus, Zeus in disgust let loose a great flood on the earth, meaning to wipe out the whole race of man; but Deucalion, King of Phthia, warned by his father Prometheus the Titan, whom he had visited in the Caucasus, built an ark, victualled it, and went aboard with his wife Pyrrha, a daughter of Epimetheus." Also, 27: "In the beginning, Eurynome, the Goddess of All Things, rose naked from Chaos, but found nothing substantial for her feet to rest upon, and therefore divided the sea from the sky, dancing lonely upon its waves." See also Stephen F. Mason, *A History of the Sciences* (New York: Collier Books, 1962), 20, regarding the Mesopotamians, who understood the Sea as an essential element supporting the Heavens.

9. Color symbolism is another very large topic; there is an interesting discussion of royal purple in John Gage's *Colour and Culture* (1993), where it is noted that the color stands not for the sea but for the brightness of the sun. Nonetheless, the murex was the secret of the seafaring Phoenicians, and the word *Phoenicia* comes from a Greek word meaning "reddish-purple."

10. Henri Pirenne, *Mohammed and Charlemagne* (Mineola, NY: Dover Publications, 2001).

11. The Rig-Veda, the oldest document of Hinduism, dates from the second millennium BC—well over three thousand years ago.

Other religious cultures long predated 1000 BC, such as Egyptian and Sumerian cults. Islam came half a millennium later.

12. Jared Diamond, *Guns, Germs, and Steel: The Fates of Human Societies* (New York & London: W.W. Norton, 1997), 165–166.

13. Ibid., 124–125.

14. Jack Weatherford, *Genghis Khan and the Making of the Modern World* (New York: Crown, 2004), xxiii–xxiv.

15. Diamond, *Guns, Germs, and Steel*, pp. 176–191.

16. See John K. Fairbank, Edwin O. Reischauer, and Albert M. Craig, *East Asia: Tradition and Transformation* (Boston: Houghton Mifflin, 1973).

17. Richard Nisbett, *The Geography of Thought, How Asians and Westerners Think Differently ... and Why* (New York: Free Press, 2004), 19.

18. Fairbank et al., *East Asia*, 242.

19. In chapter 7 we shall examine the implications of institutionalized slavery in detail.

20. G.W.F. Hegel, *The Philosophy of History,* translated J. Sibree (New York: American Home Library, 1902), 263–264.

21. Stanley Snadler, *The Korean Wars: An Encyclopedia* (Taylor & Francis, 1995), 142.

22. Hegel, *Philosophy of History,* 263–264.

23. It is true that the traditional Greek gods were *not* always allies to heroes: Odysseus is hindered by Poseidon, Aeneas is hindered by Juno, Heracles is hindered by Hera (Roman Juno), Achilles is hindered by Venus, Paris is hindered by Athena, and so on. Some may even claim that these are *not* exceptions, but just as common as gods helping heroes. Yet it is undeniable that the fundamental theme of the Greek heroes evolves around gods and that, in the end, they are helped by gods.

24. Charles de Secondat, Baron de Montesquieu, *The Spirit of Laws*, translated Thomas Nugent, ed. J. V. Prichard (London: G. Bell & Sons, 1914), Book II; *Constitution Society*, www.constitution.org/cm/sol.txt.

25. Wells, *Outline of History*, Vol. I, 150: "From what we know of mankind, we are bound to conclude that the first sailors plundered when they could, and traded when they had to."

26. It did not always result in such a separation; in Old Testament Israel, for instance, a staunch theocracy was the norm.

27. Genesis 1:26, 1:28.

28. Genesis 1:2.

29. Matthew 10:28.

30. "I know how Fortune is ever most friendly and alluring to those whom she strives to deceive, until she overwhelms them with grief beyond bearing, by deserting them when least expected.… You have given yourself over to Fortune's rule, and you must bow yourself to your mistress's ways. Are you trying to stay the force of her turning wheel? Ah! Dull-witted mortal, if Fortune begin to stay still, she is no longer

Fortune." Boethius, *The Consolation of Philosophy* (translated W.V. Cooper, 1902), Electronic Text Center, University of Virginia Library, Book II, pp. 26–29.

Chapter 2. Man and Nature: Western God vs. Eastern Tao

1. Rex Warner, *The Greek Philosophers* (New York: Mentor, 1958), 24.

2. See chapter 1 of this book.

3. Mao Zedong tried to emulate this phenomenon in 1956 with his ill-fated "Movement of One Hundred Flowers." Confident of the superiority of communism to other schools of thought, including traditional Chinese philosophy, he exhorted "Let a hundred flowers bloom; let a hundred schools of thought contend." Mao reversed this liberal policy in 1957 as communism faced mounting criticism.

4. Besides the three major fertile periods for philosophy (i.e., the Greco-Roman period, Chinese Spring-Autumn and Warring States period, and European modernity), there were three similar situations in history. In Renaissance Italy, we find many city-states vying for influence, which permitted arts and literature to flourish. In Japan, we find another period of warring states, the Sengoku era (戦国時代), stretching from the middle of the fifteenth century to the beginning of the seventeenth. In China, we find the Period of Disunity from 220 to 586 (marking, respectively, the demise of the Han dynasty to the rise of the Sui dynasty), when many kingdoms competed against each other. But these failed to produce new philosophies. The reason is most probably because both

Sengoku Japan and Disunity China were already firmly dominated by Buddhism, Taoism, and Confucianism in a circumscribed world without new input. And in the case of Renaissance Italy, despite its enormous influence on modern philosophy, it focused mostly on arts and literature due to the overwhelming influence of Roman Catholicism.

5. *Introduction to I Ching* by Richard Wilhelm www.iging.com/intro/introduc.htm.

6. This adoption is assumed to have taken place during the Ming dynasty (1368–1644).

7. Walter Demel, *China in the political thoughts in Western and Central Europe: 1570–1750,* compiled in the book by Thomas H. C. Lee, *China and Europe: Images and Influences in Sixteenth to Eighteenth Centuries* (Chinese University Press, 1991), 45–64.

8. We must not confuse the concept of yin and yang with its symbol, the *taijitu*: the former preceded the latter by nearly one and a half millennia.

9. The coat of arms of the *armigeri defensores seniores* (fourth row, third from left), a Western Roman infantry unit listed in the *Notitia Dignitatum*, dated to ca. AD 430. en.wikipedia.org/wiki/Taijitu.

10. www.estovest.net/tradizione/yinyang_en.html#t24.

11. Ibid.

12. Genesis 1:1

13. John 1:1.

14. Confucius, *The Analects*, chapter 2-1.

15. Ibid., chapter 2-2.

16. The Yin-Yang symbol has a scientific origin, namely, the observation of the sun's movement: "Observing the cycle of the Sun, ancient Chinese simply used a pole about eight feet long, posted at a right angle to the ground, and recorded positions of the shadow. The shortest shadow is found on the day of Summer Solstice. The longest shadow is found on the day of Winter Solstice. The Sun chart becomes the Yin-Yang symbol." See Allen Tsai, "Where does the Yin Yang Symbol come from?" 1999, *Chinese Fortune Calendar*. www. chinesefortunecalendar.com/yin-yang.htm.

17. Taoteking, 1.

18. In his book, *Moses and Monotheism*, Freud advances a fascinating theory connecting Akhenaten and Moses, tracing the origin of Judaic monotheism back to Egypt. If this view is valid, then the sun is at the basis of Western monotheism as well as the symbolism of Tao. See Sigmund Freud, *Moses and Monotheism*, translated Katherine Jones (New York: Knopf, 1939).

19. Exodus 3:13–14: "And Moses said unto God, Behold, when I come unto the children of Israel, and shall say unto them, 'The God of your fathers hath sent me unto you'; and they shall say to me, 'What is his name?' What shall I say unto them? And God said unto Moses, 'I AM THAT I AM': and he said, 'Thus shalt thou say unto the children of Israel, 'I AM hath sent me unto you.'"

20. Taoteking, 1.

21. Bertrand Russell, interview with *New York World,* May 4, 1924, reproduced by Will Durant, *The Story of Philosophy* (New York: Washington Square Press, 1952), 485–486.

22. As many philosophers of the Enlightenment pointed out, Joshua should have asked for the revolution of the Earth to cease, not the passage of the Sun.

23. Taoteking, 51.

24. Ibid., 5 and 62.

25. Ibid., 1. The strong warning of Taoism against confusing manifestation with essence cannot be overemphasized, since this is the most fundamental difference between the East and West. Such a warning served the East as an antidote to metaphysics and ideologies, which claim to be essence, when they are only manifestations. "The Tao that can be told is not the eternal Tao; the Tao that can be named is not the eternal Tao. The nameless is the beginning of the Universe; the named is the beginning of all creatures. Hence rid yourself of desires in order to observe the essence; but allow yourself desires in order to observe its manifestations."

26. Ibid., 14.

27. Ibid., 52: "In the beginning was the Tao. All things issue from it; all things return to it. To find the origin, trace back the manifestations."

28. Ibid., 51: "The Tao gives birth to all beings, nourishes them, maintains them, cares for them, comforts them, protects them, takes them back to itself, creating without possessing,

acting without expecting, guiding without interfering. That is why the Tao is in the very nature of things."

29. Ibid., 62.

30. In the circumscribed, continental Eastern world, dogmas were considered to be unnatural and artificial because they harmed social harmony. In Taoist texts, man is repeatedly warned "not to do anything artificial or unnatural because it is against the Tao." See Taoteking, 48 and 63.

31. It is intriguing to note that dogmas are now disappearing in the West as it has become circumscribed. In such an environment, dogma leads to alienation from the self and from nature: these will lead in turn to violence and environmental degradation.

32. Benedict de Spinoza, *Ethics,* translated E.M. Curley (UK: Penguin Books, 1996), 114. See also chapter 7 of Lao Tzu's *Taoteking*: "The Tao is infinite, eternal. Why is it eternal? It was never born; thus it can never die. Why is it infinite? It has no desire for itself; thus it is present for all beings."

33. Charles Darwin, *On the Origin of Species by Means of Natural Selection, or The Preservation of Favoured Races in the Struggle for Life* (London: John Murray, 1866), 577.

34. Ibid., 6.

35. Ibid. See also 232: "I have been astonished how rarely an organ can be named, towards which no transitional grade is known to lead. The truth of this remark is indeed shown by that old canon in natural history of '*Natura non facit saltum*.'... Why should not Nature have taken a leap from structure to structure? On the theory of natural selection, we can clearly

understand why she should not, for natural selection can act only by taking advantage of slight successive variations, she can never take a leap, but must advance by the shortest and slowest steps." See also 544: "It is, no doubt, extremely difficult even to conjecture by what gradations many structures have been perfected, more especially amongst broken and failing groups of organic beings; but we see so many strange gradations in nature, as is proclaimed by the canon, '*Natura non facit saltum*,' that we ought to be extremely cautious in saying that any organ or instinct, or any whole being, could not have arrived at its present state by many graduated steps."

36. See Arthur Oncken Lovejoy, *The Great Chain of Being: A Study of the History of an Idea* (Cambridge, Mass: Harvard University Press, 1990), 144–145.

37. Stephen Jay Gould, *The Panda's Thumb: More Reflections in Natural History* (New York and London: W. W. Norton, 1980), 68. Marx felt his own work to be an exact parallel to Darwin's. See also Stephen Jay Gould, *Ever Since Darwin: Reflections in Natural History* (New York and London: W. W. Norton, 1977), 26: Marx also wrote to Engels that Darwin's book "contains the basis in natural history for our view."

38. *Le Monde*, May 17, 1984.

39. Adolph Hitler, *Mein Kampf, Vol. 1: A Retrospect*, translated James Murphy (London, New York, Melbourne: Hurst and Blackett, 1939), chapter 11, paragraphs 7–11.

40. Darwin, *Origin of Species*, 4.

41. Ibid., 95.

42. Gould, *The Panda's Thumb*, 179. See also Ben Waggoner, "Thomas Huxley," February 1999, University of California Museum of Paleontology, www.ucmp.berkeley.edu/history/thuxley.html: In Huxley's own words, supporting Darwin: "I am prepared to go to the stake, if requisite.... I am sharpening up my claws and beak in readiness." Archbishop Wilberforce ridiculed evolution and asked Huxley if he was descended from an ape on his grandmother's side or his grandfather's. To which Huxley is said to have responded "I would rather be the offspring of two apes than be a man and afraid to face the truth." Huxley's own retelling of the story: "If then the question is put to me would I rather have a miserable ape for a grandfather or a man highly endowed by nature and possessed of great means of influence and yet who employs these faculties and that influence for the mere purpose of introducing ridicule into a grave scientific discussion, I unhesitatingly affirm my preference for the ape." Regarding *Natura non facit saltum*, Huxley said to Darwin, "You have loaded yourself with an unnecessary difficulty in adopting *Natura non facit saltum* so unreservedly."

43. Some may argue that the fact that missing links have not been found does not prove that they never existed. But it seems unlikely that such links, if they did exist, would not have been discovered.

44. Gould, *The Panda's Thumb*, 179–183; *Newsweek*, March 29, 1982, 45.

45. Confucius, *The Analects*, 9-17.

46. Ibid., 15-12.

47. Although astrology was not considered a myth—it was a very respectable and elaborate science until the seventeenth century—and augury, likewise, was an official practice in ancient Rome, they remained a divination domain.

48. A brief explanation of how one consults the *I Ching* will highlight this aspect of the book. The *I Ching* uses as its fundamental symbols the broken or yin line (--) and the solid or yang line (–). In combination with these entities, its eight trigrams (2^3) and sixty-four hexagrams (2^6) are produced. Each of the eight trigrams has a meaning. For example, three yangs ☰ represent Heaven, with the connotation of Assertiveness; and three yins ☷ represent Earth, with the connotation of Receptiveness. Among the sixty-four hexagrams, we find a hexagram of six yangs consisting of two heavens, which indicates maximum Assertiveness; and a hexagram of six yins consisting of two earths, which indicates maximum Receptiveness.

For example, by way of consulting *I Ching*, if one arrives at having six yangs (Heaven, 乾 – Qian), which constitutes the very first chapter among sixty-four chapter-hexagrams, the *I Ching* tells us that: "Heaven is in motion, the nobleman prepares himself for strenuous activities; Junzi will be assertive all day and in the evening takes precautions; Danger may be lurking but there is no risk; Be assertive all day, repeating the way of Tao; Even though one makes a leap, one is still at the bottom. Make advances, there is no danger; the force touches the limits, arrogance will bring about regrets; Fullness does not last long; the supreme virtue does not seek the foremost place." See *I Ching* chapter I: 乾 – Qian.

As a second example, the second chapter among sixty-four chapter-hexagrams is six yins (Earth, 坤 – Kun). If one comes across this sign, the *I Ching* would reveal, among others, these aphorisms: "Receptiveness has a great advantage. It is at the origin; Take the lead, one goes astray. Follow the lead, one finds his way; Remain receptive and calm, one finds luck; Receptiveness is great, all things owe to it; Do not start new enterprise, try to complete what has been started; Low-profile, no blame, no praise; Noble man will follow the way of receptiveness; Limitless is the way of receptiveness that resembles the earth; Without being strenuous, there will be achievements; Inner strength pays off, no showing off; Without purpose, one still achieves; The way knows no bound; receptive perseverance furthers and arrives at great ending." See *I-Ching* chapter II: 坤 – Kun.

49. Taoteking, 45.

50. Lynn White, Jr., "The Historical Roots of Our Ecologic Crisis," *JASA* 21 (June 1969), 42–47.

51. Ibid. Counterargument against Lynn White's paper contained in the same *JASA* journal.

Chapter 3. Mind and Body: Western Spirit vs. Eastern Man

1. Benedict de Spinoza, *Ethics,* translated E.M. Curley (UK: Penguin Books, 1996), 71.

2. Xun Zi, *Xunzi,* chapter 17, Section 1 (my own translation).

3. Genesis 1:2.

4. Charles Freeman, *The Closing of the Western Mind: The Rise of Faith and the Fall of Reason* (New York: Vintage Books and Random House, 2002), 115.

5. Edward Gibbon, *The History of the Decline and Fall of the Roman Empire*, volume 1 (Penguin Classics), David Womersley, 944.

6. H. G. Wells, *The Outline of History*, Volume 1 (New York: Doubleday), 1949, 150.

7. This is the Latin translation for Descartes' original French: "Je pense, donc je suis," which appears in his 1637 *Discourse on Method* and is often considered the starting point of Western rationalism.

8. Spinoza, *Ethics,* 161. See also 162: "What, I ask, does he understand by the union of mind and body? ... Finally, I pass over all those things he claimed about the will and its freedom, since I have already shown, more than adequately, that they are false."

9. To paraphrase Beppe Severgnini, one can say that "an Eastern mind must not feel guilty about that. The West deserves to be examined in haste and judged without pity; for centuries they have applied that treatment to the East and elsewhere." The original text written by Beppe Severgnini in his book *Inglesi* goes this way: "By the way: we must not feel guilty about that. The British deserve to be examined in haste and judged without pity; for centuries they have applied that treatment to others in Europe and elsewhere."

10. See Bertrand Russell, *A History of Western Philosophy* (New York: Simon and Schuster, 1964), 701, 703: "Philosophy in the eighteenth century was dominated by the British empiricists, of whom Locke, Berkeley, and Hume may be taken as the representatives.... In Germany, the reaction against Hume's

agnosticism took a form far more profound and subtle than that which Rousseau had given to it. Kant, Fichte, and Hegel developed a new kind of philosophy. In Kant, and still more in Fichte, the subjectivist tendency that begins with Descartes was carried to new extremes." (We are focusing solely on Kant's emphasis on Reason here. His great contribution of categorical ethics merits a separate discussion.)

11. See Ibid., 730–731: "At the end of the nineteenth century, the leading academic philosophers, both in America and in Great Britain, were largely Hegelians.…The whole, in all its complexity, is called by Hegel 'the Absolute.' The Absolute is spiritual; Spinoza's view, that it has the attribute of extension as well as that of thought, is rejected."

12. Deuteronomy 8:3, but more commonly known from Jesus' quotation in Matthew 4:4.

13. Friedrich Wilhelm Nietzsche, *Beyond Good and Evil,* translated Walter Kaufmann (New York: Vintage Books and Random House, 1966), 203.

14. In Korea, Yi Toegye (1501–1570) was the key exponent of the Korean Li School based on the primacy of Li over Ki. On the other hand, Yi Yulgok (1536–1584) was known to be the central figure of the Korean Ki School, but his view was based on harmony and complementarity between Li and Ki. The closeness in the views between Yi Yulgok and Zhu Xi is undeniable in their emphasis on Li and Ki complementarity, as with Wang Yangming and Yi Toegye in their emphasis on Li over Ki.

15. Chungdong Lyu, *Life & Philosophy of Yi T'oegye* (Seoul: Pakyoung-Mungo, ND), 60 (my translation).

16. Yinsoo Son, *The Philosophy of Yi Yulgok* (Seoul: Pakyoungsa, ND), 38 (my translation).

17. Confucius, *The Analects*, 2-6.

18. Daniel G. Amen, "Brain Systems: Physiology, Function and Associated Problems," 2006, *BrainPlace*, amenclinics.com/bp/systems/limbic.php.

19. Locke, John, *An Essay Concerning Human Understanding*, Ed. Roger Woolhouse (New York: Penguin Books, 1997), p. 307.

20. Ibid., 306.

21. Spinoza, *A Political Treatise,* introduction, the first paragraph.

22. Nietzsche, *Beyond Good and Evil,* 203.

23. Ibid., 152–153.

24. Ibid., 203.

25. Ibid.

26. Arthur Percy Noyes and Lawrence Coleman Kolb, *Modern Clinical Psychiatry* (Philadelphia: W.B. Saunders, 1963), 5.

27. W. F. Ganong, *Review of Medical Physiology*, 9th Edition (Los Altos: Lange Medical Publication, 1979), 182.

28. Charles Darwin, *On the Origin of Species by Means of Natural Selection, or The Preservation of Favoured Races in the Struggle for Life* (London: John Murray, 1866), 99–100. "This depends, not on a struggle for existence, but on a struggle between the

males for possession of the females; the result is not death of the unsuccessful competitor, but few or no offspring. Sexual selection is, therefore, less rigorous than natural selection." See also Gillian Beer's introduction in Charles Darwin, *The Origin of Species,* ed. Gillian Beer (Oxford, New York: Oxford University Press, 1996), xxvii: "Darwin came to feel that he had underestimated, or underexplained, the power of sexual selection, and in *The Descent of Man, and Selection in Relation to Sex* (New York: D. Appleton and Company, 1872) he devoted an entire volume to its action. There he emphasized that, though in almost all species the female was the choice-maker, and the males competed among themselves, in human societies the privilege of choice-making had passed to the male, with deleterious effect. Darwin's representation of nature as female in the *Origin* seems to lead his thought forward into this later phase of his argument."

29. Noyes and Kolb, *Modern Clinical Psychology*, 15.

30. Voltaire, *A Philosophical Dictionary,* vol. 5 (London: C. H. Reynell, 1824), 43.

31. B. Jowett, *Thucydides: Translated into English*, vol. I (London: Clarendon Press, 1881), 116.

32. Spinoza, *Ethics*, 87.

33. Wells, *The Outline of History*, 150.

34. Charles de Secondat, Baron de Montesquieu, *The Spirit of Laws*, translated Thomas Nugent, ed. J. V. Prichard (London: G. Bell & Sons, 1914), Tome II. Constitution Society. www.constitution.org/cm/sol.txt.

35. Lynn White, Jr., *The Historical Roots of Our Ecologic Crisis*, *JASA* 21 (June 1969), 42–47.

36. Jean-Louis and Monique Tassoul, *A Concise History of Solar and Stellar Physics* (Princeton, N.J.: Princeton University Press, 2004), as cited in en.wikipedia.org/wiki/Aristarchus_of_Samos#cite_note-1.

37. All the quotes are from Xun Zi, *Xunzi*; the first number refers to chapter and the second to the section within the chapter. The translations are my own.

38. Spinoza, *Theologico-Political Treatise*, preface.

39. Xun Zi, *Xunzi,* chapter 9, Section 69/127.

40. Spinoza, *Ethics*, final paragraph.

41. It goes the same with Confucius: "Junzi makes friends for learning; With friendship, he reinforces his virtues." Confucius, *Analects*, 12–24.

42. Confucius says the same: "The progress of Junzi is upwards; the progress of Xiaoren is downwards." Confucius, *The Analects*, 14–23.

43. Ibid., 127. See also 120: "We call good, or evil, what is useful to, or harmful to, preserving our being, that is, what increases or diminishes, aids or restrains, our power of acting."

44. Xun Zi, *Xunzi: Basic Writings,* translated Burton Watson (New York: Columbia University Press, 1963), 15.

Chapter 4. Man and Man: Western Law vs. Eastern Ethics

1. Peter H. Lee, *A History of Korean Literature* (Cambridge, UK: Cambridge University Press, 2003), p. 6.

2. Confucius, *The Analects*, 15-19.

3. Ibid., 12-22. A disciple asked about Humanity. Confucius said, "Loving your fellow men." He asked about Knowledge. Confucius said, "Knowing your fellow men."

4. Ibid., 18-6.

5. Ibid., 11-12.

6. Ibid. A disciple asked how the spirits of the dead and the gods should be served. Confucius said, "You are not able even to serve man. How can you serve the spirits?" "May I ask about death?" "You do not understand even life. How can you understand death?"

7. Confucius, *Doctrine of the Mean*, chapter 11, *Zhongwen.com*, zhongwen.com/x/zhong.htm.

8. Voltaire, *A Philosophical Dictionary*, vol. 5 (London: C. H. Reynell, 1824), 217–218.

9. William Theodore de Bary, *Asian Values and Human Rights: A Confucian Communitarian Perspective* (Cambridge, Mass.: Harvard University Press, 1998), 15. The Eastern emphasis on self-fulfillment and education explains its upholding of the state examination system throughout its long history: "Some institutions, like the mandarin class and the examination system, survived with little break from about AD 700 in the

T'ang era." Quotation from Johan Goudsblom, Eric Jones, and Stephen Mennell, *The Course of Human History: Economic Growth, Social Process, and Civilization* (Armonk, N.Y.: M.E. Sharpe, 1996), 118.

10. Here I am referring to the famous Confucian teaching: 修身齊家治國平天下

11. Voltaire, *A Philosophical Dictionary,* 217–218.

12. Ibid., chapter 1.

13. Ibid.

14. Matthew 5:17.

15. 1 Corinthians 13:13.

16. Romans 3:28.

17. Confucius, *The Analects*, 15-35.

18. Ibid., 15-28.

19. Matthew 5:3–5, 11:28–30, 6:13.

20. The First Amendment to the Constitution of the United States: "Congress shall make no law respecting an establishment of religion, or prohibiting the free exercise thereof; or abridging the freedom of speech, or of the press; or the right of the people peaceably to assemble, and to petition the Government for a redress of grievances." (December 15, 1791).

21. C. D. Herrera, *How Are Law and Ethics Related?* Philosophy & Religion Department, Montclair State University, N.J. www-hsc.usc.edu/~mbernste/tae.ethics&law.herrera.html.

22. Ibid.

23. Exodus 21:24. See also Matthew 5:38.

24. Matthew 5:44.

25. Matthew 5:38–41.

26. Confucius, *The Analects*, 14-34: "Some people say, reward bad with good. What do you think, Master? Master responded: If so, with which do you reward good? My advice shall be: Rectitude for bad; good for good."

27. Ibid., 4-3.

28. Upon comparing the *Nicomachean Ethics* of Aristotle to the moral teachings of the Bible and *The Analects*, one has the strong impression that Aristotle's ethics revolve around observation, as opposed to the prescriptive and empathetic attitude of Christian and Confucian ethics. It is true that Aristotle stressed the teleological aspect of ethics: "We are not studying in order to know what virtue is, but to become good, for otherwise there would be no profit in it." (*NE* 2.2) But again, this "becoming good" is only intended for master-citizens, having no universal ethical implications. Aristotle's main focus appeared to be on Knowledge, in the same mold with Socrates and Plato.

29. Aristotle's theory of slavery is found in Book I, chapters III–VII of the *Politics,* and in Book VII of the *Nicomachean Ethics.*

30. Aristotle, *Physics*, vol. 1. Loeb Classical Library, 1252 b 8.

31. Aristotle, *Politics*. Loeb Classical Library, 1254 b 10–14.

32. Bertrand Russell, *A History of Western Philosophy*, 1945, 184.

33. Aristotle asserted that only man has soul. What woman provides for children is matter, while man gives it soul or form.

34. Confucius, *Doctrine of the Mean,* chapter 11.

35. Quotations from Voltaire's *Philosophical Dictionary*. See *Philosophical Dictionary*, translated, with an introduction and glossary, by Peter Gay, preface by André Maurois, 2 vols. (New York: Basic Books, 1962), chnm.gmu.edu/revolution/d/273/.

36. Kangxi Emperor, Wikipedia, en.wikipedia.org/wiki/Kangxi_Emperor_of_China.

37. Richard Nisbett, *The Geography of Thought, How Asians and Westerners Think Differently ... and Why* (New York: Free Press, 2004), 12.

38. Confucius, *The Analects*, 1-1, 14-35, 14-42, 20-3.

39. Christian thinkers have long criticized Judaism for ignoring the afterlife and centering their ethics on the present life.

40. Albert Einstein, "Religion and Science," *The New York Times Magazine*, November 9, 1930.

41. Albert Einstein obituary, *The New York Times*, April 19, 1955.

42. See Einstein quotations in Victor J. Stenger, *Has Science Found God? The Latest Results in the Search for Purpose in the Universe* (Amherst, N.Y.: Prometheus Books, 2003), chapter 3.

43. Western freedom may not be entirely free of associations with religion and ideology. Self-preservation, as the most powerful

force and elemental human motivation, looks for a strong power with which to identify. The logical outcome is the creation of a supernatural being who will imbue believers with absolute conviction. Thus, individual freedom and religion (and subsequent ideologies) may share the same origin.

44. Confucius, *Doctrine of the Mean*, chapter 14. zhongwen. com/x/zhong.htm.

45. Taoteking, 10.

46. Matthew 22:21.

47. Confucius, *The Analects*, 14-28.

48. Ibid., 12-11.

49. Ibid., 12-16.

50. Ibid., 14-30.

51. The end of the *Nicomachean Ethics* declares that an inquiry into ethics necessarily leads into politics, and the two works are frequently considered to be parts of a larger treatise, or perhaps connected lectures, dealing with the "philosophy of human affairs."

52. Nirad C. Chaudhuri, *The Continent of Circe, An Essay on the Peoples of India* (New York: Oxford University Press, 1965), 211.

53. H.G. Wells, *The Outline of History*, Vol. I (New York: Doubleday, 1949), 313. Perhaps Confucius had arrived at a similar conclusion when he said: "I have been the whole day without eating, and the whole night without sleeping—

occupied with thinking. It was of no use. Better plan to learn!" See Confucius, *The Analects*, chapter 15.

54. Confucius, *The Analects*, 15-30.

55. Waphola Rahula, *What the Buddha Taught* (New York: Grove Press, 1974), 10.

56. Ibid., 51–52.

57. The intellectual metaphysicization is similar to physical metaphysation, denoting cancellous change of the part of bone in contact with a prosthesis. Application of this term to denote the Eastern phenomenon of taking metaphysical tendencies and flavors from imported Buddhism does make sense, as such a process did make the Eastern culture cancellous with its unproductive and scholastic impeachment among different schools of thought, one against another.

58. Han Yu, Wikipedia, en.wikipedia.org/wiki/Han_Yu.

59. Thomas Friedman, "One Party Democracy," *The International Herald Tribune*, September 10, 2009.

Chapter 5. Role Model: Western Hero vs. Eastern Junzi

1. Matthew 5:14–15, 5:13.

2. Lao Tzu, *Taoteking*, 11 (zhongwen.com/doo.htm).

3. "Reign of Zhen Guan" (貞觀之治).

4. Source: en.wikipedia.org/wiki/Emperor_Taizong_of_Tang.

5. His grandson, Emperor Qianlong, formally yielded the throne to his son after sixty-one years, but continued to rule behind the scenes until his death. This abdication was performed out of filial duty in deference to his illustrious grandfather, Emperor Kangxi, who had ruled for "only" sixty-one years.

6. This long era was composed of sixty-one years under Emperor Kangxi (康熙帝, 1654–1722), thirteen years of Emperor Yongzheng (雍正帝, 1678–1735), and sixty-four years under Emperor Qianlong (乾隆帝, 1711–1799).

7. Confucius, *The Analects*, 6-4.

8. Benedict de Spinoza, *Ethics*, Part IV: Of Human Bondage, or the Strength of Emotions, Appendix XXXII, translated E.M. Curley (UK: Penguin Books, 1996).

9. *Taoteking*, 48 and 49.

10. Spinoza, *Ethics*, Part IV: Of Human Bondage, or the Strength of Emotions, Proposition XVIII.

11. *Taoteking*, 18.

12. This emphasis on altruism is particularly prevalent in Japanese Confucianism.

13. Spinoza, *Ethics*, 69.

14. Ibid., 76, 77.

15. Benjamin Franklin, *Autobiography* (Applewood Books), 85–86.

16. Confucius, *The Analects*, 15-36.

17. Ibid., 2-14.

18. en.wikipedia.org/wiki/Thomas_Hobbes.

19. Ibid.

20. Albert Einstein, www.spaceandmotion.com/albert-einstein-god-religion-theology.htm.

21. *Taoteking*, 5.

22. Ibid., 3.

23. Antonio R. Damasio, *Looking for Spinoza: Joy, Sorrow, and the Feeling Brain* (Orlando, FL: Harcourt Brace, 2003), 171.

24. Stephen Jay Gould, *Ever Since Darwin: Reflections in Natural History* (New York and London: W. W. Norton, 1977), 265–266.

25. Confucius, *The Analects*, 12-1.

26. *Taoteking*, 54.

27. en.wikipedia.org/wiki/The_pen_is_mightier_than_the_sword.

28. *Taoteking*, 30.

29. Ibid., 31.

30. Mencius, 14- 48.

31. Confucius, *The Analects*, 15-22.

32. *Taoteking*, 61.

33. Ibid., 51.

34. Ibid., 22. See also chapter 78: "There is nothing more submissive and weak than water. Yet for attacking that which is hard and strong nothing can surpass it.… The weak overcomes the strong, and the submissive overcomes the hard."

35. Ibid., 66. See also chapter 71: "To know yet to think that one does not know is best; not to know yet to think that one knows will lead to difficulty."

36. Ibid., 67. See also chapter 33: "Knowing others is intelligence; knowing oneself is true wisdom. Mastering others is strength; mastering yourself is true power."

37. Ibid., 76. See also chapter 8: "The supreme good is like water, which nourishes all things without trying to. It is content with the low places that people disdain. Thus it is like Tao." And chapter 66: "All streams flow to the sea because it is lower than they are. Humility gives it its power. If you want to govern the people, you must place yourself below them. If you want to lead the people, you must learn how to follow them."

38. Albert Einstein, www.spaceandmotion.com/albert-einstein-god-religion-theology.htm.

39. Confucius, *The Analects*, 15-19.

40. Ibid., 15-21.

41. Ibid., 6-22.

42. *Taoteking*, 49.

43. Ibid., 49.

44. Ibid., 77.

45. The exact term would be "Hegemon-Barons," since they did not claim the title of king, which was still reserved only for the Zhu dynasty monarchs. During this period, the Zhu monarch had only nominal power, which was ever diminishing, as his authority as well as survival was entirely in the hands of the Hegemon-Barons. But the role of the Western barons does not quite correspond to that of the Chinese hegemons, so instead I will use the term Hegemon-King rather than simply Hegemon or Hegemon-Baron.

46. *Taoteking*, 11.

47. Ibid., 78.

48. H. G. Wells, *The Outline of History*, Vol. I (New York: Doubleday, 1949), 464.

49. Luke 6:31.

50. Confucius, *The Analects*, 15-24. "Is there one word which may serve as a rule of practice for all one's life? Is not *reciprocity* such a word? What you do not want others to do unto you, do not do to others." *Zhongwen.com,* zhongwen.com/lunyu.htm.

51. *Taoteking*, 22.

52. Ibid., 73.

53. Matthew 5:3–5, 5:11.

54. *Taoteking*, 13.

55. Luke 8:5–8, 13:21.

56. *Taoteking*, 9.

57. Matthew 6:19–20.

58. Ibid., 10:32–33.

59. Ibid., 5:29–30.

60. By rejecting absolutism, Eastern culture encourages and promotes moderation and inertia. By accepting absolutism, Western culture, until recently, has instinctively turned to activism and extremism. The twentieth-century clashes between political ideologies epitomize this tendency to favor extremism. The East's eclectic attitude toward other religions and beliefs shielded it from unnecessary ideological conflict, but also from the dynamism that powered the West after the Age of Discovery.

61. *Taoteking*, 62.

62. Ibid., 54.

63. Matthew 10:34–38.

64. Confucius, *The Analects*, 1-1.

65. Matthew 13:40–42.

66. *Taoteking*, 33.

67. Ibid., 69.

Chapter 6. Culture: Western Religion vs. Eastern Education

1. Carl von Clausewitz, *On War*, ed., translated Michael Howard and Peter Paret (Princeton, N.J.: Princeton University Press, 1976), 97.

2. Sun Tzu, *The Art of War*, chapter 3.

3. Edward Gibbon, *History of the Decline and Fall of the Roman Empire,* Volume 1, chapter 15 (audiobook).

4. en.wikipedia.org/wiki/Imperial_examination.

5. en.wikipedia.org/wiki/Imperial_examination.

6. For example, in the case of Korea, the imperial examination was first adopted in 958, during the Koryo dynasty, and remains in effect to this day—1,051 years later. The fundamentals remain intact (i.e., its meritocracy and non-discrimination), even though the name has been changed from "imperial examination" to "state examination." Even today, anyone with determination and intelligence can succeed in the state examinations to become a high government official, thus acquiring social status and freeing himself from financial worries during his lifetime. Numerous ministers and several prime ministers in Korea have been the products of the state examination system.

7. en.wikipedia.org/wiki/Song_Dynasty.

8. en.wikipedia.org/wiki/Ming_Dynasty.

9. "The examination system also served to maintain cultural unity and consensus on basic values. The uniformity of the content of the examinations meant that the local elites and ambitious would-be members of those elites across the whole of China were taught with the same values. Even though only a small fraction (about 5 percent) of those who attempted the examinations passed them and received titles, the studying and the hope of eventual success on a subsequent examination

served to sustain the interest of those who took them." See en.wikipedia.org/wiki/Imperial_examination.

10. Confucius, *The Analects*, 15-20.

11. Ibid., 15-18.

12. Ibid., 15-21.

13. Ibid., 15-31.

14. en.wikipedia.org/wiki/Heraclitus.

15. en.wikipedia.org/wiki/Carneades.

16. Dong-ho Sung, *Han Fei* (Seoul: Hongshin-Sinsu, ND), 368 (my translation).

17. Niccolo Machiavelli, *The Prince,* translated W. K. Marriott (Plain Label Books, 2007), 90, *Google Books*, books.google. com/books?id=VIAgG12gh_EC.

18. Ibid., 124.

19. Thomas Hobbes, *Leviathan*, oregonstate.edu/instruct/phl302/ texts/hobbes/leviathan-c.html# chapter XIII: "Hereby it is manifest that during the time men live without a common power to keep them all in awe, they are in that condition which is called war; and such a war as is of every man against every man.... In such condition there is no place for industry, because the fruit thereof is uncertain ... no arts; no letters; no society; and which is worst of all, continual fear, and danger of violent death; and the life of man, solitary, poor, nasty, brutish, and short."

20. Thomas Hobbes, *Leviathan*, oregonstate.edu/instruct/phl302/ texts/hobbes/leviathan-c.html# Part III.

21. Voltaire, *A Philosophical Dictionary* (London: C. H. Reynell, 1824), see section on Ignatius Loyola.

22. From this perspective, it is no wonder that Socratic faith in knowledge ultimately (or inadvertently) led the West to metaphysics and ideologies, which produced monstrous results from the perspective of a Universal ethics.

23. Fritjof Capra, *The Tao of Physics: An Exploration of the Parallels Between Modern Physics and Eastern Mysticism* (New York: Bantam Books, 1975), 50.

24. Stephen Mennell, *Asia and Europe: Comparing Civilizing Processes,* quotation from Gouldsblom, Johan, Eric Jones, and Stephen Mennell, *The Course of Human History* (New York: M.E. Sharpe, 1996), 119.

25. The Seven Military Classics (武經七書).

26. Mao Zedong, *A Single Spark Can Start a Prairie Fire, Selected Works* (Peking: Foreign Language Press, English edition, 1965), 124.

27. Sun Tzu, *The Art of War*, chapter 1.

28. Thomas Hobbes, *Leviathan*, chapter XIII.

29. Sun Tzu, *The Art of War*, chapter 13.

30. Clausewitz, *On War,* 203.

31. Sun Tzu, *The Art of War*, chapter 3.

32. Clausewitz, *On War,* 90.

33. Ibid., 177.

34. Ibid., 86: "War is merely the continuation of policy by other means. We see, therefore, that war is not merely an act of policy but a true political instrument, a continuation of political intercourse, carried on with other means. What remains peculiar to war is simply the peculiar nature of its means. War in general, and the commander in any specific instance, is entitled to require that the trend and designs of policy shall not be inconsistent with these means. That, of course, is no small demand; but however much it may affect political aims in a given case, it will never do more than modify them. The political object is the goal, war is the means of reaching it, and means can never be considered in isolation from their purpose." See 610, in which Clausewitz develops this theme further: "Once again, war is an instrument of policy. It must necessarily bear the character of policy and measure by its standards. The conduct of war, in its great outlines, is therefore policy itself, which takes up the sword in place of the pen, but does not on that account cease to think according to its own laws."

35. Sun Tzu, *The Art of War*, chapter 2.

36. Ibid., chapter 6: "Hence to fight and conquer in all your battles is not supreme excellence; supreme excellence consists in breaking the enemy's resistance without fighting." See also chapter 5: "In all fighting, the direct method may be used for joining battle, but indirect methods will be needed in order to secure victory. Indirect tactics, efficiently applied, are inexhaustible as Heaven and Earth, unending as the flow of rivers and streams; like the sun and moon, they end but to begin anew; like the four seasons, they pass away to return once more."

37. *Taoteking*, 31.

38. Clausewitz, *On War,* 75.

39. Ibid., 75–76.

40. Sun Tzu, *The Art of War*, chapter 1.

41. Clausewitz, *On War,* 75.

42. *Newsweek*, November 8, 2004.

Chapter 7. Civilization: Vasco da Gama vs. Cheng Ho

1. Robert Temple, *The Genius of China* (London: Prion Books, 1999), 186, cited by John M. Hobson, *The Eastern Origins of Western Civilization* (Cambridge, UK: Cambridge University Press, 2004), 58. Some have argued, on the contrary, that Western ships were already superior to those of the East by the sixteenth century: "Thus Chinese ships ruled the waves in East Asian waters for a long period of time until the sixteenth century when the Portuguese arrived in East Asia and found no equal to their *calivers* outside the Atlantic." Helaine Selin, *Encyclopedia of the History of Science, Technology, and Medicine in Non-Western Cultures* (London: Springer, 2006), 765.

2. en.wikipedia.org/wiki/Song_Dynasty#Economy.2C_industry.2C_and_trade.

3. Marco Polo's nickname was *"Il Milione"* (which was actually the title of his book about the East), as he frequently referred to millions of people, millions of this and millions of that materials. He was advised by his friends and contemporaries to be reasonable and to bring down "the millions" to a realistic number.

4. The modern Western view of the East is best represented by such influential thinkers as Hegel and Ranke. Hegel taught that Eastern civilization lay outside the course of world history, and that the West should not concern itself with it any further. Leopold von Ranke (1795–1886) exulted in the submission of the Eastern world to the Western "spirit." Most people, Easterners included, still remain vastly influenced by the Industrial Revolution and by the sort of prejudice expressed by Hegel and Ranke.

5. David A. Taylor, "Was Sinbad a Nanjing Sailor?" *Christian Science Monitor*, June 16, 2004.

6. The following are coincidental and circumstantial evidence that Cheng Ho (Ma Sanbao) was actually Sinbad: the names Sanbao and Sinbad; the same number of seven voyages; Cheng Ho as Ma Sanbao actually making several visits to the Persian Gulf region; Ma Sanbao was widely known as San Bao in the Muslim world and in Southeast Asia and beyond, and later worshiped in the region by the same name; and the fact that the story of "The Seven Voyages of Sinbad the Sailor," though an authentic Arab-Persian tale, was not included in the original Arabic version of the *Arabian Nights*—which was earlier than Ma Sanbao's seven voyages—but was later interpolated into the *Arabian Nights* by the European translators, which appeared after Ma Sanbao's actual voyages.

7. en.wikipedia.org/wiki/Song_Dynasty#Economy.2C_ industry.2C_and_trade.

8. The large number of ships and sailors involved in the great Chinese maritime expeditions could only mean one of two

things: preparation for war or a demonstration of strength. In the West before the nineteenth century, only a handful of major naval battles—and certainly no goodwill missions—had involved a similar magnitude of force. There was, for example, the Battle of Salamis between Greece and Persia in 480 BC; the Battle of Actium between Augustus and Mark Antony in 31 BC; and the Battle of Lepanto between the West and the Ottoman Turks in the late sixteenth century. Amazingly, from a Western perspective, there are no records of Cheng Ho's expeditions. At that time, the Mongols, although defeated and repulsed to the Mongolian hinterland, still remained a serious threat to the Ming dynasty, whose emperor looked to the south to reinforce his suzerainty. During the previous Yuan dynasty (under Mongol rule), maritime commerce had flourished between China and the Middle East. Meanwhile, Arab and Persian merchants established bases on the east coast of Africa, dominating the maritime commerce of the Indian Ocean.

9. Matthew Ricci, *China in the Sixteenth Century: The Journals of Matthew Ricci: 1583–1610*, translated Louis J. Gallagher (New York: Random House, 1953), 54–55.

10. 事大字小

11. 厚往薄來

12. It was the same with Christopher Columbus. In his second voyage on September 24, 1493, Columbus was equipped with seventeen ships and a crew of about 1,200 men to colonize the New World.

13. Wikipedia, Vasco da Gama. en.wikipedia.org/wiki/Vasco_da_Gama.

14. Neither was this phenomenon limited to the Iberian nations; rather, it became a European trend. Perhaps the best example of national support for maritime exploration and exploitation was Francis Drake (1540–1596), who was a privateer, navigator, pirate, slaver, and naval hero. Queen Elizabeth I was Francis Drake's closest associate, directly investing in and enormously profiting from his piratical enterprises and later giving orders to his maritime missions: "On 26 September 1580 *Golden Hind* sailed into Plymouth with Drake and 59 remaining crew aboard, along with a rich cargo of spices and captured Spanish treasures. The Queen's half-share of the cargo surpassed the rest of the crown's income for that entire year." See Wikipedia, Francis Drake, www.google.com/search?hl=en&q=francis+drake&aq=9&oq=francis+&aqi=g10.

15. In the meantime, Spanish conquistadors conquered a major section of the American coast, leaving only Brazil to Portugal. By 1600, most of the American coastline had been conquered by Europeans. As the Romans had made the Mediterranean *Mare Nostrum*, so the Europeans made the Atlantic theirs.

16. The basic aim of Vasco da Gama's voyage was to establish a Western sea route to India, so as to gain access to India with its invaluable spices. Mehmed II (1432–1481) of the Ottoman Empire had conquered Constantinople in 1453. His growing maritime power blocked Western access to the Black Sea as well as to the Middle East, thus allowing him to charge a premium for spices. Da Gama's quest to circumvent a trading monopoly was not unprecedented; Portugal had made similar gains in directly sourcing slaves and gold from sub-Saharan Africa under Henry the Navigator, obviating the Muslim-controlled trans-Saharan trade of these valuable goods.

17. As we read ancient history, we become familiar with stories of Mediterranean pirates. Plundering and slavery must have been one of the most lucrative and exciting enterprises of the time. Diogenes of Sinope was once captured by pirates and sold as a slave. (So was Plato, incidentally—according to a popular story, at least.) Pompey the Great made his name by waging a successful campaign against the Mediterranean pirates. Julius Caesar once became a prisoner of pirates and characteristically requested that the pirates raise the ransom for him in line with his importance. After the payment of the ransom and his release, he organized an army, captured the pirates, and executed them. In medieval Europe, after the Mediterranean pirates, there were the Viking raiders from the Nordic countries. Sailing from the Baltic Sea, they roamed the entire Atlantic coast of Europe, North Africa, and Italy. They also descended along the Volga River to the Black Sea and reached as far as Persia.

18. After the Vikings, it was the Muslim pirates who dominated the Mediterranean Sea. The Barbary pirates and privateers operating from Tripoli, Tunis, and Algiers in North Africa were particularly active until the nineteenth century, wreaking havoc on Western merchant ships. Just as Japanese pirates (Wokou) caused the evacuation of people from the coasts of Korea and China, these Barbary pirates caused emigration from a long stretch of the Spanish and Italian coastlines. It is no wonder that we find stories of the Barbary pirates in Daniel Defoe's *Robinson Crusoe* as well as in Voltaire's *Candide*. According to some statistics, over one million Europeans were captured to be sold as slaves between the sixteenth and the nineteenth centuries. One historian notes: "Between 1609

and 1616, England had a staggering 466 merchant ships lost to Barbary pirates. 160 British ships were captured by Algerians between 1677 and 1680. Slave-taking persisted into the 19th century when Barbary pirates would capture ships and enslave the crew.... Payments in ransom and tribute to the Barbary States amounted to 20% of United States government annual revenues in 1800. It was not until 1815 that naval victories in the Barbary Wars ended tribute payments by the U.S., although some European nations continued annual payments until the 1830s." See Wikipedia, Slavery, en.wikipedia.org/wiki/Slavery.

19. Winston Churchill, *A History of the English Speaking Peoples, Vol. I, The Birth of Britain*, Part 1 (audiobook). The quotation is preceded by the following insights: "The vitality of the church repaired the ruin with devoted zeal. The Vikings having a large choice of action allowed an interval of recovery before paying another visit ... buccaneering had become a steady profession. And the church was there to perpetually replenish their treasure of the house ... and a new shadow of fear spread over Christendom. No effective measures were, however, taken."

20. en.wikipedia.org/wiki/Wokou.

21. In a series of naval battles, the Japanese maritime invasion force was repeatedly defeated by Korea's Admiral Yi Sun-sin, who is often compared to Horatio Nelson. Both men met their death at the victorious moment of an epic battle.

22. This extraordinary voyage gave rise to a great debate over the need for an international date line. The returning crew

found the discrepancy of one day between their ship's log and the actual date in Spain after their circumnavigation. A delegation was reportedly sent to the Papal States to explain this phenomenon.

23. We can see the beginnings of this uniquely European phenomenon with the Vikings, whose raids involved the entire nation. Although Muslim pirates were often employed as privateers, the most famous case being Pasha Barbarossa, who became admiral of the entire Ottoman fleet, this practice was limited in time and space. The melding of national and personal interest reached a revolutionary scale with the European naval powers of Portugal, Spain, and Britain.

24. In fact, Sir Francis Drake initiated the triangular slave trade between Europe, Africa, and the New World.

25. Keith Hopkins estimates that, in Rome of the first century AD, around 300,000 to 350,000 slaves existed out of a population of about 900,000 to 950,000. Keith Hopkins, *Conquerors and Slaves: Sociological Studies in Roman History, Vol. 1* (Cambridge, UK: Cambridge University Press, 1977).

26. en.wikipedia.org/wiki/Slavery.

27. Muslim control of the Mediterranean culminated in its complete conquest of the sea under Pasha Barbarossa (1478–1546). It is quite intriguing to imagine that the three heroes—Barbarossa, Vasco da Gama, and Cheng Ho—were almost contemporaries, each roaming the Mediterranean; Africa and South Asia; and South and Southeast Asia, respectively, as their principal maritime theaters.

28. "The explorers had passed the southern boundary of the desert, and from then on Henry had one of his wishes fulfilled: the Portuguese had circumvented the Muslim land-based trade routes across the Western Sahara Desert, and slaves and gold began arriving in Portugal." See Wikipedia, Henry the Navigator, en.wikipedia.org/wiki/Henry_the_Navigator.

29. "In 1441, the first slaves were brought to Portugal from northern Mauritania. Prince Henry the Navigator, major sponsor of the Portuguese African expeditions, as of any other merchandise, taxed one fifth of the selling price of the slaves imported to Portugal. By the year 1552 black African slaves made up 10 percent of the population of Lisbon. In the second half of the 16th century, the Crown gave up the monopoly on slave trade and the focus of European trade in African slaves shifted from import to Europe to slave transports directly to tropical colonies in the Americas." See Wikipedia, Slavery, en.wikipedia.org/wiki/Slavery.

30. "An entry in his journal from September 1498 reads, 'From here one might send, in the name of the Holy Trinity, as many slaves as could be sold.' Indeed, as an ardent supporter of slavery, Columbus ultimately refused to baptize the native people of Hispaniola, since Catholic law forbade the enslavement of Christians." See Wikipedia, Columbus, en.wikipedia.org/wiki/Christopher_Columbus.

31. "The 15th century Portuguese exploration of the African coast is commonly regarded as the harbinger of European colonialism. In 1452, Pope Nicholas V issued the papal bull, granting Alfonso V of Portugal the right to reduce any 'Saracens, pagans and any other unbelievers' to hereditary

slavery which legitimized the slave trade under Catholic beliefs of that time. This approval of slavery was reaffirmed and extended in his bull of 1455. These papal bulls came to serve as a justification for the subsequent era of slave trade and European colonialism. Although for a short period as in 1462, Pius II declared slavery to be 'a great crime." See Wikipedia, Slavery, en.wikipedia.org/wiki/Slavery.

32. Piracy and slavery seemed to have gone hand in hand until the modern age: "Among the most important slave markets where Pirates operated in Mediterranean Europe were the ports of Majorca, Toulon, Marseille, Genoa, Pisa, Leghorn, and Malta. In Africa, the most important were the ports of Morocco, Tripoli, Algiers, and Tunis." See Wikipedia, Slavery, en.wikipedia.org/wiki/Slavery.

33. en.wikipedia.org/wiki/Emperor_Taizong_of_Tang.

34. Confucius, *The Analects*, 15-28.

35. Op. cit. Wikipedia, Slavery, http://en.wikipedia.org/wiki/Slavery.

36. Immanuel Kant, *Perpetual Peace: A Philosophical Essay* (New York: Macmillan, 1917), 139–142.

37. Wikipedia, Columbus, en.wikipedia.org/wiki/Christopher_Columbus.

38. In the East, only Japan had a tradition of using the coat of arms. This can be explained by Japan's having gone through the feudal system in the modern era, unlike other Eastern countries.

39. One of the natural consequences of such a culture is its emphasis on harmony: between the sovereign and his subjects; between citizens and foreigners; and among nations. Individual rights and obligations are sacrificed to this overarching concept; it was ultimately the emperor's responsibility to maintain and enhance harmony. The concept of a sovereign's "exploitation" of his subjects, or of one nation by another, cannot exist under such circumstances. Thus, the absence of institutionalized, systematic, and ruthless exploitation in the East served as the mechanism of its self-preservation, just as the pronounced existence of such practices in the West was also a mechanism for its self-preservation.

40. Wikipedia, Imperial Examination System, en.wikipedia.org/wiki/Imperial_examination.

41. In the case of Japan, because of the rise of the military Samurai class, the imperial examinations were instead reserved for rather low class officials, although the state examination system, after the demise of the Samurai class, revived the obsession for education by the entire Japanese population. In these circumstances, it was with a view to passing the state examinations for high government officials or the entrance examinations for the first rank universities and high schools.

42. en.wikipedia.org/wiki/Tang_Dynasty.

43. en.wikipedia.org/wiki/Song_Dynasty.

44. William Manchester, *The Last Lion: Winston Spencer Churchill, Volume I: Visions of Glory 1874–1932*, Part II (audiobook).

45. 孟母三遷之敎

46. en.wikipedia.org/wiki/Horace.

47. Mozi, 2-1-6.

48. Ibid., 2-2-1.

49. Ibid., 2-2-3.

50. Ibid., 2-2-7.

51. Ibid., 2-3-3.

52. 四書五經

53. Walter Demel, "China in the Political Thought of Western and Central Europe, 1570–1750," in *China and Europe: Images and Influences in Sixteenth to Eighteenth Centuries,* ed. Thomas H. C. Lee (Hong Kong: The Chinese University Press, 1991), 45–64.

54. Ibid., Water Demel, 99–128, D. E. Mungello, *Confucianism in the Enlightenment: Antagonism and Collaboration between the Jesuits and the Philosophes.*

Chapter 8. Industrial Revolution: Western Paradigm and Eastern Fundamental

1. philosophy.eserver.org/hegel-christianity.html.

2. Robert B. Marks, *The Origins of the Modern World: A Global and Ecological Narrative* (New York: Rowman & Littlefield, 2002), 156–157.

3. en.wikipedia.org/wiki/Qing_Dynasty: "In 1793, the Chinese Emperor stated to the British Ambassador Lord McCartney

that China had no use for European manufactured products. Consequently, leading Chinese merchants only accepted bar silver as payment for their goods. The huge demand in Europe for Chinese goods such as silk, tea, and ceramics could only be met if European companies funneled their limited supplies of silver into China. By the late 1830s, the governments of Great Britain and France were deeply concerned about their stockpiles of precious metals and sought alternate trading schemes with China—the foremost of which was addicting China to opium. When the Chinese regime tried to ban the Opium Trade in 1838, Great Britain declared war on China."

4. It is intriguing that the quantities of British opium exported to China multiplied about 150 times in a century, just as the quantities of cotton imported to Britain multiplied about 200 times in a century at the start of the Industrial Revolution: "Opium had started to trickle into China during the reign of his great grandfather Emperor Yongzheng but was limited to approximately 200 boxes annually. By Emperor Qianlong's reign, the amount had increased to 1,000 boxes, 4,000 boxes by Jiaqing's era, and more than 30,000 boxes during Daoguang's reign. He made many edicts against opium in the 1820s and 1830s, which were carried out by the famous Lin Zexu." See wapedia.mobi/en/Daoguang_Emperor.

5. acc6.its.brooklyn.cuny.edu/~phalsall/texts/com-lin.html.

6. en.wikipedia.org/wiki/Opium_War.

7. Before the West possessed its technological advantage, it hesitated to attack Eastern countries directly, since they were

geographically remote and the West's military superiority was not so evident. The West accepted a compromise: "In 1535, Portuguese traders obtained the rights to anchor ships in Macau's harbours and to carry out trading activities, though not the right to stay onshore. Around 1552–1553, they obtained temporary permission to erect storage sheds onshore, in order to dry out goods drenched by sea water. In 1557, the Portuguese established a permanent settlement in Macau, paying an annual rent." See en.wikipedia.org/wiki/Macau#cite_note-F7-16.

8. It remains to be seen how the ancient Eastern tribute system will manifest itself, if at all, in a world dominated by the Western paradigms of individual freedom, democracy, science, and commerce.

9. The goals of these agreements were the right of perpetual occupation and the colonization of occupied territories. These were achieved. But in the process, the old harmony was replaced by a pattern of brutal and unilateral exploitation.

10. Robert Davis, *British Slaves on the Barbary Coast*, BBC British History, www.bbc.co.uk/history/british/empire_seapower/white_slaves_01.shtml.

11. Ibid.

12. en.wikipedia.org/wiki/Sack_of_Baltimore.

13. Davis, *British Slaves*.

14. Ibid.

15. Walter Demel, "China in the Political Thought of Western and Central Europe, 1570–1750," in *China and Europe: Images and Influences in the Sixteenth to Eighteenth Centuries,* ed. Thomas H. C. Lee (Hong Kong: The Chinese University Press, 1991).

16. Immanuel Kant, *Perpetual Peace: A Philosophical Essay* (New York: Macmillan, 1917), 140–141.

17. en.wikipedia.org/wiki/Adam_Smith#cite_ref-68.

18. en.wikipedia.org/wiki/Elizabeth_I_of_England#cite_note-151#cite_note-151.

19. Ibid.

20. Instead of taking the initiative to eliminate pirates, as Pompey and Cheng Ho had done, China and Korea closed-mindedly used scorched-earth tactics, evacuating their people from coastal areas.

21. H.G. Wells, *The Outline of History: Vol. 2* (New York: Barnes and Noble Publishing, 2004), 540. "For a time Japan welcomed European intercourse, and the Christian missionaries made a great number of converts.... Then arose complicated quarrels between the Spanish Dominicans, the Portuguese Jesuits, and the English and Dutch Protestants, each warning the Japanese against the evil political designs of the others."

22. She is best known in the East as the West Dowager Empress, 西太后.

23. Benjamin A. Elman, "Imperial Politics and Confucian Societies in Late Imperial China: The Hanlin and Donglin Academies,"

Modern China, Vol. 15, No. 4. (Sage Publications, 1989), 378; see also 379–418: "The civil service examinations in turn engendered a national school system down to the prefectural level during the Song, and even further to counties during the Ming (1368–1644) and Qing (1644–1911) dynasties. These high-level public schools initially prepared candidates for the written tests devised by state-appointed examiners. Fully seven centuries before Europe, the imperial Chinese state committed itself financially to support an empire-wide school network" (381).

24. Ibid., 378.

25. Peter H. Lee, *A History of Korean Literature* (Cambridge, UK: Cambridge University Press, 2003), 6.

26. Elman, *Imperial Politics*, 391.

27. Ibid., 395.

28. Wenziyu, 以言入罪.

29. en.wikipedia.org/wiki/Qianlong.

30. Plato, *Timaeus*, 90e.

31. *The Analects*, 17-25.

32. en.wikipedia.org/wiki/Empress_L%C3%BC_Zhi.

33. www.womeninworldhistory.com/heroine6.html.

34. en.wikipedia.org/wiki/Li_Zhi_(philosopher).

35. Although the Western Roman Empire produced no female rulers, the Byzantine Empire had three official empresses

regnant: Irene, Zoe, and Theodora. Aelfgifu of Northampton in Norway, Margaret of Anjou, or Empress Matilda in England cannot be seriously considered as de facto female rulers, since their rules were either too short or not sufficiently independent.

36. en.wikipedia.org/wiki/Catherine_II_of_Russia.

37. en.wikipedia.org/wiki/Wu_Zetian#cite_ref-31.

38. Lawrence E. Harrison and Samuel P. Huntington, ed., *Culture Matters: How Values Shape Human Progress* (New York: Basic Books, 2000).

39. As Easterners put it, "The Great Wall cannot stand for strength, gumption, and glory! It represents isolation, conservatism, incompetent defense, and timidity. Ah, Great Wall, why do we still sing your praises?"

40. Demel, "China in Political Thought" (see 100, n. 15).

41. Yet, this appears to be part of Western assertiveness—that it uses these advances as reference points to evaluate, appraise, and appreciate other civilizations. For example, instead of comparing the solid establishment of the rule of law in the West with the absence of it in the East, comparing the rule of law in the West with the role of the East's meritocratic examination system, and the role of individual initiatives in the West with the extraordinary focus on education in the East, would do more justice in assessing the two civilizations. It goes the same with religion. Instead of comparing monotheistic and anthropomorphic religions in the West with their absence in the East, it would be more balanced and

appropriate to compare the Western infallible God with the Eastern ineffable Tao. Furthermore, with regard to the roles that they respectively played, comparing Western religion, which gave birth to law, with Eastern education, which gave birth to ethics, would make more sense given their weight and magnitude in each respective civilization.

42. Richard Nisbett, *The Geography of Thought, How Asians and Westerners Think Differently ... and Why* (New York: Free Press, 2004), 21. Nisbett believes that the Greeks made the difference: "The Greeks' discovery of nature made possible the invention of science. China's failure to develop science can be attributed in part to lack of curiosity, but the absence of a concept of nature would have blocked the development in any case."

43. This appears in Einstein's famous letter sent to J. E. Switzer of San Mateo, California, in 1953; see Joseph Needham, *The Grand Titration: Science and Society in East and West* (London: Allen & Unwin, 1969), 43. Gibbon expresses similar attitude regarding the Roman Empire: "Instead of inquiring why the Roman Empire was destroyed we should rather be surprised that it has subsisted for so long." Gibbon, *Decline and Fall of the Roman Empire*, 2nd ed., vol. 4, ed. by J. B. Bury (London, 1909), 174.

44. Ibid.

45. en.wikipedia.org/wiki/Tang_Dynasty#Seaports_and_maritime_trade.

46. Ibid.

47. en.wikipedia.org/wiki/Song_Dynasty#Economy.2C_industry.2C_and_trade.

48. Matthew 12:46–50.

49. Mancur Olson, "Dictatorship, Democracy, and Development," *The American Political Science Review*, 87:3 (September 1993), 573.

50. William Theodore de Bary, *Asian Values and Human Rights: A Confucian Communitarian Perspective* (Cambridge, Mass.: Harvard University Press, 1998), 19.

51. Ibid., 23–24.

52. *The Analects*, 2-14.

53. Ibid., 2-16.

54. en.wikipedia.org/wiki/Ouyang_Xiu.

55. Elman, *Imperial Politics,* 391–394.

Chapter 9. Political Economy:
Western Invisible Hand and Eastern Wuwei

1. en.wikipedia.org/wiki/Adam_Smith.

2. 实事求是

3. *The Economist*, November 7, 2009, 29.

4. Deng Xiaoping, "Building Socialism with Chinese Characteristics," June 30, 1948, www.wellesley.edu/Polisci/ wj/China/Deng/Building.htm.

5. *Taoteking*, 49 and 57.

6. Adam Smith, *The Wealth of Nations* (Chicago: University of Chicago Press, 1976), 477.

7. Adam Smith, *The Theory of Moral Sentiments*, 6th edition, 350.

8. en.wikipedia.org/wiki/The_Fable_of_the_Bees.

9. Ibid.

10. en.wikipedia.org/wiki/Joseph_Butler.

11. en.wikipedia.org/wiki/Invisible_hand.

12. Ibid.

13. en.wikipedia.org/wiki/Capitalism.

14. As indicated, Taoism uses the term "Sage" as Confucianism uses the term "Junzi" (Noble Man). Both represent the same ethical ideal. In Eastern culture, people often use the two terms combined as one "Noble Man-Sage."

15. Given the gradualism of Darwin, and Lamarck's insistence on the malleability of human nature, Karl Marx may have envisioned a Communist society motivated by altruism.

16. en.wikipedia.org/wiki/Adam_Smith.

17. en.wikipedia.org/wiki/David_Hume.

18. Adam Smith, *Moral Sentiments*.

19. In this sense, Smith's theory may be "incomplete," as insinuated in the film *A Beautiful Mind*.

20. Stephen Mitchell, *Taoteking* (New York: Harper Perennial), 1992.

21. Walter Demel, "China in the Political Thought of Western and Central Europe: 1570–1750," in *China and Europe: Images and Influences in the Sixteenth to Eighteenth Centuries*, ed. Thomas H. C. Lee (Hong Kong: The Chinese University Press, 1991).

22. *Taoteking*, 75.

23. *Taoteking*, 58.

24. Mancur Olson, "Dictatorship, Democracy, and Development," *The American Political Science Review* 87 (September 1993), 568.

25. Ibid., 569: "[F]rom the time that Sargon's Empire of Akkad during the third millennium until the time of Louis XVI and Voltaire."

26. In a dialogue with a king, Mencius explains that if a man, upon returning from abroad, found his family, whom he had entrusted to a friend, suffering from hunger and cold, he would renounce his friendship. Similarly, if a king found his chief minister in dereliction of duty, he would dismiss him; if a people discovered that their sovereign was not properly governing them, they would depose him. See Mencius 2-13.

27. Mencius, 2-15.

28. Adam Smith left evidence of his wariness of merchants and business monopolies. On this account, it is quite intriguing that Smith referred mostly to artisans and manufacturers,

not merchants and traders, in his Invisible Hand theory: "We rarely hear, it has been said, of the combinations of masters, though frequently of those of workmen. But whoever imagines, upon this account, that masters rarely combine, is as ignorant of the world as of the subject. Masters are always and everywhere in a sort of tacit, but constant and uniform, combination, not to raise the wages of labour above their actual rate.... Masters, too, sometimes enter into particular combinations to sink the wages of labour even below this rate. These are always conducted with the utmost silence and secrecy till the moment of execution; and when the workmen yield, as they sometimes do without resistance, though severely felt by them, they are never heard of by other people. In contrast, when workers combine, the masters never cease to call aloud for the assistance of the civil magistrate, and the rigorous execution of those laws which have been enacted with so much severity against the combination of servants, labourers, and journeymen." (en.wikipedia.org/wiki/Adam_Smith#cite_note-71#cite_note-71.)

29. Olson, "Dictatorship," 574–575.

30. Ibid.

31. en.wikipedia.org/wiki/Ivan_Boesky.

32. *Le secret des grandes fortunes sans cause apparente est un crime oublié, parce qu'il a été proprement fait (Le Père Goriot, II)*: "Behind every great fortune there is a crime." This Balzac quotation is a popular version of his original writing cited here in French; it explains the subtle relationship between law and ethics.

33. Matthew 19:24.

34. Mencius, 1-I.

35. *The Analects*, Yongye.

36. *The Analects*, Wei Ling Gong, 36.

37. Taoteking, 81

38. "Who will guard the guardians themselves?" When the Roman Republic became an empire, the praetorian guards became indispensable. But the empire suffered innumerable problems caused by praetorian guards who replaced or killed emperors out of greed and at times auctioned the imperial office among ambitious generals, because of greed. The empires of the East, by contrast, survived for thousands of years without the need for large numbers of royal guards, as ethics was prevalent even among the militaries.

39. *Taoteking*, 64.

40. Mencius, 1-7.

41. *The Analects*, 2-3.

42. *Taoteking*, 53.

43. In the beginning, it was very likely that only good, altruistic, missionary, and messianic visions and intentions were involved. Karl Marx and Friedrich Engels might have been fired up with altruistic enthusiasms. But their actual implementation ended up creating the most efficient system of total theft in history, as all the means of production and fruits of them belonged to a handful of Politburo members.

44. Olson, "Dictatorship," 570.

45. Ibid., 573.

46. Mencius, 1-1.

Chapter 10. The Twenty-First Century: Paradigm Shift and Global Governance

1. Konrad Lorenz, *On Aggression* (London: Routledge Classics, 2002), 230.

2. Including the negotiations on climate change. See *Le Monde*, February 20, 2010.

3. Samuel Huntington grouped Japan with the West in terms of its civilization and the possibility of alliance. Others have thought in like terms. Indeed, there are many historical features that Japan and Europe have in common, such as their feudal systems. The Daimyos are comparable to the barons of the feudal West, existing in tension with the central government. Japan has also demonstrated a strong militaristic tendency, unlike other Eastern countries. But this is only one aspect of Japan's character, and it could be better interpreted as a dualism of Japan rather than Japan's showing uniquely Western characteristics. This dualism appears to be based on its cultural mix of force and ethics. This mix has been perpetuated since World War II. Political parties replaced the Samurai class. In fact, after the brilliant Meiji Reform, Japan was presented with a number of choices: liberalism, communism, and fascism. Its alliance with Great Britain represented liberalism, although the spirit of its intellectuals

favored communism, while the body of its government favored fascism. In retrospect, Japan's choice of fascism was predictable, since rule by force went well with the character of fascism. As the Second World War brought the democratic free market to Japan, the country maintained its Samurai traditions and placed its new Samurai class—the political parties—above its bureaucrats: no ministers would come from bureaucrats, who can only climb as high as vice-ministerships. This, in the end, created a triangular hybrid configuration in Japanese politics—between parties, civil bureaucracy, and business. But in general, Japan can be grouped with the East, since its culture is essentially grounded in Buddhism and Confucianism. H. G. Wells shares this analysis: "Whatever the origin of the Japanese, there can be no doubt that their civilization, their writing, and their literary and artistic traditions are derived from the Chinese." See H. G. Wells, *The Outline of History: Vol. 2* (New York: Barnes and Noble Publishing, 2004), 539.

4. Lorenz, *On Aggression*, 39.

5. Ibid., 41.

6. Richard Leakey and Roger Lewin, *Origins: What New Discoveries Reveal About Our Species and Its Possible Future* (New York: E.P. Dutton, 1978), 256.

7. Konrad Lorenz, *Civilized Man's Eight Deadly Sins* (Madison: University of Wisconsin, 2007), 18.

8. Lorenz, *On Aggression*, 38.

9. Ibid.

10. Lorenz, *Civilized Man's Eight Deadly Sins*, 25.

11. Lorenz, *On Aggression*, 231.

12. William Shakespeare, *The Tragedy of Hamlet, Prince of Denmark*, Act II, Sc. II.

13. Mancur Olson, "Dictatorship, Democracy, and Development," *The American Political Science Review*, 87:3 (September 1993), 574.

14. The concept of enlightened self-interest is usually associated with rather narrow instances of individual volunteerism, as witnessed by Alexis de Tocqueville in nineteenth-century America. Here, by contrast, I am referring to a more general phenomenon of taking others' interests into account.

15. One interesting aspect of this rapprochement should be underlined: the Eastern assimilation of Western paradigms has been made possible by the direct impetus of the West. Without the arrival of the Western powers in the nineteenth century, the East would certainly have remained an agrarian society, with a social harmony founded on ethics, but suffering from tyranny, inertia, complacency, and widespread famine. The West, on the other hand, seems to have adopted Eastern values by the light of its own scientific and sociological discoveries. The influence of Eastern contact is debatable, although it is sure to increase with the growing interaction between the two cultures in the present climate.

16. Peter Mandelson, "We Want China to Lead," *International Herald Tribune*, February 12, 2010.

17. George Lakoff's book (with Mark Johnson), *Metaphors We Live By* (Chicago: University of Chicago Press, 1980), is an example of a Western thinker arguing for an "embodied mind" against the philosophical mainstream.

18. *Financial Times*, Editorial, February 20–21, 2010.

19. *Taoteking*, 54.

20. Confucius, *The Great Learning*, 2.

21. *Taoteking*, 64.

22. Mencius, 2-17.

23. Mencius, 2-1.

INDEX

contracts, 339–341
creation myths, 17–19, 88–89
creationism, 87–88, 89–90
crusaders, 279, 282–283
Culture Matters (Harrison), 384

D

Dai Zhen, 349
Damasio, Antonio, 245
Darwin, Charles, 89, 90–95, 136
Dawkins, Richard, 245
Deism, 59
Demel, Walter, 349–350
democracy, 44, 194, 387–388, 393–398, 411, 427–430
Deng Xiaoping, 216–218, 349, 400, 401, 402–404
Descartes, René, 112, 129
Descent of Man, The (Darwin), 136
despotism, 8, 38, 48–49, 198–201, 394–396
Diamond, Jared, 31
Diaz, Bartholomew, 316, 324
diversity, 347
domestication of plants and animals, 28–29, 31–32, 169
Donglin Academy, 372–375, 397–398

E

earth *vs.* water, 17–19
East
 birth of, 22–26
 circumscribed perspective of, 2–3, 17, 33–35, 357
 conformity of, 18, 347–349
 cultural elements of, 383–385
 geography of, 14–17
 isolation of, 368–372
 past orientation of, 196–197
 rise of, 4

ecology, 104–105, 466–467
education, 338, 344–346, 347–348
Ein Sof, 74
Einstein, Albert, 198, 243–244, 251, 268, 389
Elizabeth I (Queen), 381
Elliot, Charles, 360–362
encephalization, 134–136
end of history thesis, 462–463
enemies, treatment of, 298–301
enlightened interest, 430–431, 439
Enlightened National Interest (ENI), 448–449, 461–462, 467, 473–474
Environmental Determinism, 32–33
Essay on the Principle of Population (Malthus), 93
ethics
 Christian, 179–180
 Confucian, 179–180
 harmony and, 49–51
 invisible hand and, 419–424
 law and, 35–38, 177–179
 sword *vs.* pen and, 231
 universal *vs.* master, 183–188
 Xun Zi compared to Spinoza, 155–159
Ethics (Spinoza), 81, 82, 84, 112, 139, 152–153, 235, 236
eunuchs, 48, 199–200
Eurasian continent, centrality of, 31–32
Euthyphro (Plato), 252
exclusionism, 190–193
exploitation, 36–37, 41, 43, 132, 247, 315

F

Fable of the Bees, The (Mandeville), 407–408
fascism, 133–134

Hegemon-King, 163, 253–256
Heisenberg, Werner Karl, 270
Henry the Navigator, 334
Heraclitus, 47, 61, 97, 140, 285–287
Hero *vs.* Junzi
    equanimity *vs.* dynamism,
        261–262
    ethics and, 247–251
    as human ideals, 225, 228, 237
    human nature and, 245–247
    inclusivity *vs.* exclusivity, 258–259
    integral *vs.* dialectic attitude,
        262–263
    introversion *vs.* extroversion,
        264–266
    laissez-faire *vs.* activism, 259–261
    nature and, 241–244
    politics and, 251–253
    receptivity *vs.* assertiveness,
        257–258
    suggestion *vs.* instruction,
        263–264
    synthetic *vs.* analytical learning,
        266–268
Hero-Conqueror, 255
heroes, 282–283
Hinduism, 207, 212, 214
Hitler, Adolf, 92
Hobbes, Thomas, 83, 116, 137,
    242–243, 290–291, 299,
    426–427
Homo sapiens sapiens, 86–87
Horace, 344–345
human nature, 148–149, 154–155,
    161–164, 416–419, 479
    See also man
human races, 96–97
Hume, David, 14, 114–115, 119,
    131, 137, 186, 242, 416–417
Hundred Flowers Competing for
    Fame, 56
Huntington, Samuel, 462–463

Hutcheson, Francis, 407, 408, 410,
    419, 420
Huxley, Thomas, 87–88, 94

I

I Ching, 58–59, 60–61, 97–100,
    101–102
ideologies, 133–134, 201–202
Iliad, The, 42
Imperial examination system, 272–
    278, 338, 340, 341–343,
    347, 380, 385, 404
Inchon, 40
India, 207–208
individual initiative, 3, 36–37, 194,
    315, 339–341, 344, 386, 388
Industrial Revolution, 9, 143, 356,
    358–359
inertia, 48–49, 199
international relations, 473–474
intra-specific competition, 464–467
Invisible Hand theory
    ethics and, 419–424
    free market and, 400, 401
    human nature and, 416–418
    nature and, 414–416
    political, 425–430
    Wuwei and, 386–387, 406–413,
        420
Islam, 169

J

Japanese pirates, 329–330, 366,
    370–371
Jesus Christ, 172, 174–176, 238
Johnson, Samuel, 351
Judaism, 168–169
Junzi
    described, 146–147
    Communism and, 218
    on ethics and politics, 386–387

as separate from nature, 39–41,
42, 60, 197
should be *vs.* what man is,
147–148
See also human nature
Manchester, William, 343–344
Mandate of Heaven, 61, 318, 325,
427–428
Mandela, Nelson, 480
Mandelson, Peter, 478
Mandeville, Bernard, 407–408, 409,
420–421
Mao Zedong, 226, 297, 401–402
Mare Nostrum. See Mediterranean Sea
Maria Theresa (Empress), 381
Marx, Karl, 92
Master ethics, 183–188, 202–205,
206, 225, 247, 281, 298, 309
Mediterranean Sea, 2, 16–17, 18,
19–21
Mein Kampf (Hitler), 92
menace from within, 460–461,
465–468
Mencius, 161–162, 344, 348, 375,
437
mercantilist statism, 400–401
meritocracy, 338, 341–343, 344–
346, 404
meritocratic examination system, 3,
273–278, 338
metaphysics, 188, 189, 286
military paradigms, 296–306
mind
innate ideas *vs.* tabula rasa,
130–131
limbic system without neocortex,
132–133
neocortex without limbic system,
131–132
and relationship to body, 108–
109, 224
See also brain

Ming dynasty, 124–125
Mohammed and Charlemagne
(Pirenne), 20
Mohism, 345–346
Mongols, 21, 30, 34, 124
monotheism, 62, 64–65, 75, 192–
193, 194
Montesquieu, 43, 452
Moses, 57, 65, 75, 76, 77, 284
mourning, three years of, 122–123,
346, 379
Mozi, 345
Mungello, D.E., 350–351
mutally assured destruction (MAD),
485
mythology, 17–19

N

Natural Deism, 59
natural selection, 90–93
nature
in Eastern culture, 45–46, 61
man's supremacy over, 32–33,
44, 108
separation from, 39–41, 42, 60,
197
naval battles, 25–26
navigation. *See* seafaring
Needham, Joseph, 395
Neo-Confucianism, 118–120, 121,
123, 125, 213, 214, 348,
393–394
neocortex, 86, 109, 127–130,
135–136
Newton, Isaac, 88
Nietzsche, Friedrich
apothegms of, 66
on Christian ethics, 179, 180
on exploitation, 338
on moral scruples, 134
on philosophy, 289

557

reaction against metaphysics,
116–117

on totalitarian leaders, 188

will to power, 132–133, 288

Nisbett, Richard, 6, 195

nomadic raiders, 29–30, 357

non-evolutionary transformation,
96–97

non-interventionism, 404–406, 411,
415

North Korea, 415–416, 454

nuclear weapons, 447, 461, 466,
468, 474, 478, 483–486

Nye, Joseph, 409

O

Ocean Prohibition, 370–371

Odyssey, The, 42

Of the Power of the Intellect
(Spinoza), 236–237

old brain. *See* limbic system

Olson, Mancur, 395, 425–430, 440,
447–448, 479, 480

On War (Clausewitz), 296–306, 309

One Hundred Schools of Thought,
181–182

Opium Wars, 358, 360–362

oracles, 101–102

Origin of Species, The (Darwin), 90,
92–93

original sin, 120–122, 197

Outline of History, The (Wells), 139

Ouyang Xiu, 397

P

Pacific Ocean, 2, 16, 24

Pangu, 88–89

paradigm shift

to commerce, 452–454

to Enlightened National Interest,
461–462

to gender equality, 457–458

to interdependence, 454–455

to intranational conflicts, 456

to menace from within, 460–461

and rise of non-state actors, 458

to rule of law, 458–460

to transnational problems, 457

to wealth, 455–456

Parmenides, 182

party system, 396–398, 439–441, 445

Pax Mongolica, 21, 124–125

Pericles, 139

Perpetual Peace (Kant), 336–337, 368

Philosophy of History, The (Hegel), 39

Piazza San Marco, 1–2, 40, 41, 195

piracy, 328–331, 364–367, 370–
371, 452

Pirenne, Henri, 20

plant domestication, 28–29

Plato

and concept of God, 252

on innate ideas, 110

on knowledge, 293

and Master ethics, 183

on philosopher-king, 41, 47,
188, 189

on politics, 203, 205

on reason, 136–137

on spirit-body separation, 44–45,
47

on truth, 78–79, 182–183

on women, 376

plunder, 327–331, 337

political economy

ethics and, 432–435

greed and, 441–443

leadership and, 437–439

political parties and, 439–441

profit-making and, 435–437

political parties, 396–398, 439–441,
445

politics, 202–205, 206

philosophy of, 404–406
Taoism and, 69–72
taxes and, 425–426
western knowledge of, 351

X

Xenophanes, 78
Xiaoren
    described, 146–147
    and ethics, 156, 159–161
    and greed, 163
    heathens *vs.*, 280–281
    Junzi *vs.*, 189–190, 232–238
    politics and, 204
Xun Zi
    compared to Spinoza, 4, 149–151, 153
    on ethics, 155–159
    and Han learning, 123
    on Heaven, 151–152
    Hegemon-King and, 163, 253–256
    on human nature, 154–155, 162–164
    on role models, 159–161
    and women, 375

Y

Yang (Emperor), 273, 274
Yin Yang philosophy
    described, 57–59, 62
    attributes of in modern world, 239
    complementary opposites of, 61–63
    East-West differences and, 63, 257–268
    harmony and, 51
    as non-supernatural, 60–61
    syncretistic character of, 63–65
    traits in science, 268–270
    unity and, 46–47

Yongle (Emperor), 315
Yuan Chonghuan, 200, 201

Z

Zhang Juzheng, 373
Zhu Xi, 118–119, 120, 121, 123, 348, 397

CPSIA information can be obtained at www.ICGtesting.com
Printed in the USA
BVOW031119260413

319220BV00001B/34/P

9 781450 265423